Palgrave Global Media Policy and Business

Series Editors
Petros Iosifidis
Department of Sociology
City University
London, UK

Jeanette Steemers
Culture, Media & Creative Industries
King's College London
London, UK

Gerald Sussman
Urban Studies & Planning
Portland State University
Portland, OR, USA

Terry Flew
Creative Industries Faculty
Queensland University of Technology
Brisbane, QLD, Australia

The Palgrave Global Media Policy and Business Series has published to date (2017) 15 volumes since its launch in 2012. Concentrating on the social, cultural, political, political-economic, institutional, and technological changes arising from the globalisation of media and communications industries, the series considers the impact of these changes on matters of business practice, regulation and policy, and social outcomes. The policy side encompasses the challenge of conceiving policy-making as a reiterative process that recurrently addresses such key challenges as inclusiveness, participation, industrial-labour relations, universal access and freedom in an increasingly globalized and transnationalized world. The business side encompasses a political economy approach that looks at the power of transnational corporations in specific contexts - and the controversies associated with these global conglomerates. The business side considers as well the emergence of small and medium media enterprises.

Focusing on issues of media convergence, industry concentration, and new communications practices, the series analyses the tensions between systems based on national decision-making and publicly-oriented participatory structures and a more global perspective demarcated by commercialization, privatization and monopolization.

Based on a multi-disciplinary approach, the series tackles three key questions:

- To what extent do new media developments require changes in regulatory philosophy and objectives?
- To what extent do new technologies and changing media consumption require changes in business practices and models?
- And to what extent do privatisation, globalisation, and commercialisation alter the creative freedom, cultural and political diversity, and public accountability of media enterprises?

Editorial Advisory Board
Sandra Braman, UM-Milwaukee, USA
Peter Dahlgren, Lund University, Sweden
Charles Fombad, University of Pretoria, South Africa
Manuel Alejandro Guerrero, Universidad Iberoamericana, Mexico
Alison Harcourt, University of Exeter, UK
Robin Mansell, LSE, UK
Richard Maxwell, Queen's College – CUNY, USA
Toby Miller, City University London, UK
Zizzi Papacharissi, University of Illinois-Chicago, USA
Stylianos Papathanassopoulos, National & Kapodistrian University of Athens, Greece
Caroline Pauwels, Vrije Universiteit Brussel, Belgium
Robert Picard, University of Oxford, UK
Kiran Prasad, Sri Padmavati Mahila University, India
Marc Raboy, McGill University, Canada
Chang Yong Son, Korean Communications Commission, South Korea
Miklos Sukosd, University of Hong Kong, Hong Kong
Kenton T. Wilkinson, Texas Tech University, USA
Sugmin Youn, Seoul National University, South Korea
Roderick Flynn, Dublin City University, Republic of Ireland
Manjunath Pendakur, Florida Atlantic University, USA
Deepa Kumar, Rutgers University, USA
Winston Mano, University of Westminster, UK

More information about this series at
http://www.palgrave.com/gp/series/14699

Miguel Túñez-López
Francisco Campos-Freire
Marta Rodríguez-Castro
Editors

The Values of Public Service Media in the Internet Society

palgrave
macmillan

Editors
Miguel Túñez-López
Department of Communication Sciences
Universidade de Santiago de
Compostela
Santiago de Compostela, Spain

Francisco Campos-Freire
Department of Communication
Sciences
Universidade de Santiago de
Compostela
Santiago de Compostela, Spain

Marta Rodríguez-Castro
Department of Communication Sciences
Universidade de Santiago de Compostela
Santiago de Compostela, Spain

ISSN 2634-6192   ISSN 2634-6206 (electronic)
Palgrave Global Media Policy and Business
ISBN 978-3-030-56465-0   ISBN 978-3-030-56466-7 (eBook)
https://doi.org/10.1007/978-3-030-56466-7

© The Editor(s) (if applicable) and The Author(s), under exclusive licence to Springer Nature Switzerland AG 2021
This work is subject to copyright. All rights are solely and exclusively licensed by the Publisher, whether the whole or part of the material is concerned, specifically the rights of translation, reprinting, reuse of illustrations, recitation, broadcasting, reproduction on microfilms or in any other physical way, and transmission or information storage and retrieval, electronic adaptation, computer software, or by similar or dissimilar methodology now known or hereafter developed.
The use of general descriptive names, registered names, trademarks, service marks, etc. in this publication does not imply, even in the absence of a specific statement, that such names are exempt from the relevant protective laws and regulations and therefore free for general use.
The publisher, the authors and the editors are safe to assume that the advice and information in this book are believed to be true and accurate at the date of publication. Neither the publisher nor the authors or the editors give a warranty, expressed or implied, with respect to the material contained herein or for any errors or omissions that may have been made. The publisher remains neutral with regard to jurisdictional claims in published maps and institutional affiliations.

Cover illustration: eStudioCalamar

This Palgrave Macmillan imprint is published by the registered company Springer Nature Switzerland AG.
The registered company address is: Gewerbestrasse 11, 6330 Cham, Switzerland

Foreword

Without Value, There Is No Future

Why?

This is what many citizens ask themselves when they have to pay the Public Service Media license fee invoice, or when they see a certain amount allocated to their national broadcaster in their tax declaration, or when the news mention how much the state budget will allocate to sustain the traditional television and radio broadcasting organization.

That question is probably followed by a feeling of frustration or bitterness, in the best case by a discussion about the price, the content offered, whether it is worse or better or any different from what others offer, whether we watch it or not, or whether it is just political propaganda. In those discussions, most of the times, the citizens—people with very different sociodemographic profiles, educational backgrounds, and interests or knowledge about the media—do not talk or think like us, media scholars or professionals. They do not refer to values like universality or independence, they do not consider market competition or market failure arguments, they do not reflect on the democratic function played by their public service broadcasters or how it drives their national media industry, and they do not see the multiple positive impacts that the money invested in such an organization returns in the short, medium, and long term to the entire society.

This is the first handicap that any reflection about the future of Public Service Media needs to address: the enormous gap between the intellectual and technical reflections by scholars and PSM professionals—by the way, very much needed—and the thinking and the feelings of the citizens.

During the many years I studied and researched about PSM as a media scholar, I had the opportunity to read a vast amount of papers, book chapters, and presentations that brilliantly elaborated about the concept of Public Service Media, the values behind it, its articulation, its future challenges, the never fading threats and risks. In all those texts, the values attributed to PSM, the supposed benefits it can deliver to society, and its almost not-challenged reasons for its existence had a very significant weight. Besides, the need for transformation of PSM organizations was always an underlying and transversal issue.

Since I started to work for the European Broadcasting Union (EBU) in 2012, I have had the opportunity to see the other side of the coin. Having access to more than 100 PSM organizations in 56 countries and having met with directors-general, strategist, researchers, producers, and so on has given me the opportunity to be exposed to, and understand, how the PSM professionals think and talk about themselves. Most of the times, I have met people with a very high sense of service and professionalism. People who give their best in challenging circumstances because of the lack of resources, complicated corporate legacy and culture, and uncertainty about what the future will bring. I have met many people with a strong awareness about the need to change, who however not always had a clear picture of what the right direction should be and without the required support to design and implement such a change. I have met people that are constantly juggling between their aspirations as socially committed journalists or content producers that aim to deliver top-quality content and their resource restrictions or the limitations imposed by regulation, competition law, or many other legal, structural, and labor constraints.

When brought together, scholars and PSM professionals usually do not have any problem to connect, to exchange knowledge and expertise, to collaborate, to think and dream about a better future for Public Service Media.

In these occasions, I have however noticed a worrying phenomenon: in both cases, Public Service Media scholars and professionals share a self-reference limitation. They enjoy the talk about their subject, they feel strongly about it, they invest a lot of effort and thinking in developing new ideas about it, but with the handicap of not always looking outside of their comfort zone and their natural ecosystem. They seem to have some kind of aversion to explore what organizations from other sectors in similar risk and change situations did to overcome their difficulties and reinvent themselves to catch-up with the ever-changing society.

In my opinion, this is a huge limitation that hinders scholars and professionals' ability to come up with new approaches to PSM problems and with effective solutions. In many cases, the result is either frustration or just resignation, and a bitter feeling of not being able to cope with an increasing complexity and falling behind the multiple changes the media industry and society are experiencing. What worries me most is what usually comes next: the use of the tautology "Public service media is important because it delivers a public service, and if it would not exist, we would have to invent it."

This worries me because it lacks any sense of self-criticism and ambition, both essential elements to move forward. Is Public Service Media so important? Is that what citizens, politicians, or any other PSM stakeholder think? I am not so sure.

During the last five years, I had the privilege to lead an EBU strategic initiative called PSM Contribution to Society. Our work was focused on raising awareness among EBU members of the need to address the legitimacy and transformation challenges they face from a different angle. I could be tempted to say from a 'new angle', but the reality is that we did not invent anything that was not done before. In fact, this is something that many commercial media organizations, platforms, and non-media companies have done to evolve, adapt, and succeed. We promoted a mindset centered on the final recipient(s) of the PSM remit (the citizen, the society) and on the final deliverable: value.

The discourses, academic and professionals, about PSM are full of references to the benefits that it will supposedly be delivered to the citizens, to society, to the nation state. But the reality is somehow different. Public Service Media organizations across the world are hindered to fulfill their 'original remit' by multiple funding, legal, labor, structural, and cultural constraints. Said in a plain way: while we all talk about the value we supposedly deliver to the citizens, the reality is that the business model of PSM prevents that.

This is a risky statement; I am very much aware of that. Does PSM have a business model? Isn't it a non-profit organization? Well, assuming that PSM does not have or must have a business model is the first mistake. Any professional activity has a business model, understood as the organization of resources and capabilities to conduct an activity that delivers different types of value across an ecosystem of players.

So what is PSM's business model? Here it would be very easy to resort to all the literature and professional narrative I mentioned above. But the reality, in my opinion, and regardless whether we like it or not, is that currently PSM's business model is delivering market share figures to the political establishment for it to sign-off its budget.

Yes, you have read it well: 'selling audiences to the politicians'. Many colleagues would strongly and vehemently disagree with me on this. Some would even take some offense from my words. This is obviously not my intention, and I do not mean that this is what PSM professionals stand for or aim to achieve. But the deliberately provocative tone of my words has a very clear goal: it is a wake-up call, an invitation to break with the previously mentioned tautology and to realize that PSM needs to do better in articulating and explaining its remit. I would even go further. It is time for PSM organizations to realize that there is no future without a profound change of their business model, a change that truly accounts for and reflects the academic and professional narratives about what Public Service Media is.

Everything is about values and value. The values of public service (universality, independence, excellence, innovation, accountability, and diversity), which the EBU defined in 2012, are those guiding principles that shape how Public Service Media organizations and professionals make decisions, operate, and behave. They are important and strongly shape the identity and legitimacy of the service. But those values do not define the value PSM organizations deliver to the citizens. The concept of value is very relative, and it depends on each individual's needs. Each person has a different perception of value. What is important to me might be insignificant to you.

Public Service Media organizations, professionals, and scholars need to embrace a new mindset: without value, there is no future. If the citizens—as a collective and individually—do not obtain value from a certain organization, why would they favor that it would receive first public resources and secondly their attention? If there is the perception that the value delivered by an organization is not distinctive and exclusive and relevant enough, why support its continuity and not promote other potential substitutes? If I do not feel that a certain organization does care about me and is centered in delivering value to me, why would I care about it?

All this connects with the questions opening this prologue: why? Each citizen, each politician, each market player... any PSM stakeholder is constantly looking for an answer to that why. If clear and meaningful answers are not provided, there is no future for PSM.

This requires adopting an extremely proactive citizen-centered approach. First, this implies understanding how the society we aim to serve is structured. Fragmentation and diversity are key concepts in this area. Secondly, the societal, community, group, and individual needs must be identified. Only by meeting those needs, by providing solutions, or contributing to the solutions to people's problems, will PSM be valuable in the eyes of its stakeholders.

I would like to end by clarifying that value does not mean output. Providing 10,000 hours of news content per year have no value at all for many citizens, and yet it is a recurrent argument when researchers or PSM professionals want to talk about the democratic value delivered by a certain broadcaster. Instead, citizens will assess the value of those news depending on whether they helped them better understand the reality they live in, make their mind about issues that are important to them, feel connected to their community… and all this mostly occurs in an unconscious way. I do not know many people who ask themselves out loud all this range of questions to assess whether they are satisfied with the value their PSM delivers to them. As mentioned in the beginning, the conversation is frequently triggered by the obligation to pay for the service and focused on other aspects.

To conclude, I would like to emphasize that I strongly believe that there is a future for Public Service Media. In fact, I strongly believe that, in the current state of the world and our societies, in the Internet/information society we live in, the need for an organization whose business model is using public resources, a set of clear values, and the goal of helping all of us have a better life, regardless of who we are, has not only a great future but is also extremely fashionable.

It is the time to really articulate the concept of Public Service Media as we have described it for decades, but that got somehow distorted by many legal, market, and labor constraints. We cannot get rid of all of them, I am fully aware of that, but we can focus on delivering value, on asking ourselves what is the positive effect, the positive change that the content and services delivered will bring to the citizens.

It is time for a Public Service Media that is radically centered on delivering value.

Head of Strategy & Media Intelligence
European Broadcasting Union   Roberto Suárez Candel
Geneva, Switzerland

Acknowledgments

This book has been prepared as part of the activities of the research project "New values, governance, financing and public audiovisual services for the Internet society: European and Spanish contrasts" (RTI2018-096065-B-100), funded by the Spanish State Program of R + D + I oriented to the Challenges of Society of the Ministry of Science, Innovation and Universities (Government of Spain), Agencia Estatal de Investigación (AEI), and the European Regional Development Fund (ERDF).

One of the editors, Marta Rodríguez-Castro, holds a faculty training grant awarded by the Ministry of Education (FPU16/05234).

Contents

Part I Introduction 1

1 Introduction. The Values of Public Service Media in the Internet Society 3
Marta Rodríguez-Castro, Francisco Campos-Freire, and Miguel Túñez-López

2 Public Service Broadcasting and Democracy: Main Research Topics and Suggestions for the Future 21
Manuel Goyanes

Part II Innovation Strategies 43

3 Public Service Media in the Age of Platformization of Culture and Society 45
Tiziano Bonini Baldini, Miguel Túñez-López, and Almudena Barrientos Báez

4 Can Automated Strategies Work for PSM in a Network Society? Engaging Digital Intermediation for Informed Citizenry 59
Jonathon Hutchinson and Jannick Kirk Sørensen

5 Are Public Service Media Necessary in the Transmedia Era? 77
   Esteban Galán-Cubillo, María Soler-Campillo, and Javier Marzal-Felici

6 Public Service Media and Blockchain Technology: First Thoughts 93
   Juan Carlos Miguel-de-Bustos and Jessica Izquierdo-Castillo

7 Analysis of the Quality of the Websites of Regional Public Television Networks in the European Union: Comparative Study Between Spain, Germany, and Belgium 111
   Ana María López-Cepeda, Belén Galletero-Campos, and Vanesa Saiz-Echezarreta

Part III Governance and Regulation 127

8 The Governance of Public Service Media for the Internet Society 129
   Francisco Campos-Freire, Martín Vaz-Álvarez, and María José Ufarte Ruiz

9 Canadian Communication Policies in the Post-Netflix Era 155
   Michel Sénécal and Éric George

10 Public Service Media Interventions: Risk and the Market 173
   Marta Rodríguez-Castro, Caitriona Noonan, and Phil Ramsey

11 Media and the Internet Access Providers in an Era of Convergence 193
   Pierre-Jean Benghozi and Françoise Benhamou

Part IV Democratic Reinforcement — 215

12 Media Capture and Its Contexts: Developing a Comparative Framework for Public Service Media — 217
Marius Dragomir and Minna Aslama Horowitz

13 The Challenge of Media and Information Literacy for Public Service Media — 247
José Manuel Pérez Tornero, Alton Grizzle, Cristina M. Pulido, and Sally S. Tayie

14 Electoral Debates in Television and Democratic Quality: Value Indicators — 275
Iván Puentes-Rivera, Paulo-Carlos López-López, and José Rúas-Araújo

15 Trends on the Relationship Between Public Service Media Organizations and Their Audiences — 293
Carmen Costa-Sánchez, Barbara Mazza, and Ana Gabriela Frazão-Nogueira

16 State Media and Digital Citizenship in Latin America: Is There a Place for the Weak? — 309
Natalí Schejtman, Ezequiel Rivero, and Martín Becerra

Index — 327

NOTES ON CONTRIBUTORS

Minna Aslama Horowitz is a docent and a member of the Helsinki Media Policy Research Group at the University of Helsinki, fellow at the Institute of International Communication, St. John's University, New York, and expert on Advocacy and Digital Rights at the Central European University, Vienna. Her research projects at the University of Helsinki include a multi-method project on trust, emotions, and legacy media, as well as a multiyear, multidisciplinary project on communication rights.

Almudena Barrientos Báez is a professor at the Iriarte School of Tourism of the University of La Laguna, as well as at the Universidad Europea. She holds a degree in Tourism and a PhD with an international mention in Education. Her main research lines are tourism, communications, social media, business management, emotional intelligence, and gender.

Martín Becerra is tenured professor at the National University of Quilmes and at the University of Buenos Aires and researcher at the National Scientific and Technical Research Council (CONICET). He is doctor and magister in Information Sciences from the Autonomous University of Barcelona. He has authored books on communication policies, concentration of media, and information technologies.

Pierre-Jean Benghozi is a CNRS research director and professor at the Ecole Polytechnique in Paris, and the University of Geneva. He was a member of the ARCEP (French independent agency in charge of the regulation of telecoms) from 2013 to 2019.

Françoise Benhamou is Professor of Economics at Sorbonne Paris Nord University. She was a member of the ARCEP (French independent agency in charge of the regulation of telecoms) from 2012 to 2018.

Tiziano Bonini Baldini is Associate Professor of Sociology of Culture & Communication at the Department of Social, Political and Cognitive Sciences, University of Siena. His main current research topics are radio studies, Public Service Media, critical political economy of the media, cultural industries, and platform studies. He coedited (with Belen Monclus) the book *Radio Audiences and Participation in the Age of Network Society* (ECREA Series, 2014) and he has extensively published articles in international academic journals. He is a member of the RIPE network and has served as freelance consultant for the Media Intelligence Service of EBU.

Francisco Campos-Freire is Full Professor of Journalism in the Faculty of Communication Sciences of the University of Santiago de Compostela. His main research lines are the management of media companies, the study of the impact of social networks and innovation on traditional media, and the funding, governance, accountability, and transformation of European Public Service Media. In the professional field, he has worked as editor and director in several Spanish newspapers and television and radio companies.

Carmen Costa-Sánchez is full professor in the Department of Sociology and Communication Sciences of the University of A Coruña (UDC). She is research coordinator of the research group 'Culture and Interactive Communication'. She is winner of the outstanding doctoral award granted by the School of Communication Sciences of the University of Santiago de Compostela. She teaches corporate communication in the bachelor's degree program in audiovisual communication of the University of A Coruña. Her main research interests are corporate communication, audiovisual communication, social media, and health communication.

Marius Dragomir is the Director of the Center for Media, Data and Society, a research center at Central European University (CEU). He is also a visiting professor at CEU School of Public Policy in Budapest and Vienna. He has previously worked for the Open Society Foundations (OSF) for over a decade where he was the main editor of the research project 'Mapping Digital Media', which covered 56 countries worldwide, and the main writer of 'Television Across Europe', a comparative study of broadcast policies in 20 European countries.

Ana Gabriela Frazão-Nogueira holds a PhD in Audiovisual Communication and Journalism from the University of Santiago de Compostela (USC) and is in charge, also giving teaching support in the press, radio, and hypermedia laboratories of the Fernando Pessoa University in Porto. As a member and external collaborator of the Grupo Novos Medios of USC, the author has main research interests in infographics, journalism, visual journalism, automation of journalistic content, content design, media communication, journalistic genre, and hypermedia or journalistic content.

Esteban Galán-Cubillo is a lecturer at Universitat Politècnica de València and a researcher of the group "Communication, Art and Digital Culture" (ARTICOM). He has worked as audiovisual storyteller and he has more than 15 years of experience as producer in different TV broadcasters. He has been awarded with several academic prizes such as the 3rd National Award in Communication Audiovisual in Spain (2003). He has published articles, and participated in courses, lectures, and international conferences on communication, transmedia, TV technologies, and media. Since 2017 he runs the podcast Transmedia: comtransmedia.com.

Belén Galletero-Campos has worked as a journalist for a decade and is a professor at University of Castilla-La Mancha (UCLM). She has carried out research at Centro de Estudos de Comunicação e Sociedade (Universidade do Minho, Portugal), has led research projects for entities such as the Institute for Women of Castile-La Mancha and Plan International Foundation. She is currently participating in two state research projects. Her research interests are local media, television, and digital transition.

Éric George is a full professor at the School of Media in the Université du Québec à Montréal (UQAM), director of CRICIS, member of the Royal Society of Canada, and coeditor of the tic&société review. He is interested in the relationships between communication, capitalism, and democracy from the political economy of communications, cultural studies, and critical theory perspectives. He coordinated the publication of two volumes titled *Digitalization of Society and Socio-political Issues* that appeared in French and English in 2019 and 2020. Website: https://ericgeorge.uqam.ca.

Manuel Goyanes teaches at Carlos III University in Madrid and his main interests are in media management and sociology of communication sciences. He has written about leadership, news overload, and business models. His works have appeared in leading journals like *Scientometrics*, *Information, Communication & Society*, *Journalism*, *Journalism Studies*, *Journalism & Mass Communication Quarterly*, and so on.

Alton Grizzle is Programme Specialist in Communication and Information at UNESCO. He is a UNESCO focal point on gender and media and is co-manager of UNESCO's global actions on media and information literacy (MIL). He has a diverse education and experience in the fields of education, management, information systems, and media and communication. He has conceptualized and spearheaded many projects and coauthored and edited books and articles related to MIL, gender and media, media development, and communication for development.

Jonathon Hutchinson is Senior Lecturer in Online Communication and Media at the University of Sydney. His research explores Public Service Media, cultural intermediation, everyday social media, automated media, and algorithms in media. He is an award-winning author and his latest book is *Cultural Intermediaries: Audience Participation and Media Organisations* (2017), published through Palgrave Macmillan.

Jessica Izquierdo-Castillo is an associate professor in the Department of Sciences of Communication at Jaume I University. She is director of the research group OBCOP (Observatory of Content and Media Platforms). Her lines of research focus on the study of the media ecosystem, digital platforms, and business models. She has been a visiting scholar at different universities, such as Université Stendhal, Paris 13, Università degli Studi di Firenze, University of Vienna, and The City University of New York. She has authored many articles that have appeared in many books and national and international journals.

Ana María López-Cepeda is a professor and vice-dean of the Faculty of Communication at the University of Castilla-La Mancha (UCLM). She is specialized in public media services in Europe. She is Principal Investigator of the Research Group in Sociology of Communication at the University of Castilla-La Mancha and Principal Investigator of the research project "Indicators of profitability in the media for regional development," funded by the Government of Castilla-La Mancha. She is also part of a USC-led

R&D project about the new values, governance, financing and services of public service media.

Paulo-Carlos López-López holds a PhD in Communication and Creative Industries at the Universidade de Santiago de Compostela (USC), where he is Professor of Political Sciences at the Department of Political Sciences and Sociology. He holds a Diploma of Advanced Studies in Communication and Journalism (USC) and a degree in Journalism and Political Sciences and Public Administration (international relations). He is a specialist in political communication and transparency, with extensive experience in electoral campaigns and parliamentary management.

Javier Marzal-Felici is Doctor and Bachelor in Audiovisual Communication, Hispanic Philology, and Philosophy from the University of Valencia. He is Full Professor of Audiovisual Communication and Advertising at the University Jaume I, where he coordinates the Doctoral Program in Communication. He directs the Department of Communication Sciences and the Research Group ITACA-UJI, whose interests focus on the study of visual culture, the relationships between technology and visuality, picture theory, the political economy of communication, and the analysis of audiovisual texts.

Barbara Mazza is associate professor in the Department of Communication and Social Research at the Sapienza University of Rome, where she teaches Corporate Communication and Event Management and Communication. She is the director of the master's degree in Organization and Marketing for Business Communication and is also responsible for the sport communication of the Sapienza University. She is a member of IRNIST, International Research Network in Sport Tourism, and the local coordinator of several research projects at national and international level. Her main research interests concern the corporate communication, sport communication, and university communication.

Juan Carlos Miguel-de-Bustos is a full professor in the Department of Audiovisual Communication of the Faculty of Social Sciences and Communication at Universidad del País Vasco – EHU. He is the director of the scientific journal ZER, specialized in Communication Studies. Since 1987, he teaches Economy of Cultural Industries and Marketing. His research is focused on strategies of the cultural industries and corporate groups. He is doing research on public regional televisions and on the GAFAM (Google, Apple, Facebook, Amazon and Microsoft).

Caitriona Noonan is Senior Lecturer in Media and Communication at Cardiff University. She researches screen production and cultural policy. She is leading a funded project which examines the strategies for economic and cultural sustainability adopted by publicly funded screen agencies. With Professor Ruth McElroy, she is author of the book *Producing British Television Drama: Local Production in a Global Era* (Palgrave, 2019). More information about her research is available at www.smallnationsscreen.org.

José Manuel Pérez Tornero is Professor of Journalism at the Autonomous University of Barcelona (UAB). He is an expert in public television and in educational and cultural programs. He is director of the UNESCO Chair on Media and Information Literacy for Quality Journalism and of the Chair on News Innovation (RTVE-UAB) that promotes the Observatory for News Innovation in the Digital Society (RTVE-UAB), OI2. He is the director of the Scientific Research Group Communication and Education Cabinet at the Faculty of Communication Sciences, UAB.

Iván Puentes-Rivera holds a PhD in Communication, a degree in Advertising and Public Relations, and a master's degree in Communication from the Universidad de Vigo. He is a Professor of Communication in the Department of Sociology and Communication Sciences of the Universidad de A Coruña, Spain. He has authored several papers and reports on communication managements, mainly in the fields of political, electoral, and institutional communication and televised electoral debates, and he has a professional background working in management and political communication.

Cristina M. Pulido is a Serra Húnter Fellow at the Department of Journalism and Communication Sciences of the Autonomous University of Barcelona. She is member of the UNESCO Chair on MIL for Quality Journalism and Member of the Chair of News Innovation (RTVE-UAB) that promotes the Observatory for News Innovation in the Digital Society (RTVE-UAB), OI2. She is the director of Scientific Journal *Anàlisi* focused on Communication and Journalism Research.

Phil Ramsey is lecturer in the School of Communication and Media, and member of the Centre for Media Research at Ulster University, UK. His research on Public Service Media has addressed subjects such as public value, the shifting of linear television channels online, and the role of radio in the public sphere. His research has been published in international journals that include *Media, Culture & Society*, *Television and New Media*, *Convergence*, and the *European Journal of Communication*.

Ezequiel Rivero is a doctoral candidate in the Department of Social Sciences at the University of Buenos Aires and National Scientific and Technical Research Council (CONICET) grant holder (2016–2021) at the National University of Quilmes.

Marta Rodríguez-Castro holds a BA degree in Audiovisual Communication from the University of Santiago de Compostela and a MA degree in Media Research from the University Carlos III de Madrid. She is a PhD candidate at the University of Santiago de Compostela thanks to a grant awarded by the Ministry of Education (FPU16/05234). Her main research lines involve the regulation and values of Public Service Media. She is visiting fellow at the Center for Media, Data and Society of the Central European University.

José Rúas-Araújo is Professor of Political Communication at the Faculty of Social and Communication Sciences of the Universidad de Vigo, where he directs the Department of Audiovisual Communication and Advertising. He is the main principal investigator of the R +D + i project "DEVATv, Televised Electoral Debates in Spain: Models, Process, Diagnosis and Proposal" (Ref. CSO2017-83159-R), funded by the Ministry of Science, Innovation and Universities (MCIU) of the Government of Spain, the State Research Agency (SRA), and the European Regional Development Fund (ERDF).

Vanesa Saiz-Echezarreta is a professor and vice-dean of the Faculty of Communication at the University of Castilla-La Mancha. She is a researcher in the area of theory of communication and sociocultural analysis. She is specialized in semiotics and discourse analysis. She is member of the research group: "Semiotics, Communication and Culture," and is working in a I + D project about construction of public affairs and controversies in the mediated social sphere. She has been member of the Administrative Council of Castilla-La Mancha Media, the regional public media in Castilla-La Mancha.

Natalí Schejtman is a producer, journalist, and doctoral candidate in the Department of Social Science at the University of Buenos Aires and Fondo para la Investigación Científica y Tecnológica (FONCyT) grant holder (2018–2021) at the National University of Quilmes. She was an executive producer for Primal and worked at Canal Encuentro between 2012 and 2017.

Michel Sénécal is a full professor at TÉLUQ University, researcher, and member of the CRICIS steering committee. He is interested in the hybridization of the audiovisual sectors, the implementation of new tools for accessing the industry's products in the digital era, and the long-term development of these phenomena. He was the visiting professor at University Paris 8, Universidad Autónoma de Baja California, Sciences Po Toulouse, and the University of the Basque Country in Bilbao.

María Soler-Campillo is Bachelor in Economics from the University of Valencia, Master in Tax System from CEU-San Pablo of Valencia, and Doctor in Business and Institutional Communication from the University Jaume I (UJI). She is Assistant Professor in Audiovisual Business Administration at UJI. Her research focuses on the study of the structures of European, Spanish, and Valencian communication systems, the political economy of communication, and the management of communication companies. She is a member of the ITACA-UJI Research Group.

Jannick Kirk Sørensen is Associate Professor in Digital Media at Communication, Media and Information technologies under Department of Electronic Systems at Aalborg University, Copenhagen, Denmark. Since 2007 he has researched and discussed implications for Public Service Media of algorithmic content provision, for example, personalization and algorithmic recommendation. Having a background as a PSM journalist he teaches topics recommender systems, user experience, and computer ethics to computer engineers.

Roberto Suárez Candel is the Head of Strategy & Media Intelligence of the European Broadcasting Union since 2017. From 2012 to 2017, he was the Head of the Media Intelligence Service. Since 2015, he has led the EBU strategic initiative Public Service Media Contribution to Society. Previously, he worked as a Marie Curie postdoctoral Fellow at the Hans-Bredow-Institut für Medienforschung in Germany. As an academic researcher and lecturer, he has worked in Sweden (Stockholm University) and Spain (Pompeu Fabra University). His work was focused on communication policy, Public Service Media, and ecology of the media.

Sally S. Tayie is Doctor in Journalism and Communication from the Autonomous University of Barcelona. She is a university lecturer at the Arab Academy for Science, Technology and Maritime Transport in Cairo, Egypt. She obtained her BA and MA in Journalism and Communications from the American University in Cairo. She is also a researcher in the Scientific Research Group-Communication and Education Cabinet and a teacher in the Communication and Education Online Master's program.

Miguel Túñez-López is professor at the Department of Communication Sciences of the University of Santiago de Compostela, where he is part of the research group Novos Medios (New Media) and co-directs the research project "New values, governance, financing and public audiovisual services for the Internet society: European and Spanish contrasts." He is also Deputy Director of Social and Legal Sciences of the International Doctoral School of the USC and co-director of the scientific journal *RAE-IC*.

María José Ufarte Ruiz is a lecturer at the Faculty of Communication of the University of Castilla-La Mancha, where she teaches in the area of Journalistic Writing. She is a visiting professor at the University of La Frontera, Chile, and at the University of Rome La Sapienza, Italy, and has participated in several R +D + i projects. Her lines of research include the influence of emerging technologies on journalistic genres and new journalistic narratives.

Martín Vaz-Álvarez is a BA graduate in Journalism from the University of Santiago de Compostela (USC) and an MA graduate in Research in Journalism and Audiovisual Communication from the Autonomous University of Barcelona (UAB). He is working as a Predoctoral Fellow at the Department of Communication Sciences of the University of Santiago de Compostela through an FPU grant (ref. FPU19/06204). His research interests include the integration of new technologies, innovation, and co-creation in Public Service Media.

LIST OF FIGURES

Fig. 11.1	Duration of return on capital invested (ROI) by sector, France, average 2013–2017, number of years (Source: Fédération Française des Télécoms, 2019)	198
Fig. 11.2	Telecom operators in the content production value chain	201
Fig. 13.1	Five laws of Media and Information Literacy. Source: http://www.unesco.org/new/en/communication-and-information/media-development/media-literacy/mil-as-composite-concept/	262
Fig. 13.2	*Fake news et complotisme, comment s'y retrouver?* Source: Lumni	265
Fig. 13.3	Education aux médias et à l'information. Source: Lumni	266
Fig. 13.4	*BBC Young Reporter*—lesson plans. Source: BBC	267
Fig. 13.5	Oi2	267
Fig. 13.6	Keywords in EPRA search. Source: EPRA	269

LIST OF TABLES

Table 3.1	Periodization of PSM values	48
Table 6.1	Advantages for players involved in the cultural industries	98
Table 11.1	Top deals in technologies, media, and telecoms in France, 2018	196
Table 11.2	Investments of telecom operators, France, 2014–2018 (€ billion)	198
Table 11.3	Premier League football TV rights value (€ billions)	200
Table 12.1	Summary findings based on the comparative framework for public service media	240
Table 13.1	A brief overview of media literacy/media and information literacy development	250
Table 13.2	Context, actors, competences, and processes	254

PART I

Introduction

CHAPTER 1

Introduction. The Values of Public Service Media in the Internet Society

Marta Rodríguez-Castro, Francisco Campos-Freire, and Miguel Túñez-López

1   PUBLIC SERVICE MEDIA IN THE DIGITAL AGE: KEEPING UP WITH CONSTANT CHANGE

From the very origins of both radio and television broadcasting, public service organizations have been in charge of serving the communication needs of their citizens. Much has changed since the time when public service broadcasters operated under a monopoly regime, justified both in terms of spectrum scarcity and in relation to the importance granted to this kind of mass communication by national governments (van Cuilenburg and McQuail 2003), or with very little competition. Both the societies they serve and the market environment within which they operate have undergone major transformations that call for public service broadcasters

M. Rodríguez-Castro (✉) • F. Campos-Freire • M. Túñez-López
Department of Communication Sciences, Universidade de Santiago de Compostela, Santiago de Compostela, Spain
e-mail: m.rodriguez.castro@usc.gal; francisco.campos@usc.es; miguel.tunez@usc.es

© The Author(s), under exclusive license to Springer Nature Switzerland AG 2021
M. Túñez-López et al. (eds.), *The Values of Public Service Media in the Internet Society*, Palgrave Global Media Policy and Business, https://doi.org/10.1007/978-3-030-56466-7_1

to adopt new strategies in order to remain relevant, while enduring the core values that sustain a publicly funded media company.

Regardless of the size, market power or model adopted by a public service broadcaster in each specific context, these organizations experienced a quite challenging transformation since the mid-1990s, as online and digital media started to develop, changing the communication markets for good. Public service broadcasters then evolved into Public Service Media (PSM) organizations (Bardoel and Lowe 2007; Brevini 2010), a process that authors like Donders (2019, p. 1012) consider still a "work in progress." Their traditional activity in the radio and television market was expanded and PSM organizations launched catch-up and on-demand platforms (Rodríguez-Fernández et al. 2018), developed new ways to connect with their audiences through social media (van Dijck and Poell 2015), experimented with innovative narratives, including immersive (Gutiérrez-Caneda et al. 2020) and transmedia products (Franquet and Villa Montoya 2014) and exploited the personalization potentialities posed by the new digital environment (Schwarz 2016; Vaz Álvarez et al. 2020). This digital expansion was also accompanied by major organizational reforms, affecting the organizations' charts and newsrooms (Larrondo et al. 2016), which had to be redesigned in order to adapt to new workflows of content production; its culture, which must evolve from protectionism to a partnership framework (Głowacki and Jackson 2019); and its funding models, which in some cases (such as the license fee attached to the ownership of a television set) became unsustainable in the face of new consumption habits (Warner 2019).

In addition to the internal challenges posed by this digital transformation, Public Service Media organizations also had to face remarkable resistance to their online project from commercial media. The traditional attacks from private broadcasters were joined by the print media sector as well, as newspapers and magazines were experiencing their own digital transformation too. In this context of adaptation streams shaping the media market, public service broadcasters' digital and online activities were seen by commercial media as a constraint for the success of their new business models. Thus, numerous complaints were filed to the Directorate General of Competition of the European Commission claiming that the digital expansion of public service broadcasters was not covered by their public service remit and therefore constituted illegal State aid that was distorting the market (Donders 2015). This resulted in the update of the Commission's State aid rules to public service broadcasting in 2009. In this new Broadcasting Communication (European Commission 2009), the Commission acknowledged the right for public service broadcasters to introduce their online activities within their mission, although it also recommended the introduction of an ex ante test that would counterbalance the public value and the market impact of a proposed new service in order to decide on its approval. Since then, over ten countries have (diversely) introduced this kind of procedures (Donders and Moe 2011) to govern the digital expansion of their PSM organizations. The market approach adopted by the Commission (Brevini 2013) and materialized in this ex ante regulation added an extra layer of complexity to the PSM project across Europe, as public broadcasters had to ensure that their new services would not distort competition.

2 The Need for Legitimacy in a Challenging Environment

All the above-mentioned challenges emerging from PSM's digital transformation have recently escalated as increasing competition from digital platforms, changes on funding models, and different kind of threats from political actors are eroding PSM's legitimacy in the current media environment.

The dominance of digital platforms is disrupting all legacy media outlets. The new digital economy imposed by these technological companies is changing the way media outlets conceive their business models. Moreover, both private and public media organizations must reflect on the relationship they want to establish and develop with these tech giants, counterbalancing staying in control of their content (and its monetization) and missing the opportunity to reach wider audiences. In the online environment, the relevance of PSM organizations is still minuscule when compared with the presence, impact, and gatekeeping power of digital platforms. Even the digital project of the BBC, which is deem as one of the strongest PSM organizations worldwide, both in terms of market power and reputation, is still minimal compared to these tech giants. As summarized by Nielsen (2020a), "offline, the BBC is still a giant. Online, it is not." Of course, traditional radio and television services are still relevant (see, for instance, the increase on TV news consumption during the coronavirus crisis, in Newman et al. 2020), but in order to maintain their legitimacy in the long term (and thus survive), PSM organizations must build and safeguard their own space within the digital realm as well.

One of the main reasons behind this urgent need for PSM to be relevant online lies in the changes of media consumption, especially among young audiences, who are increasingly accessing news and media content online. A recent research conducted by the Reuters Institute for the Study of Journalism proved that "most PSMs struggle to reach younger audiences with news" (Schulz et al. 2019, p. 19), as this audience segment tends to use digital platforms such as Facebook or YouTube to be informed. Similarly, in the field of entertainment, audiences are also migrating from linear broadcasting to subscription video on-demand services, the main growth driver in the audiovisual market, according to the European Audiovisual Observatory (2020, p. 54). The consumption habits that young audiences are developing now are likely to become mainstream patterns of use in a few years (Reiter et al. 2018), so beyond the current implications for the universalism principle by which PSM organizations must attempt to reach all audiences, the problem might escalate in the future: if PSM does not reach young audiences when they are configuring their own media consumption habits, they might risk losing them for good.

This challenging task of engaging young audiences is being faced by most PSM organizations under insufficient financial conditions. According to the European Broadcasting Union (EBU 2019), PSM organizations within the European Union (EU) have still not recovered from the impact of the 2008 financial crisis and their budgets remain stagnated: in real terms (i.e., considering inflation), EU PSM institutions have lost on average 4.0% of their funding from 2014 to 2018. Besides budget constraints, PSM organizations have also experienced changes on their funding models. These institutions are mainly funded through public funds and, in some cases, also through commercial activities (such as advertising or the selling of their original productions). This mixed funding system is widely spread, although the way public funds are allocated diverges significantly from country to country. The license fee used to be the most widespread funding stream, but it has experienced some adaptations lately in order to comprehend new consumption habits. In 2013, Germany moved to a household license fee, the UK adapted its license fee in 2017 in order to include the iPlayer, therefore not limiting its payment to households with a television set, and the Italian one was linked to electricity bills as a measure to fight evasion (Warner 2019). Other countries opt to fund their PSM organizations through direct grants derived from the State budget, as is the case of Spain. This type of public funding can be problematic as it may hinder PSM's independence from the government.

Funding, therefore, can be an important weapon that governments and political parties can use to threat or constraint PSM organizations, as demonstrated by the 2017 Media Pluralism Monitor, that considers that PSM funding represents an average medium risk in the EU (Brogi et al. 2018). But governments and political parties can exert pressure and erode PSM's reputation also through direct threats and attacks targeting these institutions. The most straightforward of these attacks took place in Switzerland in 2018, with the celebration of a referendum on the funding of the Swiss PSM organization, SRR-SRG. The proposal to defund SRR-SRG was launched by youth associations of the two main right-wing political parties and was based "on the fight for advertising between public and private media, the need for greater monitoring of SRR and its lack of austerity and trust" (Campos-Freire et al. 2020). The Swiss people supported the continuance of their PSM organizations on the polls, although there was great concern about the possibility of the removal of SRR-SRG from the Swiss media environment, considering its contribution to local, public journalism.

Different articulations of these attacks have been replicated in other countries. In Germany, for instance, the right-wing populist party "Alternative für Deutschland" has fiercely attacked the media during the 2017 electoral campaign and called for the abolishment of the license fee that funds the German PSM organizations ARD and ZDF (EJO 2018). In Spain, the traditional attacks from the opposition parties against the political pressures exerted by the government party on the public broadcaster RTVE (Goyanes et al. 2020) reached a higher level of criticism when the extreme right political party "Vox" proposed to privatize regional PSM organizations, tempering its original proposal to shut them down (González 2019). Even the BBC has experienced a drop of political support in the past years, as the UK government suggested to replace the license fee for a subscription-based funding model, which would entail major implications for the PSM organization in terms of focus and competition (Nielsen 2020b).

Considering all the challenges that have just been summarized, the endurance of strong, legitimate PSM organizations built on social support seems to be a path full of financial, political, and disruptive obstacles. For PSM to be able to navigate that path, not just merely surviving but managing to prevail as the cornerstone of democratic media environments, regardless of all the changes that these environments may experience in the future, these organizations must bear in mind the values that they traditionally stood for, as well as those that are arising and must be adopted as a consequence of evolving communication needs. PSM organizations should develop innovative strategies that consider these values as their compass, guiding their activity toward the contribution that they can bring to society in very different levels. Only through the reinforcement of its values will PSM be able to navigate the storm.

3   Ensuring Core Values, Embracing Emerging Ones

The value of Public Service Media has been widely discussed by both professionals and academics. Recently, as PSM organizations became the target of increasing scrutiny, they have been forced to prove and explain the value that they provide (Martin and Lowe 2014) in order to make a case for themselves. However, demonstrating value (or, rather, values) can be a slippery task. The value of PSM is difficult to define because of its multidimensional and even subjective nature. The content and the services provided by a PSM organization can be valued differently by different people (or by different stakeholders). Likewise, this value can also be understood differently from an individual or a social point of view, or from a market perspective or a cultural one. PSM organizations must be able to understand the different dimensions that their potential value can encompass in order to better fulfill its public service remit, because it is through the creation of value (and the demonstration of such value) that they legitimize themselves in front of the citizens they serve.

The digital transition of public service broadcasters came along with a handy term that aimed at encapsulating all these different dimensions of value. The notion of "public value," originally developed by Mark H. Moore (1995) to renew public management through innovation and citizens' engagement, was first transferred from public sector management to public service broadcasting in relation to the BBC as a way to legitimize its continuance in 2004. Since then, public value has been defined in diverse ways depending on the countries, stakeholders, and interests behind such definition. Moe and Van den Bulck consider "public value" a buzzword that can serve very different functions, as "for some, it is a new regulatory concept meant to discipline public service broadcasters, while others see it as a way to 'defend' and promote what public service institutions do" (Moe and Van den Bulck 2014, p. 73). Spigelman (2014, p. 54) argued that this abstract feature of "public value" can be beneficial when used as a synonym for "public benefit, public interest or public good," or even when it is disaggregated into different types of values, as the BBC did by establishing five elements of public value (democratic, cultural and creative, education, social and community value). However, this abstraction can be detrimental in the *measuring* or assessment of public value, as the nature and complexity of PSM content and services does not allow for straightforward metrics.

Beyond this abstract sphere of public value, there have been other attempts to define and disaggregate PSM value. The original Reithian triad that guided the functioning of the BBC (and other public service broadcasters that looked up to the British corporation) almost since its foundation, based on informing, educating, and entertaining the public, is still definitely relevant for any current PSM organization, although, at the same time, these three elements on their own could barely serve all the communication needs of today's societies and should be complemented with other core values. The European Broadcasting Union developed a new framework of PSM core values, adapted to the digital environment. This framework (EBU 2012) established six essential values: universality, independence, excellence, diversity, accountability, and innovation. Universality is understood as the commitment to reach all audiences through all platforms, not leaving anyone behind in order to contribute to shaping a public sphere where everyone can be included. Independence from political and commercial forces is key for operating autonomous organizations that can be trusted by citizens. By excellence, the EBU calls for PSM organizations to work toward professionalism, integrity, quality, and the engagement of the citizens. PSM must also be inclusive and diverse, including, representing and giving a voice to all minorities that make up modern societies. As public entities, they must be transparent and accountable in its functioning. Finally, PSM organizations have to be committed to the development of innovation strategies in order to drive media change in the current digital and disruptive context.

EBU's proposal has been extremely valuable for PSM organizations. These six values constitute a framework that all Public Service Media should embrace in order to comply not only with their organizational responsibilities regulated by their respective media laws, but also with their audiences' expectations. But as the media environment is characterized by its dynamism, so have to be the value that PSM organizations create. To better understand the potential benefits than can be provided by PSM, we can establish a distinction between the core values that have been part of this institutions' mission since its origins, which would include EBU's framework, and the ones that PSM organizations should be integrating as new communication needs emerge and new value systems are developed within the society. This second type of values can be contextual (i.e., developed during a specific period, as it could be the COVID-19 pandemic), but they can more often than not become part of PSM's integral, core values. As societies grow and evolve, they become increasingly complex and so do their communication needs and their value systems. PSM has an obligation to keep up with this evolution in order to remain relevant and valuable for their public.

One example of a growing value within current societies that permeates PSM organizations is ecology and the concern for climate change. As PSM organizations are free from commercial pressures and, in principle, don't need to fight for audience figures in the same way as commercial broadcasters do, they constitute a suitable platform for the representation, debate, and understanding of climate change (Debrett 2017). Providing a space for the coverage of climate-related issues and doing so in such a way that can raise awareness and educate on this increasingly concerning field are new tasks for PSM organizations. Moreover, some of them are taking this responsibility to another level by implementing green measures within the organization. The BBC, for instance, is developing a "greener broadcasting" strategy (2018–2022) based on the idea that, as a public institution, the corporation must implement sustainability measures that aim at reducing its environmental impact. By establishing sustainability as a value that governs the BBC's production and supply chain, as well as by creating content that raises awareness on the need to stop climate change (see, for instance, the documentary *Blue Planet II*), the public corporation can innovate and find new ways to engage with an audience that increasingly cares about the health of the planet. This could even be a profitable strategy from a managerial point of view, as stated by the Director General Tony Hall: "reducing energy consumption and waste saves money which will enable us to spend more money on programmes and content" (BBC 2018, p. 3).

Some other values can be contextual, in the sense that they emerge during very specific times. The COVID-19 pandemic that stopped the world in the spring of 2020 provides an interesting case study in this regard, one that should definitely be the object of in-depth future research. By now, some reports have already highlighted the way PSM organizations have contributed to support citizens in these unprecedented times (see, for instance, EBU 2020). The pandemic drew the audiences to broadcast television and increased the consumption of news in general (Newman et al. 2020). But in the middle of this information abundance (as well as dangerous fake news and misinformation), PSM organizations proved to be reliable sources of information that citizens can trust, as proven by the increase on audience figures of PSM's evening news on an average of 20% and the fact that the reach of their online news websites more than doubled (EBU 2020).

Beyond news and the special coverage of the pandemic, PSM organizations have also engaged in other actions to support citizens. For instance, as schools were shut down, PSM organizations such as RTVE, France TV or ORF developed and broadcasted educational programming to support both teachers and students. Staying at home also required some source of entertainment: RTVE launched the site "Somos Cine" ("We are cinema"), where an extensive catalogue of Spanish films could be freely accessed; the void left on sport programming by the cancelation of all events was filled with archived sports that were rebroadcasted by, for instance, RAI in Italy; and in the UK the BBC launched "Culture in Quarantine," a virtual festival that offered diverse creative content, such as theater plays, performances, and cinema to the British audiences. In Spain, where gyms were closed and citizens were not allowed to go out to exercise during the hardest weeks of the pandemic, RTVE launched the show "Muévete en casa" ("Move at home"), a daily half an hour of exercise with the professional trainer Cesc Escolà, aimed at people of all ages who wanted to avoid physical inactivity.

The COVID-19 pandemic thus proved that Public Service Media is still a paramount agent within media ecosystems. In the midst of the crisis, PSM organizations were able to remain trusted agents that citizens turned to seeking reliable information and quality content, innovating in order to serve new communication needs that emerged in this unparalleled situation. This experience shows that the combination of core and contextual values is key for PSM organizations to remain committed to its original public service remit while innovating and exploring new ways to engage their audiences and contribute to society.

This book explores how Public Service Media provides value to different audiences and stakeholders in the Internet society. The contributions gathered in this volume are structured in three main sections, approaching (1) PSM's innovation strategies, (2) its governance and regulation, and (3) its democratic reinforcement. The analytical framework applied by the contributors is mainly based on the triangulation of the theoretical foundations, policy documents and gray literature that enables the study of organizational strategies deployed (or that should be deployed) by Public Service Media in different international contexts.

In order to provide a better understanding of the current situation of Public Service Media, in Chap. 2 Manuel Goyanes presents the results of his review of the last years' research published on this object of study. According to this literature review, the author identified four main areas that have been widely covered by communication scholars, namely the impact of digitization and new technologies on PSM, in relation to, for instance, convergence and audience participation; the funding and business models of PSM, focusing on their relation to the wider market, their effects on competition and the opportunities of mixed models; the policies and regulation that affect PSM, both in terms of national and supranational regulation (i.e., the European Union) and in relation to broader theories such as neoliberalism and multistakeholderism; and how PSM organizations can (or should) create public value and safeguard citizen's interests. Goyanes also suggests three research lines that could be interesting to delve into in further research: the provision of feasible strategies to PSM's current challenges, the quality and features of PSM's content and its relation to social media, and widening the scope of the analysis in order to include cultural and artistic variables.

After this introductory section, Part I approaches some of the main strategies that PSM organizations are developing both to push innovation forward and to keep up with fast-moving technological and digital advances. Developing a platform strategy, both in terms of building their own online platforms and algorithmic strategies and in terms of studying their relationship with third-party platforms, is a key issue that needs to be resolved for PSM to maintain its relevance. This relates to the need to build transmedia strategies that contribute to the presence of the PSM brand in every medium and platform, from radio and television to websites and social media. The possibilities that new technologies such as blockchain offer for PSM organizations are also approached in this first part of the book.

Part I starts with an approximation to the platformization of PSM. Tiziano Bonini Baldini, Miguel Túñez-López, and Almudena

Barrientos Báez approach the relation between PSM and digital platforms from a political economy perspective. After providing a periodization of the evolution from public service broadcasting to Public Service Media and the authors attached to each paradigm, in Chap. 3 the authors, Tiziano Bonini Baldini, Miguel Túñez-López, and Almudena Barrientos Báez, argue that PSM organizations must evolve into Public Service Platforms in order to keep their legitimacy in the face of greater platformization of both societies and culture.

In close connection with platformization, in Chap. 4 Jonathon Hutchinson and Jannick Kirk Sørensen explore the challenges and the opportunities posed by automated and algorithmic strategies in the production and distribution processes of media content. These AI and big data actions have been integrated by commercial media, digital platforms and social media, but PSM organizations must find their own algorithmic strategy where their core values, that is, diversity and universality, are safeguarded. The authors argue that automated and algorithmic strategies can help PSM organizations demonstrate distinctiveness and redefine traditional gatekeeping roles.

Esteban Galán-Cubillo, María Soler-Campillo, and Javier Marzal-Felici ask themselves in Chap. 5 whether PSM organizations are necessary in the transmedia scene. To answer this question, they delve into the case of the Valencian Community (Spain), where its public service broadcaster was shut down in 2013 and reopened in 2017 with the ambition to embrace the transmedia environment. Learning from the mistakes of its predecessor, *À Punt Media* is now playing a key role in maintaining a proximity media space for Valencian speakers and in providing cultural and educational content, especially for young audiences, who benefit from the transmedia strategy of the corporation. As the authors argue, this kind of innovation is essential for the sustainability of Public Service Media.

In Chap. 6, Juan Carlos Miguel-de-Bustos and Jessica Izquierdo-Castillo explore the possibilities that blockchain technology can bring to the field of PSM. Despite the fact that blockchain projects have been predominantly developed under market logics, this transparent, democratic, and secure technology has the potential to contribute to the several areas of PSM's value chain, from the management of contracts, to the identification of fake news, opening new funding possibilities through crowdfunding, and increasing audience participation. Even though there are still no PSM experiences with blockchain, the authors consider that they should start experimenting with this new technology.

In the closing chapter of this part dedicated to PSM's innovation strategies the websites of proximity PSM organizations are reviewed by Ana María López-Cepeda, Belén Galletero-Campos, and Vanesa Saiz-Echezarreta. The authors study the way the websites of regional PSM in Spain, Germany, and Belgium can provide value in different areas, such as technical innovation, accessibility, diversity, media literacy, or citizen participation. The value provided by the websites of German and Belgic PSM is deemed greater than that created by the Spanish public broadcasters, although all of them contribute to the development of a regional and local public sphere through the promotion of co-official or minority languages and the support of content targeting children and young audiences.

In Part II of this book, the focus is moved toward the organizational value PSM organizations can provide, from the point of view of governance and regulation. This part delves into the relation between PSM organizations and the broader context within which they operate. This involves both the increasing intertwining between telecom and media companies, as well as the long-established dispute between public and private media companies.

In Chap. 8, Francisco Campos-Freire, Martín Vaz-Álvarez, and María José Ufarte-Ruiz approach the different governance models that PSM organizations adopt in different EU member states, providing a solid background for the book's Part II, focusing on governance and regulation. Drawing on the genealogy of the origins of public service broadcasting and the evolution of these institutions during the past century until now, the authors provide an overview on the different ways PSM is regulated, structured, governed, and funded throughout Europe and highlight independence as a core value that needs to be strengthened in PSM governance.

Chapter 9 takes the reader to Canada. Michel Sénécal and Éric George explore the evolution of the public policy on the broadcasting and telecommunications sectors in Canada, from an original interventionist and protectionist approach, to a neoliberal one since the 1980s. Such an evolution, especially with regard to new media, has created the perfect scenario for transnational companies such as Netflix, which are not subjected to production nor distribution quotas in the same way that other media and telecommunication companies are. In this context, the authors wonder which role should Canadian PSM play in the protection of the Canadian culture, identity, and languages.

Marta Rodríguez-Castro, Caitriona Noonan, and Phil Ramsey approach Public Service Media's market impact from a positive perspective in Chap. 10. The authors apply a risk frame to explore the way PSM organizations contribute to creating and shaping creative markets, identifying two main areas where PSM's activity is key: the creation of a supply base in different national and regional contexts, especially valuable as it sustains an important labor market; and supporting digital innovation, which contributes to advancing the media market as a whole. These two types of risk taken by PSM are examples of the economic and social value these organizations generate within the media market and the digital economy.

In Chap. 11, closing this section on governance and regulation, Pierre-Jean Benghozi and Françoise Benhamou tackle one of the key concepts affecting the economics of the Internet society: convergence between media and Internet Access Providers. As telecommunication and media companies become closer together, their business models and their objectives change. According to the authors, this situation disrupts both the media market and the regulators' work, as convergence can challenge some of the core values of European digital policies, such as net neutrality, diversity, and innovation.

Part III concentrates some examples of the relation between PSM and democracy, both from positive and negative experiences. On the bright side, the promotion of media literacy, the role of PSM organizations in televised electoral debates or the way they engage with young audiences are good examples of the value PSM can bring to societies as a whole. However, there is always a risk for PSM organizations to be captured by different interests, so this democratic value must not always be taken for granted.

Minna Aslama Horowitz and Marius Dragomir open the third part of this book, dedicated to PSM's democratic reinforcement, and explore the extent to which PSM organizations are being captured by political and commercial pressures in five European countries: Finland, Spain, Belgium, the Czech Republic, and the UK. Even though media capture is a phenomenon that can affect all actors of a media system, its impact on PSM organizations is especially relevant because it targets one of their core values: their independence. In Chap. 12, the authors delve into three main questions surrounding the capture of PSM in the above-mentioned countries, namely the role PSM plays within its national media system, the public discourses that approach PSM, and the structural factors that lead to capture.

Media and Information Literacy is the subject of Chap. 13, where José Manuel Pérez Tornero, Alton Grizzle, Cristina M. Pulido, and Sally Tayie develop, first, an overview on the main initiatives developed in this field by the European Commission and the UNESCO over the past 25 years, and then explore three initiatives that link media literacy and PSM organizations: *Lumni* in France, *BBC-Bitesize* in the UK and the observatory Oi2 RTVE-UAB in Spain. The authors argue that both PSM organizations and media authorities have a major role to play in the development and monitoring of media and information literacy initiatives.

Iván Puentes-Rivera, Paulo-Carlos López-López, and José Rúas-Araújo establish in Chap. 14 a set of 50 indicators for the standardized assessment of the democratic quality of televised electoral debates. Considering these debates as powerful instruments for PSM to contribute to shaping the public opinion and to strengthen citizen participation in public issues, the authors explore key aspects in the organization and programming of electoral debates that create democratic value by balancing the need to engage large segments of audience with ensuring the credibility of the show.

In Chap. 15, Carmen Costa-Sánchez, Barbara Mazza, and Ana Gabriela Frazão-Nogueira explore the strategies deployed by three PSM organizations (RTVE in Spain, the Italian RAI, and the Portuguese RTP) in order to strengthen their relationship with young audiences, an especially difficult target for PSM. In the development of digital platforms and multimedia, interactive and innovative content is deemed key by the authors. The three case studies describe different ways for PSM to attract young audiences, including educational content, reality television or brand projects that aim at getting closer to millennials and Gen Z in such a way that they are consistent with their public service remit and values.

The closing chapter of this book approaches the situation of PSM in Latin America. Natalí Schejtman, Ezequiel Rivero, and Martín Becerra point to two different developments of Latin American state media: expansionary processes, linked to the increase of resources and of content development alternate with others of retraction, when the budgets and productive capacity of these media organizations are diminished. The authors advocate for an active role of Latin American state-media in the development of a digital citizenship that strengthens communication rights such as the universal access to diverse and pluralistic content that enables dialogue with and among citizens.

All 16 chapters contribute to a better understanding of the role that Public Service Media plays in the current media systems, as key agents for the development of the public sphere and democratic societies. It is not the purpose of this book to lay down an exhaustive list of values that PSM should comply with, but to provide some examples and experiences that highlight the contribution of these organizations to both the media environment and society as a whole. Surely many more examples of PSM value can be added to those pointed out in this book, from positive, paradigmatic cases to troubling ones that may work as negative lessons.

Despite the fact that there might be some core values that are desirable to find in every publicly funded media organization, it is not possible to develop a universal value model common for all of them, considering the major differences (in size, budget, culture, policy environments, social needs) among them. However, it is indeed desirable to raise awareness on the value creation possibilities that are enabled by strong, adaptative, open PSM organizations, for different stakeholders, in different contexts and through different means.

References

Bardoel, J., & Lowe, G. F. (2007). From Public Service Broadcasting to Public Service Media. The Core Challenge. In G. F. Lowe & J. Bardoel (Eds.), *From Public Service Broadcasting to Public Service Media* (pp. 9–26). Göteborg: Nordicom.

BBC. (2018). *Greener Broadcasting. Creating a Positive Environmental Impact*. London: BBC. Retrieved June 11, 2020, from http://downloads.bbc.co.uk/aboutthebbc/insidethebbc/howwework/reports/pdf/greener_broadcasting.pdf.

Brevini, B. (2010). Towards PSB 2.0? Applying the PSB Ethos to Online Media in Europe: A Comparative Study of PSBs' Internet Policies in Spain, Italy and Britain. *European Journal of Communication, 25*(4), 348–365. https://doi.org/10.1177/0267323110381004.

Brevini, B. (2013). European Commission Media Policy and Its Pro-market Inclination: The Revised 2009 Communication on State Aid to PSB and Its Restraining Effect on PSB Online. *European Journal of Communication, 28*(2), 183–197. https://doi.org/10.1177/0267323112470227.

Brogi, E., Nenadic, I., Parcu, P. L., & Viola de Azevedo Cunha, M. (2018). *Monitoring Media Pluralism in Europe: Application of the Media Pluralism Monitor 2017 in the European Union, FYROM, Serbia & Turkey* [Report]. European University Institute. Retrieved June 10, 2020, from https://cadmus.eui.eu/bitstream/handle/1814/60773/CMPF_PolicyReport2017.pdf?sequence=4.

Campos-Freire, F., Rodríguez-Castro, M., & Blasco-Blasco, O. (2020). Public Service Media's Funding Crisis in the Face of the Digital Challenge. In Á. Rocha, C. Ferrás, C. M. Marin, & V. M. García (Eds.), *Information Technology and Systems. ICITS 2020. Advances in Intelligent Systems and Computing*. Cham: Springer. https://doi.org/10.1007/978-3-030-40690-5_64.

Debrett, M. (2017). Representing Climate Change on Public Service Television: A Case Study. *Public Understanding of Science, 26*(4), 452–466. https://doi.org/10.1177/0963662515597187.

Donders, K. (2015). State Aid to Public Service Media: European Commission Decisional Practice Before and After the 2009 Broadcasting Communication. *European State Aid Quarterly, 14*(1), 68–87.

Donders, K. (2019). Public Service Media Beyond the Digital Hype: Distribution Strategies in a Platform Era. *Media, Culture & Society, 41*(7), 1011–1028. https://doi.org/10.1177/0163443719857616.

Donders, K., & Moe, H. (Eds.). (2011). *Exporting the Public Value Test. The Regulation of Public Broadcasters' New Media Services Across Europe*. Göteborg: Nordicom.

EBU. (2012). *Empowering Society. A Declaration on the Core Values of Public Service Media*. Geneva: European Broadcasting Union. Retrieved June 11, 2020, from https://www.ebu.ch/files/live/sites/ebu/files/Publications/EBU-Empowering-Society_EN.pdf.

EBU. (2019). *Funding of Public Service Media 2019. Public Version*. Geneva: European Broadcasting Union.

EBU. (2020). *Update: COVID-19 Crisis. PSM Audience Performance [Public Version]*. Geneva: European Broadcasting Union. Retrieved June 11, 2020, from https://www.ebu.ch/publications/research/membersonly/report/covid-19-crisis-psm-audience-performance.

EJO. (2018, April 22). Germany's AfD: With the Media and Against the Media. *European Journalism Observatory*. Retrieved June 11, 2020, from https://en.ejo.ch/media-politics/with-the-media-and-against-the-media.

European Audiovisual Observatory. (2020). *Yearbook 2019/2020. Key Trends*. Strasbourg: European Audiovisual Observatory. Retrieved June 11, 2020, from https://rm.coe.int/yearbook-keytrends-2019-2020-en/16809ce58d.

European Commission. (2009). Communication from the Commission on the Application of State Aid Rules to Public Service Broadcasting. 2009/C 257/01. Retrieved June 11, 2020, from https://eur-lex.europa.eu/legal-content/EN/TXT/?uri=celex%3A52009XC1027%2801%29.

Franquet, R., & Villa Montoya, M. I. (2014). Cross-Media Production in Spain's Public Broadcast RTVE: Innovation, Promotion and Audience Loyalty Strategies. *International Journal of Communication, 8*, 2301–2322.

Głowacki, M., & Jackson, L. (2019). Organisational Culture of Public Service Media: People, Values, Processes. Retrieved June 11, 2020, from https://www.creativemediaclusters.com/images/Glowacki_Jackson_2019.pdf.

González, M. (2019, May 21). Vox ya no pide cerrar las televisiones autonómicas sino privatizarlas. *El País*. Retrieved June 11, 2020, from https://elpais.com/politica/2019/05/20/actualidad/1558374996_861017.html.

Goyanes, M., Vaz-Álvarez, M., & Demeter, M. (2020). Political Pressures in TVE: Cascade Effects, Morphology of Manipulations and Professional and Personal Reprisals. *Journalism Practice* (online first). https://doi.org/10.1080/17512786.2020.1772098.

Gutiérrez-Caneda, B., Pérez-Seijo, S., & López-García, X. (2020). Analysing VR and 360-degree Video Apps and Sections. A Case Study of Seven European News Media Outlets. *Revista Latina de Comunicación Social, 75*, 149–167. https://doi.org/10.4185/RLCS-2020-1420.

Larrondo, A., Domingo, D., Erdal, I. J., Masip, P., & Van den Bulck, H. (2016). Opportunities and Limitations of Newsroom Convergence. A Comparative Study of European Public Service Broadcasting Organisations. *Journalism Studies, 17*(3), 277–300. https://doi.org/10.1080/1461670X.2014.977611.

Martin, F., & Lowe, G. F. (2014). The Value and Values of Public Service Media. In G. F. Lowe & F. Martin (Eds.), *The Value of Public Service Media* (pp. 19–40). Göteborg: Nordicom.

Moe, H., & Van den Bulck, H. (2014). Comparing 'Public Value' as a Media Policy Term in Europe. In G. F. Lowe & F. Martin (Eds.), *The Value of Public Service Media* (pp. 57–76). Göteborg: Nordicom.

Moore, M. (1995). *Creating Public Value: Strategic Management in Government*. Cambridge: Harvard.

Newman, N., Fletcher, R., Schulz, A., Andı, S., & Nielsen, R. K. (2020). *Reuters Institute Digital News Report 2020*. Oxford: Reuters Institute for the Study of Journalism. Retrieved June 11, 2020, from https://reutersinstitute.politics.ox.ac.uk/sites/default/files/2020-06/DNR_2020_FINAL.pdf.

Nielsen, R. K. (2020a, June 5). The World Has Changed Much Faster than the BBC. The New DG Need to Confront That. *Reuters Institute for the Study of Journalism*. Retrieved June 11, 2020, from https://reutersinstitute.politics.ox.ac.uk/risj-review/world-has-changed-much-faster-bbc-new-dg-needs-confront.

Nielsen, R. K. (2020b, March 12). Op-ed: Politics, Waning Public Attention Are Existential Threats to the BBC. *Columbia Journalism Review*. Retrieved June 11, 2020, from https://www.cjr.org/opinion/bbc-license-fee-model-conservative.php.

Reiter, G., Gonser, N., Grammel, M., & Gründl, J. (2018). Young Audiences and Their Valuation of Public Service Media. A Case Study in Austria. In G. F. Lowe, H. Van den Bulck, & K. Donders (Eds.), *Public Service Media in the Networked Society* (pp. 211–226). Nordicom: Göteborg.

Rodríguez-Fernández, M. M., Sánchez-Amboage, E., & Toural-Bran, C. (2018). Public Service Media in the Online Arena. *Revista Latina de Comunicación Social*, 73, 911–926. https://doi.org/10.4185/rlcs-2018-1288en.

Schulz, A., Levy, D., & Nielsen, R. K. (2019). *Old, Educated, and Politically Diverse: The Audience of Public Service News*. Oxford: Reuters Institute for the Study of Journalism. Retrieved June 11, 2020, from https://reutersinstitute.politics.ox.ac.uk/sites/default/files/2019-09/The_audience_of_public_service_news_FINAL.pdf.

Schwarz, J. A. (2016). Public Service Broadcasting and Data-Driven Personalization: A View from Sweden. *Television & New Media*, 17(2), 124–141. https://doi.org/10.1177/1527476415616193.

Spigelman, J. (2014). Defining Public Value in the Age of Information Abundance. In G. F. Lowe & F. Martin (Eds.), *The Value of Public Service Media* (pp. 43–56). Göteborg: Nordicom.

van Cuilenburg, J., & McQuail, D. (2003). Media Policy Paradigm Shifts. Towards a New Communications Policy Paradigm. *European Journal of Communication*, 18(2), 181–207. https://doi.org/10.1177/0267323103018002002.

van Dijck, J., & Poell, T. (2015). Making Public Television Social? Public Service Broadcasting and the Challenges of Social Media. *Television & New Media*, 16(2), 148–164. https://doi.org/10.1177/1527476414527136.

Vaz Álvarez, M., Túñez López, J. M., & Ufarte Ruíz, M. J. (2020). What Are You Offering?: An Overview of VODs and Recommender Systems in European Public Service Media. In Á. Rocha, C. Ferrás, C. M. Marin, & V. M. García (Eds.), *Information Technology and Systems. ICITS 2020*. Cham: Springer. https://doi.org/10.1007/978-3-030-40690-5_69.

Warner, M. (2019). *Funding Public Media. An Insight into Contemporary Funding Models*. Norwich: Public Media Alliance. Retrieved June 11, 2020, from https://www.publicmediaalliance.org/wp-content/uploads/2017/08/Funding-Public-Media-.pdf.

CHAPTER 2

Public Service Broadcasting and Democracy: Main Research Topics and Suggestions for the Future

Manuel Goyanes

1 Introduction

Public Service Broadcasters, commonly known by the English acronym PSBs, are public entities whose traditional mission is to provide a universal and democratic mass media service (Harrison and Woods 2001). PSB is considered as a crucial pillar of democratic societies (Jacobs et al. 2016)—mostly in Europe where its role "seems, however, wider than the purely political" (Harrison and Woods 2001, p. 480)—as it also encompasses educational, social, and cultural functions. Since its origins, PSB has been essential in fostering public and civic values, ensuring citizens' access to verified information (Scannell 2005), and preserving the common culture and welfare of societies (Arriaza Ibarra and Nord 2014; Jõesaar 2011; Scannell 2005; Suárez Candel 2011).

M. Goyanes (✉)
Universidad Carlos III de Madrid, Madrid, Spain
e-mail: mgoyanes@hum.uc3m.es

In recent years, however, the traditional role of the PSB has been questioned because of growing challenges relating to its funding difficulties (Arriaza Ibarra 2013; Collins 2011; Herzog and Karppinen 2014; Huntsberger 2014; Jõesaar 2011), raising market competition (Brink Lund and Edelvold Berg 2009; Dawes 2014; Donders 2010; García de Madariaga et al. 2013; Johnson 2013), and new technologies and digital platforms (Debrett 2009; Ejbye Sørensen 2013; Kant 2014; Sjøvaag et al. 2015; Schwarz 2016) that have disrupted their long-standing business operations. In this turbulent context, the status of public media has urged broadcasters and governments to rethink PSB's business strategies and content output to preserve citizens' rights and interests (Ginosar and Krispil 2015; Iosifidis 2011; Sjøvaag et al. 2019; Van Dijck and Poell 2015).

Despite PSB's relevant role in nourishing important values (like pluralism or diversity) in democratic societies, scant attention has been paid to the potential research clusters that compose this important literature. As the academic attention on PSB has grown exponentially in recent years because of key digital and organizational transformations (D'Arma 2018; Donders et al. 2019; Evans 2018; Keinonen and Klein Shagrir 2017; Värk and Kindsiko 2019), there is a growing pressure to provide a holistic vision on the main findings and research streams. Further, given the different research communities interested in illustrating and problematizing the main social, political, and economic challenges of the PSB, there is a growing need to scrutinize its research traditions and provide new avenues of research that address thematic gaps.

2   Main Research Topics in Public Service Broadcasting

2.1   *Digitalization and New Technologies*

2.1.1   *Digital Transition and Switchover*

Since the early 2000s, new technologies and digital developments have challenged PSB, which had to constantly adapt to new formats, services, and production routines. Transition to Digital Terrestrial Television (DTT) is a clear example of the PSB's challenges because of the several political and financial decisions implied in its deployment. The switchover required a huge economical investment and rapid technological innovation, which many countries were not prepared for and, therefore, could not handle properly. However, the main problem PSBs had to face was the arrival of multiple private broadcasters, which has led to an increment of the competition and a free market logic dominance over the media landscape—conflicting with the traditional PSB's goals and obligations (Suárez Candel 2011). More specifically, PSBs must find innovative and sustainable ways to introduce the public value in a more competitive environment in which commercial broadcasters can reach larger audiences through popular programs and the entertainment genre. "The often dry and technical debate on radio spectrum management cannot obscure what is really at stake: how to adapt and secure PSB values in the emerging media environment, irrespective of which transmission platform(s) will succeed" (Michalis 2016, p. 348). Previous studies have proven that—considering the new market-oriented logic—the PSB needs more regulation and supervision to avoid commercial and advertising activities and ensure its traditional principles and stakeholders' benefits (Evens et al. 2010).

2.1.2 Use of Social Media

As previously explained, digitalization has challenged PSBs in several important ways. In this category, the papers included have observed the challenges faced by public broadcasters trying to maintain an accurate and balanced social media presence: "with the potential for networked multimedia, the Web has challenged journalism to adapt to its capacities by, for instance, incorporating audio and video and adding polls, quizzes, comments or games to the text based news reporting" (Sjøvaag et al. 2015, p. 11). Certain studies (Horsti and Hultén 2011; Evans 2018) have analyzed the impact of the competition created by social media, which has led to the development of new strategies and practices to reach and attract more viewers and obtain enough revenue to maintain financial stability. According to some studies (Moe 2013; Stollfuß 2018; van Dijck and Poell 2015), PSB's main social media challenge is the conflict between their public character and the commercial and private interest that dominate digital platforms. According to Stollfuß (2018), the configuration and algorithm processes of social media have transformed the informational conditions and communication forms of a democratic citizenship.

These sites are characterized by their universal access and free public distribution; however, to ensure their stability, Social Networking Sites (SNS)—or other platforms including Google or YouTube—allow third-party companies to advertise their products and services, which is against the traditional principles and publicly funding of PSBs:

Apple and Google have offered to share revenues with content providers but the offered terms have not yet proven attractive. Further new business models may emerge [...] But such a business strategy depends on viewers being addressable [...] and may not do much to fund public content. [...] In consequence, advertising revenues generated from video on demand and/or sport or movie channels may not flow to fund news and public information. (Collins 2011, p. 1210)

2.1.3 Audience Participation and Engagement

This theme refers to the steady transformation of the audience's consumption and viewing habits. The new media landscape has turned the audience's role into a more active and participative one: "multi-platform productions only provide television with new forms of interactivity as the one-to-many medium is accompanied by other many-to-many mediums" (Keinonen and Klein Shagrir 2017, p. 72). One PSB strategy (and of the private broadcasters) to reach and engage more viewers is to develop more participatory and interactive contents in which spectators act as participants (Enli and Ihlebæk 2011). The aim of this tactic is to give viewers a voice and include them in the content's production, achieving loyalty and universality: "this new socio-technical landscape is empowering the viewers with both a voice—mobilized largely through social media networks—and choice—providing a plurality of content and tools that allow viewers to map their own self-directed trajectories through this multi-platform environment" (Kant 2014, p. 383).

However, some studies have shown that this strategy actually responds to private and economic interests as the audience's participation and interaction do not directly lead to a more democratic and horizontal production, but to a competition increment—a rise of the funding revenues and the audience's fragmentation. Only one of the aforementioned studies (Millanga 2014) has demonstrated that the use of new technologies, such as the mobile phone, has resulted in a more horizontal and reciprocal communication, because citizens from different population sections and conditions are able to openly discuss public and local issues. However, it is important to note that this study was conducted in undeveloped countries in Africa, where the traditional broadcasting service is characterized by complete state control. Therefore, the addition of interactive technologies has provided a voice to the different minorities and ethnicities, which does not mean that broadcasters and producers, in fact, hear these new voices.

2.1.4 Convergence

Another major line of research addresses the convergence processes and models imposed by the digital development and the multi-platform formats:

> the communication field has for years been defending a transmission model that is capable of bringing together the best of the old and new media, with the result that, in the present stage, the relation of online with traditional media has ceased to be understood in terms of replacement and subordination, and has given way to new conceptions based on complementariness and coordination. (Larrondo et al. 2012, p. 790)

Some studies focus on the convergence's impact over the journalists' work and practices (Larrondo et al. 2016; Värk and Kindsiko 2019). The confluence of different mediums, such as merging radio, television, and newspaper's headquarters in one single company, implies new routines and professional habits characterized by collaboration, cooperation, and multi-skilled attitudes, suggesting fewer degrees of specialization and higher levels of competition and workload (Larrondo et al. 2016). Others (Larrondo et al. 2012; Puijk 2015; Vanhaeght and Donders 2016) focus on the European countries' challenges to transform the PSB into PSM, or Public Service Media, which are, in essence, the need for more interaction and co-creation and the adaptation of their traditional routines and formats to the new media to reach viewers. However, this change implies more competition: "audiences of traditional media, especially the press, are declining, habits of news consumption have changed, and advertising revenues are diminishing, while there is increasing competition to retain them" (Larrondo et al. 2016, p. 278), since public and private broadcasters have access to the same services and technologies.

2.2 Business Model and Funding

2.2.1 Competition and Conflict with Commercial Broadcasters

Digitalization and technological evolution have brought several challenges to PSBs, regarding not only formats and services but also funding and financial revenues. The contemporary media environment is defined by the media's privatization:

> As more and more media content is accessed through the broadband internet, public broadcasters such as the ABC and SBS face the issue that—in contrast to their broadcast services—each incremental increase in demand for online content brings additional delivery costs, so they can face the 'curse of rising popularity' as it increases costs without increasing revenue. (Flew 2009, p. 10)

As some studies exemplify (Curran et al. 2009; D'Arma 2018), media privatization stimulates the economy and implies a higher strain to reach audiences, which broadcasters justify as a benefit for the public; if there is more competition to ensure the audience share, more innovative and quality contents will be offered to attract viewers. Nevertheless, results have demonstrated that the outcome is actually the opposite and, if there is more competition, the public broadcasting's content and production process will be less democratic. This occurs because of the soft and superficial content provided by commercial broadcasters. By trying to reach and engage more consumers, private channels offer popular and trivial content (as entertainment or popular shows) as this type of programming suits all audiences, what leads to a PSB content's reshaping to approach private broadcasters and, therefore, a lack of quality and information of the public programs. Then, the problem is to ensure the public value and citizen interest while competing with private actors. To achieve this, states and institutions have opted to public funding and media regulation to ensure a democratic and well-informed citizenship. Thus, public broadcasters receive governmental subsidies that are used to warrant programs that do not generate enough income to maintain its production, as cultural or public affairs programs do (Curran et al. 2009). Following this strategy, PSB is required to differentiate their public funding and activities from their commercial ones, as advertising or partnerships, to secure that public funding is devoted to the public interest, what means that governmental and institutional revenues are not subsidizing private interests (Flynn 2015).

Public funding has proven insufficient to ensuring a high-quality public service in the current media system. Therefore, most public broadcasters have opted for a mixed model or advertising formats. However, as Jakubowicz (2011) notes, it is necessary to guarantee the PSB principles—such as citizens' interest, content diversity, pluralism, social inclusion, and democratic values—while acquiring funding from other sources: "money is a relevant factor when one aims to make outstanding (and domestically produced) programmes" (Donders 2010, p. 69). Nevertheless, private companies have denounced this strategy as an unfair competition, since the commercial broadcasters are entirely funding by private and market operations and are competing in the same environment as public broadcasters, which also benefit from public budgets:

> The exclusive (i.e. non-competitive) access of PSBs to public funding was characterized as conferring 'privileged status' (Ward 2004: 93) upon those broadcasters. This status was challenged in a series of legal actions at the European level in the 1990s: commercial players in France, Italy, Spain, Portugal, and Ireland filed legal complaints to the effect that public funding of public broadcasters, through licence fees or direct subsidy, constituted state aid incompatible with the Treaty of Rome provisions on competition law. (Flynn 2015, p. 127)

Thus, in the case of the European Union, the solution has been to limit the public service remit to assure fair competition between public and private actors and prevent the PSB from engaging in activities aimed at economical profits.

2.2.2 Mixed Models

As previously illustrated, some broadcasters benefit from both public and private funding systems. While providing high quality, diverse, and informative content, public broadcasters engage in commercial activities and allow advertising content in their programming to avoid political intervention and institutional dependency. This is because the competitive environment created by the commercial counterparts is meant to lead to greater content diversity (Smith 2009). The most popular example of this dual system is the British Broadcasting Corporation, BBC, which was the first in combined public and private funding to assure impartiality and sufficient resources to create quality content and preserve the citizens' interest (Ramsey 2016). As some studies have explained (Donders and Raats 2015; Mjøs 2011; Smith 2009), mixed models enable PSBs to serve the public and offer local, cultural, and plural content corresponding to some of its principal values. Thus, thanks to the advertising activities and market-oriented strategies, public broadcasters can afford the costs of the production processes and the technological investment. Nevertheless, in most cases, broadcasters are under political pressure to legitimize their public character and financial model, as well as demonstrate that public funding fulfills the public's needs and requirements (Johnson 2013).

2.3 Policies and Regulation

2.3.1 Multi-Stakeholder Approach

In some European countries—such as the United Kingdom, Germany, and Sweden—public broadcasters resort to the multi-stakeholder consultation to secure diversity, plurality, and democratic values in PSB programming. This strategy's objective is to include more actors involved in the regulation and production processes to warrant the public interest and inclusion of educational and cultural content (Donders and Raats 2012; Van den Bulck and Donders 2014). However, current research has shown that the multi-stakeholder approach—while trying to ensure democracy, consensus, and a greater representation and inclusion of all society groups—has proven to be the opposite of democracy. There is a domination of some agents, especially commercial ones, which results in a prioritization of private interest over public value (Donders et al. 2019).

2.3.2 Government Regulation and Influence

One strategy to ensure democracy and preserve public interest is government regulation (Ginosar and Krispil 2015). A PSB, in its origins, should serve the public and satisfy the social and local demands and needs. Therefore, some governments must supervise and control the broadcasting practices, such as the Spanish PSB, in which the institutional regulation molds the communication field and audio-visual processes (Fernández Alonso et al. 2010). Furthermore, as Ogus (2004) explains, government supervision serves to warrant the public value by reflecting all political attitudes and correcting market failures: "identifying the market failures that justify state intervention and selecting the methods of intervention that predictably will correct that failure at least cost" (Ginosar and Krispil 2015, p. 4). Nevertheless, some studies have demonstrated that the political and ideological influence over PSB is not beneficial to democracy or the citizens but, rather, results in the media's lack of independence and autonomy that benefits private interests and political preferences (Arriaza Ibarra 2013). Moreover, in other cases—including undeveloped geographies or ex-socialist countries, such as China—the state aid control results in the ideological manipulation and rights reduction: "de-emphasis of individual equality, and the subordination of individual liberty to collective and state interests in the Chinese Constitution, as well as by the government's practice of implementing collective rights to subsistence and development ahead of civil and political rights" (Chan Chin 2012, p. 907).

2.3.3 Neoliberal Approach and Deregulation Process

Three studies analyze the PSB's deregulation processes and neoliberalism practices to avoid political intervention. As Dawes (2014, p. 707) indicates, government supervision influences media production and distribution in favor of ideological preferences:

> the construction of the public as a passive citizenry of recipients of state aid, requiring state interference and thus compromising their freedom from the state (and the legitimacy of the liberal state as one that does not interfere in the private realm), broke down the public–private distinction between politics and economy, and undermined just as much as market processes the ability of citizens to form an active public and hold political power to account.

Therefore, some broadcasters have opted for a deregulated model characterized by media independence, impartiality, and a free-market driven system, because—as Larsen (2014) notes—the market is better qualified than governments to preserve the citizens' independence. Nevertheless, Thussu (2007) argues that media autonomy—while implying more competition—threatens democracy because viewers are considered consumers, not citizens, and the production processes are submitted to the economical profit, leading to poor-quality content and a prioritization of popular genres: "public television is increasingly sold off and market competition is reshaping the values of the television news genre. The information environment, in other words, is diminishing as media markets become privatised" (Cushion et al. 2012, p. 832).

2.3.4 Small Countries, Third Democracies, and Undeveloped Nations

PSB is a central element of the European democracies, as well as other countries, including Australia, Canada, and the United States. However, in small countries or undeveloped geographies, the PSB's role has proven different. Two articles have observed the PSB's role in small countries such as Macedonia, Finland, and Serbia, where there is little space for private broadcasters and marketers as their population size is insufficient to be economically motivating. Therefore, governments of these countries have more responsibility to offer and ensure diversity, information, and high quality in PSB content. In this case, the strategy followed by public broadcasters and regulators was the opposite of other European countries. The goal was to guarantee the presence of private companies in the media landscape and ensure the commercial competition because the market failure was unaffordable to the PSB's budgets (Jõesaar 2011).

However, in non-democratic geographies and third democracies, the PSB implementation was seen by Aaron Rhodes (2007) as a path to democracy and a strategy to achieve social and political transformation: "stable, independent, and functional media are seen as a means of achieving wider democratic goals. Media-specific goals focus on establishing and supporting independent media institutions. Support to PSB reform could fall into both political and media specific goals" (Marko 2015, p. 294). The same can be said for Arab countries where PSB was an essential tool for developing democracy and citizens' participation in public affairs (Ayish 2010). The European Union and other broad institutions have guided the public broadcasting model of these nations to develop the media's independency and democracy. However, some studies (Ayish 2010; Marko 2015) have demonstrated that the media transformation did not result in political changes because the social and cultural contexts of each nation remain dominant.

2.3.5 European Union and Homogenization

The European Union is instrumental in media regulation and funding for all state members. Some studies (Just et al. 2012; Spasovska and Imre 2015; Van den Bulck and Moe 2012) analyze the EU pressures to distinguish between public and commercial financing and justify the public remit as a tool to protect democracy and warrant transparency and independence. Some studies (Donders and Pauwels 2010; Psychogiopoulou and Kandyla 2013) have demonstrated that the EU guidelines have a global and homogenic character that do not consider each nation's particularities and context, resulting in several challenges as the national features predominate over common commandments (Van den Bulck and Moe 2012). In this case, the implementation of new formats or services has failed, such as the aforementioned transition to DTT. Three articles have observed a recent transformation in the EU practices from a regulatory attitude to a free-market prevalence. This resolution has led to the implementation of an ex ante test that state members must apply to approve new services (Donders and Pauwels 2010; Van den Bulck and Moe 2012; Just et al. 2012). The tests consist of two steps—public value evaluation and market impact: "on the one hand, new media services' public value must be evaluated. On the other hand, their positive and negative effects on the market should be calculated as well. On the basis of these two components, governments have to approve the delivery of a service" (Donders and Pauwels 2010, p. 137). Following this strategy, governments clarify the PSB's role and warrant the traditional principles while avoiding the PSB's participation in commercial activities.

2.4 Public Value and Citizen Interest

2.4.1 Public Role and Citizen Interest

Since its origins, PSBs, especially in Europe, have maintained a democratic role and serve the citizens: "generally, [the] PSB can be considered as 'a major pillar of the democratic process'" (Iyengar 2009; cited in Jacobs et al. 2016, p. 3). However, as some articles explain (Esser and Majbritt Jensen 2015; Sjøvaag et al. 2019), the PSB should provide citizens with high-quality, diverse, and tolerant content; ensure universal access; and inform each societal group. As the Amsterdam Treaty on PSB (1997) declares, "the system of public broadcasting in the Member States is directly related to the democratic, social, and cultural needs of each society and to the need to preserve media pluralism'" (cited in García de Madariaga et al. 2013, p. 911). Furthermore, PSBs must address market failure, ensure citizens are well informed, and utilize public funding to ensure democracy and transparency (Sjøvaag et al. 2019). However, PSBs face several challenges because of market impact and digitalization, as previously mentioned. Thus, PSBs must find a balance between popular and soft content, which attracts large population sections (as entertainment or sensationalism), and informative and cultural programs, which help maintain PSB quality and status (Esser and Majbritt Jensen 2015).

2.4.2 Educate and Inform

Education and culture are some of the main values of PSBs. Nevertheless, this type of programming does not attract the private and commercial broadcasters because of its audience share and scant revenues that do not cover the production and distribution costs (Huntsberger 2014; Pajala 2010; Shepperd 2014; Steemers and D'Arma 2012). Therefore, educational and cultural programs are considered a market failure that PSBs should supply and provide, as follows: "there are still likely to be important gaps in market provision, and thus there continues to be a continuing justification for a strong PSB presence in this area" (D'Arma and Labio 2017, p. 2). Nevertheless, as we have seen, PSBs must find a balance between the commercial success and popularity and the public and cultural values. For this purpose, some public broadcasters have prioritized what Grummel (2009) calls edinfotainment—educational and cultural content adapted to the entertainment genre and to popular formats and programs: "educational producers adopted new programme styles and strategies to attract viewers, blending educational material with entertainment and information strategies from mainstream broadcasting" (Grummel 2009, p. 276).

2.4.3 Distinctiveness

In a more competitive and commercial environment, PSBs must differ from their private counterparts to attract viewers and ensure revenues: "incentivizes the audience to stay within the content of a vertical or create hype around it, thereby increasing the potential for generating advertising revenue" (Ejbye Sørensen 2013, p. 43). To accomplish this, some broadcasters, including the BBC, have opted for a mixed model: "distinctiveness here seems to be associated with innovation, risk-taking, the overall volume of what the report calls 'PSB genres' in peak-time (identified rather narrowly as 'including specialist factual, arts, classical music and comedy'), 'challenging genres' and programmes, as well as 'service innovation'" (Goddard 2017, p. 1902). Following this strategy, the BBC was able to create an actual brand as its quality guarantee; thus, the British broadcaster can afford different multi-platform strategies to reach larger audiences in the United Kingdom and globally: "provide brand security for viewers, visitors and documentary producers. To be a successful site, it is therefore not just the ability to produce or deliver documentary content that matters, the ability to vouch for its quality is equally important" (Ejbye Sørensen 2013, p. 39).

2.4.4 Diversity and Pluralism

These values are also two main principles of PSBs. In this case, new technologies have supposed an advantage to PSBs while their development has provided public broadcasters with advanced and economical ways to reach all groups of society: "new narrowcast and on-demand services are extending ways of delivering media services, contributing more media, rather than displacing broadcasting" (Debrett 2009, p. 816). Thus, the expression and inclusion of minorities and ethnicities are guaranteed, as well as the universal access: "from the perspective of social representation, large groups of citizens, compared to minorities, have a greater ability to organise their interests and be visible in the mass media" (Mangani Tarrini 2018, p. 284). Nevertheless, research in this area (Engelbert and Awad 2014; Ala-Fossi and Lax 2016) has proven that new technologies and services depend on economic factors, which is against PSBs' core principles and leads states and governments to regulate PSBs' online activities to truly ensure pluralism and diversity.

3 Public Service Broadcasting Research: Suggestions for the Future

The increasing challenges and difficulties of PSB and Public Service Media (PSM) in maintaining its status and position as a democratic service have enabled a new research agenda for social scientists. In this context, PSBs may be instrumental in expanding and preserving public and cultural interest in democratic societies as well as ensuring a well-informed citizenship. PSB research over the last decade shows a lack of possible strategies or solutions to face the current PSB challenges, neglect of qualitative approaches for PSB programs' quality and features, limited research on multi-platform strategies and social media management besides the BBC, and the absence of a cultural analysis in a broad sense—meaning music, cinema, or stage arts.

Suggestions for future research should address a special emphasis on possible solutions and strategies to manage the current PSB's hindrances. Furthermore, a reanalysis of the extant strategies is adopted by some broadcasters, such as the BBC as well as failed cases, to determine mistakes and causes of the current instability to identify clues as a basis for possible solutions. Beyond the controversial situation, future studies might also consider including actual spectators' critiques and perceptions to rigorously analyze the public contents' quality and features. Finally, PSB's line of inquiry should consider including other artistic and cultural values, beyond national and political sentiment and identity.

3.1 Providing Possible Strategies to Face PSB Challenges

As reflected in the qualitative analysis, the PSB's current situation is challenging because of the different obstacles public broadcasters must face. Although some studies have identified and defined the phases and inconveniences when funding PSB (Collins 2011; D'Arma 2018; García de

Madariaga et al. 2013) or adopting contents and formats to digital platforms (Ejbye Sørensen 2013; Moe 2013; Van Dijck and Poell 2015; Stollfuß 2018), this analysis rests on a superficial level, as most of the studies describe the current difficult situation for public broadcasters. However, each study offers accurate and relevant proposals to face it. Thus, research on possible solutions and strategies to properly manage the PSB's hindrances is still required.

To address and solve this critical situation, future PSB research should detect not only the challenges that threaten PSB's status and its adverse consequences, but its origins, trying to identify the strategies and actors involved. Based on previous public broadcasters' experiences, the successes as well as the failures—such as the DTT implementation or the adoption of mixed models—future research should propose alternative ways to compete with commercial broadcasters and social media sites or reconfigure the funding model. Therefore, if existing and current research has extensively proven that the PSB's current plan has failed, a line of inquiry should proceed in reanalyzing and identifying the previous mistakes to reshape PSB's tactics. Furthermore, a qualitative approach is needed to test the possible solutions on different scenarios, such as the distinct multimedia platforms or services of several public broadcasters from different countries, to ensure and validate the efficiency of the potential solutions.

3.2 Public Programs' Quality and Features

Although research on PSB is extensive, most of studies remain on political, financial, or regulatory measures (D'Arma and Labio 2017; Ramsey 2016) and few of them focus on the contents' quality and features (Evens et al. 2010; Ginosar and Krispil 2015; Iosifidis 2011; Jõesaar 2011; Moe 2010; Psychogiopoulou and Kandyla 2013). Although some previous studies have analyzed the audiences' perception germane to the PSB status (Horsti and Hultén 2011; López Olano 2017), practically no study considers the public opinion about PSB contents, program structure, and variety or quality. Moreover, regarding PSB's quality, articles included in this review consider it one of the former obligations and features of PSB, especially in Europe, but a clear definition of the chief features and elements that constitute high-quality content or services is still required. Future research should move into the analysis of the viewpoints of critics and the public regarding program themes, genres, and messages as the PSB's target audience includes citizens and not the competitors, stakeholders, or institutions. Therefore, PSB's future research questions should broaden their representative samples, including not only producers and other media professionals, but also spectators and consumers to provide a wide representation of all agents' involved and value the PSB's program content.

3.3 Social Media Management in Different Contexts

PSB research germane to digital and multi-platform strategies still deeply relies on the BBC's case (D'Arma 2018; Ejbye Sørensen 2013; Goddard 2017; Ramsey 2018; Starks 2011), because it is the most successful and international public broadcaster, leaving the question on the adoption of online strategies and services to other public broadcasters. Extant literature has demonstrated that the BBC is the main public broadcaster that has succeeded in the digital environment thanks to its mixed model, partnership with commercial broadcasters, and branding strategy. However, few studies consider the techniques employed by other public services or channels; PSBs of other nations are only mentioned relating to its difficulties and failed strategies but without delving into its causes or possible alternatives. This closed perspective regarding online formats and social media platforms prevent PSB research from discovering efficient ways to manage the technological and digital challenges, because—according to Ayish (2010) and Marko (2015)—a PSB's needs and restrictions differ from one nation to another as the political, social, and cultural features remain dominant. Concisely, future research should dig deep into the digital landscape, multi-platform services, and social network sites, as this environment is in constant and rapid evolution.

3.4 Improving Cultural and Artistic Analysis

Although education and culture are two of the main PSB obligations (Esser and Majbritt Jensen 2015; Grummel 2009; Pajala 2010; Shepperd 2014), a focus should be placed on artistic and international culture. Previous studies suggest that the cultural and educational values are best suited to political and democratic interests (Huntsberger 2014; Pajala 2010; Shepperd 2014; Steemers and D'Arma 2012); indeed, in some studies, the term "culture" refers to national or local identity (Debrett 2009; Flew 2009; Spasovska and Imre 2015). This implies a lack of a cultural analysis in a broad and general sense. Therefore, PSB future research should consider a wider and more precise definition of "culture." Moreover, the actual value that PSBs offer through high-quality cultural and educational programs should be sought by analyzing the program's content regarding national identity, democratic values, and political information, as well as contemplating other artistic and cultural forms—including stage arts, cinema, or music—that are lacking in current research.

References

Ala-Fossi, M., & Lax, S. (2016). The Short Future of Public Broadcasting: Replacing Digital Terrestrial Television with Internet Protocol? *International Communication Gazette*, 78(4), 365–382. https://doi.org/10.1177/1748048516632171.

Arriaza Ibarra, K. (2013). The Situation of National and Regional Public Television in Spain Public Media in the Crossroad. *Nordicom Review*, 34(1), 145–156. https://doi.org/10.2478/nor-2013-0048.

Arriaza Ibarra, K., & Nord, L. (2014). Public Service Media Under Pressure: Comparing Government Policies in Spain and Sweden 2006–2012. *Javnost-The Public*, 21(1), 71–84. https://doi.org/10.1080/13183222.2014.11009140.

Ayish, M. (2010). Arab State Broadcasting Systems in Transition the Promise of the Public Service Broadcasting Model. *Middle East Journal of Culture and Communication*, 3(1), 9–25. https://doi.org/10.1163/187398609X12584657078448.

Brink Lund, A., & Edelvold Berg, C. (2009). Denmark, Sweden and Norway: Television Diversity by Duopolistic Competition and Co-Regulation. *The International Communication Gazette*, 33(6), 953–962. https://doi.org/10.1177/1748048508097928.

Chan Chin, Y. (2012). Public Service Broadcasting, Public Interest and Individual Rights in China. *Media, Culture & Society*, 34(7), 898–912. https://doi.org/10.1177/0163443712452700.

Collins, R. (2011). Content Online and the End of Public Media? The UK, a Canary in the Coal Mine? *Media, Culture & Society*, 33(8), 1202–12129. https://doi.org/10.1177/0163443711422459.

Curran, J., Iyengar, S., Brink Lund, A., & Salovaara Moring, I. (2009). Media System, Public Knowledge and Democracy. *European Journal of Communication*, 24(1), 5–26. https://doi.org/10.1177/0267323108098943.

Cushion, S., Lewis, J., & Ramsay, G. (2012). The Impact of Interventionist Regulation in Reshaping News Agendas: A Comparative Analysis of Public and Commercially Funded Television Journalism. *Journalism*, 13(7), 831–849. https://doi.org/10.1177/1464884911431536.

D'Arma, A. (2018). The Hollowing Out of Public Service Media: A Constructivist Institutionalist Analysis of the Commercialisation of BBC's In-house Production.

Media, Culture & Society, 40(3), 432–448. https://doi.org/10.1177/0163443717713260.
D'Arma, A., & Labio, A. (2017). Making a Difference? Public Service Broadcasting, Distinctiveness and Children's Provision in Italy and Spain. *International Journal of Digital Television, 8*(2), 183–199. https://doi.org/10.1386/jdtv.8.2.183_1.
Dawes, S. (2014). Broadcasting and the Public Sphere: Problematising Citizens, Consumers and Neoliberalism. *Media, Culture & Society, 36*(5), 702–719. https://doi.org/10.1177/0163443714536842.
Debrett, M. (2009). Riding the Wave: Public Service Television in the Multi-Platform Era. *Media, Culture & Society, 31*(5), 807–827. https://doi.org/10.1177/0163443709339466.
Donders, K. (2010). The Benefits of Introducing European Competition Principles into National Public Broadcasting Policy. *Info. Digital Policy, Regulation and Governance, 12*(6), 56–68. https://doi.org/10.1108/14636691011086044.
Donders, K., & Pauwels, C. (2010). The Introduction of an ex ante Evaluation for New Media Services: Is 'Europe' Asking for It, Or Does Public Service Broadcasting Need It? *International Journal of Media & Cultural Politics, 6*(2), 33–148. https://doi.org/10.1386/mcp.6.2.133_1.
Donders, K., & Raats, T. (2012). Analysing National Practices After European State Aid Control: Are Multi-Stakeholder Negotiations Beneficial for Public Service Broadcasting? *Media, Culture & Society, 34*(2), 162–180. https://doi.org/10.1177/0163443711430756.
Donders, K., & Raats, T. (2015). From Public Service Media Organisations to De-centralised Public Service for the Media Sector: A Comparative Analysis of Opportunities and Disadvantages. *Javnost-The Public, 22*(2), 145–163. https://doi.org/10.1080/13183222.2015.1041227.
Donders, K., Van den Bulck, H., & Raats, T. (2019). The Politics of Pleasing: A Critical Analysis of Multistakeholderism in Public Service Media Policies in Flanders. *Media, Culture & Society, 41*(3), 347–366. https://doi.org/10.1177/0163443718782004.
Ejbye Sørensen, I. (2013). Channels as Content Curators: Multiplatform Strategies for Documentary Film and Factual Content in British Public Service Broadcasting. *European Journal of Communication, 29*(1), 34–39. https://doi.org/10.1177/0267323113504856.
Engelbert, J., & Awad, I. (2014). Securitizing Cultural Diversity: Dutch Public Broadcasting in Post-Multicultural and De-Pillarized Times. *Global Media and Communication, 10*(3), 261–274. https://doi.org/10.1177/1742766514552352.
Enli, G. S., & Ihlebæk, K. (2011). 'Dancing with the Audience': Administrating Vote-Ins in Public and Commercial Broadcasting. *Media, Culture & Society, 33*(6), 953–962. https://doi.org/10.1177/0163443711412299.

Esser, A., & Majbritt Jensen, P. (2015). The Use of International Television Formats by Public Service Broadcasters in Australia, Denmark and Germany. *International Communication Gazette*, 77(4), 359–383. https://doi.org/10.1177/1748048514568766.

Evans, S. (2018). Making Sense of Innovation: Process, Product, and Storytelling Innovation in Public Service Broadcasting Organizations. *Journalism Studies*, 19(1), 4–24. https://doi.org/10.1080/1461670X.2016.1154446.

Evens, T., Verdegem, P., & De Marez, L. (2010). Balancing Public and Private Value for the Digital Television Era. *Javnost-The Public*, 17(1), 37–54. https://doi.org/10.1080/13183222.2010.11009025.

Fernández Alonso, I., Bonet, M., Guimerà, J., Díez, M., & Alborch, F. (2010). Spanish Public Broadcasting. Defining Traits and Future Challenges Following Analogue Television Switch Off. *Observatorio (OBS*)*, 4(3). https://doi.org/10.15847/obsOBS432010351.

Flew, T. (2009). The Special Broadcasting Service After 30 Years: Public Service Media and New Ways of Thinking About Media and Citizenship. *Media International Australia*, 133(1), 9–14. https://doi.org/10.1177/1329878X0913300103.

Flynn, R. (2015). Public Service Broadcasting Beyond Public Service Broadcasters. *International Journal of Digital Television*, 6(2), 125–144. https://doi.org/10.1386/jdtv.6.2.125_1.

García de Madariaga, J. M., Lamuedra Graván, M., & Tucho Fernández, F. (2013). Challenges to Public Service News Programmes in Spain: Professionals and Viewers' Discourses Wavering Between Institutional Reform and Counter-Reform. *Journalism: Theory, Practice & Criticism*, 15(7), 908–925. https://doi.org/10.1177/1464884913508609.

Ginosar, A., & Krispil, O. (2015). Broadcasting Regulation and the Public Interest: Independent Versus Governmental Agencies. *Journalism & Mass Communication Quarterly*, 93(4), 946–966. https://doi.org/10.1177/1077699015610066.

Goddard, P. (2017). 'Distinctiveness' and the BBC: A New Battleground for Public Service Television? *Media, Culture & Society*, 39(7), 1089–1099. https://doi.org/10.1177/0163443717692787.

Grummel, B. (2009). The Educational Character of Public Service Broadcasting from Cultural Enrichment to Knowledge Society. *European Journal of Communication*, 24(3), 267–285. https://doi.org/10.1177/0267323109336756.

Harrison, J., & Woods, L. M. (2001). Defining European Public Service Broadcasting. *European Journal of Communication*, 16(4), 477–504. https://doi.org/10.1177/0267323101016004003.

Herzog, C., & Karppinen, K. (2014). Policy Streams and Public Service Media Funding Reforms in Germany and Finland. *European Journal of Communication*, 29(4), 416–432. https://doi.org/10.1177/0267323114530581.

Horsti, K., & Hultén, G. (2011). Directing Diversity: Managing Cultural Diversity Media Policies in Finnish and Swedish Public Service Broadcasting. *International Journal of Cultural Studies*, *14*(2), 209–227. https://doi.org/10.1177/1367877910382180.

Huntsberger, M. (2014). Attempting an Affirmative Approach to American Broadcasting: Ideology, Politics, and the Public Telecommunications Facilities Program. *Journalism & Mass Communication Quarterly*, *91*(4), 756–771. https://doi.org/10.1177/1077699014550089.

Iosifidis, P. (2011). Growing Pains? The Transition to Digital Television in Europe. *European Journal of Communication*, *26*(1), 3–17. https://doi.org/10.1177/0267323110394562.

Jacobs, L., Meeusen, C., & d'Haenens, L. (2016). News Coverage and Attitudes on Immigration: Public and Commercial Television News Compared. *European Journal of Communication*, *31*(6), 642–660. https://doi.org/10.1177/0267323116669456.

Jakubowicz, K. (2011). Public Service Broadcasting: Product (and victim?) of Public Policy. *The Handbook of Global Media and Communication Policy*, 210–229.

Jõesaar, A. (2011). Different Ways, Same Outcome? Liberal Communication Policy and Development of Public Broadcasting. *Trames*, *15*(1), 74–101. https://doi.org/10.3176/tr.2011.1.04.

Johnson, K. (2013). From Brand Congruence to the 'Virtuous Circle': Branding and the Commercialization of Public Service Broadcasting. *Media, Culture & Society*, *35*(3), 314–331. https://doi.org/10.1177/0163443712472088.

Just, N., Latzer, M., & Saurwein, F. (2012). Public Service Broadcasting Put to Test: Ex Post Control of Online Services. *International Journal of Media & Cultural Politics*, *8*(1), 51–65. https://doi.org/10.1386/macp.8.1.51_1.

Kant, T. (2014). Giving the "Viewser" a Voice? Situating the Individual in Relation to Personalization, Narrowcasting and Public Service Broadcasting. *Journal of Broadcasting and Electronic Media*, *58*(3), 381–399. https://doi.org/10.1080/08838151.2014.935851.

Keinonen, H., & Klein Shagrir, O. (2017). From Public Service Broadcasting to Soci(et)al TV Producers' Perceptions of Interactivity and Audience Participation in Finland and Israel. *Nordicom Review*, *38*(1), 65–79. https://doi.org/10.1515/nor-2016-0037.

Larrondo, A., Larrañaga, J., Meso, K., & Agirreazkuenaga, I. (2012). The Convergence Process in Public Audio-visual Groups: The Case of Basque Public Radio Television (EITB). *Journalism Practice*, *6*(5–6), 788–797. https://doi.org/10.1080/17512786.2012.667282.

Larrondo, A., Domingo, D., Erdal, I. J., Masip, P., & Van den Bulck, H. (2016). Opportunities and Limitations of Newsroom Convergence: A Comparative

Study on European Public Service Broadcasting Organisations. *Journalism Studies*, 17(3), 277–300. https://doi.org/10.1080/1461670X.2014.977611.

Larsen, H. (2014). The Legitimacy of Public Service Broadcasting in the 21st Century: The Case of Scandinavia. *Nordicom Review*, 35(2), 65–76. https://doi.org/10.2478/nor-2014-0015.

López Olano, C. (2017). The Model for Public Television and the Young Audience's Expectations. Differences Between Great Britain and Spain in the Perception of Qualities and Obligations. *El Profesional de la Información*, 26(4), 1699–2407. https://doi.org/10.3145/epi.2017.jul.15.

Mangani, A., & Tarrini, E. (2018). Social Pluralism in Public and Private Television Broadcasting. *Javnost-The Public*, 25(3), 282–297. https://doi.org/10.1080/13183222.2018.1463044.

Marko, D. (2015). The Role of Media Assistance in the Establishment of Public Service Broadcasting in Serbia. *International Journal of Digital Television*, 6(3), 293–309. https://doi.org/10.1386/jdtv.6.3.293_1.

Michalis, M. (2016). Radio Spectrum Battles: Television Broadcast vs Wireless Broadband and the Future of PSB. *International Journal of Digital Television*, 7(3), 347–362. https://doi.org/10.1386/jdtv.7.3.347_1.

Millanga, A. K. (2014). Mobile Phones and Participatory Communication for Poverty Eradication on Public Service Broadcasting: The Case of Tanzania Broadcasting Corporation (TBC). *Mobile, Media & Communication*, 2(3), 281–297. https://doi.org/10.1177/2050157914533695.

Mjøs, O. (2011). Marriage of Convenience? Public Service Broadcasters' Cross-National Partnerships in Factual Television. *International Communication Gazette*, 73(3), 181–197. https://doi.org/10.1177/1748048510393652.

Moe, H. (2010). Governing Public Service Broadcasting: "Public Value Tests" in Different National Contexts. *Communication, Culture & Critique*, 3(2), 207–223. https://doi.org/10.1111/j.1753-9137.2010.01067.x.

Moe, H. (2013). Public Service Broadcasting and Social Networking Sites: The Norwegian Broadcasting Corporation on Facebook. *Media International Australia*, 146(1), 114–122. https://doi.org/10.1177/1329878X1314600115.

Ogus, A. (2004). W(h)ither the Economic Theory of Regulation? What Economic Theory of Regulation? In J. Jordana & D. Levi-Faur (Eds.), *The Politics of Regulation* (pp. 31–44). Cheltenham, UK: Edward Elgar.

Pajala, M. (2010). Television as an Archive of Memories? Cultural Memory and Its Limits on The Finnish Public Service Broadcaster's Online Archive. *Critical Studies in Television*, 5(2), 133–145. https://doi.org/10.7227/CST.5.2.16.

Psychogiopoulou, E., & Kandyla, A. (2013). Media Policy-Making in Greece: Lessons from Digital Terrestrial Television and the Restructuring of Public Service Broadcasting. *International Journal of Media & Cultural Politics*, 9(2), 133–152. https://doi.org/10.1386/macp.9.2.133_1.

Puijk, R. (2015). Slow Television a Successful Innovation in Public Service Broadcasting. *Nordicom Review, 36*(1), 95–108. https://doi.org/10.1515/nor-2015-0008.

Ramsey, P. (2016). Commercial Public Service Broadcasting in the United Kingdom: Public Service Television, Regulation, and the Market. *Television & New Media, 18*(7), 639–654. https://doi.org/10.1177/1527476416677113.

Ramsey, P. (2018). 'It Could Redefine Public Service Broadcasting in The Digital Age' Assessing the Rationale for Moving BBC Three Online. *Convergence, 24*(2), 152–167. https://doi.org/10.1177/1354856516659001.

Scannell, P. (2005). Public Service Broadcasting: The History of a Concept. In A. Goodwin & G. Whannel (Eds.), *Understanding Television* (pp. 20–38). London: Routledge.

Schwarz, J. A. (2016). Public Service Broadcasting and Data-Driven Personalization: A View from Sweden. *Television & New Media, 17*(2), 124–141. https://doi.org/10.1177/1527476415616193.

Shepperd, J. (2014). Infrastructure in the Air: The Office of Education and the Development of Public Broadcasting in the United States, 1934–1944. *Critical Studies in Media Communication, 31*(3), 230–243. https://doi.org/10.1080/15295036.2014.889320.

Sjøvaag, H., Stavelin, E., & Moe, H. (2015). Continuity and Change in Public Service News Online: A Longitudinal Analysis of the Norwegian Broadcasting Corporation. *Journalism Studies, 17*(8), 952–970. https://doi.org/10.1080/1461670X.2015.1022204.

Sjøvaag, H., Pedersen, T., & Owren, T. (2019). Is Public Service Broadcasting a Threat to Commercial Media? *Media, Culture & Society, 41*(6), 808–827. https://doi.org/10.1177/0163443718818354.

Smith, L. K. (2009). Consolidation and News Content: How Broadcast Ownership Policy Impacts Local Television News and the Public Interests. *Journalism & Communication Monographs, 10*(4), 387–453. https://doi.org/10.1177/152263790901000403.

Spasovska, K., & Imre, I. (2015). Transformation of the Public Broadcasting Systems in Croatia and Macedonia as Indicators of Democratic Transformation. *International Journal of Digital Television, 6*(3), 275–292. https://doi.org/10.1386/jdtv.6.3.275_1.

Starks, M. (2011). Can the BBC Live to be 100? Public Service Broadcasting After Digital Switchover. *International Journal of Digital Television, 2*(2), 181–200. https://doi.org/10.1386/jdtv.2.2.181_1.

Steemers, J., & D'Arma, A. (2012). Evaluating and Regulating the Role of Public Broadcasters in the Children's Media Ecology: The Case of Home-Grown Television Content. *International Journal of Media & Cultural Politics, 8*(1), 67–85. https://doi.org/10.1386/macp.8.1.67_1.

Stollfuß, S. (2018). Is This Social TV 3.0? On Funk and Social Media Policy in German Public Post Television Content Production. *Television & New Media*, *20*(5), 509–524. https://doi.org/10.1177/1527476418755514.

Suárez Candel, R. (2011). Public Policy Best Practice in the Field of Digital Terrestrial Television: Lessons from Sweden and Spain. *International Journal of Digital Television*, *2*(3), 297–321. https://doi.org/10.1386/jdtv.2.3.297_1.

Thussu, D.K. (2007). News as Entertainment: The Rise of Global Infotainment. London: SAGE.

Van den Bulck, H., & Donders, K. (2014). Of Discourses, Stakeholders and Advocacy Coalitions in Media Policy: Tracing Negotiations Towards the New Management Contract of Flemish Public Broadcaster VRT. *European Journal of Communication*, *29*(1), 83–99. https://doi.org/10.1177/0267323113509362.

Van den Bulck, H., & Moe, H. (2012). To Test or Not to Test: Comparing the Development of ex ante Public Service Media Assessments in Flanders and Norway. *International Journal of Media & Cultural Politics*, *8*(1), 31–49. https://doi.org/10.1386/macp.8.1.31_1.

Van Dijck, J., & Poell, T. (2015). Making Public Television Social? Public Service Broadcasting and the Challenges of Social Media. *Television & New Media*, *16*(2), 148–164. https://doi.org/10.1177/1527476414527136.

Vanhaeght, A. S., & Donders, K. (2016). Moving Beyond the Borders of Top–Down Broadcasting: An Analysis of Younger Users' Participation in Public Service Media. *Television & New Media*, *17*(4), 291–307. https://doi.org/10.1177/1527476415595871.

Värk, A., & Kindsiko, E. (2019). Knowing in Journalistic Practice: Ethnography in a Public Broadcasting Company. *Journalism Practice*, *13*(3), 298–313. https://doi.org/10.1080/17512786.2018.1424022.

PART II

Innovation Strategies

CHAPTER 3

Public Service Media in the Age of Platformization of Culture and Society

Tiziano Bonini Baldini, Miguel Túñez-López, and Almudena Barrientos Báez

1   PUBLIC SERVICE MEDIA'S CHANGING VALUES

In 2007, Gregory Ferrell Lowe and Jo Bardoel edited a fundamental book for Public Service Media studies: *From Public Service Broadcasting to Public Service Media*. This text compiled an accurate selection of papers presented at the conference of RIPE@2006. The introduction by Bardoel

---

T. Bonini Baldini
University of Siena, Siena, Italy
e-mail: tiziano.bonini@unisi.it

M. Túñez-López (✉)
Department of Communication Sciences, Universidade de Santiago de Compostela, Santiago de Compostela, Spain
e-mail: miguel.tunez@usc.es

A. Barrientos Báez
Iriarte School of Tourism, University of La Laguna,
San Cristóbal de La Laguna, Spain
e-mail: almudenabarrientos@iriarteuniversidad.es

© The Author(s), under exclusive license to Springer Nature Switzerland AG 2021
M. Túñez-López et al. (eds.), *The Values of Public Service Media in the Internet Society*, Palgrave Global Media Policy and Business, https://doi.org/10.1007/978-3-030-56466-7_3

and Ferrell Lowe clearly identified the most important challenge for Public Service Broadcasting (PSB) in the media context of the time: the transition to Public Service Media (PSM).

> The core challenge facing public service broadcasting [PSB] today is the transition to public service media [PSM]. (…) A key dimension is the necessity of moving beyond the transmission model that has deeply conditioned professional thought in broadcasting. In the multimedia, digitized environment public service providers must mature a character of thought that privileges being effective public service communicators. (Bardoel and Ferrell Lowe 2007, p. 9)

This introduction by Bardoel and Farrell Lowe was so successful that today, 12 years later, PSB has lost its traction in favor of the PSM term. The rethinking of PSB's role and future was not only the consequence of this book, of course. The argument made by Ferrell Lowe and Bardoel represented one of the first of a widely distributed rethinking of PSB.

The 12 years following the publication of Bardoel and Farrell Lowe's book were an extremely challenging period for Public Service Media companies. Since the economic crisis of 2008, many Public Service Media companies have suffered budget cuts from which they have been unable to recover, and in some cases, like in Hungary, national government control has increased rather than decreased. In the meantime, the rise of social media has attracted increasing shares of advertising investment to the latter, draining resources to those PSM companies, such as Rai in Italy, whose budgets depend heavily on advertising revenues. Not only the economic budgets of PSM organizations have decreased. In many European countries the time dedicated to programs produced by PSM on television and radio has also decreased. The attention of audiences, especially the younger ones, has gradually shifted toward social media, which provide on-demand infotainment contents able to remediate the PSM offer (Instagram and YouTube remediate the flow of TV, Spotify playlists remediate the flow of music radio stations, Facebook and Twitter remediate TV and radio news, Twitch begins to replace the broadcast on the network of offline and online events). In this emerging technological context, it is increasingly difficult for PSM to convince its users of the legitimacy of the license fee.

The loss of the economic value of PSM audiences and the general loss of audience share have prompted PSM companies and its scholars to review the value of these companies for society in order to legitimize their existence in the eyes of citizens. What is the use of PSM in a media ecosystem where citizens have a wide choice of cultural content outside the PSM system? What is the use of PSM if there are fewer people following it? To answer these questions, PSM scholars have proposed a change of perspective on the role of public service in society and have begun to assess the value of PSM for society no longer in terms of audience size, but rather in terms of PSM ability to contribute to the well-being of a society (PSM *contribution to society*, see Bardoel and d'Haenens 2008; Trappel 2014; EBU 2014) and to foster democratic audience/citizen participation (Enli 2008), leading some scholars to talk about a "participatory turn" in PSM (Bonini 2017).

Vaz et al. (2020a) analyzed four co-creation products issued on PSM: (1) the series *El Ministerio del Tiempo*, in RTVE; (2) the joint project of RTÉ with the supermarket chain ALDI; (3) the Talents project ZDI, created by ZDF, a quest that combines opportunities for the development and financing of young German creators, solving their own needs for innovation; and (4) the collaboration of SBS with Viceland, aimed at young people to project themes and content. The authors concluded that in this type of co-creation the project has the capacity to promote different values of the PSMs such as representation, participation, innovation, and diversity of content.

This debate makes it clear that there is an ongoing transition from the values traditionally associated with PSM in the twentieth century. This transition toward the definition of a new social role for PSM in the digital age is still at an early stage but has already found its way into many official documents, including those of the European institutions. EBU (European Broadcasting Union) published the documents *Empowering Society. A Declaration on the Core Values of Public Service Media* (2012) in which a new set of values for PSM is envisioned (universality; independence; excellence; diversity; accountability; innovation) and *EBU Vision 2020. Connecting to a networked society* (2014) in which this transition toward the social benefits of PSM is highly emphasized.

The values associated with the public role of PSM throughout the history of public broadcasting have changed a great deal, depending on the historical, political, technological, and economic contexts that PSM have experienced. In Table 3.1 we try to summarize the most evident changes in the values associated with PSM. We propose to divide the evolution of PSM values into three different paradigmatic shifts: the first is the one that informed public broadcasting during the era of the radio-television

Table 3.1 Periodization of PSM values

Public service paradigm	Periodization	Features	Values	PSM audience "affordances"
PSB	1920–1989 circa	Monopoly Audience as a (passive) citizen	Inform, educate, entertain	Listen, watch, read, write (letters), call (phone-in calls from 1940s)
PSB	1989–2004	Broadcasting market competition Competition for advertising Audience as a (passive) commodity	Entertain, inform, educate Audience competition	Listen, watch, read, write, call, send emails and SMS
PSM	2004–2020	Multimedia market competition Audience as an (active) citizen/prod-user to be engaged	Entertain, inform, educate Interaction/connection/Participation Social benefits of PSM (Return on society) EBU values (2012)— Universality; independence; excellence; diversity; accountability; innovation	Listen, watch, read, call, send emails and SMS, produce, post, tweet, share, upload/download, comment, like, chat, crowdfund, meet

monopoly: PSB aimed at paternalistically serving the audience. The second corresponds to the liberalization of mass communication in Western countries, a period that saw public service for the first time being forced to compete for audience attention with other private actors. The third paradigm shift occurs with the rise of social media and their transformation into online platforms. In this new era, PSM has to take into account not only the mere attention of the audience but also include new metrics of their emotional involvement (Arvidsson and Bonini 2015).

The next section will analyze why PSM are facing a new phase in their history today, and therefore why a further semantic extension of the boundaries of their meaning is needed: from Public Service Media to Public Service Platforms. We will focus on the consequences of the third paradigm shift described in this section and illustrate how the rise of online platforms represents a threat to the stability of PSM, but at the same time provides an opportunity for them to renew their aims and their legitimacy.

2   From Public Service Media to Public Service Platforms

2.1   The Rising Power of Online Platforms

Since the end of the first decade of the twenty-first century, the development of Web 2.0 and social media have been characterized by the rise of a particular technological infrastructure: the platform.

According to Srnicek (2017), tech companies like Google, Facebook, Amazon, Netflix, Spotify, Airbnb, and Uber, despite (not) making profits by selling different services, share a common feature: they all frame themselves as "platforms" driven by algorithms based on data infrastructures. Gillespie (2010) was one of the first media scholars to detect and understand their attempt to position themselves as new intermediaries, in order "to establish a long-term position in a fluctuating economic and cultural terrain" (2010, p. 348). In 2006, when Google bought YouTube, the description of this service in the company's press releases marked an important semantic transformation: YouTube was no longer described as just a "website," a "company," or a "community," but as a "distribution platform for original content creators and large and small advertisers" (Gillespie 2010, p. 348). From that moment on, technology companies appropriated this term to describe their service as an "open" and "neutral" space, taking up the original meaning of platform, an open and flat space, which anyone can climb on, without differences or discrimination. Again according to Gillespie (2010), technology companies use this term as part of a broader rhetorical strategy to publicly present their services as pure intermediaries, neutral aggregators connecting content producers and consumers, without interfering or changing the processes of cultural production and consumption: in short, without any responsibility for the content in circulation.

Yet, behind this seemingly so neutral term lurk several implications, which scholars from different disciplines have tried to bring to the forefront of the debate on the role of technologies in today's society. Probably the most important aspect is that what we define as a platform is far from representing a neutral space. On the contrary, the rhetorical force of this definition lies in making invisible both the logic with which a platform puts people, producers, and consumers in contact, and the power relationships that are established between those who participate in it.

To shed light on the subtle mechanisms by which platforms shape content and relationships in today's digital society, the recent work by Dutch sociologists José van Dijck et al. (2018) is helpful. This group of researchers argue that digital platforms constitute a technological and economic infrastructure that influences not only the cultural industries, but society as a whole and, for this reason, they proposed the definition of the platform society to describe the society in which we live: a society in which "social and economic traffic is increasingly channeled by an (overwhelmingly corporate) global online platform ecosystem that is driven by algorithms and fueled by data" (2018, p. 4).

In this type of society, few private companies have accumulated a huge amount of data on our behavior and a great asymmetry of knowledge between users and platforms has been created. Big international tech corporations already represent the new intermediaries of cultural and creative industries. Their influence on the economy and society has been demonstrated by the latest waves of protest and social conflicts caused by the introduction of services like Uber and Airbnb in many Western cities, as well as by the use of networking sites such as Facebook, Twitter, Instagram, and WhatsApp for political propaganda and computational politics (Tufekci 2014; Cho et al. 2020). van Dijck et al. (2018) also identify three main mechanisms as driving forces underlying this platform ecosystem: datafication, commodification, and selection.

The process of platformization of culture (Nieborg and Poell 2018) and society (van Dijck et al. 2018) is transforming all global and national cultural and creative industries, not just Public Service Media companies. The online platforms owned by big tech corporations (principally GAFAM—Google, Apple, Facebook, Amazon, Microsoft, but not only) are putting enormous pressure on various economic sectors, including that of legacy media. Cultural and creative industries are increasingly dependent on these platforms, as demonstrated by Nieborg and Poell (2018). The ongoing platformization of culture and society extends its dominance over the previous intermediaries of the cultural and creative industries: the old traditional cultural intermediaries (Bourdieu 1984), including PSM, are quickly losing the centrality of their role. This also happens because the technologies they use for the production and circulation of content (antennas, rotary presses, web sites) are not as efficient as online platforms—driven by algorithms—are at extracting and managing data.

In order to cope with this new challenge, legacy media and PSM companies are under pressure to optimize their content for multisided online platforms in order to maximize user traffic and/or advertising revenue. They are increasingly pressed to render themselves compliant with the platforms, or to directly turn themselves into platforms. According to Sørensen and Hutchinson (2017), "the use of external third-party web services for media content delivery, media recommendation, audience behavior measurement, and sale of advertisement, makes PSM organizations increasingly integrated in and dependent on the global business ecology of web services."

2.2 Platforms as Media

We have always been accustomed to thinking of the media in the traditional forms of newspapers and broadcasting, as publishers of audiovisual, sound, or paper content. A newspaper, a television channel, or a radio stands out from other companies because they make editorial choices, selecting and discarding certain content according to professional logic. Traditional media are recognized as gatekeepers of information and cultural industries in general. If these are the media, then platforms like Facebook, Instagram, WhatsApp, Netflix, and Spotify apparently cannot be considered media. Yet Netflix, Spotify, Facebook, and YouTube are not just content aggregators, but exercise editorial control over the content they aggregate through their moderation policies (Gillespie 2018) and their recommendation algorithms. In addition, some of these companies have started producing original content, not just aggregating other people's content. Netflix produces original TV series, and Facebook and Google finance local journalism programs and plans to support journalism's business models, to shelter from criticism that they are disrupting journalism; Spotify has bought original podcast production companies and threatens the music industry to acquire its own music artists. Certainly, however, GAFAM's interests in the cultural industries are still limited and do not represent the majority of their revenue. As political economist Dwyne Winseck (2019) argues, "with the exception of Netflix, GAFAM+ do not own the rights to a catalogue of content, at least not in a way that is core to their business, and they do not exchange rights for products of cultural production." Winseck argues that technology companies should be assimilated to telecoms, while Napoli and Caplan (2017) argue that they should be considered media companies. The debate sees many scholars from the political economy of the media, media studies, Creative and cultural industries studies, cultural studies and emerging platform studies discussing each other, without finding a convergence.

Surely platforms are not media like the previous ones and they certainly have many economic interests in sectors other than the media industry. Yet, if we ask ourselves what a media outlet is and try to question traditional definitions of media, we could argue that online platforms are also media. If we shift the focus from the product that media offers (the content) to the position that media occupies in society, we will see how much easier it is to consider platforms as media.

A medium, according to this definition, is not distinguished by what it produces (in the case of newspapers, information) but by the position it occupies, by its being an intermediary between two or more subjects. This definition of media is very similar to the definition of online platforms given by economy scholars, who first began to talk about platforms to describe the nascent digital economy. According to Rochet and Tirole (2003) platforms are two-sided markets, that is, they act as intermediaries connecting two "sides" of the same market.

All these platforms could also be understood in the same way that the Italian media scholar, Fausto Colombo (2003), defined the media, as socio-technical apparatuses that play a role of mediation in communication between different actors. This definition is not much different from what Srnicek (2017, p. 43) defined as "platform": "digital infrastructures that allow two or more social groups to interact with each other." If we distinguish the technologies designed for communication from their specific function/position of intermediaries, we can also accept that online platforms, once they have acquired the role of intermediaries between two or more actors or between two or more social groups, can act as media companies.

2.3 *IF Platforms Are Media, THEN Public Service Media Can Be Platforms Too!*

If PSM companies have so far produced audiovisual content suitable for broadcasting, why can't the same companies today also produce TV series for on-demand consumption, or use recommender systems and other services such as apps and video games, while maintaining the public values they are inspired by today? Why can't it be a public model of online platforms like Spotify or Netflix, funded by license fees rather than by speculative finance? If, in terms of abstract logic, this argument seems to be reasonable, in terms of practice, at least so far, it is a little less so.

In the age of broadcasting there were mainly three existing macro-models of media ownership: (1) state-owned PSM companies or partially independent ones (see the media systems described by Hallin and Mancini 2004), funded by license fee, government funds, advertising, private donations, or a mix of these sources; (2) private companies, funded through advertising and/or subscriptions and private investments; and (3) cooperative or non-profit institutions, owned by a group of organized citizens, which gave life to community media, independent of both the market and the state (Servaes 1999, p. 260 in Carpentier et al. 2003, p. 244).

Despite the growing process of media liberalization that took place in Europe after the fall of the Berlin Wall, public service and community media are still an important alternative to commercial media in many countries of the world today. In the field of online platforms, however, the presence of public or community actors is much more limited or even non-existent. Most platforms are privately owned, driven by market values, fueled by venture capital, and aimed primarily at building monopolies to become economically viable, as was clearly argued by venture capitalist and ultra-libertarian Peter Thiel (2014).

In the Western audiovisual media ecosystem, there are practically no alternatives to the platform capitalism represented by Facebook, Netflix, Twitter, Spotify, Amazon Music, Audible, and YouTube. But the current predominance of private platforms is neither natural nor irreversible. Governments and public institutions can also develop their own platforms, as van Dijck et al. (2018, p. 160) argue: "Besides being exemplary and demanding users, governments can also be proactive as platform developers."

In the field of on-demand audiovisual content, some large PSM companies have recently launched their online platforms or upgraded their old websites into on-demand platforms, with more or less successful imitations of the models on which they are based (e.g., Netflix). In the United Kingdom, the BBC was one of the first public service companies to develop its proprietary platform for on-demand consumption. In 2007 it created the iPlayer, an internet streaming, catchup television and radio service, which was replaced in 2018 by the BBC Sounds application; in Italy, in 2017, the public broadcaster RAI launched its own video and audio content platforms (Rai Play and Rai Play Radio). According to Sørensen and Hutchinson (2017), other PSM companies that have developed online platforms with recommendation algorithms are NRK (Norway), RPT (Portugal), YLE (Finland), and ZDF (Germany).

Changes in public habits seem to be pushing PSM organizations to develop content strategies opposed to Video On Demand (VOD) to retain audiences on the move and as a reaction in each country to the global subscription platforms of, mainly, Netflix, HBO, or Amazon and the more recent Disney+ or AppleTV. OFCOM director Sharon White asked British broadcasters BBC, ITV, and Channel 4 to collaborate on the development of a common service to gain scale and compete with global technology giants (Council of Europe 2019, p. 49) and some channels such as RTVE in Spain have partnered with private networks (Atresmedia and Mediaset) to create a new HbbTv Service, LovesTV.

After analyzing a total of 56 Public Service Media companies in Europe, Vaz et al. (2020b) concluded that in European PSMs, the elements of recommendation are present in almost a third of all PSMs that present a Video on Demand platform. These 16 PSM organizations are: ARD (Germany), BBC (United Kingdom), Channel One (Russia); ERT (Greece), ETV ERR (Estonia), France TV (France), HRTi (Croatia), NPO (Holland), RAI (Italy), RTCG (Montenegro), RTÉ (Ireland), RTP (Portugal), RTS (Switzerland), TVM (Malta), YLE (Finland), and ZDF (Germany). As recommendation systems develop, it is necessary to assess their impact on the values that define the PSM because, as Fields et al. (2018) point out, the idea that PSM values offer different scenarios for applying recommendation systems underpins the need for initiatives that help to clearly include them in Public Service Media objectives.

The examples are still limited but, most importantly, none of the platforms developed by PSM seems to wonder what it means to design an online platform that is not profit-oriented and that is able to respect the public values inscribed in the contracts that PSM companies have signed with their governments. So far, PSM who have developed online platforms have done so by trying to emulate existing business models in terms of aesthetics and functionality (Bonini and Mazzoli 2020).

The difference between market-oriented and value-oriented platforms should lie in the way the platform selects, filters, and cares for content: what are the principles and editorial rules that govern the curatorial work of a platform? Are these principles oriented toward maximizing the audience or contributing to society? How should automatic content curation powered by algorithms on an online public service platform look like?

What user data management policy should a public service platform adopt? Do the laws of each state on data protection policies allow arbitration of a common action to all the PSM in Europe that define recommendation strategies in the framework of the public service?

So far, hardly anyone among media scholars (with a few exceptions, see Taylor 2014; Sørensen and Schmidt 2016; Sørensen and Hutchinson 2017) seems to have addressed these issues, both among professionals and PSM experts. Sørensen and Hutchinson (2017) distil their understanding of important challenges involved in algorithmic development for PSM in five dimensions: reach and distinctiveness; provision of diversity; transparency; user sovereignty and the attention economy; dependency. Apart from few exceptions, research on what challenges await PSM companies in their transition to become platforms is still in its infancy, yet it is of vital importance for their future.

It is not long before the global audience that once consumed content and services produced according to public service values and standards is permanently confined—or locked in—in the walled gardens of online commercial platforms. If PSM do not want to lose their role as intermediaries of content and services aimed at improving citizens' knowledge and well-being, they will have to change again.

In 2007 Bardoel and Farrell Lowe proposed that PSB should evolve into PSM. Today, we agree with Bonini and Mazzoli (2020) that PSM companies should turn themselves into public service platforms (PSPs), capable of directing the management of user data and the development of recommendation algorithms toward those values of benefit to society that we have described in the first part of this chapter.

The existence of these platforms could better legitimize the demand, now seen by many citizens as anachronistic, for a license fee for PSM, and could provide citizens with a greater cultural diversity of content and services than those offered by the dominant platforms. It is good for the health of a democracy that platforms, media, and publishers with different goals and editorial logics continue to exist.

3 Conclusions

In this chapter, we have proposed a historical perspective in order to analyze the paradigm changes occurring within the debate on the values of Public Service Media, dedicating special attention to the paradigm change envisioned by Ferrell Lowe and Bardoel in 2007. Considering the processes of the platformization of culture (Nieborg and Poell 2018) and the wider process of the platformization of society (van Dijck et al. 2018), we have argued that PSM organizations are at a turning point in their history, and that a further semantic extension of the boundaries of their meaning is needed: from Public Service Media to Public Service Platforms, as highlighted by Bonini and Mazzoli (2020). If platforms are media, then Public Service Media can be platforms, too.

Hopefully, this chapter aimed at opening up a debate on the future of PSM in the age of the platform society. In this particular period, platforms driven by algorithms resting on data infrastructures have enormous competitive advantages compared to traditional PSM companies, which are less efficient in gathering, analyzing, and managing data. Therefore, in the future, if PSM companies do not embrace the challenge of platformization, they may risk being marginalized or even disappear, with unknown consequences for society and democracy.

Acknowledgments This chapter is part of the activities of the research project (RTI2018-096065-B-100) of the Spanish State Program of R + D + I oriented to the Challenges of Society of the Ministry of Science, Innovation and Universities (MCIU), State Research Agency (SRA), and the European Regional Development Fund (ERDF) on "New values, governance, financing and public audiovisual services for the Internet society: European and Spanish contrasts."

References

Arvidsson, A., & Bonini, T. (2015). Valuing Audience Passions: From Smythe to Tarde. *European Journal of Cultural Studies, 18*(2), 158–173. https://doi.org/10.1177/1367549414563297.

Bardoel, J., & d'Haenens, L. (2008). Reinventing Public Service Broadcasting in Europe: Prospects, Promises and Problems. *Media, Culture and Society, 30*(3), 337–355. https://doi.org/10.1177/0163443708088791.

Bardoel, J., & Lowe Gregory, F. (2007). From Public Service Broadcasting to Public Service Media: The Core Challenge. In G. F. Lowe, G. Ferrell, & J. Bardoel (Eds.), *From Public Service Broadcasting to Public Service Media, RIPE@2007* (pp. 9–26). Göteborg: Nordicom.

Bonini, T. (2017). The Participatory Turn in Public Service Media. In M. Glowacki & A. Jaskiernia (Eds.), *Public Service Media Renewal: Adaptation to Digital Network Challenges* (pp. 101–116). New York: Peter Lang.

Bonini, T., & Mazzoli, E. (2020). *Public Service Media in a Platform Society: Theorizing 'Convivial' Public Service Platforms*. Paper Presented at RIPE Conference 2020, Geneve.

Bourdieu, P. (1984). *Distinction*. Cambridge, MA: Harvard University Press.
Carpentier, N., Lie, R., & Servaes, J. (2003). Is There a Role and Place for Community Media in the Remit? In T. Hujanen & F. Lowe Gregory (Eds.), *Broadcasting and Convergence: New Articulations of the Public Remit, RIPE@2003* (pp. 239–254). Göteborg: Nordicom.
Cho, J., Saifuddin, A., Martin, H., Billy, L., & Jonathan, L. (2020). Do Search Algorithms Endanger Democracy? An Experimental Investigation of Algorithm Effects on Political Polarization. *Journal of Broadcasting & Electronic Media*. https://doi.org/10.1080/08838151.2020.1757365.
Colombo, F. (2003). *Introduzione allo studio dei media*. Rome: Carocci.
Council of Europe. (2019). *Yearbook 2018/2019. Key Trends. Television, Cinema, Video and On-Demand Audiovisual Services—The Pan-European Picture*. European Audiovisual Observatory. Retrieved April 17, 2019, from https://rm.coe.int/yearbook-keytrends-2018-2019-en/1680938f8e.
EBU. (2012). *Empowering Societies. A Declaration of the Core Values of Public Service Media*. Geneva: EBU Press. Retrieved April 19, 2019, from https://www.ebu.ch/files/live/sites/ebu/files/Publications/EBU-Empowering-Society_EN.pdf.
EBU. (2014). *EBU Vision 2020. Connecting to a Networked Society*. Geneva: EBU Press.
Enli, G. (2008). Redefining Public Service Broadcasting: Multi-platform Participation. *Convergence, 14*(1), 105–120. Redefining Public Service Broadcasting: Multi-platform Participation. https://doi.org/10.1177/1354856507084422.
Fields, B., Jones, R., & Cowlishaw, T. (2018). The Case for Public Service Recommender Algorithms (pp. 22–24). In Fratrec 2018. Retrieved April 19, 2020, from https://piret.gitlab.io/fatrec2018/program/fatrec2018-fields.pdf.
Gillespie, T. (2010). The Politics of 'Platforms'. *New Media & Society, 12*(3), 347–364. https://doi.org/10.1177/1461444809342738.
Gillespie, T. (2018). *Custodians of the Internet*. Princeton: Princeton University Press.
Hallin, D., & Mancini, P. (2004). *Comparing Media Systems: Three Models of Media and Politics*. Cambridge: Cambridge University Press.
Napoli, P., & Caplan, R. (2017). Why Media Companies Insist They're Not Media Companies, Why They're Wrong, and Why It Matters. *First Monday, 22*(5) https://doi.org/10.5210/fm.v22i5.7051.
Nieborg, D., & Poell, T. (2018). The Platformization of Cultural Production: Theorizing the Contingent Cultural Commodity. *New Media & Society.*. https://doi.org/10.1177/1461444818769694.
Rochet, J. C., & Tirole, J. (2003). Platform Competition in Two-Sided Markets. *Journal of the European Economic Association, 1*(4), 990–1029. https://doi.org/10.1162/154247603322493212.

Sørensen, J. K., & Hutchinson, J. (2017). Algorithms and Public Service Media. In *Public Service Media in the Networked Society RIPE* (pp. 91–106). Nordicom.
Sørensen, J. K., & Schmidt, J. H. (2016). *An Algorithmic Diversity Diet? Questioning Assumptions behind a Diversity Recommendation System for PSM*. Paper presented at RIPE@2016 Conference, Antwerp University, Antwerp, September 23.
Srnicek, N. (2017). *Platform Capitalism*. Cambridge: Polity Press.
Taylor, A. (2014). *The People's Platform: Taking Back Power and Culture in the Digital Age*. London: Fourth Estate.
Thiel, P. (2014, September 12). Competition Is for Losers. *The Wall Street Journal*. Retrieved February 24, 2019, from https://www.wsj.com/articles/peter-thiel-competition-is-for-losers-1410535536.
Trappel, J. (2014). What Media Value? Theorising on Social Values and Testing in Ten Countries. In G. F. Lowe & F. Martin (Eds.), *The Value of Public Service Media* (pp. 127–144). Göteborg: Nordicom.
Tufekci, Z. (2014). Engineering the Public: Big Data, Surveillance and Computational Politics. *First Monday*, 19(7) https://doi.org/10.5210/fm.v19i7.4901.
van Dijck, J., Poell, T., & De Waal, M. (2018). *The Platform Society: Public Values in a Connective World*. Oxford: Oxford University Press.
Vaz, M., Túñez, M., & Fraçao-Nogueira, A. (2020a). *Co-creating value in European Public Service Media. An Analysis of 4 Successful Co-creation Experiences in Public Television*. CISTI—15ª Conferencia Ibérica de Sistemas y Tecnologías de Información. Proceedings. Sevilla.
Vaz, M., Túñez, M., & Ufarte, M. J. (2020b). What Are You Offering? An Overview of VODs and Recommender Systems in European Public Service Media. In Á. Rocha, C. Ferrás, C. M. Marín, & V. M. García (Eds.), *Information Technology and Systems. ICITS. Advances in Intelligent Systems and Computing* (p.1137).Cham:Springer.https://doi.org/10.1007/978-3-030-40690-5_69.
Winseck, D. (2019). *Digital Dominance and Vampire Squids: Why Big, Powerful Platforms Are Not Media Companies and How to Regulate Them*. Paper presented at the International Association of Media and Communication Researchers, Madrid, Spain.

CHAPTER 4

Can Automated Strategies Work for PSM in a Network Society? Engaging Digital Intermediation for Informed Citizenry

Jonathon Hutchinson and Jannick Kirk Sørensen

1 Introduction

This chapter will focus on the changing processes of content production within Public Service Media given the impact of the network society, especially that of automated and algorithmed media ecosystems. The contemporary media ecosystem for Public Service Media is one that operates within an increasingly automated space through the implementation of recommender systems that suggest the media we should be exposed to, chatbots that are to some extent providing our news exposure and diversity, and media that is not only distributed algorithmically, but indeed

---

J. Hutchinson (✉)
University of Sydney, Camperdown, NSW, Australia
e-mail: jonathon.hutchisnon@sydney.edu.au

J. K. Sørensen
Aalborg University, Copenhagen, Denmark
e-mail: js@es.aau.dk

© The Author(s), under exclusive license to Springer Nature Switzerland AG 2021
M. Túñez-López et al. (eds.), *The Values of Public Service Media in the Internet Society*, Palgrave Global Media Policy and Business,
https://doi.org/10.1007/978-3-030-56466-7_4

59

created through increasingly automated processes that draw on mathematical calculations. The purpose of this chapter is to highlight the digital intermediation processes that content producers, which includes journalists, undertake to effectively operate in this space. We argue that these online content producers are digital intermediaries that operate in a number of evolving and responsive ways to ensure media diversity remains high through the remit of Public Service Media.

If we cast this production process to other industries momentarily, it becomes easier to understand the continual evolution of digital intermediaries. Pilots, for example, are constantly adjusting the wings of their aircraft as they come in for landing, even though the aircraft is predominantly flown by its onboard computer. This example demonstrates the effective use of humans within the automated process, that works alongside the machine for the ultimate outcome of the passengers: a safe landing. So too in content production are digital intermediaries adopting new production techniques and methodologies to operate effectively within a system that increasingly functions in an automated space. In the aero industry, this is for safety. In the Public Service Media sector, it is to ensure media diversity through increased techniques for visibility.

In many ways, this new Public Service Media digital intermediary function is still developing through new roles and job descriptions. Journalists have become data journalists. Content producers are now online content producers. Research by Sherwood and O'Donnell (2018) also confirms that industrial roles are changing beyond PSM alone, where those who were once employed as "journalists" are now part of the larger "entertainment" industry: a representation in itself that describes the shift of producer roles from one specific role to one that functions within the broader ecosystem.

Given the changing make-up of online content producer roles and the environment in which they work, the Public Service Media digital intermediary needs to in many ways embody the producer, developer, and analyst roles in one. For example, what might happen if Public Service Media were to close down the audience measurement space? Would that result in every journalist becoming responsible for the performance of their content? Do they also become responsible for the algorithms on which they operate? In most instances, journalists manage the meta data as a digital intermediary, for example tagging images and videos for increased exposure—this is an optimization process. But what about the broader picture? Journalists may have control over internal algorithms of the Public Service

Media organization, but they have little control of how these algorithms operate in the commercial space. In this context, they are competing against incredibly skilled commercial operators to effectively function as they are employed to by the socially responsible Public Service Media sector.

The introduction of algorithms in media content production and exposure challenges the established division of work between journalists, editors, audience researchers, program schedulers, and marketing people. That division was motivated by the scarcity of space to expose content—for example, through newspaper pages or slots in the broadcast schedule, by segmenting strategies to shape and predict audiences (Ang 1991), but also by the limited access to audience data. The division of work often created tensions in the media companies, for example, when journalists needed to convince editors about publishing, or when editors had to argue with audience researchers, program schedulers, and marketing people about the best dissemination strategy for different content. The centralized gatekeeping structure was not only caused by the cumbersome information exchange, but it also mirrors organizational power conflicts. As digitalization proceeds, dramatic changes thus take place at the management level of public service broadcasting and media organizations.[1]

While we currently see adjustments to PSM management structure, we will in this chapter suggest a more radical change as a thought experiment. Audience performance data for digital media easily can be provided to both editors and journalists. Some PSM organizations such as YLE in Finland already do so via dashboard accessibility for all journalists. The next step would let content producers decide on the exposure of their content. This could be obtained by letting content producers create so-called business rules for the algorithm when and to whom the content should be shown, or by letting journalists create and curate channels. Such an idea would represent a shift from a manual and centralized strategic gatekeeping of content exposure, to an algorithmically based collective, and co-creative version, of the PSM programming identity. The algorithm would be used for decentralized content programming. By allowing and encouraging content producers to look into the algorithm and explore its potential for content exposure optimization, PSM would be delegating the labor to those who have the deepest insights in the content, namely content creators. Furthermore, they will establish a better understanding of their audiences, and further develop that audience relationship. The production, accounting, and development processes would thus be embedded in the same person ensuring fast feedback loops and rapid innovation cycles.

2   Public Service Media and the "Network Society" of 2020

> all nodes of a network are necessary for the network's performance. When nodes become redundant or useless, networks tend to reconfigure themselves, deleting some nodes, and adding new ones. Nodes only exist and function as components of networks. The network is the unit, not the node.
> (Castells 2004)

The increasing digitization of media environments, especially within recent times, has spurred a great number of research inquiries into its implications across a spectrum between positive and negative. At the height of caution of contemporary digital media, Striphas (2015) described the complications of passing cultural production toward machines through automation cultures, the increasing opaqueness of algorithms within a black-boxed society (Pasquale 2015), and the inherent bias of algorithms (Noble 2018) and inequality. This has been extended into our contemporary societies via the impact of power and politics as a result of automation and algorithmic culture (Bucher 2018). While the other side of the debate highlights the benefits of increased connectivity for marginalized groups, such as First Nation folk, who engage in shared recognition which is "the collective sense of anger and frustration experienced by Indigenous people when traumatic events in the public domain act as reminders of ongoing colonialism" (Carlson et al. 2017, p. 1). Through its social, cultural, and political uses, it is clear that digital media has transformed our societies beyond normative bad or good scenarios, but indeed challenge and support how we communicate collectively and individually.

Institutionally, publics have experienced a significant transformation of information providers, creators, and curators. A traditional model was top-down hierarchical and institutional, which, while having significant inhibitions, provided media content that was professional and had passed the scrutiny test of content makers and editors. The recent transformation away from institutionally based content providers and toward platform providers has shifted the gatekeeping role from institutions and toward the so-called custodians of the internet (Gillespie 2018). Indeed, we have seen research that points to hard types of platform filtering administered by automation and algorithms. Pasquale (2015) spoke of the implications on our societies from so-called black boxes, while Noble (2018) highlighted the racist and negative profiling acts of algorithms. Platforms have spawned new content production models (Hutchinson 2019), economies, and subcultural processes that have appealed to larger and highly niche audiences. The role of automation, algorithmic culture, and recommendation has become a burden of choice, built on systems "which are derived from an analysis of aggregated user data to lead people toward certain objects and away from others" (Cohn 2019, p. 5).

A number of governmental inquiries have been undertaken to understand the implications of this shift toward digital platforms as increasingly powerful stakeholders in the shaping of culture, society, economics, and politics. The Australian Competition and Consumer Commission (ACCC) recently delivered its 2019 report into the Digital Platforms Inquiry suggesting a number of items such as limiting the merging power of the "tech giants" and monitoring markets in which digital platforms operate. New Zealand has developed its NetSafe project for online safety, Brazil has moved on its General Data Protection Law, while Germany has implemented its *Netzwerkdurchsetzungsgesetz* (network Enforcement Act) to protect the user of the ever-growing digital platform providers.

Public Service Media (PSM) has continued to operate within such markets with a number of responses to the evolving digital media landscape. The earlier developments of sharing content across social media as a means of distribution and engaging in conversation with users in spaces such as Facebook and Twitter (Jackson 2010) have evolved considerably. The use of algorithms is increasingly used for not only content production but also distribution (Sørensen 2019); for example, chatbots are also being used within the news sector at the BBC and the ABC. In many cases, these technological advances have assisted producers to find new voices to communicate with previously marginalized users, to use innovative production techniques and engage in new distribution technologies such as recommender systems (Álvarez et al. 2020). Yet the PSM obligations remain the same.

While the innovation continues to develop in alignment with digital media technologies, PSM are still subject to historical arguments such as economically crowding out commercial providers and remaining in the liberal side of politics as described through conservative media publications (Holmes 2020). Beyond these well-trodden historical arguments, Campos-Freire et al. (2020, p. 671) highlight PSM is also in a crisis of "legitimacy, business model, audience, innovation and transformation required to adapt to the current digital ecosystem, which is dominated by the changes in the access and consumption ways available to citizens, as well as by the new telecommunications global players." This then asks the question, why does PSM need to remain relevant in this iteration of the network society?

PSM has been at the fore of innovation since its inception in the early twentieth century. From radio development, extended cultural practices, the shift toward not only being a content procurement broadcaster but also an exhaustive media service, and its recent foray into algorithmic practices, PSM is not only the exemplary media institute but a social innovation institution. It is within this contemporary moment that we see the need for PSM to lead the way in inclusive, diverse, and social good innovation: through innovative automation practices. The general deception and antagonism that have been delivered through misinformation practices of late leave users wanting a beacon of hope through innovative PSM practices.

3 Digital Intermediation: Automation

With the proliferation of digital platforms as a central source of connectivity, information, and engagement for a majority of users in Western societies, a number of practices have emerged for online content producers, curators, and distributors. Certainly, within the commercial services, the concept of visibility has become a central focus to increase exposure, which is often converted into other forms of capital including social and economic capital. Cotter (2019) highlights how social media users play the visibility game, particularly on platforms such as Instagram and YouTube, to maximize exposure in an algorithmic engineered exposure model. "'Playing the game' captures disciplinary normalization via algorithms that treats visibility as a reward (Bucher 2012), but also asserts influencers' role in directing and making sense of their own behavior through interpretations of the game" (Cotter 2019, p. 900). This approach by online content producers in and of itself highlights the sort of environment and strategies that have been developed to cut through the signal to noise ratio on digital platforms, which have been further clouded through commercial imperatives of digital platforms.

Digital intermediation (Hutchinson, forthcoming) is the combination of several interventions by non-human actors on the creation of cultural artefacts on digital platforms. It describes the combination of the technologies, agencies, and automation on online content production, often by digital influencers, to increase visibility and thereby exposure. The increased exposure intrinsically determines the capital value (economic, cultural, social, or combination of all three) of the online media content based on the engagement of the audience members. Technology refers to the combination of platforms, connectivity, data and databases, and surrounding peripheral devices (smartphones, smart homes, Internet of Things, etc.). Agencies refer to the designated firms that intermediate between online content producers and platform providers, often referred to as Multichannel Networks (MCN). From facilitating collaboration between high-profile digital influencers, through to increased visibility upon platforms, MCNs operate as digital intermediaries to increase exposure.

The third and most significant digital intermediation intervention for this chapter is *automation*. In relation to media content, we can observe automation applied in at least three ways. For editorial content, automation is applied as (1) "robot journalism" (Kim and Kim 2017; Dörr 2016; Montal and Reich 2017), that is, software systems that compose and publish news articles based on automatically gathered information, as (2) recommender systems that select and compose presentation of content to users in a semi-automated or fully automated manner, and as (3) systems that assist journalists in making sense of data, that is, big data journalism. The EBU "Next Newsroom" report (EBU 2019) suggests that in the context of PSM, big data journalism is not so much about automating news production as the costs exceed the value. Rather, big data is about the use of data to produce novel journalistic stories, for example, based on analysis of statistical data. Furthermore, AI can be used for fact checking and to prevent citing fake news.

If we turn to the related field of advertising, Thomas (2018, p. 35) makes the observation that automation falls into two arenas within this industry: the programmatic publisher side, and the selective consumer disposition. "On the industry side, there is 'programmatic' advertising—which we can define broadly as the automation of the sale and delivery of digital advertising, where the appearance of advertising on a website is controlled by software rather than direct human decision-making. On the consumer side, there are the filtering technologies of adblocking, designed to enable users to remove unwanted ads from websites or other Internet applications." Within both of these perspectives of media automation, there is a reliance of programming and tools, which ultimately decide which content is seen, and which is not. It is of course premised by commercial motivation, especially in the advertising industry, so what might that look like in a PSM environment, which is legislatively required to perform a particular societal function?

To begin to answer this question, we can return to the work of Perry et al. (2015), who argue for the development of the "third wave cultural intermediaries": the folk who engage in cultural production for reasons beyond personal gain. It is in this sense that we may be able to connect the digital intermediation programmatic approach with that of the third-wave cultural intermediaries. This is certainly not the approach of the commercial sector, but how might it be possible to incorporate PSM principles into digital intermediation automation? And what would the dimensions of that inclusion look like?

4   Public Service Media Algorithmic Strategies

We will begin this examination of digital intermediation and automation in context of PSM by looking at the strategies applied so far by Public Service Media organizations. Beginning with the European Broadcasting Union's early work on a strategy for the digital media environment (EBU Digital Strategy Group 2002), public service broadcasters have tried to position themselves in the emerging new media landscape with much more competition and less control over the value-chain from rights over production to distribution (Chalaby and Segell 1999). While "innovation" is often promoted as a core PSM quality, concerns have also been voiced both internally in the organization and externally from commercial media and media politicians that PSM's new digital services endeavors should not go too far. Moe (2007, 2011) presents examples where PSM legitimacy has been challenged, for example, in cases where PSM organizations wanted to produce online games. Furthermore, the eternal problematic relationship between commercial media and PSM organizations has not been eased by digitalization. Rigorous media regulation "tests" and assessments have been implemented politically to prevent new digital PSM services to distort the business of commercial media. Finally, PSM practitioners within new media complain that the organizational structure and financial resources are now bound by the PSM production of content aimed for linear dissemination (broadcast TV and radio) (cf. Sørensen 2011, 2013, 2019). Getting PSM management's resources for the development of digital or algorithmic projects within PSM organization has traditionally been difficult and projects have typically isolated technical projects without a close relation to the PSM business. Donders (2019) thus describe via four phases how PSM organizations have tried to move from the hype of new media toward integrated digital distribution strategies.

Identified by the European Broadcasting Union (EBU) as crucial for PSM's continuation,[2] algorithms and big data have had EBU's attention through a number of conferences, workshops, and other means of knowledge distribution (EBU 2018). Big Data or AI is however typically approached as tools to support the legacy mode of mass-media production and not as a way to redefine the business of PSM, for example, how AI can help audience measurement (EBU 2017) or predict audience demands (EBU 2016). The new technologies are thus approached as ways to improve the existing business of Public Service Media, with an emphasis on "consumer experience" and "audience behavior," but also seen as part of "a culture of change which integrates this new dimension [big data] into our daily work" (EBU 2016). The EBU "Next Newsroom" (2019) report takes a similar approach: When we look at how the word "citizens" is used by sources quoted in the report, we see that citizens are rendered as someone to be served with PSM content that they hopefully find valuable, and can act upon in society—the idea of the engaged citizen. The idea of citizen journalism (Sambrook 2005; Nip 2006; Flew 2009) has disappeared. It is a one-way communication: The "citizen-user" is the receiver of information, only expressing his or her opinion very indirectly via tiny clicks in the big algorithmic clickstream.

But how could we imagine an "algorithmic strategy"? Should it be different for PSM than for commercial media and content aggregators (i.e., social media)? A traditional commercial media company may gauge an algorithmic strategy by asking, for example, how algorithms may challenge the editorial quality control, which type of staff will be needed, how the relationship with readers/viewers/listeners/users may change, how the quality of the output product will develop (the "tone of voice"), and how will the brand identity transform. On top of these questions, discussions particular to Public Service Media emerge. At stake is both PSM organizations' political-economical legitimacy in the media market balancing between giving users (and politicians) value for money and not disturbing commercial media. Also maintaining core PSM values such as providing for diversity, ensuring universal access, and avoiding bias is at stake. The diversity of the content exposure in algorithmic recommender systems challenges the Public Service Media in two ways (cf. Sørensen and Schmidt 2016): first, automated systems require consistent definitions and mark-up of content, forcing human editors to explicitly define what previously have been unspoken, namely the criteria that are applied in the human editorial curation of content to construct diverse programming. Secondly, as the computational processes in recommender systems are so many and complex that a transparent accounting for the logic and data that produced a specific recommendation to a specific user is impossible to produce. An algorithmic strategy for PSM must accept the basic loss of control caused by recommender systems, or it must limit the influence of the recommender systems. Sørensen (2019) finds in a cross-institutional study of nine European PSM organizations' implantation of recommender systems that the latter is the preferred choice. Álvarez et al. (2020) have offered an overview of the implementation of personalized recommendation at European PSM websites. Recommender systems are mostly curated or steered manually by editors via different business rules, and in many cases algorithmic recommendations are not shown on prominent position on the webpages.

5   Attempts to Implement PSM Values in Algorithms

With the growing influence of recommender systems and other types of algorithmic systems in the production, exposure, and consumption of media content, both PSM practitioners and scholars discuss the possibilities for representing core PSM editorial principles in algorithms. An example could be how to represent PSM's obligation to present a diverse and fair array of ideas, viewpoints, and worldviews to users in a personalized system (cf. Sørensen and Schmidt 2016)? Should a diversity diet be enforced, ensuring that users either are exposed to or even consume diverse content (cf. Helberger (2012)), or should users just be nudged navigated to consume in a diverse way (cf. Burri (2013, 2016))? Sørensen and Schmidt (2016) suggest that the process of defining "diversity" in a machine-readable form will reveal not only hitherto unspoken disagreements among editors on the definition of diversity, but will also highlight a paradigmatic conflict between computer scientists and journalists on the basic understanding of diversity. The term "PSM value" could thus easily be misunderstood in this context as it could wrongly indicate something measurable, while in reality being an unspecified and partly unarticulated social construction of the PSM programming mission. It is thus not an easy computer programming task to extract PSM values and implement them in an algorithm. Often the ideas for "PSM algorithms" remain just intentions not operational for computer scientists (cf. e.g., Fields et al. 2018). Therefore PSM data scientists and programmers typically implement a standard commercial recommender system, but augment that with business rules that manually ensures the exposure of specific editorially selected content elements that are seen as important for fulfilling the PSM programming policy and identity (Sørensen 2019).

6   Digital Intermediation as a PSM Strategy?

We have so far outlined the concept of digital intermediation to describe the environment in which Public Service Media now exists—one that functions through a number of technologies, agencies, and automation. We have also outlined the sorts of strategies that Public Service Media is beginning to adopt, particularly in the European context. We now turn our attention to explore how digital intermediation can be adopted by Public Service Media as a means to embody the approach of digital intermediation while adhering to the legislated requirements to, for example, innovate, provide voice for marginal communities, and provide and procure a diverse range of content production.

The concept of digital mediation and third-wave cultural intermediaries presented in the beginning of this chapter may conflict with PSM values and traditions as it embodies a radical marketplace concept where individuals propagate messages by the means of networked algorithms, for example, in a social network. One may furthermore object that this algorithmically managed marketplace is not a level playing field as it is controlled by platforms with advertising interests, and that it is based on dynamics of surveillance capitalism (Zuboff 2019). While the distorted power relation in surveillance capitalism indeed is a concern, we here assume a technical infrastructure in the context of PSM detached from the dynamics of surveillance capitalism. However, for digital media in the context of PSM, its contribution to surveillance capitalism is another question (cf. Sørensen, Van den Bulck & Kosta 2020, Sørensen and Van den Bulck 2018). The scope here is to discuss the potentials of digital intermediation in relation to PSM, leaving the discussion of the wider implications of the idea for later contributions. Zuboff (2019) does, however, inspire our discussion as her capitalism-approach to the analysis of companies' data collection strategies highlights the dynamics between individual content producers and gatekeepers such as editors, algorithms, or platforms.

Understanding the dynamics of the black-boxed algorithms and their interplay with social action is thus the key to success for individual digital intermediaries, for example, represented by the social media role, the "Influencer." Conversely, PSM represents a centralized gatekeeping editorial process that not only follows specific editorial values and policies, but also—traditionally—is a schedule for publishing, namely the broadcast programming. The two strategies of content dissemination appear incompatible. However, the personalized on-demand exposure of PSM content offers an opportunity for integrating some dynamics from the third-wave digital intermediaries into PSM publishing that can resolve an old conflict. Traditionally, a conflict exists between content producing journalists and editors that commission and select stories. As gatekeepers, editors sometimes prioritize differently than journalists. This prioritization can be motivated by coordination and merging of several journalists' individual contributions into one coherent story. This process can however also annul the diversity of individual journalists or contributor views and observations. With algorithmic curation of personalized news and media content, the gatekeeper function of the editor can however be questioned at least as a mechanism of reducing and merging content. Individual content producers—journalists—could be granted access directly to feed content into the algorithm and given the opportunity to learn its dynamics. That would mimic the dynamic of content exposure on social networks in the world of PSM, but still with editorial control and high-quality content as objective. In some cases, this principle has already been introduced by some PSM organizations, for example, by letting content producers add "tags" to the content thereby influencing how the content will be exposed in the personalized interface. The idea presented here is however more radical, as it enables individual PSM journalists to explore the algorithm of curating personalization systems, while granting them insights into its dynamics.

7 Conclusion

While the mass-media approach to AI seems to dominate the managerial thinking, are there any examples of "third wave cultural intermediaries" being invited by PSM? Is there an opportunity for real participatory citizen-centered construction of news and media content in the age of algorithms, or does the nature of the AI technology automatically reinforce existing power structures? To help answering that question we may look how the World Wide Web in its infancy was perceived by many scholars as a tool for freedom of thought (and expression) and as the perfect consumer choice platform (cf. Shapiro 1999) but the reality turned out to be different. With AI and automation, we could pose a similar hypothesis: Automation may help existing modes of PSM production and dissemination, but it is more likely that the determining development will take place outside these institutions.

The use of different types of algorithmic systems offers to PSM organizations the opportunity to incrementally improve different aspects of the services: Personalization technologies may increase the user loyalty consumption of content or the exposure of the diversity of the PSM catalogue of content. Likewise, chatbots may offer new forms of communication that may be appreciated by certain user groups. Also automatically generated content—robot journalism—may expand the news coverage. All these services are already being implemented by private media—and already perfected by social media and other digitally born media. By implementing above-mentioned technologies, PSM organizations at most show competitiveness.

As we have shown in this chapter, PSM organizations have an opportunity to demonstrate distinctiveness in comparison with both traditional commercial media and social commercial media. It requires however to acknowledge the role of the content producer as more than a person constantly feeding editors or algorithms with content items. Content producers should be acknowledged as "third wave cultural intermediaries" collaborating with and exploring algorithms for the sake of not personal gain but public good. This approach would acknowledge the skills embedded in content producers as well as it would allow for a much closer contact between media persons and their audiences, not unlike phone-in radio programs. This idea presents a diversion from the traditional centralized gatekeeping of Public Service Broadcasting (PSB). It allows also the diversity of the PSM content creators to be exposed more clearly and it counteracts the harmonizing effect of all produced content passing through a centralized editorial board with strategic media planning. Implications of applying "third wave cultural intermediaries" to PSM production and exposure can be many, and both positive and negative. Further research must discuss the concept in detail, approached from the existing theoretical frameworks for constructing PSM both as a political-economical institution and as a social-cultural phenomenon.

Notes

1. In the case of Danish Broadcasting Corporation (DR) an internal conflict about strategic decision making for digital media led to the retirement of Head of Digital Media, cf.: https://www.dr.dk/om-dr/nyheder/aendringer-i-dr-medier-det-digitale-omraade-integreres-i-resten-af-organisationen (accessed 2020-03-29).
2. In the "EBU Big data week report" (2016) EBU President Jean-Paul Philippot is quoted: *"integrating big data into PSM's strategies and changing internal cultures are crucial to 'revisiting our DNA' and adapting the public remit to the digital world."*

References

Álvarez, M. V., López, J. M. T., & Ruíz, M. J. U. (2020). What Are You Offering?: An Overview of VODs and Recommender Systems in European Public Service Media. In Á. Rocha, C. Ferrás, C. E. Montenegro Marin, & V. H. Medina García (Eds.), *Information Technology and Systems* (pp. 725–732). Cham: Springer International Publishing.

Ang, I. (1991). *Desperately Seeking the Audience*. London, New York: Routledge.

Bucher, T. (2012). Want to be on the top? Algorithmic power and the threat of invisibility on Facebook. *New Media & Society, 14*(7), 1164–1180. https://doi.org/10.1177/1461444812440159

Bucher, T. (2018). *If...then: Algorithmic power and politics*. New York: Oxford University Press.

Burri, M. (2013). Contemplating a 'Public Service Navigator': In Search of New (and Better) Functioning Public Service Media. *SSRN Electronic Journal.* https://doi.org/10.2139/ssrn.2364951.

Burri, M. (2016). Nudging as a Tool of Media Policy. In K. Mathis & A. Tor (Eds.), Nudging—Possibilities, Limitations and Applications in European Law and Economics (pp. 315–341). Cham: Springer International Publishing. https://doi.org/10.1007/978-3-319-29562-6_16.

Campos-Freire, F., Rodríguez-Castro, M., & Blasco-Blasco, O. (2020). Public Service Media's Funding Crisis in the Face of the Digital Challenge. In Á. Rocha, C. Ferrás, C. Montenegro Marin, & V. Medina García (Eds.), *International Conference on Information Technology & Systems* (pp. 671–680). Cham: Springer International Publishing. https://doi.org/10.1007/978-3-030-40690-5_64.

Carlson, B. L., Jones, L. V., Harris, M., Quezada, N., & Frazer, R. (2017). Trauma, shared recognition and indigenous resistance on social media. *Australasian Journal of Information Systems, 21*.

Castells, M. (2004). Informationalism, networks, and the network society: A theoretical blueprint. In M. Castells (Ed.), *The network society: A cross-cultural perspective* (pp. 3–45). Cheltenham, UK; Northampton, Mass.: Edward Elgar Publishing.

Chalaby, J. K., & Segell, G. (1999). The Broadcasting Media in the Age of Risk: The Advent of Digital Television. *New Media & Society, 1*(3), 351–368. https://doi.org/10.1177/14614449922225627.

Cohn, J. (2019). *The Burden of Choice: Recommendations, Subversion, and Algorithmic Culture*. New Brunswick: Rutgers University Press.

Cotter, K. (2019). Playing the visibility game: How digital influencers and algorithms negotiate influence on Instagram. *New Media & Society, 21*(4), 895–913.

Donders, K. (2019). Public Service Media Beyond the Digital Hype: Distribution Strategies in a Platform Era. *Media, Culture & Society, 41*(7), 1011–1028. https://doi.org/10.1177/0163443719857616.

Dörr, K. N. (2016). Mapping the field of Algorithmic Journalism. *Digital Journalism, 4*(6), 700–722. https://doi.org/10.1080/21670811.2015.1096748

EBU. (2016). *Big Data Week Insights*. Retrieved June 3, 2020, from https://www.ebu.ch/files/live/sites/ebu/files/Publications/Reports/EBU_Big_Data-Week-Insights.pdf.

EBU. (2017). *The Future of Audience Measurement. Key Challenges*. Retrieved June 3, 2020, from https://www.ebu.ch/files/live/sites/ebu/files/Publications/MIS/login_only/audiences/EBU-MIS_The-Future-of-Audience-Measurement-Key-Challenges.pdf.

EBU. (2018). *Big Data Initiative Activity Report 2017–2018*. Retrieved June 3, 2020, from https://www.ebu.ch/publications/activity-report/login_only/activity-report/big-data-initiative-activity-report-2017-18.

EBU. (2019). *News Report 2019 – The Next Newsroom*. Retrieved June 3, 2020, from https://www.ebu.ch/files/live/sites/ebu/files/codes/news_report_2019/downloads/ebu-news-report-2019.pdf.

EBU Digital Strategy Group. (2002). *Media with a Purpose – Public Service Broadcasting in the Digital Era*. Retrieved June 3, 2020, from http://www.ebu.ch/CMSimages/en/DSG_final_report_E_tcm6-5090.pdf.

Fields, B., Jones, R., & Cowlishaw, T. (2018). The Case for Public Service Recommender Algorithms. *FATREC Workshop*, 22–24. Retrieved from https://www.piret.gitlab.io/fatrec2018/program/fatrec2018-fields.pdf.

Flew, T. (2009). A Citizen Journalism Primer. In S. Priya (Ed.), *Citizen Journalism: A Social Revolution* (pp. 1–22). Icfai Univerisity Press. Retrieved from https://eprints.qut.edu.au/10232/14/apo-nid69021-37921.pdf.

Gillespie, T. (2018). *Custodians of the Internet: Platforms, content moderation, and the hidden decisions that shape social media*. Yale University Press.

Helberger, N. (2012). Exposure Diversity as a Policy Goal. *Journal of Media Law, 4*(1), 65–92. https://doi.org/10.5235/175776312802483880.

Holmes, J. (2020). *On Aunty*. Sydney: Macquarie University Press.
Hutchinson, J. (2019). Digital First Personality: Automation and Influence Within Evolving Media Ecologies. *Convergence: The International Journal of Research into New Media Technologies* (Online First). https://doi.org/10.1177/1354856519858921.
Jackson, L. (2010). Facilitating Participatory Audiences: Sociable Media and PSM. In G. F. Lowe (Ed.), *The Public in Public Service Media* (pp. 175–188). Gothenburg: Nordicom.
Kim, D., & Kim, S. (2017). Newspaper companies' determinants in adopting robot journalism. *Technological Forecasting and Social Change*, *117*, 184–195. https://doi.org/10.1016/j.techfore.2016.12.002
Moe, H. (2007). Commercial Services, Enclosure and Legitimacy. Comparing Contexts and Strategies for PSM Funding and Development. In G. F. Lowe & J. Bardoel (Eds.), *From Public Service Broadcasting to Public Service Media* (pp. 51–69). Götenborg: Nordicom, Göteborg Universitet.
Moe, H. (2011). Defining Public Service Beyond Broadcasting: The Legitimacy of Different Approaches. *International Journal of Cultural Policy*, *17*(1), 52–68. https://doi.org/10.1080/10286630903049912.
Montal, T., & Reich, Z. (2017). I, robot. You, journalist. Who is the author? Authorship, bylines and full disclosure in automated journalism. *Digital journalism*, *5*(7), 829–849.
Nip, J. Y. M. (2006). Exploring the Second Phase of Public Journalism. *Journalism Studies*, *7*(2), 212–236. https://doi.org/10.1080/14616700500533528.
Noble, S. U. (2018). *Algorithms of Oppression: How Search Engines Reinforce Racism*. New York: NYU Press.
Pasquale, F. (2015). *The Black Box Society: The Secret Algorithms that Control Money and Information*. Cambridge: MIT Press.
Perry, B., Smith, K., & Warren, S. (2015). Revealing and Revaluing Cultural Intermediaries in the 'Real' Creative City: Insights from a Dairy Keeping Exercise. *European Journal of Cultural Studies*, *18*(6), 724–740. https://doi.org/10.1177/1367549415572324.
Sambrook, R. (2005). *Citizen Journalism and the BBC*. Nieman Reports December 15, 2005. Retrieved June 3, 2020, from https://niemanreports.org/articles/citizen-journalism-and-the-bbc/.
Shapiro, A. L. (1999). *The Control Revolution*. New York: PublicAffairs.
Sherwood, M., & O'Donnell, P. (2018). Once a Journalist, Always a Journalist? Industry Restructure, Job Loss and Professional Identity. *Journalism Studies*, *19*(7), 1021–1038. https://doi.org/10.1080/1461670X.2016.1249007.
Sørensen, J. K. (2011). *The Paradox of Personalisation. Public Service Broadcasters' Approaches to Media Personalisation Services*. PhD thesis, University of Southern Denmark.

Sørensen, J. K. (2013). PSB Goes Personal: The Failure of Personalised PSB Web Pages. *MedieKultur, 29*(55), 43–71. https://doi.org/10.7146/mediekultur.v29i55.7993.

Sørensen, J. K. (2019). Public Service Media, Diversity and Algorithmic Recommendation: Tensions Between Editorial Principles and Algorithms in European PSM Organizations. INRA at RecSys 2019: 13th ACM Conference on Recommender Systems Copenhagen, Denmark, Copenhagen, Denmark Published in CEUR Workshop Proceedings, 2554, 6–11. Retrieved from http://ceur-ws.org/Vol-2554/paper_01.pdf.

Sørensen, J. K., & Hutchinson, J. (2018). Algorithms and Public Service Media. In G. F. Lowe, H. Van den Bulck, & K. Donders (Eds.), *Public Service Media in the Networked Society RIPE@2017* (pp. 91–106). Nordicom, Göteborg Universitet: Göteborg.

Sørensen, J. K., & Schmidt, J.-H. (2016). An Algorithmic Diversity Diet? Questioning Assumptions behind a Diversity Recommendation System for PSM. Presented at the RIPE@2016. Retrieved from https://www.researchgate.net/publication/308721307_An_Algorithmic_Diversity_Diet_Questioning_Assumptions_behind_a_Diversity_Recommendation_System_for_PSM

Sørensen, J. K., & Van den Bulck, H. (2018). Public Service Media Online, Advertising and the Third-Party User Data Business: A Trade Versus Trust Dilemma? *Convergence: The International Journal of Research into New Media Technologies, 26*(2), 421–447. https://doi.org/10.1177/1354856518790203.

Sørensen, J. K., Van den Bulck, H., & Kosta, S. (2020). Stop Spreading the Data: PSM, Trust and Third-Party Services. *Journal of Information Policy, 10*, 474–513. https://doi.org/10.5325/jinfopoli.10.2020.0474

Striphas, T. (2015). Algorithmic culture. *European Journal of Cultural Studies, 18*(4–5). https://doi.org/10.1177/1367549415577392.

Thomas, J. (2018). Programming, filtering, adblocking: advertising and media automation. *Media International Australia, 166*(1), 34–43. https://doi.org/10.1177/1329878X17738787.

Thurman, N., & Schifferes, S. (2012). The Future of Personalization at News Websites. *Journalism Studies, 13*(5–6), 775–790. https://doi.org/10.1080/1461670X.2012.664341.

Van den Bulck, H., & Moe, H. (2017). Public Service Media, Universality and Personalisation Through Algorithms: Mapping Strategies and Exploring Dilemmas. *Media, Culture & Society, 40*(6), 875–892. https://doi.org/10.1177/0163443717734407.

Zuboff, S. (2019). "We Make Them Dance": Surveillance Capitalism, the Rise of Instrumentarian Power, and the Threat to Human Rights. In R. F. Jørgensen & D. Kaye (Eds.), *Human Rights in the Age of Platforms* (pp. 3–51). MIT press, Cambridge, Massachusetts, USA.

CHAPTER 5

Are Public Service Media Necessary in the Transmedia Era?

Esteban Galán-Cubillo, María Soler-Campillo, and Javier Marzal-Felici

1 Introduction

It all began on 29 November 2013, a date we will never forget. The truth is, we do not know why it happened that day, since there is nothing in particular in this history that had not forewarned us. The true tale itself is so extraordinary that it might be a worthwhile television production itself. The shutdown of a public radio and television corporation was broadcast live with the state security forces looking on, narrated live by a reporter in a corridor backed by a strikingly white-textured wall that suddenly turned green and then dark, just before photographers appeared in the image

---

E. Galán-Cubillo (✉)
Universitat Politècnica de València, Valencia, Spain
e-mail: egalan@upv.es

M. Soler-Campillo • J. Marzal-Felici
Universitat Jaume I, Castelló, Spain
e-mail: solerm@uji.es; marzal@uji.es

trying to immortalize those last seconds of broadcast. At that moment, in the room known as the television corporation's Control Central, the electricity was cut off and all of the technical apparatus stopped working abruptly, some of which would be rendered useless forever after that action was taken. The general electricity power cut stopped hundreds of devices from working in a second, and it was also felt physically in the stomachs of hundreds of workers who then joined the statistical ranks of the unemployed in Spain. In 2013, unemployment in Spain came to well over six million people. The number of Valencian citizens that were left without a public communication service was just one million fewer. The situation was not easy for anybody, but with the country gradually showing cracks and a quarter of the active population unemployed, perhaps the closure of a public communication service could be seen as a necessary way of rationalizing expenditure to maintain the public services that our heads of government said truly mattered to the citizens: education and health care. The autonomous regional government's ideologically conservative official discourse stated that the public broadcaster was being closed in order to keep schools and hospitals open. The exceptional nature of the event served as a warning of the real danger faced by other public media in Spain and the rest of Europe, as well as to identify the void that the Valencian communication service effectively left on shutting down the public radio and television corporation (López Olano 2018). In this context and to avoid future temptations to close or privatize, it is worth posing the following question: Are public communication services necessary in the transmedia age?

1.1 The Need for Public Media

The process of digitalizing the media is a phenomenon that is now complete. Television has morphed into a hybrid with the Internet, and today it is possible to consume television content via traditional means or mobile devices. This digitalization has transformed the medium of television, which has become much more permeable to new forms of production and circulation of content (Salaverría 2018, p. 26). Every day, YouTube shows us how any individual can attract global audiences from their own bedroom (Gómez Domínguez 2019). It is in this context that audiovisual public media coexist. In the European Union, they have been set up based on a dual model in which public service acts as a counterbalance to privately owned media, but in the twentieth century public media are faced with the difficulty not only of providing quality public service content but also of the need to involve the audience in it. Today, one cannot talk of public service television without effective participation from the citizens (EBU / UER Report 2015; Gómez-Mompart et al. 2015; Ribas et al. 2016; Wilson 2016). These new flows are becoming expensive to implement because public media are very regulated and they thus depend on legislation, which is inevitably always a step behind the social reality (Zallo 2016). Furthermore, it is not a simple task to modify the organizational culture due to very human factors such as conservative attitudes, the fear of change, or professional inertia. With this in mind, on a European level one of the greatest difficulties detected in maintaining public media's relevance is the introduction of participation as one of the broad values in terms of legislation, governance, innovation, the creation of content, and an evaluation of the social contribution to the public service. In addition to this difficulty, there is the de-legitimization of the public sphere being suffered by democracies, aggravated by populisms, and the instability generated by changes in business models in the media. Amid this panorama of generalized crisis, which affects audiovisual public service, it would seem to be essential to reinvent the media strategy and take on a far-reaching transformation in which the transmedia narrative necessarily comes into play (Ellis and Greenbank 2015; Quintas-Froufe and González-Neira 2016). Let us examine the reasons why.

1.2 Public Service in the Transmedia Age

Transmedia is a concept that has become popular over the last 15 years, with its forerunner found in the concept of multimedia. Stemming from the latter term, and mainly fostered by Henry Jenkins, the term *transmedia* has been coined to describe the different way of circulating content today (Jenkins et al. 2006, 2015). The target is no longer a simple information receiver, but somebody who acts and re-disseminates the content. Nevertheless, linear narratives are still perfectly valid; the new media (social networks, instant messaging, and streaming platforms) coexist with the old (television, radio, and cinema). Even so, although the events we have mentioned took place in a traditional medium, it is important to be aware that today, once we have created content then the audience also has it and may disseminate it whatever way they see fit via different platforms and at a speed never before seen in the history of humanity. In a few seconds, an image or video can travel around the world and become viral.

The concept of transmedia narrative therefore describes a multitude of options available to the creator to construct their story. Until recently, stories were linear, one-directional, and linked to the medium through which they were going to be communicated. Now, however, a story can travel via different media and be enriched with contributions from the community at which it is targeted. Transmedia is an adjective that we can add to the term *storytelling* and which ultimately defines a radical change in our way of communicating. Narration or storytelling intertwines with technology and social participation, so that citizens cast aside their traditionally passive role, opening up a sphere of activism by creating content and participating in fora that often become public service proximity media capable of channeling citizen participation into social changes (Scolari 2018).

Even so, despite these new possibilities, the concept of transmedia raises some controversy because it is understood that the narrative can be cut up and therefore lose some of its unity. One transmedia strategy, however, does not necessarily involve cutting up the narrative; rather, each medium has to contribute something that is valuable and distinctive in itself. Each part must be narratively conclusive, while at the same time containing a clue (which may be implicit) that suggests to the audience that there is something further that they can access to enrich or complement the story.

1.3 From the Transmedia Project to the Product

Any audiovisual production entails great complexity. Thus, when an audiovisual product is included in a transmedia strategy, its complexity multiplies, and as a result the number of professionals involved also multiplies, swelling the budget necessary to produce it. These organizational difficulties would seem to put transmedia productions out of the reach of all but national and international television corporations or big entertainment franchises. However, there is a type of transmedia production called "project transmedia," which involves drawing up a strategy for an audiovisual production through which we can work on a final deliverable, which may be a documentary, a film, or a series. At the same time, we use new media to distribute the necessary materials for the project's pre-production, which until now were hidden (evaluations, location profiles, costume trials, etc.). These materials can be gamified via the social networks and hence serve to build or strengthen a community around the project.

Project transmedia involves putting together a strategy through which the different contents generated to create the main deliverable become independent products at the same time (podcasts with evaluations, profile on Instagram with costume trials, instant messaging to identify and gain loyalty among groups and organizations interested in our project, etc.). In the project transmedia strategy, parts of the production that until now were hidden now become visible, being turned into audiovisual contents that complement and add value to the final product. The project's transmedia narrative enables the creative leap needed by any audiovisual production without excessively increasing its complexity. Hence, it would seem that in the current panorama of limited budgets for public media, the project transmedia format could be the appropriate one to implement new narratives, foster citizen participation, and innovate with new technologies and languages in an audiovisual public service. Implementing a "project transmedia" strategy in a public medium also enables greater efficiency in adapting to the panorama of audience fragmentation and to the demand for content, especially from the younger public, who seek formats with which they can interact via their mobile phones.

2   The Case of À Punt Mèdia

For some time now, it has been common to hear voices protesting that the cost per citizen of a paid subscription to a platform is lower than the maintenance costs for public media, and that with the Internet and the wide range of educational, cultural, and scientific content on offer within our reach, public television is no longer necessary (Campos-Freire 2016; Marzal-Felici and Soler-Campillo 2016). Very much on the contrary, it is precisely that excess supply that makes public radio and television corporations more necessary than ever, in order to preserve cultural diversity and identity while ensuring universal access to the content. In this context, in addition to the traditional aims of public service related to promoting culture and language, the quality of information and the construction of a public space, there is also the aim of fostering innovation and creativity. Thus, public communication platforms are called on to lead in implementing disruptive technological tools that open up new approaches to the news and ways for citizens to participate, with the aim of guiding them toward pro-social ends (Miguel et al. 2017).

In the case of the Valencia Community region, the disappearance of the public radio and television service (RTVV) brought home to people the strategic worth of proximity public media as a motor for the audiovisual sector and creative industries (Galán et al. 2018). The closure also served to affirm the need to protect cultural identity, which in the case of the Valencia Community region is intimately linked to the use and promotion of Valencian as a co-official language in the territory. The existence of public radio and television corporations has been decisive for the growth of different cultural industries that generate wealth and employment. Nor should it be forgotten that regional public radio and television corporations are a fundamental tool to project cultural and linguistic identity. They should therefore also aspire for their proximity content to be distributed in some cases outside the region, too (CVMC 2017).

Finally, it should be remembered that the General Law on Audiovisual Communication of 2010 indicates that citizens have the right "to receive audiovisual communication in conditions of cultural and linguistic pluralism by means of protecting European and Spanish works, as well as those in different official languages, and Spanish cultural manifestations" (Azurmendi et al. 2011). With this perspective, proximity media should be understood as an instrument to bolster the social and cultural fabric, and therefore as an investment aimed at ensuring the quality of our democracy.

The old public radio and television corporation (RTVV), which shut down abruptly in 2013, was an archetypal example of one of the main problems suffered by European public television: dependence on the government, a lack of quality content, no transparency, and insufficient funding, aggravated by the financial crisis in 2008 and also by unprecedented political corruption (Marzal-Felici and Soler-Campillo 2016). À Punt Mèdia was launched four years after the shutdown. Its objective from the outset has been to take advantage of the situation as an opportunity to adapt the new public service platform to the new communications ecosystem. À Punt Mèdia has been founded within a public communications space that in many senses could be considered to be a paradigm of adaptation to the new environment: the content is articulated using a transmedia strategy that promotes and encourages citizen participation. Today, it is a public communication platform with nearly 500 employees, an annual budget of over 50 million euros and a potential audience of 5 million citizens. The case of À Punt Mèdia is unique because it has had the opportunity to implement its operational structure according to the requirements of the new multiplatform environment. The launching of a public communications service to be adapted to the new communication environment in the Internet soon came up against an added difficulty: its employees mostly came from the old radio and television model, and have therefore had to adapt their work routines to the new digital environment, which requires more multiskilled job profiles. To do so, they have created new professional profiles such as data journalist, social networks expert, audiovisual editor, and more.

However, the most significant change has been to unify the workspace into a single newsroom in which content is produced for television, radio, the Internet, and the social networks, all in coordination (Soler-Campillo et al. 2019). The production and content-editing software has also been unified and the Dalet Galaxy platform has also been adopted, which enables tasks to be centralized, such as taking in audiovisual material, step outlines, and management of documentary archives. Working in a single newsroom enables a great many professionals from different disciplines to be included in the same physical space, such as producers, documentary makers, IT engineers, and so on, thereby helping work routines to take on a multidisciplinary perspective. This multidisciplinary profile is especially relevant when developing interactive content for mobile devices. Adapting content to the contexts of consumption via new interactive windows poses one of the fundamental challenges of the new corporation, because as happens in other territories such as Catalonia, Galicia, and the Basque country, one of the purposes of the public corporation is to normalize the use of the regional language. The use of Valencian in the content consumed via the social networks and mobile devices is practically insignificant. Therefore, À Punt Mèdia has set itself the task of trying to reverse this situation as much as possible as a priority basis for its activity. The new patterns of audiovisual consumption have taken up video as the preferred format for internauts. The youngest generations spend more time consuming content via new devices than via general viewing TV, and those habits are also occurring as regards radio. In order to adapt to this new situation, À Punt Mèdia has made an effort for its audiovisual creations to have an itinerary that does not end (and sometimes does not even begin) with being broadcast openly. Open content is transformed into online content that can be consumed, commented, and shared at any time from any place and screen.

The most important point is that À Punt Mèdia is now a reality that began its radio broadcasts in December 2017 and television broadcasts in June 2018. Furthermore, À Punt Mèdia's *à la carte* content platform has also been created, which has exclusive content for children. The website and children's and youth's platform are often used to première programs. Great progress has been made by the fact that À Punt Media's schedule for children has been developed from the outset on the multimedia platform, adapting to the forms of online consumption that are mostly used among the youngest people today. *La Colla* is a children's community via À Punt Media that brings together the world of content, programs, and entertainment online, on the radio, or on the street, as well as all of the television programs for the little ones. *La Colla* has its own mobile application for IOS and Android, and the content is available in the Smart TV ecosystem of the communication space (Arjona 2019, p. 26).

The series on the platform *La Colla* can be seen *à la carte* online or on its own app, which can be downloaded for free. The content is divided into the age ranges it is aimed at (pre-school or children's) and there is a third section on the website to identify content in English. As for the content for the youth audience, the educational program *Rosquilletres* stands out, in both television and radio versions. *Rosquilletres* is a contest in which compulsory secondary school students (young teenagers and pre-adolescents) from schools all around the Valencia region compete by pitting their spelling skills against each other with Valencian words. There is also a musical section where the competitors have to see a video clip of songs by Valencian music groups who sing in Valencian; they have to correctly answer questions about the song they have heard. "The programme is used in secondary schools as a tool to boost learning of the Valencian language. In fact, it has created a link among *Valencià* teachers' professional associations due to its usefulness in linguistic matters. During the 2018–2019 season, 420 students from schools around the entire Valencia Community region took part" (Arjona 2019, p. 28).

Together with the children's schedule, another aspect that À Punt Mèdia has been working on as a priority is the news services. The old Canal 9 received a lot of criticism, and it has to be said often justifiably so, due to its bias and lack of objectivity in addressing information about politics or current affairs. This is why the heads of À Punt Mèdia have taken special care to distance themselves from the old practices of political manipulation, taking care to be independent and meticulous in the new services. An effort has also been made to include new languages and offer reports on in-depth topics that can be consumed via the website. There is noteworthy news coverage that is carried out via programs with special interactive formats of social significance, for example, related to corruption, evictions, and suicides.

The transmedia strategy is also used in producing programs like *69 raons* (*69 reasons*), which À Punt Mèdia co-produces in association with the audiovisual company from Castellón, Saó Produccions. The 30-minute program is a combination of fiction and reality to reflect on matters of concern to adolescents as regards affective and sexual relations. The format is an adaptation of the program *Betevé* from the Barcelona municipal television corporation. It is called *Oh My Goig!* (*Goig* means *joy* in Valencian) and is a pioneer in addressing sexuality for youths on public television. It has been broadcast since 2016. The program offers content adapted to the social networks, talks in schools, and television programs lasting 30 minutes that are first posted on the website and YouTube before being broadcast openly so as to stimulate debate in the social networks. In each chapter, matters related to the sexuality of youths are posed and debated.

Una habitació pròpia (*A room of my own*) also stands out among the programs scheduled due to its visual attractiveness and educational value. The literary pundit Irene Rodrigo heads the program, which can be found on television, radio, street posters, and content in the social networks. Like *69 raons*, there is also close collaboration with the regional *Conselleria* (Education Department), by which activities in schools are linked to the content in this multiplatform format. The strategy to introduce the format for *Una habitació pròpia* was gradual. It began on the radio, continued on television, remained on the streets with posters about the books and authors it dealt with, then fostered interaction in the social networks, and now it also organizes activities and workshops that are carried out in secondary schools. This program helps À Punt Mèdia lend visibility to its commitment as a public medium to disseminate literature and culture. In order to work on this kind of relationship with schools, universities, and social and cultural groups, the Department of Social Projection has been created, which works to streamline interlocution with relevant professional associations. Maintaining these communication channels with educational institutions has enabled them to create initiatives to receive ideas from universities that may help connect with a younger audience. One of the most noteworthy initiatives has been the *Festival Talent Universitari*, organized by the À Punt Mèdia public communication platform together with the Valencian university system and the private audiovisual sector. In its first two editions, the contest has achieved a total participation of 30 projects, of which 5 have been selected and presented by students to be broadcast by the public communication channel. This activity is also part of a collaboration agreement between universities and the CVMC (Valencia Media Corporation, which founded and supervises À Punt Mèdia), by which common activities are organized periodically such as seminars, courses, and talks related to education for students and professional refreshers for the employees of À Punt Mèdia. Using these training activities and the forum for presenting audiovisual formats, universities and À Punt Mèdia work together to promote culture, science, and knowledge so as to lend visibility to the work of artists, teachers, and researchers, making a commitment to an equal presence of men and women while doing so.

3   Discussion

The rise of populist movements has benefited from a generalized rise in fake news that has found its way through the social networks: an underground relativism that makes it more necessary than ever for there to be quality public media with sufficient social relevance to counterbalance populist discourses. The crisis in the public media exemplified by the closure of RTVV and the creation of À Punt Mèdia (López Olano 2018) has clearly shown the fragility of the current democratic system. There is still much to do in Spain, since a state regulatory authority is yet to be created, and where applicable audiovisual committees for autonomous regions to supervise the work of public and private media (Donders 2011). The television Corporation À Punt Mèdia has set up its own Audience Council, whose purpose is to oversee compliance with the public service of communication and ensure that complaints and suggestions from citizens are effectively addressed by those responsible for this medium. In the time that the radio and television have completed their first months of broadcasting since 2017 and 2018 respectively, the Audience Council (2019) has seen a significant contribution made by À Punt Mèdia to recover and normalize the use of Valencian as a language of public use. Work has also been done to strengthen regional unity and stimulate culture, essentially through entertainment programs. Nevertheless, some shortcomings have been detected as regards the scarce economic resources the medium has at its disposal and the circumstance of having only one channel in an age of fragmented audiences, which makes it difficult to adapt to consumption patterns increasingly aimed at more specific content.

4   Conclusions

As we know, the communication products we consume are the result of a combination of different media. We are thus in a scenario of convergence in which the dominant screen is increasingly the one on mobile phones. In this context, is it still necessary for there to be public communication services? Should they adapt to the new environments of consumption? Let us see.

Every day, we read a news item which we then look into further through a video, which we then share in a social network in which we can end up signing to show support for a citizen-based proposal linked to the information. In addition to this change in consumption habits, in many new households there are no longer traditional television sets or transistor radios. This means that for Public Service Media to be relevant, it must aim its productions at the new windows. These new windows enable and encourage interaction from the user. They therefore open up the door to creativity that is to be found not only among traditional content creators but also among the audience, who can also create and propose content and even new media and communication channels. Hence, the role of public service communication should be to articulate communities and lead creation strategies that enable citizens' activity in the Internet to be geared toward social ends. Creativity is no longer the domain of the creators that work for the industry. There are increasingly more people in the audience who can create and put forward content fundamentally aimed at new platforms. Under these circumstances, the hybridization of consumption and creation interfaces has collaborated up to the point that they are sometimes indistinguishable. Using an instant messaging app, we can launch a meme that will go around the world in a few seconds or see the highlights of the latest Champions League final.

The commitment to recovering the public radio and television service in the Valencia Community region has been implemented via a transmedia strategy in an attempt to be relevant in the current scenario and to have a presence in today's media and the media of the future. This transmedia strategy involves defining content linked to topics that straddle the group's different media and establishing a series of strategic actions linked to them. The aim must be to inform and entertain using the same media used by the users, in other words radio and television, but also new devices. Television, radio, and cinema are still very relevant media, but today they coexist with new screens that also need multimedia content. The transmedia scenario calls for a change of model in which the audience become users and decide at all times if they wish to be active or not. To do so, it would seem to be necessary to bolster the management of proximity public communication media with staff and material resources from the R&D&i department or service. Innovation is essential in order to design strategies that make the presentation of content more attractive and which stimulate participation from citizens in creating and proposing content. The public service must have active participation from citizens in order to ensure that its social and educational projection meets the demands of the society that finances public media with its taxes.

Following the explanations above, the reply to the initial question of whether a public communications service is necessary in the transmedia age would seem to be clear. In order to halt the growing mistrust among citizens toward mass media, it is necessary for traditional media to cast off some of the traditional routines (journalism using statements, exclusive use of government sources, lack of contrasting information) so that they may provide innovative, quality content that can be shared in the social networks, while at the same time acting more and more as the dominant media platform. It is necessary to appeal more and more to citizens' responsibility when they share information whose source's reliability and truthfulness they have not been able to verify. New levels of commitment from citizens must be sought, and the audiovisual content should become a catalyst for social activism. It is a question of helping citizens to articulate themselves as regards initiatives related to culture, associations, and education. This can only be done in a credible, sustained way over time by managing public policies, which must lead the public information services. The wave of fake news that has fueled phenomena such as Brexit, the electoral success of populist parties in many European countries, and alarms about COVID-19 all reminds us of the importance of having quality information and entertainment. In the case of COVID-19, the continual rumors about new contagions and alarms about baseless remedies appearing in order to combat the epidemic have all plunged us into a kind of neo-Middle Ages in communication, where each individual inhabits their own bubble in which we comfortably give all our data to today's equivalent of the feudal lord, the technological giant in question (Facebook, Instagram, or YouTube), in exchange for everything that the algorithm thinks we might or must think. Therefore, if the importance of the citizen is not to be reduced to a simple click, the result of an algorithm designed thousands of kilometers away, then we need quality public communication spaces. In the case of regional television corporations such as À Punt Mèdia, we believe that the commitment must be to produce proximity content that ensures pluralism and diversity for citizens. In an ever more global world, it is increasingly important to respect diversity or even simply respect citizens as such and not as goods to be sold to an advertiser or a technological giant for the price of a few clicks.

Acknowledgments This work has been carried out as part of the research project "Citizens' participation and public communication media. Analysis of the experiences of audiovisual co-creation in Spain and in Europe (PARCICOM)" (code RTI2018-093649-B-I00) under the management of Javier Marzal-Felici, funded by the 2018 Call for R&D&I Projects "Research Challenges" by the state R&D&i program aimed at Challenges for Society, for the 2019–2021 period.

References

Arjona, E. (2019). *La programación infantil en À Punt Mèdia. El cumplimiento de valores y la proyección educativa*. Trabajo Final de Máster. Castellón: Universitat Jaume I de Castelló.
Azurmendi, A., López, N., & Manfredi, J. L. (2011). La reforma de la televisión pública en el nuevo marco legal audiovisual (Ley 7/2010, General de la Comunicación Audiovisual) de cobertura nacional. *Derecom, 5*, 1–24. Retrieved June 3, 2020, from https://dialnet.unirioja.es/servlet/articulo?codigo=4799974.
Campos-Freire, F. (2016). *Situación actual y tendencias de la radiotelevisión pública en Europa*. Santiago de Compostela: Universidad de Santiago de Compostela / FORTA. Retrieved June 3, 2020, from https://www.academia.edu/34087686/Situación_actual_y_tendencias_de_la_radiotelevisión_pública_en_Europa.
Corporación Valenciana de Medios de Comunicación. (2017). *Llibre d'Estil de la Corporació Valenciana de Mitjans de Comunicació*. Burjassot (Valencia): Corporació Valenciana de Mitjans de Comunicació & Generalitat Valenciana. Aprobado el 07/09/2017 por la CVMC. Retrieved June 3, 2020, from https://www.cvmc.es/wp-content/uploads/2017/12/Llibre-destil-CVMC_web.pdf.
Donders, K. (2011). *Public Service Media and policy in Europe*. Londres: Palgrave Macmillan.
EBU / UER. (2015). *Public Service Media. Contribution to Society*. Le Gran-Saconnex, Switzerland: Media Intelligence Service, European Broadcasting Union.
Ellis, R., & Greenbank, M. (2015). *Watching the Devices: Do we Watch Video Differently on Smaller Screens?* Esomar Congress, 150–157, Dublin.
Galán, E., Rodríguez, A., & Marzal, J. (2018). *Contenidos transmedia para la radiotelevisión de proximidad*. Pamplona: Eunsa.

Gómez Domínguez, P. (2019). *L'audiovisual públic europeu i Youtube*. Barcelona: Observatori de la Producció Audiovisual. Retrieved from http://hdl.handle.net/10230/36289.

Gómez-Mompart, J. L., Gutiérrez-Lozano, J. F., & Palau-Sampio, D. (2015). Los periodistas españoles y la pérdida de la calidad de la información: el juicio profesional. *Comunicar, 45*, 143–150. https://doi.org/10.3916/C45-2015-15.

Jenkins, H., Clinton, K., Purushotma, R., Robison, A., & Weigel, M. (2006). *Confronting the Challenges of Participatory Culture: Media Education for the 21st Century*. Chicago: The MacArthur Foundation. Retrieved June 3, 2020, from https://www.macfound.org/media/article_pdfs/JENKINS_WHITE_PAPER.PDF.

Jenkins, H., Ford, S., & Green, J. (2015). *Cultura transmedia. La creación de contenido y valor en una cultura en red*. Barcelona: Gedisa.

López Olano, C. (2018). *RTVV: Paradigma de la triple crisis de las televisiones públicas*. Valencia: Tirant Lo Blanch.

Marzal-Felici, J., & Soler-Campillo, M. (2016). Retos de la futura radiotelevisión pública de la Comunidad Valenciana. Un espacio para la aplicación de buenas prácticas públicas. In G. Orozco & M. Francés (Eds.), *Nuevos modelos mediáticos. Diversidad, usuarios y ventanas* (pp. 121–134). Madrid: Síntesis.

Miguel, J. C., Zallo, R., & Casado, M. A. (2017). Las televisiones autonómicas públicas y privadas. In E. G. Montes (Ed.), *Televisión Abierta. Situación actual y Tendencias de futuro de la TDT*. Madrid: Colegio Oficial de Ingenieros de Telecomunicación. Retrieved June 3, 2020, from https://www.coit.es/informes/television-abierta-situacion-actual-y-tendencias-de-futuro-de-la-tdt-ano-de-publicacion.

Quintas-Froufe, N., & González-Neira, A. (2016). Consumo televisivo y su medición en España: camino hacia las audiencias híbridas. *El Profesional de la Información, 25*(3), 376–383. https://doi.org/10.3145/epi.2016.may.07.

Ribas, J. V., Finger, C., & Ferreira, G. (2016). Televisão pública no contexto de convergência midiática. *Revista Lumina, 10*(2) https://doi.org/10.34019/1981-4070.2016.v10.21285.

Salaverría, R. (2018). De la televisión al audiovisual transmedia: tecnologías, audiencias y lenguajes. En E. Galán, A. Rodríguez & J. Marzal-Felici, *Contenidos transmedia para la radiotelevisión de proximidad* (pp. 23–32). Pamplona: Eunsa.

Scolari, C. A. (2018). *Libro Blanco. Alfabetismo transmedia en la nueva ecología de los medios*. Barcelona: Transliteracy & Ars Media. Retrieved June 3, 2020, from http://transmedialiteracy.upf.edu/sites/default/files/files/TL_whit_es.pdf.

Soler-Campillo, M., Galán Cubillo, E., & Marzal-Felici, J. (2019). La creación de À Punt Mèdia (2013–19) como nuevo espacio público de comunicación. *Revista Latina de Comunicación Social, 74*, 1801–1817. Retrieved from http://www.revistalatinacs.org/074paper/1411/94es.html.

Wilson, S. (2016). In the Living Room: Second Screens and TV Audiences. *Television and New Media*, *17*(2), 174–191. https://doi.org/10.1177/1527476415593348.

Zallo, R. (2016). *Tendencias en comunicación. Cultura digital y poder.* Barcelona: Gedisa.

CHAPTER 6

Public Service Media and Blockchain Technology: First Thoughts

Juan Carlos Miguel-de-Bustos and Jessica Izquierdo-Castillo

1 INTRODUCTION

Blockchain technology works with block structures. Each block contains its own information and metainformation from other blocks, so that all pieces are linked together and self-managed in a network. This technology is at the base of crypto currencies, with Bitcoin and Ethereum being the most popular.

> A blockchain is a shared ledger of transactions between parties in a network, not controlled by a single central authority. You can think of a ledger like a record book: it records and stores all transactions between users in chronological order. Instead of one authority controlling this ledger (like a bank),

J. C. Miguel-de-Bustos (✉)
Universidad del País Vasco-EHU, Bilbao, Spain
e-mail: jc.miguel@ehu.eus

J. Izquierdo-Castillo
Universidad Jaume I, Castellón, Spain
e-mail: jizquier@com.uji.es

© The Author(s), under exclusive license to Springer Nature Switzerland AG 2021
M. Túñez-López et al. (eds.), *The Values of Public Service Media in the Internet Society*, Palgrave Global Media Policy and Business, https://doi.org/10.1007/978-3-030-56466-7_6

an identical copy of the ledger is held by all users on the network, called nodes. (Carson et al. 2018)

This can mean a substantial change in the Internet and its applications. Winfield (2017) talks about the transition from an Internet of data to an Internet of value. Thus, the first generation was a revolution in terms of access and content creation, thanks to interconnection. This allowed the content to be duplicated and distributed at virtually no cost, which has created an ecosystem where it is very difficult to assign authorship to the works and, therefore, to remunerate the creators of that content. Added to this is the difficulty in managing the individual data that remains in the hands of larger platforms, such as GAFAM (Google, Apple, Facebook, Amazon, Microsoft) (Miguel-de-Bustos and Izquierdo-Castillo 2019). This first generation "was great for distribution, but terrible for value" (Potts and Rennie 2017, p. 5). The second generation based on blockchain can create structural protocols that allow the creation and transaction of value. Therefore, it would allow the creation of a new distribution platform that will be able to "reshape the world of business and transform the old order of human affairs for the better" (Leodolter 2017, p. 253). In general terms, this technology enables five types of transaction and/or actions (Catalini and Gans 2017): (a) atomic, (b) identity verification, (c) production chain monitoring, (d) online reputation, and (e) auctions.

Blockchain performs transactions between the nodes of the network, and the information of these transactions is saved in blocks, once the net itself validates it through miners. The miner receives some kind of remuneration. This recorded information becomes immutable, guaranteeing trust in the network. The information is associated with a hash (used for actions such as user validation and authentication), and the blocks are related to each other, so that if someone were to change a block, alarms would go off, because all nodes share the same information. Any attempt to change a block is detected, and it is also impossible to modify it. Hackers would have to change the block in all its nodes, which is impossible, especially if there are multiple nodes. They would also have to change all subsequent blocks, because there is a specific hash that relates one block to the previous one. They would have to change 51% of all the blocks simultaneously, because they are generally regulated by consensus.

The costs associated with blockchain technology are mainly affected by verification costs and networking costs (Catalini and Gans 2017). The verification costs refer to the costs that are incurred when a transaction takes place. This verification is recorded in data, such as the date of the transaction, the items transacted (e.g., content versus money), buyer/seller data, conflict resolution rules (guarantee), and so on. The exchanged elements can refer to any type of element: intellectual property, property ownership, currencies, information, votes, and so on. This allows entry barriers to be lowered and competitiveness to increase, as well as making possible an increase in innovation and a decrease in pirated practices and fake news, and so on, and, above all, it makes it possible to diminish the power of the platforms that characterize the Internet economy. This occurs because blockchain reduces the operating costs of the exchange networks, and allows the creation of digital platforms, where the benefits are not obtained at the cost of an increase in their power, as happens with the GAFAM. The costs associated with verification are ascribed to the work of the miners, who are responsible for carrying out complex computing tasks to ensure the existence of a consensus. The networking costs refer to costs that take place when the market is managed without the need for intermediaries. In this sense, blockchain allows the use of a specific currency, with which members can make payments and establish contracts accepting the veracity of the data they share.

In this way, blockchain is characterized by being a transparent, digital, democratic, secure, consultable, and decentralized technology that allows instantaneous transactions and is irreversible in its annotations (Deloitte 2017; Allayannis and Fernstrom 2018; Writght and De Filippi 2015). In the blockchain, the network itself acts as an intermediary, so it does not need a central point of control and does not allow any annotation without the consent of the entire network. Therefore, it operates in a context of free-trust. For this reason, it is at the base of digital currencies, since it allows the use of tokens as an alternative monetary mechanism. And it also permits other applications, such as smart contracts.

Due to its characteristics and operation, blockchain presents a transformative potential for business models in all industries (Wirtz et al. 2016; Weking et al. 2019), essentially for cultural industries (Rennie et al. 2019).

2 Blockchain in Cultural Industries

Blockchain technology makes it possible to change the economic models that the Internet introduced for cultural industries. These models are often based on websites financed by advertising, given the impossibility of charging for content (Potts and Rennie 2017). However, blockchain may allow better protection within the area of content creation. This technology makes it possible to license and sell rights without intermediaries, and to obtain income more easily and transparently in transactions.

Nonetheless, this disappearance of intermediaries must be qualified. To think that all mediators disappear would be simplistic. As new activities appear—verification of blocks, platforms where smart contracts are registered, and so on—there is a simultaneous disintermediation together with re-intermediation. Therefore, to think that GAFAM or banks are going to disappear as intermediaries is also reductionist, since both sectors are the ones that dedicate most resources to the implementation of the blockchain technology. GAFAM do this, for example, by offering cloud services—Amazon—while banks use blockchain technology to carry out transactions among themselves. In fact, *Forbes* magazine includes GAFAM among the largest companies with blockchain activity (Del Castillo and Schifrin 2020). Alongside them are the world's leading banks, Apple hardware maker—Foxcon—and diamond company DeBeer. This is also demonstrated by a study on patents in relation to blockchain (Lee 2018): the largest number is in start-ups (60%), although the majority of the start-ups only own one patent; financial services (20%) and traditional technology companies (13%); the remaining 7% are among companies from multiple sectors, including gaming, sales, information technology, and cultural industries.

In the academic field, blockchain has attracted the interest of numerous scholars, although to date there have been few works focused on its application to the cultural industries.[1] On the set of works collected by the Blockchain Library, only 1.1% belongs to cultural industries, specifically to media and music (Blockchain Library 2017).

Also on a theoretical level, Xu et al. (2019) establish that any industrial activity can obtain three advantages in the application of blockchain: increase the efficiency of the main activity; reduce transaction costs; and make intellectual property and payments more transparent. Transferring this to cultural industries, blockchain can be applied in four directions: (a) financing, with special consideration in crowd funding; (b) data registration and data access; (c) monitoring products throughout the value chain; (d) smart contracts can be used within the organization and outside, in relation to other organizations.

On the other hand, for O'Dair et al. (2016), blockchain could contribute specific benefits to the cultural industries in four areas: (a) it allows the attribution of ownership of works—this is especially useful nowadays, when attributing intellectual property rights in a univocal way is complex, since more agents intervene, such as the case of a media work; (b) ease of payment with greatly reduced prices; (c) transparency in all the activities making up the value chain; and (d) the possibility of new forms of financing, while facilitating those already working, such as crowdfunding. At the base of these improvements we find smart contracts, which can be specified to implement any type of financing. John Davies (2019) expresses himself in similar terms when referring to the creative industries and adds a fifth aspect related to scarcity, since the existence of a unique work can be guaranteed through blockchain.

Lansiti and Lakhani (2017) define blockchain as a foundational technology, capable of creating a new basis (foundations). It is interpreted as an economic infrastructure, which allows ownership of a cultural product to be assigned to whomever it corresponds to, and enables adaptation, production, and distribution contracts, including the corresponding public aid. It is a technology for decentralization, which allows new coordination systems that facilitate transactions. It is not only a system of financial exchanges, it also makes it possible to establish reputation systems (Davidson et al. 2016).

We consulted about twenty blockchain projects related to cinema and television.[2] All projects are privately owned and all place an emphasis on creation. Some allow the development of projects, including fundraising, and then distribute the funded projects (Singular DTB and FilmChain). Some are more Netflix-like platforms, such as Binge and Slate. Few offer different cultural industries at the same time, like Ara Blocks. This particular case permits the dissemination of books, music, and television. There are also those that integrate various players in the value chain. For example, MovieChain involves suppliers, distributors, creators, and users and gives them the possibility of interacting. As does Bond, where there are only creators, investors, and users, and which also offers the possibility for anyone to act in all three ways. In the case of TV-TWO, the specific feature is that you can choose to watch the ads and get paid for doing so. Another good example of integration is offered by Imusify, since it offers discussion forums, curators that elaborate a playlist, new artists, established artists, crowdfunding activities, transactions, and so on (Imusify n.d.). In all projects, the promoter of the blockchain system receives remuneration, although not always explicitly. This can range from 4% (as in Bucky) to 30% (as in Bond).

Cultural industries present structures that can benefit from the advantages of blockchain. Multiple contacts associated with the distribution and dissemination of content, problems with intellectual property, the multiplicity of platforms with the same content, geolocation problems, copyright, and so on, are some of the actions that may be linked to a decentralized and secure system. In fact, Griffith (2018) identifies numerous aspects that can be improved by the application of blockchain (see Table 6.1).

Traceability is one of the characteristics of blockchain. Up until now, it has been difficult to guarantee the moral and economic rights of creators. In the case of content, this traceability allows the permanent attribution of intellectual property, which implies that falsification and impersonation are not possible. Furthermore, it enables a direct relationship between creators and consumers, and therefore instant remuneration through a micro-payment (eMusic 2019). The rights management companies lose importance, and the creators and owners benefit from not having to pay the significant part of their income that was destined to them. Another fundamental advantage is the disappearance of fake news, since you can

Table 6.1 Advantages for players involved in the cultural industries

Players	Blockchain advantages and possibilities
Creators	• The traceability offered by blockchain allows the attribution of intellectual property rights and instant remuneration. • The costs of collective rights management companies decrease. • Direct relationship between creators and artists. • No counterfeiting. • Elimination of fake news and censorship. • Improved payments for rights holders.
Distributors	• The importance of the curator increases. • Fight against online piracy. • A blockchain equivalent to Amazon.
Consumers	• Willingness to pay micro amounts for content. • Implantation of the *contentmeter* (like a taximeter). • Users can decide not to accept advertising or to accept it and be remunerated. • Consumers decide on their data, and can also charge for its use. • They can act as a curator, through program lists. • Other rewards may come from the time spent playing video games. • Rewards for watching entertainment content.

Source: Elaborated by the authors from various sources, especially Griffith (2018)

determine the origin of the content. The same happens with censorship, since there is no intermediary between creator and consumer. Forms of recognition of prestige can also be established, which can contribute to generating income.

In relation to cultural industries, we should consider that until now we have fundamentally known four types of media business models: free model, financed by advertising—such as general digital terrestrial television (DTT); pay per item (cinema, pay per view television); flat rate (cable, over the top such as Netflix or Spotify); or a mixture, such as the off-line press, in which an amount is paid per copy, but somewhat less than the real cost, because one part is financed by advertising. Now they could all coexist, and the micropayments per time consumed would be added. The possibility of coexistence of all models allows us to think of new business models.

With these new models, intermediaries (e.g., distributors) might disappear. In a blockchain network, theoretically each node can have several roles, including the users' and the creators'. This allows payments and collections to be established immediately, and also in a transparent and verifiable way at all times (traceability). Other intermediaries that might disappear are the rights management entities, since remuneration originates from the moment the content is consumed and is then distributed among the rights holders.

Insofar as there are multiple contents within a system, curators and recommendation systems are needed (Li and Palanisamy 2019). Currently, recommendation systems are generally created inside the platforms, and they are at the service of the objectives that those platforms want to achieve. In the case of blockchain networks in media content, curators would have four functions (4S's) (Dé Regil 2016): Search, Select, Sense-Making and Share. Dale (2014) considers a curator to be a mix of an Aggregator and a Distillator, both of which are responsible for bringing together all kinds of content from inside or outside the network.

Curators search for content, establish a selection, and bring it to the blockchain system; or they can also act as such within the system. Thus, if there were curators in Netflix, their mission would be to discover and to make lists with transparent and objective criteria, independently from the platform. They act as a kind of meta-aggregator, who selects. For this purpose, they must provide multiple metadata (tags) and multiple selection and recommendation mechanisms. However, this does not exclude other types of curation, such as the chronological presentations of a director's films, or even a playlist, for example. They can also provide trends, such as what content is most viewed, which can be a mechanism to help consumption. In this same sense, Dale (2014) considers five types of curator: aggregators (Google), simplifiers (*The Information*, a small-paid newsletter that sends few articles per month, with high added value), trend identifiers (Google Trends), mashup (mix of music merged into one), and chronological (that classifies chronologically). We can also differentiate them by objectives. Thus, we would find, on the one hand, curators who design the business plan, the blockchain system—represented in the white papers—and the smart contracts (Rodrigues 2018). On the other, there would be those who discover artists or content and are remunerated for it (Upadhyay 2019).

In addition, blockchain can also serve to combat piracy. If it allows the establishment of monetization mechanisms with micro prices, that is, if it is easy and cheap, why hack? (Butts 2018). In fact, academic institutions, together with Sony Music, Warner, Netflix, Spotify, and more than 200 other members, established the Open Music Initiative, with the purpose of improving the attribution of ownership of the works, as well as the remuneration of their authors, all of this using blockchain technology.

The case of Amazon allows us to understand a blockchain system of media content, even if it does not use this technology. The company offers products from its own brands, but the company is fundamentally a distributor that connects different manufacturers in a network. There could be multiple producers, movies and shows, library owners, distributors, televisions, streaming platforms, and so on; in addition, micropayments could be applied, those who have the rights could be remunerated, and so on.

Therefore, blockchain implies transformations in the business models of the cultural industries. And this has its consequences for consumers. For example, crowdsourcing financing models can be integrated, or micropayments can be used. This allows users to pay and receive microamounts, adapted to the cultural content. Micropayments could be managed by *contentmeters*, which would collect the sum of the micropayments in a period. Besides, these micropayments could be applied only for the time viewed, for example, half a chapter.

In this sense, just as the flat rate has become widespread on the Internet to respond to techno-socio-economic changes (Howell 2015), today it is possible to pay very small amounts. Flat rates have big advantages, but they are inefficient from the point of view of consumer cost: "with a platform like Netflix, you pay the same amount whether you watch a few hours of TV each month or hundreds. This is inefficient from a cost standpoint for users" (Nasdaq 2017). This does not mean that flat rates cannot be implemented in a blockchain system, although some advantages would be lost, since, with micro-prices, rate discriminations could be established to attend to different groups of consumers (Moser et al. 2018); or complex prices as well, which consider explicit variables such as costs, quantity demanded, novelty/age of the user, and so on.

One of the contributions of blockchain is the creation of reward systems for end users. This is the case of Vuulr and Spokkz. This reward can come from contributions in spreading content, through comments, criticism, generation of metadata, and so on, and they can be essential when structuring a blockchain system. The rewards can be monetary—charging for advertising, for commenting on content, for establishing playlists, for forwarding and suggesting consumption, and so on—but they can also be in terms of reputation. Pazaitis et al. (2017) suggest that Wikipedia could have worked even better if it had implemented some reward system in terms of reputation, because it would have increased the incentives to collaborate. In some cases, the reward can be economic, such as that offered by TV-TWO, where users can choose the ads and get paid for it.

Together with all these advantages, we can add others directly linked to advertising players (Pärssinen et al. 2018). In a blockchain system, marketing actions are more measurable. Advertisers can obtain greater transparency in the results of the impact of their ads. And as in entertainment or news content, intermediaries—in this case advertising agencies—also lose their importance.

3   Reflections on the Public Service Media

Blockchain activity in cultural industries is still low and is in the initial phase (Del Castillo and Schifrin 2020). The number of Public Service Media (PSM) interested in its applications is even lower.

The development of blockchain initiatives in PSM will depend on development and experimentation in the field of cultural industries, and especially in television. Public television poses a certain problem: a person would directly pay a creator—for example, a producer—an amount for certain content, but the willingness to pay for this content (for a movie, music, etc.) must be studied. This consideration is important, especially at this moment when gratuitousness (with the enormous costs of privacy, fake news, etc.) is so well established and when there are numerous platforms becoming consolidated among users (Netflix, Disney+, HBO, etc.)

It is true that many projects include advertising as a way of obtaining resources, which can then be exchanged for content. But we should not think that this advertising, financing mechanism is exempt of problems. Some of these problems could be solved (such as fake news), but others would surely emerge, and these are perhaps difficult to predict at present. What does seem clear is that blockchain can mean enormous changes in the way media content is produced, distributed, and consumed. And, of course, in the way a national or regional public television is produced, distributed, consumed, and governed.

Blockchain technology is defined as a technology that allows the elimination of intermediaries. But again, as in the case of the Internet in recent years, there is a further process of re-intermediation, since, as some intermediaries disappear, new ones appear. In the case of blockchain technology, some of the new intermediaries could be the technical developers that allow the implementation and design of the networks using this technology. In this process of re-intermediation, someone might think that the days of public television are numbered, since everything can be automated. But it is hard to believe that a technology, not even blockchain, can solve all problems without generating any new ones, or that it could be capable of solving and managing small conflicts.

Furthermore, when proclaiming the disappearance of intermediaries, the possible role of already consolidated players (GAFAM, Disney, Time Warner) is not being considered, and nor is the use of blockchain that they are going to carry out. In other words, you can read that blockchain can mean the end of the banks, yet they are the ones who most investigate, and make the greatest use of this technology in many types of transactions. That is why any simplifying interpretation that considers the disappearance of intermediaries must be avoided, as this will be balanced by the appearance of new ones. For a long time at least, many of the existing ones will be transformed, and this opens a field of research focusing on new gatekeepers. GAFAM will undoubtedly undergo transformation and continue to occupy those positions.

In this scenario, a perfect decentralization that eliminates intermediaries must also be nuanced. Blockchain allows transparency and diversity, without the need of an organization as we know it—television, radio. But the problem arises of how to guarantee the promotion of values that constitute the essence and definition of PSM.

Moreover, we might think that content can be more global and more universal, that is, that media content can be accessed regardless of the country of consumption; and that media content, amateur content, journalistic content, and all kinds of books, music, radio, and so on could be consumed in the same place. But shouldn't we consider that the existence of aid for the production and consumption of certain content that maintains and complies with the requirements and objectives demanded—by public television, for example—is increasingly necessary?

At the same time, a geographical tension is emerging. Public Service Media refers to a territory in which values are promoted. Most of the values are common to all PSM (transparency, plurality, promotion of languages, identities, universal access, etc.) but the way of providing them is different. Despite all the values being common, it does not seem easy to transcend the national space, and multiple public media will continue to exist. In the written media, there are more or less global media—*Financial Times*, *The Wall Street Journal*, *The New York Times*, and so on—that coexist with media referring to a national space. In this sense, one might ask whether any transnational experiment, on a larger or smaller scale, is possible. Here the public service institutions would constitute one of the new curators, especially in relation to the content being consumed directly through the Internet, because they could even offer external content, from other Public Service Media organization.

On the other hand, Public Service Media faces various challenges, such as financing, attractive programming, attracting younger generations, transparency, and so on. In this sense, blockchain promises great advantages and there is a certain euphoria that enhances its development. However, as the World Economic Forum (2018) points out, it is difficult to believe that a single technology offers the perfect solution to all problems. Specifically, they cite one company—Stem Desintermedia—for the distribution of royalties to creators. Even what is held up as an advantage, transparency, could turn out to be problematic for some of the parties involved.

At present there are no experiences in the implementation of blockchain systems in Public Service Media. In general, it can be said that its application can be done in aspects related to the organization, for example, with the types of contracts that already exist (production, broadcasting, creation, etc.) including tenders. But where this technology can be most applied in a new way is in relation to participation and financing. Bonini and Pais (2017) show the direction of possible uses. They have conducted research to observe the willingness to use part of the canon (20%) paid in Italy to finance television and public radios. The results show the approval of citizens, who are willing to pay an additional 5% to decide which content benefits their 20% mandatory canon contribution. This experiment implies a certain form of crowdfunding, applied to this increase in the canon price. What is more, even the 20% of the fee that people would assign to certain programs can also be considered as a form of crowdfunding. This would be indirect, because it is not a voluntary contribution but a mandatory one, but it is the way it is assigned, since citizens would choose the programs to which they give the amounts. This forms part of a debate on crowdfunding for publicly owned activities. This is an area in which academic studies are beginning to be made, many of them in Great Britain (Davis and Cartwright 2019) and other countries (Lee et al. 2016). This does not mean that crowdfunding would be used to replace existing forms of public financing, but it could be a complementary means at a time when public television in Europe is going through difficult times in terms of financing.

Another new scenario of blockchain application concerns participation. There are many documents that analyze the practices of public television as a mechanism for strengthening participation in the political debate,[3] as well as works that analyze participation in news information on public television (Franquet et al. 2013). For example, Ana López-Cepeda et al. (2019) analyze discursive participation on social media through comments on radio and television programs. McNair et al. (2002) also analyze the participation of audiences in political programs.

It is necessary to go further and establish a set of practices that encourage audience participation. In fact, one of the missions of PSM is precisely to promote political participation, that is, to promote the existence of a public sphere. Therefore, the application of blockchain in PSM should guarantee participation at all levels. It is thus possible to think of a ladder of participation, with multiple steps. With respect to participation, the use of social media is seen as an opportunity, and it is desirable to start experimenting with the possibilities of blockchain, especially through the creation of symbolic remuneration systems for those who vote, contribute content, comment, and so on.

As public television platforms will be used, blockchain-based participatory mechanisms could be designed, both vertically and horizontally. Vertically, where public media could report and consult. For example, reporting on programming projects, program rankings, change in the canon, and so on. And consultation can also be done with respect to programming, future changes in the fee, how to incorporate the results of the surveys, and so on. Citizens can respond to inquiries, vote, and assess programs or the degree of compliance of the Public Media to their values, and so on. Another form of participation would be acting as curators, through the creation and establishment of playlists. In addition, there should be another type of participation through proposing the allocation of certain amounts to the programming, as noted above. And participation can also be designed horizontally, since citizens can exchange comments and opinions among themselves.

This can already be done through current social media. What blockchain adds is transparency. Everyone involved in the network could see both vertical and horizontal opinions. Besides, reward mechanisms could be established for the most active people in terms of comments and suggestions. Reward systems could also aim to acquire merchandise (T-shirts with the logo of PSM, merchandising, trips, etc.). One could also imagine a program in which the most active people take part to express their opinions on different aspects of programming.

4 Conclusions

Most blockchain projects that affect cultural industries are carried out under a market logic (the search for economic or financial profitability). Public Service Media respond to another logic—social profitability—based on the set of missions and values that characterize them. Many of these can be enhanced by the implementation of blockchain technology, especially those that are located in the field of organization, programming, and audience.

At the organizational level, transparency is facilitated in tenders, in contracting production companies and in monitoring the production of entertainment content. In the area of programming, independence can be guaranteed, because the information in the blocks cannot be changed, which eliminates any attempt at censorship that might occur.

Innovation and support for the media industry are basic principles of Public Service Media. Experimenting with blockchain technology is one of the axes that contribute to achieving that goal. In addition, with blockchain this support to the media industry is carried out in a transparent way, and to the extent that access to the block is facilitated, it allows orders to be carried out without favoritism.

However, it is in the field of participation where blockchain can be more easily implemented. For example, establishing systems of collecting opinion on some programs, projects, and so on, and even on issues related to financing and governance.

One of the obstacles to the implementation of blockchain in Public Service Media is that the funding comes from compulsory contributions. There are no projects in the cultural industries that contemplate this type of financing. It is a mandatory flat rate. In the case of Spain, where there is no license fee, the obligation exists because it is the parliamentary institutions that approve a certain budget for financing. However, starting from the obligation, some system could be articulated to allow the assignment of a certain part of the financing, to allocate it to specific programs, for example.

In any case, since the objectives, principles, and values that characterize Public Service Media are numerous, the experiments that must be started should also be numerous, so that they can be carried out in the best possible way. If participation mechanisms are implemented, Public Service Media could then be seen as everyone's media.

Notes

1. When talking about cultural industries we are referring to news, radio, television, books, film, and music. Therefore, it is a more restrictive catalogue of all the activities of the creative industries.
2. One relevant source is the White Papers of blockchain projects that are published at https://icobench.com/. However, that source does not have an exhaustive character. Some recommendations are as follows: White papers of Moviechan, Vuulr, Bond, Bucky, Spokkz and Tv-Two, Singular DTB, FilmChain, Binge, and Slate and Ara Blocks.
3. Strategies of Public Service Media as regards promoting a wider democratic participation of the individuals' compilation of good practices. A report prepared by the Group of Specialists on Public Service Media in the Information Society (MC-S-PSM), November 2008 Directorate General of Human Rights and Legal Affairs Council of Europe Strasbourg, June 2009.

REFERENCES

Allayannis, G., & Fernstrom, A. (2018). An Introduction to Blockchain. *Darden Case* No. UVA-F-1810. Retrieved from https://ssrn.com/abstract=3050049.

Blockchain Library. (2017). Most Cited Blockchain Publications. Retrieved June 4, 2020, from https://blockchainlibrary.org/2017/10/most-cited-blockchain-publications/.

Bonini, T., & Pais, I. (2017). Hacking Public Service Media Funding: A Scenario for Rethinking the License Fee as a Form of Civic Crowdfunding. *International Journal on Media Management*, 19(2), 123–143. https://doi.org/10.1080/14241277.2017.1298109.

Butts, T. (2018, April 3). Need to Know: How Will Blockchain Impact The Media & Entertainment Industry? *TVtechnology*. Retrieved June 4, 2020, from https://www.tvtechnology.com/expertise/how-will-blockchain-impact-the-media-entertainment-industry.

Carson, B., Romanelli, G., Walsh, P., & Zhumaev, A. (2018, June 18). Blockchain Beyond the hype: What Is the Strategic Business Value? *McKinsey Digital*. Retrieved from https://www.mckinsey.com/business-functions/mckinsey-digital/our-insights/blockchain-beyond-the-hype-what-is-the-strategic-business-value.

Catalini, C., & Gans, J. S. (2017, September 2). *Some Simple Economics of the Blockchain*. Rotman School of Management Working Paper No. 2874598. MIT Sloan Research Paper No. 5191-16. https://doi.org/10.2139/ssrn.2874598.

Dale, S. (2014). Content Curation: The Future of Relevance. *Business Information Review*, 31(4), 199–205. https://doi.org/10.1177/2F0266382114564267.

Davidson, S., De Filippi, P., & Potts, J. (2016). Economics of Blockchain. https://doi.org/10.2139/ssrn.2744751.

Davies, J. (2019, June 21). Visions and Reality – Can Blockchain Allow Us to Rethink the Creative Industries?. *NESTA*. Retrieved June 4, 2020, from https://www.nesta.org.uk/blog/visions-and-reality-can-blockchain-allow-us-rethink-creative-industries/.

Davis, M., & Cartwright, L. (2019). *Financing for Society: Assessing the Suitability of Crowdfunding for the Public Sector*. Report. University of Leeds.

De Régil, E. (2016, October 7). ¿Qué hace un content curator? *El documentalista audiovisual*. Retrieved June 4, 2020, from https://eldocumentalistaudiovisual.com/2016/10/07/que-hace-un-content-curator/.

Del Castillo, M., & Schifrin, M. (Eds.). (2020). Forbes Blockchain 50. *Forbes*. Retrieved June 4, 2020, from https://www.forbes.com/sites/michaeldelcastillo/2020/02/19/blockchain-50/#3cce51907553.

Deloitte. (2017). *Blockchain @ Media A new Game Changer for the Media Industry?* Retrieved June 4, 2020, from https://www2.deloitte.com/content/dam/Deloitte/tr/Documents/technology-media-telecommunications/deloitte-PoV-blockchain-media.pdf.

eMusic. (2019). *eMusic. Redefining Music Distribution Through Blockchain.* White Paper. Retrieved June 4, 2020, from https://token.emusic.com/assets/pdf/eMusic_White_Paper_EN.pdf?d=1584441026235.

Franquet, i., Calvet, R., Villa Montoya, M. I., & Bergillos García, I. (2013). Public Service Broadcasting's Participation in the Reconfiguration of Online News Content. *Journal of Computer-Mediated Communication, 18*(3), 378–397. https://doi.org/10.1111/jcc4.12014.

Griffith, E. (2018, May 25). 187 Things the Blockchain is Supposed to Fix. *Wired.* Retrieved June 4, 2020, from https://www.wired.com/story/187-things-the-blockchain-is-supposed-to-fix/.

Howell, B. (2015, December 16). Flat-Rate Pricing: The Internet Has Changed and So Should Our Pricing Models. *America Enterprise Institute.* Retrieved June 4, 2020, from https://www.aei.org/technology-and-innovation/telecommunications/flat-rate-pricing-internet-changed-pricing-models/.

imusify. (n.d.) *White Paper.* Retrieved June 4, 2020, from https://imusify.com/whitepaper.pdf.

Lansiti, M. & Lakhani, K.R. (2017). From The Truth About Blockchain, *Harvard Business Review, 95,* 118-127. Retrieved June 4, 2020, from https://hbr.org/2017/01/the-truth-about-blockchain.

Lee, A. (2018, January 12). Lockchain Patent Filings Dominated by Financial Services Industry. *PatentVue.* Retrieved from http://patentvue.com/2018/01/12/blockchain-patent-filings-dominated-by-financial-services-industry/.

Lee, C. H., Zhao, J. L., & Hassna, G. (2016). Government Incentivized Crowdfunding for One-Belt, One-Road Enterprises: Design and Research Issues. *Financial Innovation, 2*(2), 1–14. https://doi.org/10.1186/s40854-016-0022-0.

Leodolter, W. (2017). *Digital Transformation Shaping the Subconscious Minds of Organizations.* Springer.

Li, C., & Palanisamy, B.. (2019). Incentivized Blockchain-Based Social Media Platforms: A Case Study of Steemit. *WebSci '19: Proceedings of the 10th ACM Conference on Web Science, June,* pp. 145–154. New York: Association for Computing Machinery. https://doi.org/10.1145/3292522.3326041.

López-Cepeda, A. M., López-Golan, M., & Rodríguez-Castro, M. (2019). Participatory Audiences in the, European Public Service Media: Content Production and Copyright. *Comunicar, 60,* 93–102. https://doi.org/10.3916/C60-2019-09.

McNair, B., Hibberd, M., & Schlesinger, P. (2002). Public Access Broadcasting and Democratic Participation in the Age of Mediated Politics. *Journalism Studies, 3*(3), 407–422. https://doi.org/10.1080/14616700220145623.

Miguel-de-Bustos, J. C., & Izquierdo-Castillo, J. (2019). Who Will Control the Media? The Impact of GAFAM on the Media Industries in the Digital Economy. *Revista Latina de Comunicación Social, 74*, 803–821. https://doi.org/10.4185/RLCS-2019-1358en.

Moser, S., Schumann, J. H., Von Wangenheim, F., & Frank, F. (2018). The Effect of a Service Provider's Competitive Market Position on Churn Among Flat-Rate Customers. *Journal of Service Research, 21*(3), 319–335. https://doi.org/10.1177/2F1094670517752458.

Nasdaq. (2017, November 7). Streaming Television on the Blockchain. *Nasdaq.* Retrieved June 4, 2020, from https://www.nasdaq.com/articles/streaming-television-blockchain-2017-11-07.

O'Dair, M., Beaven, Z., Neilson, D., Osborne, R., & Pacifico, P. (2016). *Music on the Blockchain.* Blockchain For Creative Industries Research Cluster, Middlesex University, Report N° 1. Retrieved June 4, 2020, from http://www.mdx.ac.uk/__data/assets/pdf_file/0026/230696/Music-On-The-Blockchain.pdf.

Pärssinen, M., Kotila, M., Cuevas, R., Phansalkar, A., & Manner, J. (2018). Is Blockchain Ready to Revolutionize Online Advertising? *IEEE Access, 6.* https://doi.org/10.1109/ACCESS.2018.2872694.

Pazaitis, A., De Filippi, P., & Kostakis, V. (2017). Blockchain and Value Systems in the Sharing Economy: The Illustrative Case of Backfeed. *Technological Forecasting & Social Change, 125*, 105–115. https://doi.org/10.1016/j.techfore.2017.05.025.

Potts, J., & Rennie, E. (2017). *Blockchains and Creative Industries.* https://doi.org/10.2139/ssrn.3072129.

Rennie, E., Potts, J., & Pochesneva, A. (2019). Blockchain and the Creative Industries: Provocation Paper. *RMIT Blockchain Innovation Hub.* Retrieved June 4, 2020, from https://apo.org.au/node/267131.

Rodrigues, U. R. (2018). Law and the Blockchain. *Iowa L. Rev, 104*, 679. Retrieved June 4, 2020, from https://ilr.law.uiowa.edu/print/volume-104-issue-2/law-and-the-blockchain/.

Upadhyay, N. (2019). *Transforming Social Media Business Models Through Blockchain.* Bingley: Emerald Group Publishing.

Weking, J., Mandalenakis, M., Hein, A., Hermes, S., Böhm, M., & Krcmar, H. (2019). The Impact of Blockchain Technology on Business Models – A Taxonomy and Archetypal Patterns. *Electronic Markets.* https://doi.org/10.1007/s12525-019-00386-3.

Winfield, A. (2017, November 20). How Blockchain's 'Web of Value' Could Oust the New Big Media. *Forbes.* Retrieved June 4, 2020, from https://www.forbes.

com/sites/sap/2017/11/20/how-blockchains-web-of-value-could-oust-the-new-big-media/#9e0320692712.

Wirtz, B. W., Pistoia, A., Ullrich, S., & Göttel, V. (2016). Business Models: Origin, Development and Future Research Perspectives. *Long Range Planning*, 49(1), 36–54. https://doi.org/10.1016/j.lrp.2015.04.001.

World Economic Forum. (2018). Creative Disruption: The Impact of Emerging Technologies on the Creative Economy. *WEF*, February. Retrieved June 4, 2020, from https://www.weforum.org/whitepapers/creative-disruption-the-impact-of-emerging-technologies-on-the-creative-economy.

Wright, A. & De Filippi, P. (2015). *Decentralized Blockchain Technology and the Rise of Lex Cryptographia*. https://doi.org/10.2139/ssrn.2580664.

Xu, M., Chen, X., & Kou, G. (2019). A Systematic Review of Blockchain. *Financial Innovation*, 5(1), 27. https://doi.org/10.1186/s40854-019-0147-z.

CHAPTER 7

Analysis of the Quality of the Websites of Regional Public Television Networks in the European Union: Comparative Study Between Spain, Germany, and Belgium

Ana María López-Cepeda, Belén Galletero-Campos, and Vanesa Saiz-Echezarreta

1   Quality and Public Service Media

Television emerges in Europe with a public service vocation in the form of a monopoly justified by the scarcity of the radio spectrum. Nevertheless, when the first private television networks appear in the eighties, this rationale fades away, and new reasons are searched that explain the maintenance of media of public ownership. The theory of the three functions of public television gains force (to inform, educate, and entertain) (López Cepeda 2015), at the same time that their features are defined (Roel Vecino 2005): universality, cultural responsibility, and independence.

A. M. López-Cepeda (✉) • B. Galletero-Campos • V. Saiz-Echezarreta
University of Castilla-La Mancha, Ciudad Real, Spain
e-mail: Ana.LopezCepeda@uclm.es; belen.galletero@uclm.es; Vanesa.Saiz@uclm.es

© The Author(s), under exclusive license to Springer Nature Switzerland AG 2021
M. Túñez-López et al. (eds.), *The Values of Public Service Media in the Internet Society*, Palgrave Global Media Policy and Business, https://doi.org/10.1007/978-3-030-56466-7_7

The new media scenario creates the need to redefine the concept of Public Service Broadcasting, first by playing a role in the digital development and the promotion of convergence (Prado and Fernández 2006) and later, by adapting to online environment such as the web or the mobile phone (Gómez Domínguez 2016). We witness the transition from the concept of Public Service Broadcasting (PSB) to the Public Service Media (PSM) and more recently, to the concept of Public Service Media in the Internet (PSI).

Proximity Public Service Broadcasting faces different challenges in a moment where there is an important legitimacy crisis with critiques about the media model, funding system, and with complaints of informative manipulation, patronage, and instrumentalization (Izquierdo Castillo and López Rabadán 2016; Marzal Felici et al. 2017). This situation has created a resentment of quality in a very significant manner in the past years, a trend that impacts the European continent, and more specifically the Mediterranean model (Hallin and Mancini 2004; Marzal Felici and Zallo Elguezabal 2016). However, the relevance of quality is indisputable, due to its relationship with credibility (Gómez Mompart et al. 2013), social development, and democracy (De la Torre and Téramo 2015).

In line with this situation, there are studies about quality indicators and media of public ownership that analyze the concept from a wide perspective. The UNESCO in 2012 published a report on quality indicators of public broadcasting networks, where 188 indicators are defined based on nine axes: management transparency, cultural diversity, geographic coverage and platforms offer, public pattern of journalism, independence, public nature of funding, audience satisfaction, experimentation and innovation of language, and technical standards (Bucci et al. 2012). The European Broadcasting Union presented in 2014 a self-assessment tool for public corporations (PSM Values Review: The Tool), "so to stablish a framework of measurable intangible indicators of quality, transparency, accountability, innovation, universality and independence" (Valencia Bermúdez and Campos Freire 2016, p. 62). There, quality is measured using fiscalization mechanisms, professional education, and the opinion of the audience.

2 Quality and Proximity Public Service Media

Regional media of public ownership face these quality challenges at the same time they must comply with the standards of proximity media. These can be identified with the presence of the journalist in the place of events, or through standards of veracity, contrast, coherence, and equity (Pérez Curiel et al. 2015), besides their engagement to society (Chaparro et al. 2016). Local media have turned into intermediaries and stakeholders of the social relationships established inside and outside of a specific collective (López García et al. 1998). Among the features that characterize local journalism, there outstand the closeness between the citizen and the institutions of the government, created contents based on incidents and social, economic, sports, cultural and political events, interest of the media in the space where it expresses itself, and its responsibility toward the society it addresses to (Martínez Juan 2003).

However, the arrival of the Internet also influenced the way quality is measured in these media. Like Caldevilla (2013, p. 170) emphasizes, according to what Colin Sparks (2002) states, among the advantages of the local media online, there is the breach of the geographical barriers, thus broadening the potential audience, even competing directly with stronger media at a national or international scope.

In this chapter we conceive the online quality of proximity media of public ownership from a double perspective: on the one hand, the websites must comply to standards of quality and serve as an indicator of the enforcement of the proximity public service; and secondly, they must operate as a meeting point between institutions and their communities of reference. The systematic observation of websites (of 27 entities: 11 German, 3 Belgian, and 13 Spanish) to confirm their quality was based on four dimensions: accessibility, technical innovation, participation, and literacy. It is assessed whether the websites convey the commitment of the network in terms of diversity; whether the websites are conceived as new platforms of access and consumption of content, beyond the corporate information offered or the mere complement of the forms of conventional rebroadcasting; whether they operate as a space of interaction with publics, especially about listening to their needs, protection of their rights, and fostering participation; and lastly, whether there are tools aimed to increase the population awareness about the public service function of these media.

2.1 *Technical Information: From Radio and Television Broadcasting to Platforms*

One of the effects of digitalization has been the transformation of the concept of medium into platform, as a "space of convergence where a specific interactive technology models a continuous flow of multimedia information" (Díaz Arias 2017, p. 82). Public Service Media cannot be considered only in terms of their linear broadcast anymore, but instead in terms of their adaptation to this new context and their transformation into suppliers of reproducible audiovisual content on different devices and available for their re-utilization anytime and anywhere (Ramsey 2018).

These new consumption patterns, quite distanced from the traditional view at home (Rigby et al. 2018), have been assimilated in a natural manner by the younger public, but can be less familiar for whom the television consumption started with the analogic broadcast. This scenario requires that the websites of the public corporations provide thorough information about all the access routes to their content available. The most complete explain in detail how to access the broadcast through satellite, cable, antenna, IPTV, streaming, how to tune the radio in the digital platform and by radio frequency, and in what alternative mediums (mobile applications) can it be either viewed or listened on demand. Very significant differences are observed between the Central European and the Spanish entities, whose websites lack this information in some cases (*Canal Extremadura* or *À Punt—Corporació Valenciana de Mitjans de Comunicació*) or either provide succinct and basic data (*Castilla-La Mancha Media, Radiotelevisión Canaria, Radiotelevisión del Principiado de Asturias*).

The media has endeavored to diversify and adapt their contents to the different platforms, especially, smartphones and tablets. For now, the information in proximity media of public ownership about the compatibility with voice assistants is minor. On the opposite side, the website of *Radiotelevisión Canaria* in Spain still does not even have a mobile-responsive design. In general, we can talk about a poor level of innovation in the Spanish context, where 30% of autonomic television networks have not developed an application, which represents a difference compared to the German websites, which offer several applications, specialized by themes (*Norddeutscher Rundfunk* has N-Joy, NDR Kultur, and NDR EO) or for the different platforms. All German corporations and two out of the three Belgian ones (*Vlaamse Radio—in Televisieomroep* and *Radio Télévision Belge Francophone*) have a platform available for mobile consumption.

All the proximity European television and radio networks (in Spain, Germany, and Belgium) understand their websites, to different extents, as another way to access their programming. In this line, they all offer "on demand" access to their public. Sometimes, there are well organized multimedia libraries; in others, the users are directed to the websites of the different programs where the content is stored. However, the complete broadcast cannot be always found in these repositories, but instead only some contents or programs. A complementary service that very few websites offer is the ability to record the spaces and rebroadcasted contents that are only offered live. *Saarländischer Rundfunk* and *Deutschlandfunk* (ARD) provide free software to record the online content.

The task of the media when it comes to offering events and rebroadcasts live through Internet is one of the activities that allow to legitimate its public service function. Some significant examples are the rebroadcasts of the parliamentary debates (*Westdeutscher Rundfunk*, in Germany) or proximity sports or cultural events (*Castilla-La Mancha Media, Corporació Catalana de Mitjans Audiovisuals*, in Spain).

2.2 Accessibility

One of the pillars of the public service, together with independence, the creation of community and quality, is its universal nature (Freedman and Curran 2016), which must be translated into easy access—technological and geographic, social and cultural—for all kinds of collectives, in order to reach every citizen without exclusion. However, this cannot be guaranteed without an adequate dissemination about the adaptation of the content for people with different abilities.

An example of good practices is grouping, in a unique section, all the formulas to access these contents translated into sign language, subtitles, or audio-description. The television networks that dedicate a complete section to these matters are the Spanish networks *Radio Televisión de Andalucía*, *Corporació Catalana de Mitjans Audiovisuals*, and *Radiotelevisión del Principado de Asturias*; the German networks *Mitteldeutscher Rundfunk*, *Westdeutscher Rundfunk*, *Saarländischer Rundfunk*, and *Norddeutscher Rundfunk*; and the Belgian networks *Vlaamse Radio-in Televisieomroeporganisatie* and *Radio Télévision Belge de la Communauté Française*. In a less exhaustive level of development, we must refer to other websites where the news can be listened to, like *Euskal Irrati Telebista* (Spain). It is relevant to mention that some radio and television broadcasting networks understand accessibility as an intuitive web design that allows people with poor digital competencies to browse through their websites without hurdles. This is specifically indicated by Ra*dio Televisión de Andalucía, Corporació Catalana de Mitjans*

Audiovisuals (Spain), or*Vlaamse Radio—in Televisieomroeporganisatie* (Belgium). Among their objectives, there is to improve the experience of the user in such a way that is easy to find what they are looking for, across contents that are clear and well-structured in terms of wording.

On the other hand, we cannot talk about universality only when referring to the mode the message can be received, but also when ensuring that said message can be understood. It is all about fostering routes so that information can also be within the reach of people with low literacy or suffering specific learning issues or reading comprehension handicaps. Some German television networks offer contents in a simple language. These texts are written following readability rules that make them more understandable for people with no reading habits or who have the problems mentioned earlier. This wording implies that themes that could be difficult for some collectives, such as local elections or the functioning of institutions, are translated into a way that favors understanding and promotes citizen participation.

2.3   Languages, Attention to Dialects, and Cultural Minorities

The language of the website is highly connected to the coverage scope and, in general, the websites of the proximity Public Service Media can be read in a single language, except for those Spanish communities with co-official languages, where the websites can be read in both languages completely. The most singular case is that of *Deutsche Welle* (ARD), due to the particular features of this network oriented to the audience abroad, which allows to choose in its website among 30 different languages and, moreover, it changes the content depending on the language chosen, for a greater personalization.

Together with this policy of offering a multilingual platform, we must also consider the role of these public media when it comes to preserving cultural minorities, thus differentiating in front of any commercial offer. Among their purposes, in an even more pronounced manner in the proximity entities, there is the care for the tangible and intangible patrimony of the local-based, since their existence is based on becoming invigorating agents of their immediate environment, either through measures like the specific support to the audiovisual industry, or by granting a privileged space to the specific features of each region. It is not only about keeping a structure of sections that distributes information by regions, but instead about paying special attention to minorities.

The protection and dissemination of a dialect was detected in the *Radiotelevisión del Principado de Asturias* or in the *Corporació Catalana de Mitjans Audiovisuals* (both based in Spain), which broadcast in Aranese. The website of *Norddeutscher Rundfunk* (Germany) offers a section dedicated to promoting Low German through informational and fiction contents, but also through initiatives like literary contests or a dictionary where citizens are encouraged to collaborate to incorporate terms used in the Northern region of the country. The German network *Rundfunk Berlin-Brandenburg* goes one step further, with a specific section to keep the language and culture of the Sorbian people, a minority of Slavic origin located in the Federal States of Saxony and Brandenburg. The VRT in Belgium advocates a strong focus in the productions and talent of the area in its website, as well as its will to strengthen the sense of community among its audience, something that is done through the promotion of music, rebroadcasting events, and the festivity of the Flemish community on 11 July, among many other initiatives.

2.4 Children and Youth

In Spain, the content targeted at children in the autonomous public radio and television broadcast is scarce. Only in 4 out of the 13 regional media an actual preference to incorporate this audience is observed, with the creation of a club that favors that children and teenagers become part of a community. The oldest one is *Club Xabarín* from the Galician television network, broadcasting since 1994. The most recent are *Club Super3* (2009) by *Corporació Catalana de Mitjans Audiovisuals*, *Hiru 3* (2011) by EITB, and *La Colla* (2018), in the Valencian television network. This sort of digital communities generate transmedia universes, because besides providing access to contents, they also offer discounts, call for participation, and engage their members in offline activities like parties or campaigns. In short, they represent a place of digital and face-to-face meeting, a place of creation and relationship with their peers.

The VRT (Belgium) keeps a private label since 1997 on Internet, *Ketnet Junior* and *Ketnet*, for children and teenagers, respectively. Both have their equivalent mobile application. According to what is mentioned in the website, the priorities of this brand include in-house productions, socially relevant programs for children in their daily life—"like falling in love, having a sick family member, bullying at school or having fun with friends." They turn into an invigorating and social cohesion element through actions, campaigns, and activities.

The offer scope is much wider in Germany, where 54% of radio television broadcasts of ARD have a space targeted to children. The formats are diverse. SWR has developed a children's network—*Kindernetz*—similar to the Spanish clubs mentioned earlier, but it does not only nourish from entertainment, but also provides informational contents through *Infonetz*, an archive of news for children about different subjects like history, rights, the European Union, culture, or media. The *Kinder* website of WDR broadcasts news for children, both in German and French, and provides two in-house applications, *ElefantenApp* and *MausApp*. In the case of MDR, a safe site is offered for children's browsing, at the same time it redirects parents to websites that provide advice about childhood and technology. *Deutschlandfunk* keeps *Radio Kakadu* to listen through Spotify or podcast. *RBB Kinder und Familie*, from the Berliner firm, constitutes a repository of all the children and family programs of the network. Finally, *Bayerischer Rundfunk* includes the website *BR Kinder*, which gathers some visual and sound content. The *Klaro* project stands out as a distinctive element, where students of the fourth grade of Elementary School suggest a theme, generate questions, and from the radio station they formulate them to the corresponding experts and develop information pieces, in a joint production model. We are facing an initiative in which the television plays an active role of intermediation between citizens, institutions, and expert sources.

2.5 *Diversity*

Interesting initiatives are found that aim to protect diversity and vulnerable collectives, however, they are not many. The Belgian corporation VRT develops an active policy to fight the underrepresentation of collectives that may suffer discrimination due to gender, origin, age, disability, sexual identity, and poverty reasons, six axes in which the corporation focuses intensively. In fact, its Studies Department, in collaboration with the universities of Antwerp and Amsterdam, monitor the level of fulfillment of these objectives on diversity. On the other hand, the German network WDR indicates that its goal is to reflect the intercultural mix in programs and inside the work force, as part of a modernization process and of openness in the society. Furthermore, it specifies that this philosophy of integration constitutes the baseline to elaborate a programming for everybody. In order to guarantee its fulfillment, there is the figure of the commissioner for integration and intercultural diversity.

Another initiative of interest is the Talent Workshop 2018 of *Westdeutscher Rundfunk*, an educational project where 13 young journalists from 11 countries participated, which represented a meeting forum between very different cultures in order to suggest new ideas for the network.

2.6   *Relationship with the Audience*

The ombudsman figure or the reader, viewer, or listener defender has a long history in the media sphere (Rodríguez-Martínez et al. 2017). It is conceived as one of the accountability tools which also represents an indicator of quality. More than half of regional public radio television broadcasting networks in Spain, Germany, and Belgium have an explicit figure for advocacy as well as many others with equivalent authority.

The advocacy figure involves three essential functions: self-regulation, opening out, and the creation of opinion (Oliveira 2007, p. 6). The former is the most conventional, which allows to supervise the workflow of journalists and the fulfillment of ethics standards, set forth in the deontological codes, style books, and the rest of regulations. This is a model that can be found in German entities, where the figure of the external viewer ombudsman is assigned to a lawyer, whose responsibility focuses on the fight against corruption and the conflict of interests. In the cases of HR, MDR, and *Deutschland Radio*, information about this figure is provided, as well as contact information.

A second function that can be fulfilled by the figure of the ombudsman is the opening out, since it is a space aimed to promote the direct participation of citizens in the public radio television broadcast networks. Even though there are multiple instances of participation from the organized civil society through entities such as the Citizen Council (Valencia), the Communication Council (Asturias), or the Advisory Council (Extremadura, Andalusia), the Radio Broadcast Councils of the ARD are not always known and neither of easy access for the general public, especially in the Spanish cases.

One of the most common channels for the public to approach radio television broadcasting networks is through complaints, corrections and the rectification rights, that are usually not accepted in an anonymous manner. This is the reason why in several media, the information about advocacy is reduced to a form or email to which the complaint or comment can be sent to, without representing too much difference between this section and the general contact information, like in the Canary Islands, Extremadura, or the Balearic Islands (Spain). In some cases, slightly more information is provided when there is a link to the rules of procedure with the ombudsman, like the Spanish network EITB.

Finally, the third function attributed to this figure is that of elaborating a meta-mediatic discourse (Oliveira 2007), namely, to promote critical thinking and to encourage an open and plural debate about media in the contemporary context. To widen this view, there are ideas like that of the Belgium corporation VRT which includes explanatory videos in the web of the ombudsman, about what impartiality is. On the other hand, the Belgian RTBF also suggests a collegiate figure, a mediation committee, which not only gathers complains but that it is defined as "a privileged space for listening and keeping a dialogue" with the public, to provide an answer to everything that is not understood. One of the interesting aspects of this committee is that it also includes cultural mediation and education on media literacy among its missions. In line with this function of proximity public service, the German network Rundfunk Berlin-Brandenburg invites, since 2018, to barbecues in different community spaces to meet with citizens beyond the digital boundaries.

This link between the audience ombudsman and media literacy is perceived in the websites that show a more elaborated content. An example is the blog of the Audience service in the Catalan corporation or the Ombudsman space in *Canal Sur* (both in Spain), with contents that aim not only at ensuring accountability, but also at widening the knowledge about how media works. The opening endeavor is also observed in the framing of *Telemadrid*, which includes the Ombudsman inside the participation office. Furthermore, this network incorporates the themes received at the debate spaces where the listener or the viewer who suggests the subject is invited to participate.

2.7 Media Literacy: How to Explain and Add Value to the Public Service

Undoubtedly, the media literacy is a substantial element of the fulfillment of the public service mission. Like Pérez-Tornero et al. (2018) indicate, it is necessary to establish more accurate indicators to know whether the public entities are complying with this function in relation to several aspects: education about the media context, acquisition of practical competencies in the use of media, strengthening of the abilities for critical thinking, and fostering of communication and participation competencies. For now, the German and Belgian corporations are the ones doing most in all these areas.

Their option for education is significant and understands literacy as a transversal element, which appears in the section "About us" through material elaborated with which the public, beyond getting to know the structure and the organization chart, can approach to what public service means. In general, the Spanish media offer corporate information focused more on the organizational structures rather than the modes of work and values.

The most generalized tool to carry out a media literacy are the practices and internship programs, as well as the visits to facilities and the attendance to programs, usually oriented to education centers. Depending on the information published in their websites, one of the most complete programs is offered by the German network *Westdeutscher Rundfunk* which has designed media workshops for different age groups, where students produce their own TV programs, downloadable didactic material, and a specific website *Schule Digital*, where there is training on digital media literacy (augmented reality, identification of fake news, 360°), using gamification as a resource. Another interesting model is that of the German network *Deutsche Welle* which is committed to media literacy focusing on the defense of freedom of expression and journalism (#mediadev), including a wide educational program at different levels.

Like in Germany, also in the Belgian networks there is interest in education. For instance, *Radio Télévision Belge Francophone* and *Vlaamse Radio—in Televisieomroeporganisatie* offer training programs for education centers. Furthermore, the former designed a simple resource that becomes a good tool: gathering and organizing in the same section "Education in media," contents about media that have been broadcasted through different programs in the past years. In addition, this network is committed to literacy through the INSIDE program, which is built based on questions of the audience and internal reflections and whose purpose is to explain the editorial choices and professional practices. Moreover, it includes a debate between professionals and the guest public, a direct way to encourage participation.

In contents of media literacy, the project *Sogehtmedien* is a great initiative, sponsored by 11 German corporations. The offer scope is wide, with materials about how media work, as well as glossaries, critical content to promote thinking, tutorials to acquire practical technical and journalistic skills, specialized teaching material to work in the classroom, games, and so on.

Finally, an increasing concern to educate about fake news is noteworthy: some television networks belonging to ARD (Germany), including BR and SWR, offer tutorials to identify misinformation online. Likewise, the autonomic public televisions in Spain have launched a decalogue to identify fake news, through the Federation of Autonomic Radio and Television Entities (FORTA). In the Basque case (EITB, in Spain), there is also a weekly section managed by the Big Data Expert of the University of Deusto to inform about possible fake news. In Belgium, RTBF offers its citizens the tool *Faky* to fight against misinformation. The novelty is that it is available in the website *faky.be*, but also an application that can be installed directly in smartphones is provided. VRT (Belgium) has created, together with several specialized centers (*Mediawijs*, IMEC, *Voetweg 66*, and *Arteveldehogeschool*), the tool *EDUbox* that helps youngsters identify manipulated information. There is the videogame *Fake Finder*, in SWR (Germany) among the noteworthy initiatives. The user receives several messages in order to discover whether they are true or fake news. In Spain, CARTV (Aragon) has opted to broadcast a false documentary "Desmontando a Goya" [Dismantling Goya] to fight against fake news (López Cepeda et al. 2019).

With the transformation of the media ecosystem, the public radio television networks needed to explain the society the raison d'être of the public service and what their function is, a function that cannot be replaced by commercial models. A formula to influence and reinforce their position in this ecosystem is the promotion campaigns, which have initiated both ARD in Germany with the slogan "We are yours. ARD," as well as FORTA in Spain with "I see it."

3 Conclusions

The presence and popularity of new audiovisual operators require that proximity public media reinforce their legitimacy and readapt their contents to the digital environment. The new consumptions advance a loss of relevance of the linear radio television broadcasting, to make room to new fragmented formats and platforms for sharing online videos. However, this requires a dissemination endeavor from corporations about the options available to access content, besides an effort to develop new channels, like mobile applications, and products with innovative narratives to reconnect with young audiences. Although some have already made progress in this sense, the web should be promoted as a consumption platform and place of reference of the active public, beyond its classical functions of repository or corporate element.

In general, relevant differences are appreciated between the proximity entities of Northern and Central Europe as well as the Spanish ones, especially when it comes to offering technical information or in the adaption to the different platforms, where the former are more advanced than those of the Mediterranean model. Likewise, a greater concern about media literacy is observed in the German and Belgian television networks, even though the problem of fake news positions the Spanish networks closer to the Central European model.

The possibility to offer an accessible content to all kinds of collectives and the concern to include diversity at the same time that the genuine feature of each region is promoted constitute differentiating aspects that distinguish proximity Public Service Media. In a competitive context, with a wider scope of offers and certain political and budget questionings of public media, one of the pillars must be working to improve the reception and comprehension of content.

The relation with the audience plays an essential role, although its effectiveness, for now, is subjected to a better knowledge of the media, a participatory culture, and a critical spirit that has still a long way to go. The ombudsman figure can become a valid option so that citizens can demand social responsibility to media. In the first place, they can be a way to incorporate concerns and approaches suggested by the public; they help to improve the credibility and reliability agreement with media and, finally, involve a reflective activity that directly impacts the connection of the entity with its communities of reference, thus contributing to the joint construction of a meta-journalistic discourse.

In the new media scenario, the local media must make the most of all the technological potentialities, using them for a greater approach to their audience, foster participation, complement broadcasting with added value, engage with diversity, and protect the cultural identity of their spaces. In order to do so, they have different mechanisms that, even though they are not present to the same extent in the countries studied, they represent new ways of understanding the audiovisual public service, establishing the standards of quality in terms of innovation, social responsibility, and literacy in the proximity context.

REFERENCES

Bucci, E., Chiaretti, M., & Fiorini, A. M. (2012). *Quality Indicators for Public Broadcasters: Contemporary Evaluation.* UNESCO. Retrieved June 4, 2020, from https://unesdoc.unesco.org/ark:/48223/pf0000216616_eng.

Caldevilla, D. (2013). Nuevas fórmulas de periodismo: Periodismo de proximidad 2.0. *CIC. Cuadernos de Información y Comunicación, 18*, 165–176. https://doi.org/10.5209/rev_ciyc.2013.v18.41722.

Chaparro, M., Olmedo, S., & Gabilondo, V. (2016). El Indicador de la Rentabilidad Social en Comunicación (IRSCOM): medir para transformar. *CIC. Cuadernos de Información y Comunicación, 21*, 47–62. https://doi.org/10.5209/ciyc.52944.

De la Torre, L., & Téramo, M. T. (2015). La calidad de la información periodística: estrategias para su observación. Coincidencias y divergencia entre los medios y el público. *Estudios sobre el Mensaje Periodístico, 21*, 135–144. https://doi.org/10.5209/rev_esmp.2015.v21.50666.

Díaz Arias, R. (2017). *La información periodística en televisión.* Madrid: Síntesis.

European Broadcasting Union (EBU). (2014). *PSM Values Review: The Tool.* Retrieved June 4, 2020, from https://www.ebu.ch/publications/position-paper/open/guide/psm-values-review-the-tool.

Freedman, D., & Curran, J. (2016). *A Future for Public Service Television: Content and Platforms in a Digital World.* Goldsmiths: University of London.

Gómez Domínguez, P. (2016). Era digital y televisión autonómica: un estudio comparativo de las plataformas web, aplicaciones móviles y redes sociales de TV3 y BBC One. *Communication & Society, 29*(4), 85–106. https://doi.org/10.15581/003.29.4.sp.85-106.

Gómez Mompart, J. L., Gutiérrez Lozano, J. F., & Palau Sampio, D. (Eds.). (2013). *La calidad periodística. Teorías, investigaciones y sugerencias profesionales.* Bellaterra: Universitat Autònoma de Barcelona; Castelló de la Plana: Universitat Jaume I; Barcelona: Departament de Comunicació de la Universitat Pompeu Fabra. València: Universitat de València.

Hallin, D., & Mancini, P. (2004). *Comparing Media Systems: Three Models of Media and Politics.* Cambridge: Cambridge University Press.

Izquierdo Castillo, J., & López Rabadán, P. (2016). Nuevos retos y dificultades para los medios de comunicación públicos de proximidad. *adComunica. Revista Científica de Estrategias, Tendencias e Innovación en Comunicación, 11*, 19–21. https://doi.org/10.6035/2174-0992.2016.11.

López Cepeda, A. M. (2015). *Nuevos y viejos paradigmas de la televisión pública. Alternativas a su gobierno y (des)control.* Salamanca: Comunicación Social.
López Cepeda, A. M., Ufarte Ruiz, M. J., & Murcia Verdú, F. (2019). *Medios audiovisuales de servicio público y desinformación. Principales políticas y estrategias contra las noticias falsas. En XI Congreso Latina de Comunicación Social.* Tenerife: La Laguna.
López García, X., Galindo, F., & Villar, M. (1998). El valor social de la información de proximidad. *Revista Latina de Comunicación Social, 7,* 1–5. Retrieved from http://www.ull.es/publicaciones/latina/a/68xose.htm.
Martínez Juan, A. (2003). Los retos del periodismo local en la red: hacia una definición del espacio local en la era global. *Sala de prensa, 59.*
Marzal Felici, J., & Zallo Elguezabal, R. (2016). Presentación: Las televisiones públicas de proximidad ante los retos de la sociedad digital. *Comunicación y sociedad, 29*(4), 1–7. https://doi.org/10.15581/003.29.4.1-7.
Marzal Felici, J., López Rabadán, P., & Izquierdo castillo, J. (Eds.). (2017). *Los medios de comunicación públicos de proximidad en Europa. RTVV y la crisis de las televisiones públicas.* Valencia: Tirant Humanidades.
Oliveira, M. (2007). *El defensor del telespectador: un reto meta-televisivo. XXX Congreso Internacional de Comunicación.* Pamplona: Universidad de Navarra. Retrieved June 4, from https://repositorium.sdum.uminho.pt/bitstream/1822/29758/1/MO_reto_metatelevisivo.pdf.
Pérez Curiel, C., Gutiérrez Rubio, D., Sánchez González, T., & Zurbano Berenguer, B. (2015). El uso de fuentes periodísticas en las secciones de Política, Economía y Cultura en el Periodismo de Proximidad Español. *Estudios sobre el Mensaje Periodístico, 21,* 101–117. https://doi.org/10.5209/rev_ESMP.2015.v21.50661.
Pérez-Tornero, J. M., Giraldo-Luque, S., Tejedor-Clavo, S., & Portalés-Oliva, M. (2018). Propuesta de indicadores para evaluar las competencias de alfabetización mediática en las administraciones públicas. *El profesional de la información, 27*(3), 1699–2407. https://doi.org/10.3145/epi.2018.may.06.
Prado, E., & Fernández, D. (2006). The Role of Public Service Broadcasters in the Era of Convergence. A Case Study of the Televisión de Catalunya. *Communication and Strategies, 62,* 49–69.
Ramsey, P. (2018). It Could Redefine Public Service Broadcasting in the Digital Age: Assessing the Rationale for Moving BBC Three Online. *Convergence: The International Journal of Research into New Media Technologies, 24*(2), 152–167. https://doi.org/10.1177/2F1354856516659001.
Rigby, J. M., Brumby, D. P., Cox, A. L., & Gould, S. J. (2018). Old Habits Die Hard: A Diary Study of On-demand Video Viewing. In *Extended Abstracts of the 2018 CHI Conference on Human Factors in Computing Systems.* https://doi.org/10.1145/3170427.3188665.

Rodríguez-Martínez, R., López-Mari, A., Merino-Arribas, A., & Mauri-Ríos, M. (2017). Instrumentos de rendición de cuentas en España. Análisis comparativo en Cataluña, Galicia, Madrid y Valencia. *El profesional de la información*, 26(2), 255–266. https://doi.org/10.3145/epi.2017.mar.12.

Roel Vecino, M. (2005). TVE versus BBC. Dos modelos informativos enfrentados. Propuesta para una información responsable. In Fundación COSO (Ed.), *Información para la paz: autocrítica de los medios y responsabilidad del público* (pp. 543–558). Valencia: Fundación COSO.

Sparks, C. (2002). La influencia de Internet en los medios de comunicación convencionales. In J. Vidal Beneyto (Ed.), *La Ventana Global: ciberespacio, esfera pública mundial y universo mediático*. Madrid: Taurus.

Valencia Bermúdez, A., & Campos Freire, F. (2016). Indicadores de valor para las RTV autonómicas: rendición de cuentas en EITB, CCMA y CRTVG. *Coomunication & Society*, 29(4), 59–70. https://doi.org/10.15581/003.29.4.59-68.

PART III

Governance and Regulation

CHAPTER 8

The Governance of Public Service Media for the Internet Society

Francisco Campos-Freire, Martín Vaz-Álvarez, and María José Ufarte Ruiz

1 Shared National and European Regulation

The governing structure of public audiovisual media defines itself and evolves through their respective creation and operation acts, according to the legal-administrative tradition of each country and the Europeanizing influences required by community treaties or the recommendations of the Council of Europe. Culture and communication affairs are shared competences—as established by the Treaty on the Functioning of the EU—and European bodies act on the regulations of the countries through Directives, Communications, and Recommendations, but the models, structures, and

---

F. Campos-Freire (✉) • M. Vaz-Álvarez
Department of Communication Sciences, Universidade de Santiago de Compostela, Santiago de Compostela, Spain
e-mail: francisco.campos@usc.es; martin.vaz.alvarez@usc.gal

M. J. Ufarte Ruiz
Universidad de Castilla-La Mancha, Ciudad Real, Spain
e-mail: MariaJose.Ufarte@uclm.es

© The Author(s), under exclusive license to Springer Nature Switzerland AG 2021
M. Túñez-López et al. (eds.), *The Values of Public Service Media in the Internet Society*, Palgrave Global Media Policy and Business, https://doi.org/10.1007/978-3-030-56466-7_8

government philosophies of Public Service Media (PSM) are inherited by the states.

The conception of government and governance of these public communication institutions, beyond the definition and theoretical precision, responds to the legal tradition and the democratic political culture of each of the respective states (Pavani 2018). Europe does not have a single model of public audiovisual media because their origin, regulation, and configuration respond to the socio-political characteristics of each of the states. It is a diverse set of state models and regional nationalities, which converge or diverge in certain characteristics (regulation, values, financing, governance, or organizational structure).

The diversity and divergence of models make them difficult to compare, which has been a major challenge to social sciences that some studies have approached. Despite this, there are relevant contributions in the academic literature on different categorizations by Hallin and Mancini (2004), Brüggemann et al. (2014), Büchel et al. (2016), Pavani (2018), Donders (2012), Połońska and Beckett (2019), and more generically also in studies on audiovisual media and the European public sphere.

Regarding the diversity of models, however, narratives about a common audiovisual space, the European public sphere(s), and its relationship to the object and ideal of Public Service Broadcasting (PSB) in the European Union are almost continuously present in the political debates and academic literature of the last half century: Habermas (1989, 2001), Arendt (1958), Blumler (1985), Garnham (1986), Collins (1990), Keane (1991), Curran (1991), Livingstone and Lunt (1994), Schlesinger (1998), Eriksen (2004), Fossum and Schlesinger (2007), Bardoel and d'Haenens (2008), Brüggemann and Schulz-Forberg (2009), Lowe (2010), Thomas (2010), Iosifidis (2011), Michalis (2011), Donders (2012), Fuchs (2014) Adam (2015), Burri (2015), Horowitz and Car (2015), Freedman and Curran (2016), Pavani (2018), among other contributions.

Historically, PSM organizations have been organized and developed in Europe according to the radioelectric space of each country, its political tradition, and the meta-paradigm values of the different state configurations, as expressed by Giorgia Pavani (2018), with their respective diversity of traditions of authoritarian (dictatorships) or democratic regimes, models, degrees of decentralization, and the formation of different symbolic state or meso-state communication spaces (de Moragas Spà and Garitaonandia 1995) such as those in Germany, Spain, or Belgium (Donders et al. 2019).

The legal framework for broadcasting in Europe is originally linked to the scarcity and intervention of the transmission system and to the broadcasting technology, which is carried out through radio signals with statewide terrestrial coverage. Satellite transmission, in the late 1970s and early 1980s, interconnected the headends of local cable networks and households with international television signals. The emergence of the Internet and the digitization of radio signals represent another milestone in the overall transformation of the communication system for audiovisual services.

This evolution of the broadcasting system opens the door successively to deregulation of the state's broadcasting monopoly, to cross-border television, and to the convergence of various systems and operators. This evolution, in some cases with a certain delay, has to be adapted and approved by their respective audiovisual legal framework, resulting in each state developing its own more or less centralized model—according to its constitutional configuration and territorial decentralization—and with a dual nature, of public and private competence.

State, supra-state, meso-state, or sub-state institutions are aware of the importance—and therefore of their instrumentalization—of media systems for the construction of symbolic communication spaces in the context of globalization (Flew and Waisbord 2015). Hence, the resistance of state and meso-state institutions to the homogeneous standardization of their policies on public media, over which the European supranational bodies (Council of Europe, European Parliament, and European Commission) can't transcend beyond pronouncements, forums, parliamentary debates, communications, directives, and recommendations (culture of tolerance, repudiation of hate speech, role in the information society, pluralism and diversity, financing, digitalization, etc.) that are diluted in the sovereignty of states (Pavani 2018).

The result of pressure and state safeguards has been Protocol 29 attached to the 1997 Treaty on the Functioning of the European Union (TFEU), a political declaration recognizing the autonomous right of states to organize and finance a PSM system to meet the democratic, social, and cultural needs of their respective societies (Nitsche 2001). This declaration provides the basis for the European Communications 2001/2009 (C320/5 of 15-11-2001 and C257/01 of 27-10-2009) which support the state-aid system for financing public audiovisual services in the face of pressure and complaints from private commercial operators under competition law.

The European audiovisual space, which is defined by the Green Paper Television Without Frontiers (1984) and regulated by the Television Without Frontiers Directive (1989) and its successive revisions of 2007, 2010, and 2018, is articulated between the emphasis on the cultural media ideal of Europeanization, as a decisive factor for unification and integration (Schlesinger 1998), and the economic pragmatism of deregulation of the transnational commercial mass market.

In the face of this dialectic reality and the pressure of private media lobbies on European communication directives and policies, PSM resists under the protection of the prerogatives and interests of the states (Michalis 2011), although losing funding, audience, influence, and legitimacy (Arriaza Ibarra et al. 2015). This is detrimental to the need to refund it for the Internet society (Brevini 2010; Burri 2015) as it still acts in defense of professional standards of quality journalism and contributes to the protection of a democratic public opinion formation against emerging populism (Stromback 2017; Mitchell et al. 2018).

In short, the reforms of the different state legal frameworks respond, on one hand, to an endogenous dynamic specific to each nationality; and on the other, to the exogenous need to adapt to the successive transpositions of the European regulations that have emerged from the Television Without Frontiers Directive 89/552/EC and its three subsequent counterpart regulations of 2007/65/EC, 2010/13/EU and 2018/1808/EU. The national prevalence of this regulatory duality makes historical sense given that the public broadcasting system emerged and was put in place in most states before the Treaty of Rome itself, and did not take on a cross-border legal spirit until the end of the 1980s.

2 Genealogy of Public Service Broadcasting

The Royal Charter of the British Broadcasting Corporation (BBC), an organization formed in 1922, was established in 1927 and from that date on was renewed every ten years. The latest one spans from January 1, 2017, to December 31, 2027. The Royal Charter, a legal institution of medieval origin that protects the independence of institutions, determines the regulation, governance, financing, and management model of British public broadcasting.

The BBC, which was the world's first public television when it began regular broadcasts in 1936 and in its current global reach, maintained its monopoly until 1954, when the private consortium of regional broadcasters ITV began national broadcasting as its third channel. In addition to the BBC, which is financed through a license fee paid by British households, the British public broadcasting model is complemented by another non-profit corporation, Channel Four Corporation (C4C), which was set up to manage the fourth channel, from 1982 onward, made of content produced by independent, advertisement-funded companies. Channel Four, after depending on the Independent Broadcasting Authority, is established as an independent non-profit company with public service obligations.

In addition to the general principles of informing, educating, and entertaining, which are the founding values of John Reith (BBC's first general manager), the BBC promotes the territorial and cultural cohesion of the four nations that constitute the United Kingdom. This strategy includes its disconnected regional coverage and support for the creation in 1982 (one day before Channel Four) of *Sianel Pedwar Cymru* (S4C), Wales' own public service channel, funded through advertisement, public resources, and the free contribution of the BBC's broadcasts.

Cultural and linguistic diversity is also present in the structure of Ireland's public broadcasting model, which began its emissions in 1926, four years after the proclamation of the Republic's independence. Ireland has two public corporations, *Raidió Teilifís Éireann* (RTÉ) and *Teilifís na Gaellige* (TG4), in English and Gaelic, respectively. The state-run RTÉ was established in 1960 as an independent non-profit corporation, funded by a tax paid by households and advertising. TG4 began broadcasting in 1996, was a subsidiary of RTÉ until 2007, and now, incorporated as an independent non-profit company, depends on advertising and government contributions to help sustain the Irish language in the counties and towns that still speak it.

The regulation and structure of German public broadcasting, which began in 1925 through the *Reichs-Rundfunk-Gesells* (RRG), is based on the integration of the regional broadcasters that are grouped together for state coverage. It was this decentralized integration that inspired the creation of the ARD's confederal institutional consortium, following the end of the Second World War and the liberation by the Allied troops of the domain of nationalization under the Nazi regime, in which broadcasting depended directly on the Ministry of Propaganda.

The ARD was set up in 1950, initially bringing together six regional broadcasters (NWDR of North Germany, SWF, BR of Bavaria, HR of Hesse, *Radio Bremen*, and SDR of Baden-Württemburg); later, SFB of

West Berlin, NDR of North Germany, SR of Saarland, WDR of North Rhine-Westphalia, and the international channel *Deutsche Welle* (DW) were added. The regional German radio stations also promoted the first television broadcasts and created the state channel *Das Erste*, which was very influential in providing information and entertainment, also in the eastern part of the GDR, which was controlled by the censorship of the communist regime. After the German reunification, the GDR's public broadcaster was integrated into the anatomy of the ARD, which was restructured into the current nine broadcasting corporations, alongside the international DW. Previously, in 1963, the state channel ZDF was established by an agreement between the central government and the different *Länder*.

The German audiovisual system operates under the regulation of the State Broadcasting Treaty, revised 22 times until 2019, by means of parliamentary agreements between the central government and the 16 *Länder*, which also includes the respective interstate operating agreements of ARD, ZDF, the public funding system, private televisions, the protection of minors, and Internet tele-media.

The Austrian public broadcaster, which emerged in 1924, suffered in 1938 the intervention of the Nazi regime and its control from Germany until the liberation of the Second World War, was unified from 1958 into a state and regional radio and television company (*Österreichischer Rundfunk*, ORF), becoming a public corporation in 2001, under the supervision of a 35-member multi-representative council, which was responsible for electing its governing body.

French public broadcasting has a hybrid historical tradition, with seven stages of integration, segregation, and organizational reintegration of channels according to the alternation of the country's governing political parties: *Radiodiffusion National* (1939–45), *Radiodiffusion Française* (1945–49), *Radiodiffusion Télévision Française* (1949–64); *Office de Radiodiffusion Télévision Française* (1964–75), segregation (1975) and partial privatization (TF1, in 1987), and reintegration in 2000 of Channels France 2, 3, and 5 into France TV, which is completed in 2010 in a joint entity absorbing the holding that grouped 40 companies together. The reintegration continues in 2019–20 under a holding company of *France TV, Radio France, France Médias Monde, Institut National de l'Audiovisuel, TV5 Monde*, and *Arte*.

The governance system of French public audiovisual media is divided between the influence of governments and parliamentary political parties.

In 1989, under the mandate of Minister Jack Lang, who belonged to the government of the socialist Michel Rocard, the French Audiovisual Council (CSA) was created as an independent regulator in charge of choosing and controlling the governance of public media. President Nicolas Sarkozy then changed the regulations and reserved the election of the CEO of *France Télévisions* for the government. Later, his successor François Hollande returned to the previous model of involving the CSA in choosing and controlling the governance of *France Télévisions*.

While the changes in the name of the French public broadcaster are linked to the ups and downs of traffic regulations in France's fifth republic, as well as to the sensitivities of the ruling conservative or socialist parties, in Italy the trajectory of political parallelism is no less pronounced. The first public broadcasting group was created in Italy in 1924 as *Unione Radiofonica Italiana*, which the Mussolini government transformed into *Ente Italiano per le Audizioni Radiofoniche*. After the Second World War, the name *Radio Audizioni Italiane* (RAI) was adopted, and the first television trials began, regularizing its broadcasts from 1954.

The audiovisual reform of 1975, known as Law 103, transferred control of RAI's governance from the government to the Parliament, dividing among the main political parties (Christian Democracy, Socialist Party, and Communist Party) the hierarchical leadership of each of their respective three channels (Richeri and Balgi 2015), consolidating a practice of political intervention and manipulation known as *lottizzazione* (Hanretty 2009). This resulted in a distribution and political influence on the governance of Italian public media that the subsequent regulations of 1990s, 2015, and 2017 have not managed to clear up.

Televisión Española (TVE) was born in 1956 as the "television of the regime" under the dictatorship of Francisco Franco, who won the war in 1936–39. It followed the official guidelines of *Radio Nacional de España* (RNE, created in 1937 in Salamanca, at the height of the civil war, by General Millán-Astray, who rose up against the Republic) and of the cinematographical documentary newsreel NO-DO (founded in 1942, for its mandatory broadcast in cinemas). Three Spanish audiovisual media institutions that, together with the printed press, were the instruments of Franco's ideological, political, and governmental propaganda, controlled, conditioned, and subjugated until the democratic transition in 1976 (Bustamante 2006; Palacio 2005; Montero and Paz 2011).

The Spanish Constitution of 1978 enshrines freedom of expression, which gives way to the first democratic regulation of 1980s RTVE Statute and, 25 years later, to its main reform through the law 17/2006 of the state-owned radio and television, after other intermediate sequences of lights and shadows due to the loss of its monopoly (1983), private competition (1989), crisis, employment regulations, complaints of politicization and manipulation, change of the funding system (2009), and new governance scheme (2017). In general, the regulation and governance of Spanish public broadcasting since 1980 responds to the political framework of conservative and socialist bipartisanship, while the 2017 state reform introduces a multi-party concept, as a reflection of the new fragmented reality of parliamentary representation. However, the 2017 reform of RTVE's governance is still blocked in 2020 due to the lack of agreement between political forces.

At the end of 1982, the third channel of the Spanish public audiovisual service was created. Through its respective law of 1983, 13 public radio and television stations in the Autonomous Communities of Spain were created, 12 of which were grouped together in the Federation of Autonomous Radio and Television Organizations (FORTA), an association similar to the German ARD. The regulation of this Spanish regional autonomous model adopted a legal and governance framework similar to that of RTVE.

In Portugal, public broadcasting was born under the so-called *Estado Novo*, another dictatorship—as in Italy, Spain, and Greece—which in this case was the longest-lasting in twentieth-century Europe (1926–74), until the so-called military revolution of the carnations, which gave way to its nationalization and development under the new democratic regime, and since 2004 possesses a new, more independent funding and governance model. The Portuguese national radio was created in 1935, dependent on the Post, Telegraph and Telephone Company, and in 1955 *Radiotelevisão Portuguesa* (RTP) was created as a state company with a small private participation. In the 1990s, it lost its monopoly when the Cavaco Silva government gave entry to private television (the SIC).

The Belgian public broadcasting system (RTBF in French, VRT in Dutch, and BRF in German) was set up as a unit by the National Radio Institute (NIR/INR) in 1930, and currently follows its own federal constitutional model, consisting of three distinct cultural and linguistic communities (French Walloon, Dutch Flemish, and German-speaking on the German border) with their own meso-state media institutions. This Belgian political and media structure was consolidated by the constitutional reforms of 1979, 1990, and 2000 (Donders et al. 2019), which were developed into three media laws: the *Décret sur les Services de Médias Audiovisuels* (2003) for the French Community; the *Dekret über die Audiovisuallen Mediendienste und die Kinovorstellung* (2005) in the German-speaking Community; and the *Decreet betreffende de Radio-omroep en de Televisie* (2009) in the Flemish Community.

Unlike other countries, where the state is the creator of public broadcasting, in the Netherlands it was religious and socio-political associations who started this service from 1920, and then, in 1930, the government allocated frequencies and resources for its broadcasts. In 1969 the *Nederlandse Omroep Stitching* (NOS) was established, which brought together the regional stations of the various associations and was responsible for the coordinated production of news and entertainment, as well as another entity (NTR) for the education and minority services. In 2000–02 the government integrated some 25 broadcasting associations into what is now the *Nederlandse Publike Omroep* (NPO), which was also joined by the NOS; and in 2010 this was reduced to nine organizational associations, spread through the two institutions (NOS and NTR).

The Nordic countries, which are part of Nordivision's own network of associations set up in 1959, have created and developed their public broadcasting based on the model of the British BBC, although implementing their own specific features. Founded in 1926, *Yleisradio OY* (YLE) is Finland's public broadcasting company, and began television broadcasting in 1958, maintaining its radio and television monopoly until 1995 and 1992, respectively.

Denmark established *Danmarks Radio* (DR), the state-owned public broadcasting company, in 1925. It began its television broadcasts in 1951, after having its frequencies and content under the intervention of the Nazi occupation forces. In 1988 the Danish government broke DR's monopoly but did not privatize the service, creating a publicly owned commercial company (TV2) (which remains the same despite a failed privatization attempt in 2001) to compete with the state-owned group, with a focus on regional and local broadcasting.

Public broadcasting in Sweden emerged in 1925, and television broadcasting began in 1957. Until 1970, the ownership of the organizations that performed public services was shared by associative movements, industries, and newspaper companies. In 1993, the Parliament approved their nationalization and in 1997 the Swedish government established the Foundation for the Management of Public Service Radio, Television and Audiovisual Education (*Förvaltningsstilftelsen för* SR, SVT, and UR), a public foundation for the management of *Sveriges Radio AB* (SR), *Severiges TV* (SVT), and *Utbildningsradio* (educational service). The radio management body was initially divided between the state and regional broadcasters, but in 1993 the two entities were merged into *Sveriges Radio*.

Public broadcasting in Greece, in addition to being subject to the occupation of the country by the Nazis, also suffered political intervention from 1967 to 1974, through the Dictatorship of the Colonels, and closed in 2013 due to the economic crisis. Radio broadcasting in this country began in 1938 with the National Radio Foundation, and television emissions began in 1965. With the recovery of democracy in 1974, the management of radio and television was unified, and the state corporation *Eliniki Radiofone Tileórasi* (EPT) was created. Conservative Prime Minister Andonis Samarás closed it down between 2013 and 2015 because of the economic crisis, restructuring the public service into a new company (NERIT) with a much smaller workforce. With the victory of Syriza in 2015, Prime Minister Alexis Tsipras promoted the recovery of the old corporation and all its previous workers.

First the Nazi occupation, and then the control of the radio and television committees of the communist parties in the people's republics in Eastern Europe also weighed on their respective broadcasting systems until democracy was restored and independent state enterprises were created. With regard to the organizational structure, in some of these countries, such as Poland and the Czech Republic, radio and television companies are kept separate.

In Hungary, for its part, the government of Viktor Orbán brought together all state media (radio, television, internet, and news agency) in the state-owned company MTVA in 2011. The government's dependence on the MTVA, through the CEO and the Montágh Advisory and Supervisory Board, as well as the control of the appointment of the president and the board of directors of the *Telewizja Polska* (TVP) by the Polish government of Kaczynski in 2015, reflect the difficulty of sustaining the independence of these PSM organizations. Difficulties that arose in 2000–01 also provoked the strike and lockout in its own facilities by the workers of *Ceská Televize* (CT) to denounce the appointment of a director close to Prime Minister Václav Klaus: a crisis that later transcended in a popular demonstration of more than 100,000 people and in a legal reform in 2005 to reinforce its independence.

3 Structures and Organizational Systems

The different historical political traditions of creation and regulatory development of European public service broadcasters shape a variety of typologies in structures, government systems, and forms of governance. At least seven aspects condition and influence the variety of typologies of public media: the administrative framework regulating their corporate and business structure; the scope of territorial and cultural broadcasting; the funding systems; the dependence and independence in regard to the political and social evolution of the states and communities in which they develop; the traditional and emerging values of public service; the transformation of transmission technologies; and the conditioning factors of the production models.

Broadcasting in Europe emerges as a state initiative, linked to postal and telecommunications organizations, and in some cases (in the Netherlands) promoted by cultural, social, religious, and political associations. Hence the reason that the constitutional and management structures are public bodies, non-profit state enterprises, public foundations, or public limited companies. In other words, structures that combine public and private administrative law for the management of radio and television companies. Due to their complexity and increasing size, these structures evolved toward integration through holding companies and unified corporations of converging audiovisual services.

With regard to the specific area of issue, which is original starting point of its creation in each of the states and other territorial demarcations, in Europe we find seven models of organization and development. Firstly, centralized public radio and television stations (BBC, France TV, RAI, RTVE, ORF, RTP, RTÉ, Yle, ZDF, DR, SVT) which broadcast to the entire territory of the state and some incorporate certain degrees of decentralization through regional disconnection windows in certain time slots. Secondly, public broadcasters created for federal and regional areas (the ARD of the German *Länder* and the associated corporations in the FORTA of the Autonomous Communities of Spain), coexisting with state organizations of the first model (ZDF and RTVE, respectively). Thirdly, public broadcasters created by independent political, linguistic, and cultural communities, as is the case in Belgium, where three such organizations coexist (RTBF, VRT, and BRF).

A fourth category corresponds to organizations providing associated state and regional public audiovisual services, such as the Netherlands

(VPO) and Switzerland (SRG-SSR), the latter outside the European Union. A fifth category would correspond to audiovisual organizations in states with two languages, English and Irish, which until 2007 were integrated into the state-run RTÉ radio and television. From that year onward, TG4 Gaelic became independent as a non-profit organization. There are various regions that implement this fifth model: public broadcasters in Belgium, Switzerland, and three Autonomous Communities in Spain (Catalonia, the Basque Country, and Galicia) with co-official languages in each country.

Although they have lost their presence in recent years, a sixth group still includes many local televisions, linked to municipal or meso-state public organizations, especially in the United Kingdom and Spain (Kevin 2015). As the seventh case, there are publicly owned commercial broadcasters (Channel 4 in the United Kingdom and TV2 in Denmark) which are supported by advertising and coexist with other state models (BBC and DR respectively) of license-fee funding for households or citizens and businesses.

Funding impacts public audiovisual governance systems insofar as it affects their sustainability, management capacity, and the independence of its governance. There are five types of funding for public audiovisual media, three from public sources, and two from commercial sources, which in some countries are combined to varying degrees; the former mostly in Finland, Sweden, or Norway; while the latter splits by 50% in Poland or Malta. In 2018, public funds in the European Union represented some 33.180 million euros and accounted for 77.8% of the funding. Commercial revenues (advertising and production sales), however, barely exceeded 20% (EAO 2019).

Public funding can take place through fees paid by households and businesses, by citizens and companies, and through direct contributions or transfers from the states to public corporations. Sixteen countries had radio and television fees in 2018: Austria, Belgium (French community), Czech Republic, Germany, Denmark, France, the United Kingdom, Greece, Hungary, Ireland, Italy, Poland, Portugal, Romania, Slovenia, and Slovakia (EAO 2019). Finland replaced in 2013 the collection of the broadcasting fee per household with an individual tax that citizens pay through their income tax return and is derived directly to the public broadcaster.

The third type of public funding, through contributions or transfers included in the general budgets of other states, is more dependent on governments and therefore makes the governance bodies of public audiovisual services less independent than they would be through contributions made directly by citizens. The difference lies in the direct dependence on each source of funding (citizens or governments), multi-annuity and accountability. Those corporations that are directly funded by citizens have greater capacity for independence because the source of the economic resources is not conditioned by the source of the general state budgets, which are drawn up by the governments in office (López-Cepeda et al. 2019).

The technologies of production and transmission (digitalization and the Internet) have made it possible to transcend not only the local territorial sphere itself into the global space (Hemer and Tufte 2005) but also other forms of access and participation in the processes of communication, creating both new needs and challenges for reinventing the strategies, structures, and funding resources of organizations adapted to these possibilities of glocalization and the demands of co-creation that public audiovisual services have to face in order to fulfill their mission in the twenty-first century (Iosifidis 2010; Burri 2015; Horowitz and Car 2015; Horz 2016; Hutchinson 2017).

4 Governance Typology

The concept of governance is incorporated into the management and administration of public broadcasting as a paradigm for strengthening its independence and connection with the pluralism of increasingly open societies. It is the adaptation of their government system, centralized and monopolized by the state, to new forms of relationship that are more flexible and competitive in order to try to sustain their legitimacy. The concept of governance was incorporated into regulation and scientific literature in the two final decades of the twentieth century and the first decades of the twenty-first (Council of Europe 1996, 2006, 2007, 2012a, 2012b; Ferrell Lowe and Bardoel 2007; European Commission 2011; Iosifidis 2010; EBU 2012; Głowacki and Jackson 2014; Wagner and Berg 2015).

This concept is also evolving in parallel with the renaming of the European Directive 89/552/EEC as Television Without Frontiers, its revision through the Audiovisual Media Services Directive 2007/65/EC and the recognition by the European Broadcasting Union (EBU 2012) of governance as a key factor in ensuring six main values of public audiovisual service: universality, independence, excellence, diversity, innovation, and accountability.

Governance is a pervasive concept with many different meanings, but it is not exactly a substitute for, or synonymous with, government, but rather the evolution of a capacity, a qualification, an articulation mechanism, or a faculty of government. Governance is a power and an instrument that allows the governing system to be linked to groups related to the organization, facilitating their participation, transparency, and democratic control (Schmitter 2018).

The degree and quality of governance depends not only on its regulation but also on its implementation and the political culture of the actors involved. Corporate governance is its axis of articulation and its application in the context of a society that is increasingly complex and demanding in its transparency. That is why in today's organizations the government system is being transformed into governance. This is the challenge of adaptation and transformation of traditional public service broadcasting organizations.

The board of directors and the senior executive management are the two main parts of the corporate governance structure of companies (Baysinger and Hoskisson 1990; Kose and Lemma 1998; Strebel 2011), each of them headed by a president and a general manager or CEO, who are responsible for the strategy and control functions and the coordination of the productive operations, respectively. Senior management carries out the operational execution and is accountable to the board of directors; thus, the separation of the dual functions (chairman and CEO) is an essential factor of control and good corporate governance. However, in some companies, the highest representation of this duality of functions is assumed by the same executive president.

The board of directors is the representation of the General Shareholders Meeting, which, due to its public status, is embodied by the state, through the representatives of the citizens. In the democratic system, such representation emanates from the Parliament, and from this framework arises the compositional nature of the main governing body of public companies, which is materialized through various direct and indirect elective procedures. These procedures, depending on the democratic culture of the country, reflect the influence of governments, the weight of proportional quotas of parliamentary parties, or the protection of independence against the politicization of governance.

The corporate structure is based on the normative framework of the respective countries' regulations and on the two classic pillars of agency and stakeholder theories (Michael and Jensen 1976), that is, the delegation of responsibilities and functions of the founders as well as the execution and connection of the parties related to the organization. In addition to the board of directors and executive management, other internal and external bodies, codes of good governance, systems of accountability, corporate social responsibility, quality audits, reports on contributions of public value, and so on are also a part of it. Another part of this corporate structure, especially in the current context of the Internet, is the weight of the direct relationship between organizations and their audiences and society in general.

The articulation and improvement of this whole system is what corresponds to good governance. But in Public Service Media, the weight of traditional systems of centralized and politicized power still prevails over the mechanisms of good governance, as they are interfered by an overexposure to the influences of political parties and organic elites of socioeconomic, professional, cultural, and religious representation (Gliddon 2006; Bronstein and Katzew 2018; López-Cepeda et al. 2019).

The name, structure, composition, representation, powers, qualifications, mandate periods, and election system of the governing bodies vary from country to country. In contrast to the appointment following parliamentary proportionality, which reflects the political transmission chain of the governance system in Mediterranean countries, the central and northern European states are extending co-optation through more diversity and independence of social, cultural, ethnic, religious, and territorial representations. In Germany, a ruling by its Constitutional Court in 2014 prohibits more than a third of government representatives in governance bodies. Mandates of less or more than four years (three, five, and six years respectively) seek to avoid the influence of ordinary legislature periods with the corresponding electoral processes. And the non-intervention of the government or Parliament in the selection and election of presidents and CEOs also seeks to avoid political influence and strengthen their independence.

Eight types of statutory bodies and frameworks (five internal and three external) make up the governance structure of European public broadcasting. The internal bodies are: supreme management control boards, management boards or teams, advisory and hearing boards, ombudsmen and professional committees. Of an external nature are the monitoring and control committees of the Parliaments, the audit interventions of the State Treasuries, and the accountability of the fulfillment and contribution of public values to society.

The governance of ORF in Austria, as a public corporation, is organized around its trust structure, consisting of a board of 35 trustees, 6 of them represented according to parliamentary proportionality, 9 elected by the federal government, 9 representatives of the regional states, 6 of the general council, and 5 of the corporation's works council. This council elects the CEO and supervises the execution of his management team. In addition, there is a 30-member hearing council representing the country's social, cultural, religious, and economic diversity as well as the obligations of its values charter and accountability for the social contribution of its public value.

The Broadcasting and Telemedia Council of the ZDF, consisting of 60 members from different socio-cultural representations of society and audiences, is the highest body of the German public broadcasting system. It is followed by ARD's Broadcasting Council, made up of representatives of the nine *Länder* broadcasters and the international channel Deutsche Welle (DW).

These *Länder* corporations have councils of between 17 and 50 members, with parliamentary election and quotas of political proportionality in some cases, and of representation or socio-cultural background in others. The board of directors of the federal ZDF, for its part, consists of 12 members, 8 of whom are elected by the Telemedia Council and 4 by the Länder. The *Kommission Zur Ermittlung des Finanzbedurfs der Rundfunkanstalten* (KEF) is the external body that determines the economic needs and the financing system of public service broadcasting.

The BBC Board of Directors, established in 2017 under the Royal Charter approved in 2016, replaces the BBC Trust (a supervisory trust operating since 2010 and consisting of 12 trustees) as the highest representative of its internal governance, which is shared with the external control of OFCOM, the regulatory office for converging general communication services. The BBC Board consists of 15 members, 6 of them independent, 4 representatives of the nations (England, Scotland, Wales, and Northern Ireland), 3 corporation directors and the Director-General. The latter is chosen by the government and are all appointed by The Queen-in-Council. The BBC Board elects the Director-General and OFCOM oversees its performance as a public service.

The Irish government appoints 6 of the 12 members of the *Raidió Teilifís Éireann* (RTÉ) board, including the CEO; four others are elected by the Parliament and two are employee representatives. The RTÉ and BBC audience boards are the communication channel for viewers and listeners. Foundation Management for SR, SVT, and UR is the highest authority responsible for public broadcasting in Sweden, consisting of a board of 13 directors, including the chairman and deputy chairman, appointed by the government upon proposal of the Parliament. The board of directors of the Foundation appoints the directors of the management board.

A foundation is also the corporate regime of the *Nederlandse Publike Omroep* (NPO), the parent corporation of the two associations of public broadcasting in the Netherlands, governed by a supervisory board which elects and controls the management team. The origin of television in the Netherlands and its governance is directly related to the tradition of "pillarization" (Post 1989; Cécilia 2005) or social and religious stratification in the Netherlands, Belgium, or Austria, where different pillars or strata (Catholics, Protestants, unions, and industries) divide up institutions and representations.

The supervisory board of *Yleisradio* (YLE) is the highest representation and control body, consisting of 21 members elected by the Parliament, who in turn appoint the board of directors (of seven positions and one staff representative) and the CEO of the company, who selects its own management team. The 11 members of the executive board of the state-owned company Danish DR are elected for four-year terms; the chairman and two others are appointed by the government, six by the Parliament, and two on behalf of the employees. The CEO and its management team are elected by the board of directors.

The Parliament of the Walloon-Brussels Federation elects the 13 members of the board of directors of the RTBF, according to their quotas of political proportionality; and the government of that community appoints two other commissioners. The board of directors, for its part, elects its president and vice-president, as well as the general manager of the company, who heads the management team. In accordance with political proportionality, the 12 members of the VRT are also appointed by the government of the Flemish Community for a period of five years.

Rádio e Televisão de Portugal (RTP) has a fairly balanced governance structure, with its *Conselho de Opinião* inspired by the higher collective bodies of social representation in Northern Europe and by the audience councils. This 32-member Opinion Council elects 4 of the 6 members of the *Conselho Geral Independente*, jointly with the government (two each), which chooses the remaining two members (after hearing the opinion of the external independent regulator, the *Entidade Reguladora da Comunicação*) and the three components (one of which is the CEO) of the *Conselho de Administração*. Its structure is completed with a Fiscal Council composed by three financial controllers, ombudsman, and a functioning code of ethics.

The board of directors of the *France Télévisions* (FTV) group, with 14 members plus a chairman, is elected for five-year terms, with 5 members proposed by the government and 2 by the Parliament, 5 on a proposal from the *Conseil Supérieur de l'Audiovisuel* and 2 staff representatives. The presidency of this Council is held by the CEO, who heads the management team, Delphine Ernotte. The governance structure of this group is formed by the FTV Foundation, which carries out sponsorship and media literacy activities, as well as the declaration of values, charter, code of ethics, and financial performance report.

Seven members hold the boards of *Eliniki Radiofonia Tileórasi* (EPT) of Greece and *Radiotelevisione Italiana* (RAI), elected by their respective Parliaments on the basis of proportionality. It is this RAI body that proposes the general manager of the Italian corporation, upon a parliamentary agreement in which the position is negotiated jointly with that of the chairman of the board.

The status of CEO and chairman of the board of directors is also typical of the regulatory framework of the Spanish Broadcasting Corporation RTVE, although the situation of temporariness and crisis is the characteristic of its system of governance, which did not achieve sufficient support in the Parliament for its renewal in 2018. In light of this, the socialist government of Pedro Sánchez decided to appoint a provisional administrator who has already been in office for more than two years despite the demands for normalization by the various parliamentary forces and the News Council made up of professionals from these PSM (Goyanes et al. 2020).

The governance structure of the Spanish public radio and television system, both of the state and of the Autonomous Communities, is made up of administrative boards elected according to proportionality quotas by their respective parliaments, for periods of four, five, and six years, depending on the case; advisory boards of socio-cultural representation and audiovisual boards in Catalonia and Andalusia, with external control powers. In 5 of the 13 Autonomous Communities with public broadcasting services, the CEO is appointed directly by the government, while in the remaining Autonomous Communities, the system of parliamentary election by absolute majority is imposed, since the reinforced majority invoked by the respective regulatory laws cannot be reached.

5 Governance and Values for the Internet Society

The current challenge for Public Service Media to recover and maintain both their relevance and their legitimacy, due to social changes and audience behavior on Internet platforms and society, lies not only in improving their governance systems through new forms and examples of good governance, but also in reinforcing and updating the essential values of public service (Blaug et al. 2006; Enli 2008; Burri 2015; Horowitz and Car 2015; Arriaza Ibarra et al. 2015; Brink Lund and Ferrell Lowe 2016; Tremblay 2016; Michalis and Nieminen 2016; Trappel 2016; Freedman and Curran 2016).

Linking governance and values means reinforcing within PSM the principles of universality, independence, excellence, diversity, responsibility, and innovation (EBU 2014) together with other emerging issues related to pluralism, credibility, transparency, participation, cohesion, citizenship, diversity of identities, cultural intermediation, respect, communication of values, authenticity, media literacy, open innovation, creativity, co-creation, reputation, equality, parity, integration versus xenophobia, verification versus fake news, constructive journalism, and solutions versus polarization.

Just as public service values are necessary for the Internet society, independence is indispensable, as it is the most required and important intrinsic value of governance for the reputation, credibility, trust, and legitimacy of public broadcasting (Karppinen and Moe 2016) but also surely the most difficult to manage. It is related to governance (Rhodes 1997; Głowacki 2014; Nowak 2014; Tremblay and Brunelle 2015), funding (Ala-Fossi 2012; Lowe and Berg 2013), decision-making, content pluralism, management, and democratic culture of the relation between politics and media (Hall 1992; Jakubowicz 2008; Bardoel and d'Haenens 2008; Hallin and Mancini 2004; Carpentier 2011; Meyerhofer 2012; Nissen 2014).

In short, improving the governance of public audiovisual media, in addition to the re-evaluation of traditional and emerging values that are required from PSM, still needs to strengthen its independence, overcome the polarization of its politicization, sustain its funding, increase its participation and transparency, get closer to culture and creativity, improve its communication with society, increase its innovation, and not give up its presence in all the networks and Internet platforms available. The overall balance, after a deep look through their genealogy and structure, and with some corporations being more efficient than others, is that these organizations are still burdened by the traditional system of government in order to transform their governance, despite efforts being noted in incorporating this narrative.

Research Acknowledgments This chapter is part of the activities of the research project (RTI2018-096065-B-I00) of the Spanish State Program for R&D&I oriented to the Challenges of Society of the Ministry of Science, Innovation and Universities (MCIU), State Research Agency (AEI) and the European Regional Development Fund (ERDF) on "New values, governance, funding and public audiovisual services for the Internet society: European and Spanish contrasts."

References

Adam, S. (2015). European Public Sphere. In G. Mazzoleni (Ed.), *International Encyclopedia of Political Communication* (pp. 1–9). New York: Wiley.

Ala-Fossi, M. (2012). Social Obsolescence of the TV Fee and the Financial Crisis of Finnish Public Service Media. *Journal of Media Business Studies, 9*(1), 33–54. https://doi.org/10.1080/16522354.2012.11073535.

Arendt, H. (1958). *The Human Condition*. Chicago, IL: University of Chicago Press.

Arriaza Ibarra, K., Nowak, E., & Kuhn, R. (Eds.). (2015). *Public Service Media in Europe: A Comparative Approach*. New York: Routledge.

Bardoel, J., & d'Haenens, L. (2008). Reinventing Public Service Broadcasting in Europe: Prospects, Promises and Problems. *Media, Culture & Society, 30*(3), 337–355. https://doi.org/10.1177/2F0163443708088791.

Baysinger, B., & Hoskisson, R. E. (1990). The Composition of Boards of Directors and Strategic Control: Effects on Corporate Strategy. *Academy of Management Review, 15*(1) https://doi.org/10.5465/amr.1990.4308231.

Blaug, R., Horner, L., & Lekhi, R. (2006). *Public Value, Politics and Public Management*. London: The Work Foundation.

Blumler, J. (1985). Broadcasting Finance and Programme Quality: An International Review. *European Journal of Communication, 1*(3), 343–364. https://doi.org/10.1177/2F0267323186001003006.
Brevini, B. (2010). Towards PSB 2.0? Applying the PSB Ethos to Online Media in Europe: A Comparative Study of PSBs' Internet Policies in Spain, Italy and Britain. *European Journal of Communication, 25*(4), 348–365. https://doi.org/10.1177/2F0267323110381004.
Brink Lund, A., & Ferrell Lowe, A. (2016). Public Service Broadcasting. In G. Mazzoleni (Ed.), *The International Encyclopedia of Political Communication*. The Willey Blackwell-ICA.
Bronstein, V., & Katzew, J. (2018). Safeguarding the South African Public Broadcaster: Governance, Civil Society and the SABC. *Journal of Media Law, 10*(2), 244–272. https://doi.org/10.1080/17577632.2018.1592284.
Brüggemann, M., & Schulz-Forberg, H. (2009). Becoming Pan-European? Transnational Media and the European Public Sphere. *The International Communication Gazette, 71*(8), 693–712. https://doi.org/10.1177/2F1748048509345064.
Brüggemann, M., Engesser, S., Büchel, F., Humprecht, E., & Castro, L. (2014). Hallin and Mancini Revisited: Four Empirical Types of Western Media Systems. *Journal of Communication, 64*, 1037–1065. https://doi.org/10.1111/jcom.12127.
Büchel, F., Humprecht, E., & Castro-Herrero, L. (2016). Building Empirical Typologies with QCA: Toward a Classification of Media Systems. *The International Journal of Press/Politics, 21*(2), 209–232. https://doi.org/10.1177/2F1940161215626567.
Burri, M. (2015). *Public Service Broadcasting 3.0: Legal Design for the Digital Present*. London: Routledge.
Bustamante, E. (2006). Radio y Televisión en España: historia de una asignatura pendiente de la democracia. Gedisa, Barcelona. ISBN: 84-9784-163-8.
Carpentier, N. (2011). *Media and Participation: A Site of Ideological-Democratic Struggle*. Chicago: The Chicago University Press.
Cécilia, M-C. (2005, March). Las Iglesias, el Estado y la "pilarización". *Le Monde Diplomatique en español*. Retrieved June 13, 2020, from https://mondiplo.com/las-iglesias-el-estado-y-la-pilarizacion.
Collins, R. (1990). *Television: Policy and Culture*. London: Unwin Hyman.
Council of Europe. (1996). Recommendation No. R (96) 10 of the Committee of Ministers to Member States on the Guarantee of the Independence of Public Service Broadcasting. Retrieved June 13, 2020, from https://rm.coe.int/CoERMPublicCommonSearchServices/DisplayDCTMContent?documentId=090000168050c770.
Council of Europe. (2006). Declaration of the Committee of Ministers on the Guarantee of the Independence of Public Service Broadcasting in the Member

States. Retrieved June 13, 2020, from https://eos.cartercenter.org/uploads/document_file/path/216/Committee_of_Ministers_-_Declaration_of_the_Committee_of_Ministers_on_the_guarantee_of_the_independence_of_public_service_broadcasting_in_the_member_states.pdf.

Council of Europe. (2007). Recommendation Rec (2007)3 of the Committee of Ministers to Member States on the Remit of Public Service Media in the Information Society. Retrieved June 13, 2020, from https://wcd.coe.int/ViewDoc.jsp?id=1089759.

Council of Europe. (2012a). Recommendation CM/Rec(2012)1 of the Committee of Ministers to Member States on Public Service Media Governance. Retrieved June 13, 2020, from https://wcd.coe.int/ViewDoc.jsp?id=1908265.

Council of Europe. (2012b). Declaration of the Committee of Ministers on Public Service Media Governance. Retrieved June 13, 2020, from https://wcd.coe.int/ViewDoc.jsp?id=1908241.

Curran, J. (1991). Rethinking the Media as a Public Sphere. In P. Dahlgren & C. Sparks (Eds.), *Communication and Citizenship: Journalism and The Public Sphere in the New Media Age* (pp. 1–31). London: Routledge.

Donders, K. (2012). *Public Service Media and Policy in Europe*. Londen: Palgrave Macmillan.

Donders, K., Van den Bulck, H., & Raats, T. (2019). Public Service Media in a Divided Country: Governance and Functioning of Public Broadcasters in Belgium. In E. Polanska & C. Beckett (Eds.), *Public Service Broadcasting and Media Systems in Troubled European Democracies* (pp. 89–107). London: Palgrave Macmillan.

EAO. (2019). *Yearbook 2019/2020 Key Trends. Television, Cinema, Audiovisual Services. The Pan-European Picture*. Strasbourg: European Audiovisual Observatory. Retrieved from www.obs.coe.int.

EBU. (2012). *Declaration on the Core Values of Public Service Media*. Geneva: European Broadcasting Union. Retrieved June 13, 2020, from http://www3.ebu.ch/files/live/sites/ebu/files/Knowledge/Publication%20Library/EBU-Empowering-Society_EN.pdf.

EBU. (2014). *Public Service Values. Editorial Principles and Guidelines*. Retrieved June 13, 2020, from https://www.ebu.ch/publications/position-paper/login_only/guide/public-service-values-editorial.

Enli, G. S. (2008). Redefining Public Service Broadcasting. Multi-Platform Participation. *Convergence: The International Journal of Research into New Media Technologies, 14*(1), 105–120. https://doi.org/10.1177/2F1354856507084422.

Eriksen, O. (2004). Conceptualizing European Public Spheres. General, Segmented and Strong Publics. *Arena Working Papers, 3*. Retrieved June 13, 2020.

European Commission. (2011). *INDIREG. Indicators for independence and efficient functioning of audiovisual media services regulatory bodies*. Retrieved from http://www.indireg.eu/.
Ferrell Lowe, G., & Bardoel, J. (Eds.). (2007). *From Public Service Broadcasting to Public Service Media*. Göteborg: Nordicom.
Flew, T., & Waisbord, S. (2015). The Ongoing Significance of National Media Systems in the Context of Media Globalization. *Media Culture & Society, 37*(4), 620–636. https://doi.org/10.1177/2F0163443714566903.
Fossum, J., & Schlesinger, P. R. (2007). *The European Union and the Public Sphere. A Communicative Space in the Making?* London: Routledge.
Freedman, D., & Curran, J. (2016). *A Future for Public Service Television: Content and Platforms in a Digital World*. London: Goldsmiths University of London. Retrieved June 13, 2020, from https://futureoftv.org.uk/wp-content/uploads/2016/06/FOTV-Report-Online-SP.pdf.
Fuchs, C. (2014). Social Media and the Public Sphere. *TripleC: Communication, Capitalism & Critique, 12*(1), 57–101. https://doi.org/10.31269/triplec.v12i1.552.
Garnham, N. (1986). The Media and the Public Sphere. In P. Golding, G. Murdock, & P. Schlesinger (Eds.), *Communicating Politics: Mass Communications and Political Process*. Leicester: Leicester University Press.
Gliddon, P. (2006). Programmes Subjected to Interference: The Heath Government, Broadcasting and the European Community, 1970–1971. *History, 91*(303), 401–424. https://doi.org/10.1111/j.1468-229x.2006.00372.x.
Głowacki, M. (2014). New Public + New Media = New Governance? The Council of Europe´s Approach to Governance in European Media. In M. Głowacki & L. Jackson (Eds.), *Public Media Management for the Twenty-First Century: Creativity, innovation and interaction (Chapter 10)*. London: Routledge.
Głowacki, M., & Jackson, L. (2014). *Public Media Management for the Twenty-First Century: Creativity, Innovation and Interaction*. London: Routledge.
Goyanes, M., Vaz-Álvarez, M., & Demeter, M. (2020). Political Pressures in TVE: Cascade Effects, Morphology of Manipulations and Professional and Personal Reprisals. *Journalism Practice* (Online First). https://doi.org/10.1080/17512786.2020.1772098.
Habermas, J. (1989). *The Structural Transformation of the Public Sphere: An Inquiry into a Category of Bourgeois Society*. Cambridge: MIT Press.
Habermas, J. (2001). Why Europe Needs a Constitution. *New Left Review, 11*, 5–26.
Hall, S. (1992). The Question of Cultural Identity. In S. Hall, D. Held, & T. McGrew (Eds.), *Modernity and Its Futures (Chapter 6)*. Cambridge: Polity Press/Open University.
Hallin, D. C., & Mancini, P. (2004). *Comparing Media Systems: Three Models of Media and Politics*. Cambridge University Press.

Hanretty, C. (2009). The Political Independence of Public Service Broadcasters (Thesis). Florence: European University Institute. Retrieved June 13, 2020, from https://cadmus.eui.eu/bitstream/handle/1814/13213/2009_Hanretty.pdf?sequence=2.

Hemer, O., & Tufte, T. (Eds.). (2005). *Media and Glocal Change: Rethinking Communication for Development*. Buenos Aires-Sweden: GLACSO-Nordicom.

Horowitz, M. A., & Car, V. (2015). The Future of Public Service Media. *Medijske Studije/Media Studies*, 6(12), 2–9.

Horz, C. (2016). Networking Citizens: PSM and Participatory Audience Initiatives in Europe. Presented at the RIPE@2016 Conference.

Hutchinson, J. (2017). *Cultural Intermediaries. Audience Participation in Media Organisations*. London: Palgrave Macmillan.

Iosifidis, P. (2010). *Reinventing Public Service Communication: European Broadcasters and Beyond*. London: Palgrave Macmillan.

Iosifidis, P. (2011). The Public Sphere, Social Networks and Public Service Media. *Information, Communication & Society*, 14(5), 619–637. https://doi.org/10.1080/1369118X.2010.514356.

Jakubowicz, K. (2008). Participation and Partnership: A Copernican Revolution to Re-Engineer Public Service Media for the 21st Century. Presented at the RIPE@2008 Conference: Public Service Media in the 21st Century: Participation, Partnership and Media Development. Retrieved June 13, 2020, from http://citeseerx.ist.psu.edu/viewdoc/download;jsessionid=0D6985A63BFA0D59E437F074949CA81A?doi=10.1.1.664.4823&rep=rep1&type=pdf.

Karppinen, K., & Moe, H. (2016). What We Talk About When Talk About "Media Independence". *Javnost-The Public*, 23(2), 105–119. https://doi.org/10.1080/13183222.2016.1162986.

Keane, J. (1991). *The Media and Democracy*. Cambridge: Polity Press.

Kevin, D. (2015). *Television in the Regions: Spain and the United Kingdom*. Strasbourg: European Audiovisual Observatory.

Kose, J., & Lemma, W. S. (1998). Corporate Governance and Board Effectiveness. *Journal of Banking & Finance*, 22(4), 317–403. https://doi.org/10.1016/S0378-4266(98)00005-3.

Livingstone, S., & Lunt, P. (1994). The Mass Media, Democracy and the Public Sphere. In *Talk on Television: Audience Participation and Public Debate* (pp. 9–35). London: Routledge.

López-Cepeda, A. M., Soengas-Pérez, X., & Campos-Freire, F. (2019). Gobernanza de las radiotelevisiones públicas europeas: poder estructural centralizado y politizado. *El Profesional de la Información*, 28(6) https://doi.org/10.3145/epi.2019.nov.18.

Lowe, G. F. (Ed.). (2010). *The Public in Public Service Media*. Göteborg: Nordicom.

Lowe, G. F., & Berg, C. E. (2013). The Funding of Public Service Media: A Matter of Value and Values. *The International Journal on Media Management*, 15(2), 77–97. https://doi.org/10.1080/14241277.2012.748663.

Meyerhofer, L. (2012). Balancing Between Democratic Accountability and Market Pressure: Public Service Media's Transboundary strategies. Presented at RIPE@2012 Conference.

Michalis, M. (2011). La política europea de comunicación y su impacto en los medios de radiodifusión. In F. Campos Freire (Ed.), *El nuevo escenario mediático* (pp. 29–47). Salamanca: Comunicación Social.

Michalis, M., & Nieminen, H. (2016). Public Media in the Late 2010s: Values, Governance and Policy. *International Journal of Digital Television*, 7(3), 269–272. https://doi.org/10.1386/jdtv.7.3.269_2.

Michael C., & Jensen, A. (1976). Theory of the Firm: Governance, Residual Claims and Organizational Forms. *Journal of Financial Economics (JFE)*, 3(4).

Mitchell, A., Simmons, K., Matsa, K. E., Silver, L., Shearer, E., Johnson, C., et al. (2018, May 14). In Western Europe, Public Attitudes Toward News Media More Divided by Populist Views Than Left-Right Ideology. *Pew Research Center*. Retrieved June 14, 2020, from http://www.journalism.org/2018/05/14/in-western-europe-public-attitudes-toward-news-media-more-divided-by-populist-views-than-left-right-ideology/.

Montero, J., & Paz, M. A. (2011). The Spanish Civil War on Televisión Española during the Franco era (1956–1975). Communication & Society, ISSN 0214-0039, ISSN-e 2174-0895, Vol. 24, N°. 2, págs. 149–197.

de Moragas Spà, M., & Garitaonandia, C. (1995). *Decentralization in the Global Era: Television in the Regions, Nationalities and Small Countries of the European Union*. London: John Libbey and Co.

Nissen, C. S. (2014). Organisational Culture and Structures in Public Media Management: In Search of a Model for the Digital Age. In M. Glowacki y L. Jackson (eds.) *Public Media Management for the Twenty-First Century: Creativity, Innovation, and Interaction* (Chapter 5). London: Routledge.

Nitsche, I. (2001). *Broadcasting in the European Union: The Role of Public Interest in Competition Analysis*. The Hague: TMC Asser Press.

Nowak, E. (2014). Between Economic Objectives and Public Remit: Positive and Negative Integration in European Media Policy. In K. Donders, C. Pauwels, & J. Loisen (Eds.), *The Palgrave Handbook of European Media Policy* (pp. 96–109). Basingstoke: Palgrave Macmillan.

Palacio, M. (2005). *Historia de la Televisión de España*. Gedisa: Barcelona.

Pavani, G. (2018). *The Structure and Governance of Public Service Broadcasting*. London: Palgrave Macmillan.

Połońska, E. & Beckett, C. (2019). *Public Service Broadcasting and Media Systems in Troubled European Democracies*. Palgrave Macmillan. ISBN 978-3-030-02710-0.

Post, H. (1989). *Pillarization: An Analysis of Dutch and Belgian Society*. Avebury: Gower Publishing Company.

Rhodes, R. A. W. (1997). *Understanding Governance. Policy Networks, Governance, Reflexivity and Accountability*. Buckingham: Open University Press.

Richeri, G., & Balgi, G. (2015). The Final Days of the RAI Hegemony: On the Sociocultural Reasons Behind the Fall of the Public Monopoly. *Journal of Italian Cinema and Media Studies*, *3*(1–2), 63–79. https://doi.org/10.1386/jicms.3.1-2.63_1.

Schlesinger, Ph. R. (1998). Europeidad y medios: identidad nacional y esfera pública. *Estudios sobre las Culturas Contemporáneas*, *IV*(7), 25–64. México: Universidad de Colima.

Schmitter, P. C. (2018). Defining, Explaining and, Then, Exploiting the Elusive Concept of "Governance". *Fudan Journal of the Humanities and Social Sciences*, *12*, 547–567. https://doi.org/10.1007/s40647-018-0236-9.

Strebel, P. (2011). In Touch Boards: Reaching Out to the Value Critical Stakeholders. *Corporate Governance: International Journal of Business in Society*, *11*(5), 603–610. https://doi.org/10.1108/14720701111177000.

Stromback, J. (2017). Does Public Service TV and the Intensity of the Political Information Environment Matter? *Journalism Studies*, *18*(11), 1415–1432. https://doi.org/10.1080/1461670X.2015.1133253.

Thomas, B. (2010). PSB and the European Public Sphere. In P. Iosifidis (Ed.), *Reinventing Public Service Communication: European Broadcasters and Beyond* (pp. 63–75). London: Palgrave Macmillan.

Trappel, J. (2016). Taking the Public Service Remit Forward Across the Digital Boundary. *International Journal of Digital Television*, *7*(3), 273–295. https://doi.org/10.1386/jdtv.7.3.273_1.

Tremblay, G. (2016). Public Service Media in the Age of Digital Networks. *Canadian Journal of Communication*, *41*(1), 191–206. https://doi.org/10.22230/cjc.2016v41n1a3062.

Tremblay, G., & Brunelle, A. M. (2015). La gouvernance des systèmes de communication dans les sociétés de la connaissance: défis et enjeux. Presented at *Colloque International Panam VII*, Montréal (Quebec), 16 and 17 of July.

Wagner, M., & Berg, A. C. (2015). *Legal Focus: Governance Principles for Public Service Media*. Geneva: European Broadcasting Union. Retrieved June 13, 2020, from https://www.ebu.ch/files/live/sites/ebu/files/Publications/EBU-Legal-Focus-Gov-Prin_EN.pdf.

CHAPTER 9

Canadian Communication Policies in the Post-Netflix Era

Michel Sénécal and Éric George

It is September 2017. The Canadian Heritage[1] Minister announces the future directions of the programs, legislations, and organizations under the federal government's responsibility, including the mandate of the Canadian public broadcaster (Government of Canada 2017a). She thus takes the opportunity to publicize a concluded deal between the Liberal government and Netflix, the most active multinational online streaming platform in the country. The creation of Netflix Canada, the first branch outside of the United States, inaugurates a permanent presence of the

---

This article was translated from French to English by Siavash Rokni, Doctoral Candidate in Communication at Université du Québec à Montréal (UQAM).

M. Sénécal (✉)
TÉLUQ University, Quebec, QC, Canada
e-mail: michel.senecal@teluq.ca

É. George
Université du Québec à Montréal, Montréal, QC, Canada
e-mail: george.eric@uqam.ca

© The Author(s), under exclusive license to Springer Nature Switzerland AG 2021
M. Túñez-López et al. (eds.), *The Values of Public Service Media in the Internet Society*, Palgrave Global Media Policy and Business, https://doi.org/10.1007/978-3-030-56466-7_9

platform in the country. It guarantees the injection of $500 million for original works in Canada over the next five years, $25 million of which is allocated to French-language creations. The platform commits to ensuring the discoverability of Canadian productions among its subscribers in Canada and around the world (Government of Canada 2017b). In return, the agreement exempts Netflix from any form of taxation of its activities by the Canada Revenue Agency. The minister proudly affirms that the Canadian government will be seeking this type of engagement from other foreign digital platforms, the majority of which are American. Does not this agreement, the terms of which have remained confidential,[2] inaugurate major transformations in public policy in the communication and culture sectors in Canada, and Quebec?

This is the question at the heart of the analysis that is presented in this text. First, these new orientations are located and examined in the historicity of arguments formulated throughout the evolution of Quebec's and Canada's media spaces using the political economy of culture and communication as a critical lens. Next, transformations in the audiovisual industries and public policies associated with them are emphasized in relation to the deployment of digital networks, beginning with the Internet. Finally, their future is contemplated by looking at the way Netflix tries to influence public policy in its favor and by exploring the regulatory solutions that are proposed by the review panel examining the broadcasting and telecommunication legislative framework (2020).

1 An Indispensable Return to History

Historically, when looking at cases such as wired and wireless telegraphy, postal mail, and the printing press, we observe that the Canadian government has intervened very quickly in regulating the means of communication since the nineteenth century. While the forms of interventionism may have varied according to the goals of the political party in power (sometimes conservative, other times liberal), two major historical phases can be structurally distinguished. The first is under the banner of an increasingly active Keynesian state, as an economic agent from the period between the two world wars until the 1980s. The second is characterized by a state resolutely at the service of the private sector within the context of the rise of neoliberalism.

1.1 State or States[3]

As early as the 1920s, two central ideas defined the state interventionism that accompanied the structuring of the radio industry. First, following examples from previous infrastructures such as the railroad and the telegraph, the decision to map out the *Canadian territory* from east to west was made. The implementation of these means of communication thus traced the contours of a physical territory and national politics, due to their area of propagation, and forged an identity relationship with their usage, thanks to their symbolic importance. They played a detrimental role in the constitution of a specific national political territory to the extent that the term "technological nationalism" was used to characterize the phenomenon (Charland 1986).

Subsequently, it was deemed necessary to block the overflow of American radio waves in the Canadian media space, a relatively porous one due to the geographical proximity of the United States and the power of its broadcasting systems. The assertion of the territorial boundaries and the protection of a media space still in construction went hand in hand with the establishment of national policies regulating the Canadian broadcasting and telecommunications. Thus emerged the objective of *Canadianizing* the media space in order to counter what was already called at the time the *Americanization* of the airwaves. Such an attitude characterized itself in the edification of a public service system that included private and public organizations. In the 1930s, the Canadian government intended to manage the waves spectrum as a collective public good. It created a national universal public radio service in both official languages (English and French) with the Canadian Broadcasting Corporation (CBC)/Société Radio-Canada (SRC). Similar initiatives were implemented at the provincial level, especially in Quebec. However, with the exception of educational broadcasting, strictly within provincial jurisdiction, all initiatives were rejected by the federal government because of its constitutional preponderance in the regulation of broadcasting and telecommunications.

Decades later, the discourse of political legitimacy was still based on the necessity to maintain a sovereign culture and media space in the face of the American neighbor, to constitute a public service that is widely accessible and independent of commercial imperatives, and to ensure a relatively stable financial support for creation in the media and culture domains. To do this, a regulatory framework perpetuating these efforts was instituted and one of its flagship measures has since been the creation of the Canadian Radio-television and Telecommunication Commission (CRTC) in 1968 (Government of Canada 1968). The federal government established this regulatory body for the Canadian broadcasting system with the mandate "to safeguard, enrich and strengthen the cultural, political, social and economic fabric of Canada" and "encourage the development of Canadian expression by providing a wide range of programming that reflects Canadian attitudes, opinions, ideas, values and artistic creativity" (Government of Canada 1991).

Two types of measures have since been taken by the federal government for framing media practices. On the one hand, *restrictive* measures respond to certain protectionism of national identity by imposing limits to the broadcasting of foreign production (of which the majority are from the United States) on Canadian airwaves: hence the *quota policies*. The audiovisual broadcasting regulation, for example, obligates broadcasters to obtain a license under certain conditions. One of them forces TV stations to broadcast a certain percentage of Canadian content, between 50% and 60% during primetime (in the evenings), depending on the type of license granted. In the same spirit, constraints are imposed on the foreign ownership of Canadian companies set at 20% for the license holder and 33% for the holding company (CRTC 1987). On the other hand, *incentive* measures aim to ensure universal access to broadcasting and telecommunication services at reasonable cost and to subsidize national and local production in both official languages (feature films, television programs, recorded music, etc.), thanks to various forms of direct (grants) or indirect (tax credit, tax breaks) financing. This normative framework contributed to the development of the notion of *cultural exception*, first enshrined in the free trade agreement signed with the United States in 1987, then in 1992 with the United States and Mexico, and also in the agreement on the *Convention on Cultural Diversity* (UNESCO 2005), to which Canada is a signatory.

Without these measures, the Canadian system, composed of public, private, and community sectors since the Broadcasting Act of 1991, would not have been the diverse system that it is today (Government of Canada 1991). Contrary to the United States, where private companies have played a predominant role, or countries such as France, where the (quasi) monopoly of the state persisted until the 1980s, the Canadian system favored the cohabitation of public and private structures similar to those in the British broadcasting system for a long time. This coexistence began to take place in an increasingly competitive context with the proliferation of specialized broadcasting services and the diversification of technological platforms. However, it was due to this diversity that public institutions were set up, whether that be the regulatory bodies (CRTC), public broadcasting services (e.g., CBC/SRC, Télé-Québec, TV Ontario, etc.), or funding agencies for culture and media production (e.g., Telefilm Canada, Société de développement des entreprises culturelles du Québec, Canada Media Fund, etc.).

1.2 *The Neoliberal Turn of the 1980s*

In the 1980s, public policy took a "neoliberal" turn under the pretext that the liberalization of the communication sector and its participation in the dynamics of the global economy responds to social and cultural interests better. The role of the state was modified to the "supporter" of the changes resulting from this economic logic. Nevertheless, because of the small size of the Canadian markets in North America (anglophone, and especially francophone), their proximity to the United States, and the near impossibility of producing profitable works given high costs, public institutions continued to play an important role. This orientation favored certain institutions, at the forefront of which was Telefilm Canada, a major player in audiovisual production mainly catering to the specialized private television services, to the detriment of others, such as CBC/SRC.

From the 1990s onward, following public policies under the banner of convergence, competition between the cable and the telecommunication sectors was introduced at the very moment of the arrival of the Internet. This was a meteoric shift. In 1998, 36% of Canadian households (4.3 million households) had access to the Internet (Dickinson and Ellison 1999). Yet, in the following year, the CRTC avoided regulating the Internet, presuming that (1) there is no reason to apply broadcasting laws, since the majority of the services offered on the Internet consisted mainly of alphanumeric text; (2) "there is no apparent shortage of Canadian content on the Internet today. Rather, market forces are providing a Canadian Internet presence that is also supported by a strong demand for Canadian product"; (3) the new media "have not had any detrimental impact on conventional radio and television audiences." The Commission is of the view "that the effect of new media on television audience size will be limited at least until such time as high-quality video programming can be distributed on the Internet"; and (4) there "is no evidence that the Internet has had any negative financial impact on the advertising revenues of traditional broadcasters" (CRTC 1999a).

The CRTC order "exempts from regulation, without terms or conditions, all new media broadcasting undertakings that operate in whole or in part in Canada. New media broadcasting undertakings are those undertakings that provide broadcasting services delivered and accessed over the Internet" (CRTC 1999b). Under the pretext of being "readily adaptable to scientific and technological change" (CRTC 1999c), the commission supported the unconstrained emergence of these new platforms instead of adapting its laws to regulate their activities. This order was further renewed in 2006, 2009, 2012, and 2015.

During this period, failing to impose quotas on digital services accessible by the Internet, the CRTC "simply reduced the Canadian content and optional services quotas from local stations and simplified the licensing process by consolidating licenses for television programming services" by reducing the number of categories (Prescott 2015). In short, in order to encourage competition with new actors, the CRTC rather lightened the regulatory burden on Canadian broadcasters (CRTC 2015a, 2015b).[4]

2   A Changing Situation: New Questions

Twenty years later, the situation has evolved. Video contents transmitted through high-speed Internet networks occupy most of their bandwidth. Meanwhile, a large portion of television programming nowadays is distributed by Internet access providers to the detriment of traditional operators, cable and satellite distributors, and others. In fact, with a household penetration rate increase from 83.9% to 89% between 2013 and 2017, Internet access in Canada has been continuously growing (CRTC 2019, p. 27).[5] Over the same period, the number of subscribers to traditional television distribution services began to decline, with the rate of household subscribers falling from 81.5% to 72.3%. Meanwhile, 2017 was the first year that households spent more money on Internet access ($54.17) than on cable television ($52.80) (*ibid.*, p. 23), another indicator of the changes in the Canadian media landscape. Despite these trends, changes appear to be relatively slow. In 2018, for instance, 80% of Canadians watched television and 83% listened to the radio provided by traditional channels, while 56% of them consumed Internet-based television services and 63% streamed music on YouTube in the same year (*ibid.*, p. 129).

In regard to the foreign video-on-demand platforms, 70.1% of the English-speaking and 52% of the French-speaking population in Canada had subscribed to Netflix in 2018,[6] while 22.3% and 14.3% of them respectively had Amazon Prime Video subscriptions. During the same year, among Canadian services, 16.1% of the anglophone population subscribed to Crave (Bell),[7] while 21.1% and 14.7% of francophones subscribed to Tou.tv.Extra (SRC) and Club Illico (Québecor) respectively (CMF 2020, p. 6). These figures show that even if there are real modifications in consumption habits, particularly among those between 18 and 34 years of age,[8] substitution of services is proving to be taking longer than in the United States.

These changes have been causing significant disruptions. First, by exonerating Netflix and other foreign services from Goods and Services Tax (GST), the federal government has suddenly deprived itself and the provinces of approximately $100 million in annual tax revenues. Consequently, this has created inequalities in treatment, since the equivalent Canadian digital services (ex. Club illico, Crave, Tou.tv Extra) are required to charge their customers these taxes (Bergeron 2018). In other words, Ottawa has created an unfair regime by indirectly subsidizing a foreign company through a tax break to the detriment of traditional Canadian broadcasters. Meanwhile, the federal government has loudly and clearly announced its wish for a Creative Canada in its framework by investing "in Canadian creators, cultural entrepreneurs and their stories" and strengthening "public broadcasting and support local news" (Government of Canada 2017a).

The exemption granted to Netflix and other web majors operating in Canada has caused an outcry among provincial governments, directors and producers associations, private production companies, artists' unions, and organizations committed to culture and public service principles. While having divergent interests, these cultural and media players agree on the dangers of, on the one hand, accepting confidential unilateral negotiations by multinational companies with the central government, and on the other, bartering a tax exemption that would otherwise enrich public funds dedicated to audiovisual production. The 2017 declaration by the Coalition for Culture and Media, promoting the continuity, fairness, and support of the media and culture sectors in Canada, is an example of the organized protest that the federal government's position has faced (Coalition for Culture and Media 2017). Similarly, in 2019, Quebec adopted Bill-105 allowing the collection of Quebec Sales Tax (QST) from digital platforms, which is also applicable to all providers of intangible goods and online services including those established abroad (Government of Quebec 2018).

Beyond the Netflix case, the commercial success of such streaming platforms relies, in Canada as well as other countries, on the fact that they benefit from the lack of regulation of their activities. In this way, they not only avoid quotas, but also circumvent media chronology[9] to which traditional broadcasters are subject. Thus, Netflix can decide to present a film on its platform that it has produced or of which it bought the rights, regardless of whether or not it has been shown in cinemas or broadcasted on other media. This privilege allows the company to expand its catalogue more quickly and attract a wider customer base who, wishing to access films and series before their usual timelines, subscribe to digital services. Changes to the media chronology and movie windowing[10] would have a direct impact on value chains and the rules of the competition between players with unequal prerogatives.[11]

If the arrival of the Internet puts the basis of *restrictive* measures into question because of the apparent abundance in the diversity of cultural productions on the digital platform, then *incentive* measures appear to be more sustainable in the new environment. In order to promote their application, the Canadian government must once again defend the principle of cultural exception in the renegotiations of the free trade agreement between Canada, the United States, and Mexico. The new deal maintains the cultural exemption clause and integrates it into the digital realm. However, if needed, Washington can use the same clause to initiate retaliatory measures if it deems that Canada poses an economic threat. This clause has never been evoked in the past. However, with an agreement that now includes digital technologies, certain analysts have a more or less pessimistic view of the future (Bourgault-Côté 2018a).

Returning to Netflix now, the company with "a strong market value and a significant financial capacity that can hardly be competed with" is contributing to the globalization of cultural industries (Claus 2017, p. 20). All of this began when the Californian company, originally proposing the rent and purchase of DVDs in the United States, developed an online distribution service in 2007 and extended it abroad, starting with Canada in 2010. Today, its success is clearly international with a presence in more than 190 countries and a total of 167 million subscribers in 2019 (Netflix 2020). That said, certain major culture and communication industries in the United States such as Warner Media have decided not to offer their services abroad systematically. HBOMax, for example, was not launched in Canada following the extension of the exclusive long-term agreement between Warner Bros. and Bell Canada regarding Crave, its streaming service. However, like Netflix, other multinationals such as Amazon Prime Video, Apple TV, and Disney + are expanding internationally. Thus, there is clearly a rupture from strong association with notions such as national territory and media space on which public policies have been built upon so far.[12] In addition, the globalization of flow has taken various configurations. In the past ten years, one of the most striking trends in the growth of film and TV production in Canada has been that foreign production has taken the top place in dollar spent in the country, growing from $1770 million between 2007 and 2008 to $3757 million between 2016 and 2017 (CMPA 2017, pp. 15 and 81).

3   PUBLIC POLICY ACCORDING TO NETFLIX

The analysis following the 2017 signed agreement between the Canadian government and Netflix reveals a possible reorientation in public policy. The agreement required Netflix, as we remember, to invest $500 million in the Canadian film and television series production over a five years' period.[13] Only two years later, the company announced that it had already surpassed that amount (Brousseau-Pouliot 2019). It has been especially active in English Canada where it had already developed ties with CBC during the co-production of *Anne with an E* and with Corus entertainment for the first two seasons of *Travelers*. Since 2017, the series *Riverdale*, *The Umbrella Academy*, *The Order*, and *Altered Carbon* have all been filmed in Canada. Consequently, Netflix has opened production branches in Toronto and Vancouver by renting film studios. Its growth in Québec has been slower, focusing on the shooting of two films, *Murder Mystery* and *Jusqu'au déclin*, as well as the recording of comedy shows for its "Comedians of the World" series. *Murder Mystery,* partially shot in Montreal and Italy, is a comedy that takes place in the United States and Europe with two great American stars. Released in 2019, it was the most viewed film of the year on the platform in the United States. As for the film *Jusqu'au déclin*, the director, the writers, and the main actors are all from Quebec. Moreover, the film was shot in Quebec with workers from the province, and all the production, including its translation and English dubbing, was likewise done there. Released in 2020,[14] the film is the first authentic production from Quebec stamped with "Netflix Original," showing that the platform is reproducing the approach that it is already using elsewhere in the world by favoring co-production. But it is very difficult to see all these films and series as authentic Canadian or Quebec productions.

Understanding the rationale behind establishing a sustainable presence, through participation in local production, leads to important insights into the public policy strategies and the transformations that multinationals such as Netflix are envisioning with regard to the culture and communication sectors. Nevertheless, the local nature of this productions must be questioned. For example, neither the television series *Travelers* nor the film *Murder Mystery* has anything Canadian or Quebecois in them besides the fact that they were shot in Canada and therefore contribute to maintaining employment in Canadian and Quebec audiovisual industries. Moreover, the agreement between Netflix and Ottawa allows Netflix to account for all its investments in domestic productions, regardless of the proportion of Canadian content in the production.

This situation is not new, but it reveals the historical distinction between national economic order and national cultural order. The first is clearly more present in Netflix's investments during the last two years in Canada. In addition, it is not certain that all Netflix productions can be considered Canadian according to Telefilm's criteria. Indeed, to qualify as Canadian content, a production must meet strict criteria, including the number of significant Canadian artists in the production. Netflix's agreement with Ottawa does not subject it to the same Canadian content criteria as national media producers and distributors since the deal only requires monetary investments of the company in the country. For example, Netflix's film *Murder Mystery* counts as a Netflix investment in Canada under its agreement, but would probably not qualify as Canadian content.

Therefore, all comparisons between Netflix's investments and those linked to traditional mechanisms that audiovisual companies from Canada and Quebec have to follow for obtaining local financing are risky. However, it seems that, by injecting $250 million in production in Canada and Quebec per year for two years, Netflix has positioned itself in roughly the same range as the mainstream public television channel Ici Radio Canada, who invested $259 million in 2017–2018 (Brousseau-Pouliot 2019).[15]

Furthermore, more than ever, Netflix's strategy and the Canadian government's response bear witness to the penetration of the corporate sphere in that of the government (Musso 2019). Thus, above all, the government accompanies the private sector in order to attract investments and bends to the industry's conditions. In fact, the bridge between governments and the private sector has been expanded (staff exchanges, lobbying, confidential bilateral agreements, partnerships, etc.).

Finally, even though Quebec has created, notably according to its linguistic specificity, its own institutions as a "distinct society," Netflix refuses to distinguish it from Canada by claiming its inability to provide province-by-province investment figures. Despite its particular linguistic and cultural characteristics, Quebec is considered on an equal footing with the other provinces, which are, however, more homogeneous.

In short, existing regulation allows foreign platforms such as Netflix to distribute content directly in competitions with domestic television companies, which are still subject to national regulations. Moreover, they do not have to provide information related to their Canadian activities to the CRTC, do not pay taxes, and neither contribute to the Canadian public funding program for television and cinema, nor offer a minimum quota of Canadian content productions. Meanwhile, they are active on Canadian soil. Will this situation last?

4   And Now...

On the one hand, several public affairs analysts, journalists, and political commentators highlight the "dangerous links" that the federal government has maintained behind closed doors with web multinationals since 2017. "According to the register of lobbyists [...] consulted, there are 99 communication reports for Amazon and 37 for Google, including one with the Prime Minister himself. These two giants, as well as Microsoft and Netflix, want to influence the policies of the Trudeau government, including redesigning the Copyright Act and the Broadcasting Act" (Foisy 2017). In fact, "in the past 12 months, Netflix or a firm representing the company has met with Canadian decision-makers eight times" (*idem.*). This troubling proximity puts the federal government's will to regulate these multinationals and its real independence in facing their lobbying efforts into doubt.

On the other hand, long-term analysis from the past leads us to the conclusion that the promotion of cultural and linguistic diversity in the media, both traditional and emerging, has gone hand in hand with the right of the state to financially support content producers. Consequently, the freedom to implement regulatory instruments and support cultural policies has been considered as an overarching principle that goes against the idea that cultural production is like any other commodity and that it can be subjected to the laws of the market.

However, on the eve of the federal budget tabling in March 2018, after receiving several criticisms from cultural and political circles in relation to the tax inequities benefiting Netflix and other foreign-based services, the then Canadian Heritage Minister suddenly turned into a critic of the GAFAM (Google, Apple, Facebook, Amazon, Microsoft), arguing that they are a worrying threat and stating that they have to "respect our cultural politics, and also better distribute the benefits of their business model" and finally adding that "the Netflix deal has always been a transition […] deal, a way to get short-term money" (Bourgault-Côté 2018b). Was this a clear retreat on the question or an electoral maneuver of the Canadian Liberal Party in the run-up to the federal elections in the fall of 2019? These questions were indeed addressed during the electoral campaign and the debate between the leaders of the five major political parties, all of whom pledged to tackle fiscal inequalities. Subsequently, the new Canadian Heritage Minister, again from the Liberal Party, appeared to be open to the taxation of web giants.

Meanwhile, a group of experts mandated by the federal government in 2018 submitted their findings in a report titled *Canada's Communications Future: Time to Act* in 2020. Breaking from the previous policy of 1999, they recommended that all companies broadcasting and distributing content in the country have the same financial and regulatory obligations. Their proposal to replace the term "broadcasting undertaking" with "media content undertaking" is indicative of the envisioned modifications, since it establishes a regulatory terminology that no longer distinguishes between the types of media technologies used for distributing audiovisual works. In fact, the group proposes "to bring all those providing media content services to Canadians—whether online or through conventional means, whether foreign or domestic, whether or not they have a place of business in Canada—within the scope of the Broadcasting Act and under the jurisdiction of the CRTC" (Broadcasting and Telecommunications Legislative Review Panel 2020). Based on this principle, their report insists on going beyond the application of the federal tax (GST) to services provided by foreign companies by requiring them to contribute to the development of Canadian audiovisual industries. It is suggested that these companies allocate a percentage of their revenues to the Canadian Media Fund (CMF), just like cable companies and other television services who spend 5% of their revenue to fund Canadian production. This is how, thanks to these royalties, the CMF has succeeded in spending $346 million to the production of audiovisual works from 2018 to 2019 (Castonguay 2020).

5 Conclusion

At the moment of concluding this text, it is impossible to predict what position the Canadian government will adopt in view of the expert panel's recommendations. Their implementations will consist of introducing strong political choices that are based on a new vision representative of a set of collective interests rather than following the desires of the transnationals of this world.

The case of Netflix proves to be particularly emblematic of the type of governmental decisions that are essentially financially motivated. The international dimension of Netflix and its investment promises have raised, among the main actors in the culture and communication industry, as much hope for the investment of new money in their respective sectors (television, cinema, etc.) and "discoverability" (CRTC 2016) of their work on a global scale, as concerns about the overdetermination of these new business models in the prescription of a tailor-made cultural production model giving priority to commercial ambitions.

Finally, have financial challenges taken precedence over social, cultural, and political ones that have led, for almost a decade, the construction of the media space and cultural sovereignty of Canada, and particularly of Quebec? What is the real legitimacy of the domestic cultural production actors in the definition of national cultural politics? To what extent is it possible to backtrack once the "majors" of the web such as Netflix, nothing but a Trojan Horse, start dictating the way forward for the financing of audiovisual production?

In fact, Canadian and Quebec societies are in a pivotal period for saving their regulatory heritage, defending their cultural sovereignty, and maintaining a regulated public system. In short, on the eve of the adoption of new policies in the communication and culture sectors, discussions are initiated both regarding the future of the public broadcasting organization, the SRC/CBC, and the entire audiovisual system. Far from being an anecdotal episode in Canadian media history, there will have been a before and an after Netflix anyway!

Notes

1. Department that oversees, among other things, cultural and media industries.
2. "Netflix and Ottawa have exchanged just under 733 pages of emails in the months preceding the announcement of the Creative Canada Policy Framework […] the major part of these exchanges rests unknown since 660 pages (90%) are completely and 64 of them are partially redacted!" (Roy 2018). Furthermore, the Investment Canada Act (ICA) prohibits the federal government from disclosing the terms of the agreement without Netflix's authorization.
3. Formulation of Graham Spry, president of the Canadian Radio League, who had to ensure the application of the proposals carried out by the Royal Commission of Radio Broadcasting (1928). Spry wanted to signify that Canada has to choose between either establishing strong public policy in the culture and communication sectors, or letting the United States establish itself as the dominant player in this sector.
4. The development of the Internet led to questioning the relevance of national frontiers. The presence of large groups dominating market liberalization in Canada appears to be more relevant since they, starting with Bell, Quebecor, Rogers, and Telus, are supposed to be able to compete with the large international media groups.
5. The statistics available in May 2020 are essentially those that were produced between 2017 and 2018.
6. In 2018, Netflix had 7.7 million subscribers in Canada (about 54% of the households) and pocketed an estimated $1 billion, or 11.5 % of the $8.74 billion total revenue of the Canadian television market (Winseck 2019).
7. The subscription rate was only 4.5% for French speakers before the launch of Crave in French, in 2020.
8. In 2019, the percentage of households in Quebec subscribing to Netflix increased to 75% upon adding people between ages of 18 and 24 (CEFRIO 2019).
9. Media chronology defines the order of diffusion and the deadlines according to which the various modes of exploitation of a cinematographic work can take place, starting from the date of theatrical release.
10. The movie windowing defines the various modes of film distribution: theaters, video sell-through, video rental, pay-per-view, video on demand, internet rental, internet sell-through, pay television, and television (basic free).
11. Netflix acted more like a film company by giving itself the right to distribute its production as it sees fit. It should be remembered that Canada has always been part of the U.S. domestic film market and also that, unlike

broadcasting, there is no specific legislation for the film industry in Canada and Quebec. Regulation is more a matter of tacital agreements between industry players, since negotiating power seems to be mainly in the hands of distributors.
12. This rupture partially began with media technologies such as cable or direct-to-home satellite, which made it possible to receive more and more programming from overseas.
13. The amount of $500 million represents the value of Netflix's gross investment in Canadian productions (i.e., before the calculation of tax credits). Netflix is eligible for Canadian tax credits on the same basis as other producers.
14. In theaters for screening as part of the Quebec Cinema festival in February 2020 and then on the platform.
15. In 2018, the production of screen-based content in Canada (film, television, filming and visual effects) totaled $8.9 billion. About half of this amount ($4.77 billion, or 53%) represented foreign films shot in Canada and visual effects contracts from Canadian studios. The other half ($4.16 billion, or 47%) was Canadian content production by film and television producers. With some $250 million investments per year, Netflix thus represents about 3% of the country's content production industry.

References

Bergeron, M. (2018, February 28), Fiscalité : Netflix, Google et Facebook pas inquiétés, La Presse. Retrieved June 4, 2020, from https://www.lapresse.ca/affaires/economie/canada/201802/28/01-5155550-fiscalite-netflix-google-et-facebook-pasinquietes.php.

Bourgault-Côté, G. (2018a, October 26). Libre-échange: une limite à l'exception culturelle. *Le Devoir*. Retrieved June 4, 2020, from https://www.ledevoir.com/culture/539928/une-exception-culturelle-avec-des-limites.

Bourgault-Côté, G. (2018b, March 14). Ottawa hausse le ton face aux géants du Web. *Le Devoir*, 14/03/2018. Retrieved June 4, 2020, from https://www.ledevoir.com/politique/canada/522578/melanie-joly-face-aux-geants-du-web.

Broadcasting and Telecommunications Legislative Review Panel [chaired by Janet Yale]. (2020). Canada's communications future: Time to act. Ottawa, Government of Canada. Retrieved June 4, 2020, from https://www.ic.gc.ca/eic/site/110.nsf/eng/00012.html.

Brousseau-Pouliot, V. (2019, September 26). Productions canadiennes: l'engagement de Netflix réalisé en moins de deux ans. *La Presse*, Dossier. Retrieved June 4, 2020, from https://www.lapresse.ca/affaires/entreprise

s/201909/25/01-5242874-productions-canadiennes-lengagement-de-netflix-realise-en-moins-de-deux-ans.php.

Canada Media Funds—CMF. (2020). Closer, Wider, Faster: Annual Trends Report in the Audiovisual Industry. Retrieved June 4, 2020, from https://trends.cmf-fmc.ca/wp-content/uploads/Key-Trends-2020-Report-by-the-Canada-Media-Fund-1.pdf.

Canadian Media Producers Association—CMPA. (2017). Profil 2017. Rapport économique sur la production de contenus sur écran au Canada. Retrieved June 4, 2020, from https://www.aqpm.ca/85/profil.

Castonguay, A. (2020, January 30). Mettre au pas les géants du Web: l'héritage de Steven Guilbeault? *L'Actualité*. Retrieved June 4, 2020, from https://lactualite.com/politique/mettre-au-pas-les-geants-du-web-lheritage-de-steven-guilbeault/.

CEFRIO. (2019). Portrait numérique des foyers québécois, *NETendances 2019*, *10*(4). Retrieved June 4, 2020, from https://cefrio.qc.ca/media/2288/netendances-2019_fascicule-4_portrait-numérique-des-foyers-québécois_final.pdf.

Charland, M. (1986). Technological Nationalism. *Canadian Journal of Political and Social Theory*, *10*(1-2), 196-220. Retrieved June 4, 2020, from http://www.ctheory.net/library/volumes/Vol%2010%20No%201%20-%202/VOL10_NOS1-2_4.pdf.

Claus, S. (2017). Le débat sur la mondialisation culturelle à l'heure du "numérique": le cas de Netflix au Canada et au Québec. *COMMposite*, *19*(2). Retrieved June 4, 2020, from http://www.commposite.org/index.php/revue/article/view/257.

Coalition for Culture and Media. (2017). Declaration for the Sustainability and the Vitality of National Culture and Media in the Digital Era. Retrieved June 4, 2020, from https://www.standingforculture.info/.

CRTC (Canadian Radio-television and Telecommunications Commission). (1987). Television Broadcasting Regulations, 1987, SOR/87-49. Ottawa, Government of Canada. Retrieved June 4, 2020, from https://laws-lois.justice.gc.ca/eng/regulations/sor-87-49/index.html.

CRTC (Canadian Radio-television and Telecommunications Commission). (1999a). Public Notice CRTC 1999-84 May. Ottawa, Government of Canada. Retrieved June 4, 2020, from https://crtc.gc.ca/eng/archive/1999/pb99-84.htm.

CRTC (Canadian Radio-television and Telecommunications Commission). (1999b). Public Notice CRTC 1999-197. Exemption order for new media broadcasting undertakings. Ottawa, Government of Canada. Retrieved June 4, 2020, from https://crtc.gc.ca/eng/archive/1999/pb99-197.htm.

CRTC (Canadian Radio-television and Telecommunications Commission). (1999c). Broadcasting Notice of Consultation CRTC 2019-91. Ottawa,

Government of Canada. Retrieved June 4, 2020, from https://crtc.gc.ca/eng/archive/2019/2019-91.htm.
CRTC (Canadian Radio-television and Telecommunications Commission). (2015a). Broadcasting Regulatory Policy CRTC 2015-86. Ottawa, Government of Canada. Retrieved June 4, 2020, from https://crtc.gc.ca/eng/archive/2015/2015-86.htm.
CRTC (Canadian Radio-television and Telecommunications Commission). (2015b). Broadcasting Regulatory Policy CRTC 2015-96. Ottawa, Government of Canada. Retrieved June 4, 2020, from https://crtc.gc.ca/eng/archive/2015/2015-96.htm.
CRTC (Canadian Radio-television and Telecommunications Commission). (2016). Discoverability summit. Content in the Age of Abundance. 10-11 May. Retrieved June 4, 2020, from http://discoverability.ca/.
CRTC (Canadian Radio-television and Telecommunications Commission). (2019). Communications Monitoring Report 2019. Ottawa, Government of Canada. Retrieved June 4, 2020, from https://crtc.gc.ca/pubs/cmr2019-en.pdf.
Dickinson, P., & Ellison, J. (1999). Branchés sur Internet. *Tendances sociales canadiennes*, 55, 8-11. Ottawa, Statistique Canada. Retrieved June 4, 2020, from http://www.statcan.gc.ca/pub/11-008-x/1999003/article/4786-fra.pdf.
Foisy, P.-V. (2017). Google, Amazon, Microsoft et Facebook à l'assaut du gouvernement canadien. *Radio-Canada*, 31/10/2017. Retrieved June 4, 2020, from https://ici.radio-canada.ca/nouvelle/1064360/netflix-facebook-microsoft-google-web-lobby-lobbysime-trudeau-ottawa.
Government of Canada. (1968). *Canadian Radio-television and Telecommunications Commission Act*. Ottawa: Ministry of Justice.
Government of Canada. (1991). Broadcasting Act. Ottawa, Ministry of Justice. Retrieved June 4, 2020, from https://laws-lois.justice.gc.ca/eng/acts/b-9.01/FullText.html.
Government of Canada. (2017a). Creative Canada Policy Framework. Ottawa, Government of Canada. Retrieved June 4, 2020, from https://www.canada.ca/en/canadian-heritage/campaigns/creative-canada/framework.html.
Government of Canada. (2017b). Launch of Creative Canada—The Honourable Mélanie Joly, Minister of Canadian Heritage. September 28. Ottawa, Government of Canada. Retrieved June 4, 2020, from https://www.canada.ca/en/canadian-heritage/news/2017/09/creative_canada_-avisionforcanadascreativeindustries.html.
Government of Quebec. (2018). An Act to improve the performance of the Société de l'assurance automobile du Québec, to better regulate the digital economy as regards e-commerce, remunerated passenger transportation and tourist accommodation and to amend various legislative provisions. Bill n°150, approved on June 12, 2018, Quebec.

Musso, P. (2019). *Le temps de l'État-Entreprise: Berlusconi, Trump, Macron*. Paris: Fayard.

Netflix. (2020). Company Profile. Retrieved June 4, 2020, from https://www.netflixinvestor.com/ir-overview/profile/default.aspx.

Prescott, S. M. (2015, March 25). CRTC Dramatically Shifts Canadian Television Regulation. *Communication Bulletin, Fasken*. Retrieved June 4, 2020, from https://www.fasken.com/fr/knowledge/2015/03/communicationsbulletin-20150325/.

Roy, J.-H. (2018, January 28). 733 pages de courriels entre Netflix et le gouvernement fédéral. Retrieved June 4, 2020, from http://jhroy.ca/2018/01/courriels-netflix-gouv-federal/.

UNESCO. (2005). Convention on the Protection and Promotion of the Diversity of Cultural Expressions. October 20, UNESCO. Retrieved June 4, 2020, from http://portal.unesco.org/en/ev.php-URL_ID=31038&URL_DO=DO_TOPIC&URL_SECTION=201.html.

Winseck, D. (2019). Growth and Upheaval in the Network Media Economy in Canada, 1984-2018, report. Canadian media Concentration Project—CMCRP. Retrieved June 4, 2020, from http://www.cmcrp.org/wp-content/uploads/2019/12/Growth-and-upheaval-in-the-network-media-economy-1984-2018-REPORT-10122019.pdf.

CHAPTER 10

Public Service Media Interventions: Risk and the Market

Marta Rodríguez-Castro, Caitriona Noonan, and Phil Ramsey

This chapter focuses on the relationship between Public Service Media (PSM) and the market through the lens of risk. Much discussion of PSM posits their positive cultural and social influence, while discussions of 'market impact' have often functioned to tighten control on PSM organizations and limit their remit and scale. Indeed, the discussion of market impact has often been deployed strategically as a rationale to slim down

M. Rodríguez-Castro (✉)
Department of Communication Sciences, Universidade de Santiago de Compostela, Santiago de Compostela, Spain
e-mail: m.rodriguez.castro@usc.gal

C. Noonan
Cardiff University, Cardiff, UK
e-mail: noonanc@cardiff.ac.uk

P. Ramsey
Ulster University, Belfast, UK
e-mail: pt.ramsey@ulster.ac.uk

© The Author(s), under exclusive license to Springer Nature Switzerland AG 2021
M. Túñez-López et al. (eds.), *The Values of Public Service Media in the Internet Society*, Palgrave Global Media Policy and Business, https://doi.org/10.1007/978-3-030-56466-7_10

173

organizations perceived as bloated and slow. However, discussing the market role of PSM organizations is important for a number of reasons, not least as a useful discursive frame for the financing of PSM and, for instance, their impact on national advertising markets. A discussion of market impact also recognizes the increasingly blurred line between linear broadcasting and digital media, with PSM activities increasingly focused on the latter. Seismic changes have happened in the infrastructure of broadcasting and audiences today expect interactivity and online services. Whereas in the past regulators such as the European Commission were more 'restrictive' of PSM's online efforts (Brevini 2013), today it seems archaic to approach public media as relating to 'off-line' content distribution alone. Therefore, it is a matter of public value and of survival for PSM to engage with the opportunities and challenges of the digital market.

Furthermore, market impact re-centers questions of power within the media market at a critical juncture in the evolution of information and digital infrastructures and the uncertainty which accompanies that change. Much policy discourse assumes that PSM organizations are omnipotent agents within their national media markets, and in many national cases they remain central media organizations enjoying high audience share. However, in key strategic ways their power has diminished. The growth of 'super indies' (very large international independent production companies) and the aggressive localizing strategies adopted by transnational media companies like Netflix and Disney means there are new formations of power. Added to this are technology companies like Apple and Amazon entering the market for television content, with both deep financial pockets and access to large-scale technical infrastructure. Today, these are powerful actors within media markets, as they leverage national resources and crowd out competition. However, policymakers can seem reluctant or ill-equipped to intervene in these forms of market impact.[1]

This chapter considers the interventions and innovativeness of PSM, not as activities which distort market competition, but as actions which create and sustain markets thereby expanding the terms of public support (see, e.g., EBU 2019). Of course, some will argue that positioning these organizations as market players may erode the distinctiveness of PSM, however, as we develop below, there are significant ways that PSM organizations through their operations and resources contribute strategically to media markets and the protection of national/local economic interests in ways that are often unlikely to be matched by commercial players.

Recognizing that uncertainty and change are fundamental features of both sectoral and national interests, we adopt a lens which repositions market impact in terms of the active role that PSM organizations play in negotiating and partly mitigating the economic *risks* of the broadcasting market.[2] We find the frame of risk a useful one to apply in the context of PSM, and we recognize the work of Beck (1992) on the 'risk society' which critically considers processes of modernization and the role of the state therein. As Hjort (2012) argues, risk is at the nexus of an interdisciplinary conversation which allows for a deeper understanding of media making that goes beyond national context or a specific policy frame and therefore we draw on it as a valuable comparative lens. In the context of the broadcast market, "the digitization of television has considerably increased the sources of uncertainties and the levels of risks for the rapidly expanding number of players involved in broadcasting" (Chalaby and Segell 1999, p. 354). The speed of change and the technical, political, and cultural complexities of the broadcasting market generate substantially more threats. At the same time the number of stakeholders extracting value from content has risen rapidly: for example, high-end dramas leverage value for a range of stakeholders, both within and outside broadcasting (McElroy and Noonan 2019).

In this context PSM organizations are *perceived* to be affluent and secure in relation to other stakeholders. Despite the widespread cuts to their budgets, their modes of funding are deemed less precarious compared to the financial risks faced by commercial players, especially where PSM organizations are funded from license fees or taxation. This is augmented by the fact that in many contexts they still enjoy high levels of public reach, trust, and recognizability. Whilst this doesn't make PSM exempt from risk, they are perceived as better able to negotiate its impact but also mitigate other forms of risk that circulate within the market. Therefore, this chapter considers some ways in which the PSM system is a space where some of the structural risks of production are being redistributed through a range of wider policy initiatives. By assuming this risk, publicly funded organizations are performing a vital function which then underpins many of the market activities of commercial stakeholders and national strategies for economic growth.

This chapter identifies two key areas of risk that PSM organizations are actively negotiating and/or as part of a change to their remit and responsibilities: first, in creating and sustaining a supply base of indigenous content, and second, in contributing to innovation capacity. In both of these policy agendas, PSM organizations are instrumental to the shaping of markets. Whilst we don't argue that all PSM organizations are engaging in these equally, or even delivering effectively on these agendas, we want to highlight the important contribution that PSM makes to creative economies and to economic and cultural activity within nation states more generally. We identify the different ways this market role is being realized and point to the tensions in this new set of expectations where PSM organizations are simultaneously required to do both less and more in economic terms. The chapter concludes by arguing that by undermining the scale and funding of PSM their capacity to assume that risk is weakening, and that this will have implications for the entire marketplace.

1 Conceptualizing Market Impact

In Europe, the establishment of public service broadcasters was justified first on the basis of spectrum scarcity, and second, on the basis of spectrum limitations (Bonet et al. 2008). Indeed, a look back at the history of the establishment of broadcasting casts light on the origins of the perpetual debates around how PSM should be justified, when for many decades in the twentieth century the principle of publicly owned–and–run broadcasting systems held sway (though there were detractors from this position) (Burri 2017, pp. 11–12). However, as technology developed, and latterly digital media started to thrive, spectrum limitations were no longer seen as a valid argument, and criticism of PSM's continuance started to intensify (Sieg and Stühmeier 2015; Aigner et al. 2018). This has placed ever greater scrutiny on the sources of funding for PSM, the way in which it is used, and the implications of those activities for other players in the market. Around the world, PSM organizations operate under a variety of funding systems. However, a recurring theme in many settings is the overt scrutiny from some quarters of their impact on the market.

A key issue in understanding how the market impact of PSM has been considered is the concept of market failure, a concept which "tends to be used in two different ways" (Doyle 2013, p. 92):

> In one sense it refers to any failure by the market system—the unbridled forces of demand and supply—to allocate resources efficiently. In another sense, it may refer to the failure of the market to advance socially desirable goals other than efficiency, eg. preserving democracy and social cohesion. (Doyle 2013, p. 92)

It is the latter understanding which has been the focus of media policy debate since the liberalization of broadcasting, when broadcasting markets opened up under the influence of a shift toward neoliberal economics (Potschka 2012, p. 11). However, as digitization and the Internet started to favor the emergence of new media services, this concern was reinforced (Van den Bulck and Donders 2014, p. 85). Often, this has become a debate about whether *public broadcasting should only provide what the market does not*: this can be termed the *crowding-out hypothesis*, advocated by those who argue that "services readily available on the market should be delivered not through state intervention but free entrepreneurship" (Van den Bulck and Donders 2014, p. 85).

Such arguments have been driven by market fundamentalist accounts of society (e.g., Booth 2016; Peacock 2004), where PSM appears at best anachronistic, and at worst a distorting factor that holds back private media organizations from reaching their full potential. These fundamentalist accounts have not, however, remained in the economic textbook. Indeed, there is a tradition of economists playing a direct role in influencing broadcasting policy (Barwise and Picard 2014, p. 8). Accounts have continually cropped up in many international settings where politicians, often on the Right of the political spectrum, have targeted PSM funding. For example, the Trump administration in the USA (2017–2021) repeatedly tried to eliminate federal funding for PSM (Benton 2019); in Australia, PSM has faced sustained political pressure (Meade 2018), with the ABC's "real funding… [decreasing] by 28%" since the 1980s (ABC 2018); and in June 2018 Denmark's right-wing government introduced a "controversial" media settlement which increased subsidies to the press but reduced "total public funding of media by €54m" resulting in a 20% cut in funding for DR, the main PSM organization, while subsidies available to the press were increased (Schrøder and Ørsten 2019). For many PSM organizations worldwide there is a substantial and recurring threat to their financial viability.

Both the theoretical accounts and political actions we have addressed here are often predicated on the idea that media goods *should not play* any public role, but rather should be treated like other kind of good. However, as copious amounts of scholarship contend, PSM ought not be seen in that way: in a persuasive example Sehl et al. (2020) looked at the possible influence between PSM budgets and commercial media and pay TV revenues. They found no correlation between them, nor between PSM's news reach and commercial news reach or paying for online news. As such, they concluded that there was little support for the crowding out argument. On the contrary, their analysis did show that in some cases the existence of a strong PSM correlates with strong commercial media (Sehl et al. 2020).

Across Europe PSM organizations have been required to justify their activities, and planned expansions, with reference to—among other areas—their impact on the market and under the terms of the public value tests (Donders and Moe 2012). This has happened in relation to specific decisions (e.g., the move of BBC Three online, see Ramsey 2018) but has also seen PSM organizations provide systematic details of their broader impact on the economies where they are based (e.g., BBC 2013) or provide defenses of their value for money (e.g., ABC 2018). Indeed, some PSM organizations have also increased their use of economic arguments to defend themselves from the attacks of commercial media. D'Arma (2018a, p. 9) explains how the BBC started to fight the "crowding out" argument by focusing on how the public broadcaster prompts a "race to the top" along with commercial media. He points out that it is transnational Internet companies that are really crowding out the media environment, and that the BBC "began to challenge increasingly widespread perceptions of its activities as inhibiting private sector expansion by placing growing emphasis on its enabling role in the growth of the wider creative sector" (D'Arma 2018a, p. 9), a point we take up later.

In the move toward the quantification of the economic impact of PSM on the broader economy, PSM organizations have often sought to measure their impact in terms of a multiplier effect: this entails measuring "the level an economy will grow following a change in the level of investment" (McElroy and Noonan 2019), where the economic return of each amount of money is measured, and then used as a means of justifying that investment. As such, examples of PSM organizations that have used multipliers to evidence their economic impact include:

- the BBC in the UK, which generates "two pounds of economic value for every pound of the licence fee" (BBC 2013, p. 4);
- VRT in Belgium, where "€1 in public funding generates 2.51 euro" (Raats et al. 2018);
- TG4 in Ireland, where "€1 invested … in the creative industries in Ireland, it was worth almost €2 to the Irish economy" (TG4 2018, p. 17);
- S4C in Wales, where "every £1 invested by S4C in the economy in Wales and the UK creates a total value of £2.09" (S4C 2017).

A measurement of the economic contribution of PSM has also been used in the arguments for *new* PSM services. For example Monk et al. (2019), argued in relation to the prospect of establishing a PSM organization for Cornwall in the UK—a region that has a strong cultural and linguistic identity distinct to that of Britishness or Englishness—that "Investment in a PSM for Cornwall would have a significant positive economic impact both through direct activity and indirect and induced multipliers."

On the one hand this points to the positive contribution of PSM organizations relative to their size and their capacity to grow the economy beyond the creative market. However, as has been argued in the film and television production literature (Ramsey et al. 2019), solely measuring economic impact can be something of a 'blunt instrument', where it doesn't take into account the broader social impact. As D'Arma (2018b) has pointed out, the BBC did try to widen out the use of the multiplier effect in its foundational document on public value. There, the BBC (2004, p. 29) argued:

> Part of the BBC's public value is indirect. Through its relationships with other organisations, the BBC can have a 'multiplier' impact on society. For example, the BBC's recent Big Read collaboration with libraries and book publishers reawakened interest in reading.

Indeed, the BBC did through *Building Public Value* (BBC 2004) set out a broad argument for how the institution's contribution to public value could include aspects like 'Social and community value' and 'Cultural and creative value', values echoed in work by the European Broadcasting Union (EBU 2012). However, when the public value framework was applied in actuality in the regulation of the BBC's services, the overwhelming focus on quantitative data at the expense of qualitative data limited its efficacy for capturing the complexity of broadcasting's social and cultural value. Furthermore, the placing of evidence into the public domain that their activities have positive economic impact does not necessarily protect PSM organizations from criticism: instead evidence-based arguments often fall on deaf ears amongst politicians and policy-makers. Therefore, rather than just focus on discrete economic indicators like the multiplier as a signal of market impact, we consider more nuanced forms of market interventions that PSM organizations perform, when they act as a driving force of local industry and national economic sustainability, through engaging with some of the risks of the media market.

2   Shaping the Market

In this section we consider the contribution PSM makes to the economy when viewed in terms of risk: supporting a diverse and abundant supply base, and cultivating innovation. We regard these areas as instrumental both to the realization of a sustainable creative ecology and to delivering public value. We echo Mazzucato and O'Donovan (2016, p. 101) who, in relation to the BBC, argue that instead of "beginning with a market failure framework … we view the BBC through a market creation and market shaping framework." Criticizing the market failure lens, they suggest that such an approach "is misplaced as it does not capture the BBC's leadership role in the UK's incredibly vibrant culture industry—producing high quality affordable services, with a strong notion of public value that goes beyond a notion of public good" (Mazzucato and O'Donovan 2016, p. 102). Therefore, we extend this rationale to explore how PSM organizations—across different national settings and policy imperatives—can make substantial contributions to the economic goals and market formations of different nations.

2.1   Sustaining a Supply Base

The growth of the independent sector has been a critical economic goal within policy. The independent production sector is politically and economically attractive because it is characterized by entrepreneurship, encourages competition in the market, and is associated with 'good work'. In political and market terms the ideal scenario would be a plentiful number of indies and freelancers, who are varied in terms of skills and geography, thereby providing choice, competition, and innovation. However, this ambition is often tempered by the reality of what is a large number of financially fragile production companies and precarious labor structures, the latter vividly exposed during the Covid-19 pandemic (McElroy 2020). This precarity and the accompanying consolidation of companies into 'super-indies' risks diminishing the supply base of television production and this has significant implications for domestic production (Doyle 2019). In part this lapse in the supply base is a cultural risk, as a nation can become invisible on global scale, however, it is also a market concern as fewer production companies are independent and indigenous and therefore profits flow outward from the nation. In a number of overlapping ways PSM organizations are a direct way of sustaining domestic capacity in production especially from smaller and regional independent producers.

This value is delivered partly through the commissioning strategies of PSM, especially in their commissioning of original productions with PSM, often the most important sources of original content in many national markets. For example, Donders et al. (2020) outline the cultural and economic value of commissioning strategies that lead to domestic programming which is sourced locally and is distinctive. We extend that role to consider the labor markets which these commissions underpin. Voluminous returning series (the soap opera being one example) offer workers access to regular work in their locale and the opportunity for progression and development. For example, TG4's production of the Irish language soap opera *Ros na Rún* (1996–) supports around 150 jobs in the rural economy of Spidéal and provides "really good employment and a training ground for people to learn the ropes" (Interviewee from Screen Producers Ireland, as cited in McElroy et al. 2018). Developing a creative labor market is sometimes framed by national policy-makers as part of a transition to a more complex market structure, which will in turn generate greater economic value and local market growth. By offering occupational stability and professional mobility these productions form a base from which a sustainable creative labor market can develop.

The relevance of PSM's organizations in the shaping of the labor market can also be evidenced with the drastic example of a closure. When the PSM organization of the Valencian Community (Spain), RTTV, was shut down in 2013 (see Chap. 5), the unemployment rate of the Valencian audiovisual sector rose to 90%, 60% of the journalists of the region were jobless, and over 150 production and advertisement companies closed down as well (CECUV 2015). The PSM organization proved to be essential for the sustainability of the Valencian creative industries, one of the main reasons behind its reestablishment in 2016.

Crucially, in the quest to lure international investment, the labor market is often a prominent part of the package promoted by nations, alongside other forms of 'soft money' (see Ramsey et al. 2019). However, what is overlooked are the ways PSM organizations shoulder the financial burden and risk of creating and sustaining this labor market both through commissioning content and other activities such as training and apprenticeships. Other broadcasters and stakeholders are then able to leverage this investment alongside a broad range of other fiscal incentives. In her evidence to the UK House of Lords (Parliament) 2019 inquiry on public service broadcasting, Philippa Childs, head of the production union Bectu, told the committee that publicly funded broadcasters were "providing the training and skills that the likes of Netflix and others are then happily accepting" (House of Lords 2020). Therefore, we argue that PSM organizations contribute directly on the promises of labor policy within the creative and digital economy.

PSM organizations have also become critical elements within strategies for creative clustering and local development policies. In the UK, for instance, the development of a creative hub of television production in Cardiff was predicated on the building of the BBC's studio at Roath Lock in the city (McElroy and Noonan 2019). Elsewhere in Brussels, there are plans for the development of 'a creative and vibrant new Brussels district for an innovative media ecosystem' (Mediapark.brussels 2020) which will include office space, housing, and leisure facilities, anchored by new headquarters for both Belgian public broadcasters, VRT and RTBF. But as Komorowski et al. (2018) suggest in their overall analysis of the project, "the success of government-driven clusters is not guaranteed." Both the British and Belgian initiatives use publicly funded media organizations as central tenants of these predominantly commercial sites in order to leverage potential gains. The benefits of scale to the surrounding creative ecosystem and the accumulated knowledge, expertise, and resources which PSM organizations contain are leveraged by a range of neighboring bodies.

In parallel to this strengthening of creative economies, on occasion there is political expectation on PSM organizations to address regional inequalities in areas often beset by industrial decline. In the UK this has been part of a decade-long policy drive to decentralize and relocate activities to areas out of London and the south of England and to alter the natural movement of creative and labor markets by helping to develop significant creative activities in regions that do not, and may never, benefit from larger infrastructure or large-scale employers from the private sector. Substantial strategic interventions, such as the BBC's relocation of some functions to Salford (Greater Manchester), are regarded as an accelerator of this process. These interventions have been presented politically as a way of promoting efficiencies (through lower cost studios, post-production facilities, and wages in these regions), even when the actual data supporting this rationale can be problematic (Kemeny et al. 2020). In 2019 following a very competitive bidding process by several cities in the UK,

Channel 4 (a commercial PSM organization) announced its intention to build a new national headquarters in Leeds, with smaller hubs in Bristol and Glasgow. Staff from their current central London office are being distributed across these sites as a way of shifting the location patterns of economy activity in the long-term. In this strategy PSM organizations are seen as mobile and politically desirable for the places they 'land' furthering the creative professionalization of local economies.

Therefore, PSM are critical to widening and deepening the supply base of companies and labor from which all players in the media benefit. They grow the domestic creative economy by investing in indigenous independent production and contribute to the development of a skilled freelance workforce. They often undertake these activities as a counter to the centralizing tendency of the market. This offers a different understanding of pluralism and diversity which merges economic and social objectives and is in direct response to wider market risks.

2.2 Supporting Digital Innovation

Another area where we can view the contribution of some PSM organizations to the market is in terms of their structured approaches to innovation at a time when there is a fusion of several technologies in the media market including broadcasting, telecommunications, and computing. For some PSMs, innovation is embedded in their mission and organizational structures and it can extend beyond the media market to national systems of innovation and digital infrastructure (e.g., the BBC's role in the establishment of digital television, alongside other commercial PSM organizations and commercial broadcasters). Media innovation is continuous and requires continual investment, expertise, and resources, which PSM are perceived as well-placed to deliver.

Innovation is also part of the social function of PSM (Evans 2018; Fernández-Quijada et al. 2015; Zaragoza Fuster and García Avilés 2020), and as a route to integrating public value in a digital future characterized by interactivity, personalization, and platform migration, which is of course not without its issues. In this PSM is attempting to reconcile technological advances with other public goals such as reaching young people, solving issues like misinformation (e.g., BBC Blue Room), enhancing access to minority communities, but also building research and development (R&D) capacity. Viewed in these terms, innovation can be seen as part of the public good, as PSM organizations can assume the financial risks that private media might be unable or unwilling to take. When new knowledge is created and shared with other market actors, it can offer commercial entities additional resources. This return from PSM innovation to the market is partly evidenced by Netflix's CEO Reed Hastings, who acknowledged that the BBC iPlayer "really blazed the trail" for his company by getting "people used to this idea of on-demand viewing" (Williams 2014). Indeed, this statement is recognition of the risks taken in the changing culture by the PSM, which then allows the market to capitalize.

Here we offer a further situated example of innovation interventions in action. In 2015, VRT (the Flemish public service broadcaster) established a new project, VRT Sandbox. It was aimed at "organizing innovative collaborations with start-ups and entrepreneurs" (VRT 2020). Through the program, the PSM organization sought to find synergies that could accelerate innovation both within VRT and the wider media and technology market. This collaboration project offered Flemish and international start-ups the chance to develop their products in a safe environment, with access to the public broadcaster's content and tools, its workers—who can coach and advise them—and VRT's contacts network. One of the last projects tested in 2020 was *Just in Time*, a collaboration between *Fallound* and VRT Radio and VRT Pilootzone. The project was described as "the VRT podcast app on the go." By combining Fallout's patented technology and the VRT Radio's content, *Just in Time* offered a curation of short fragments of audio content available in its own app. The main asset of this project was its playlists, tailored according to the interest of the users and the time they have available. After this experience, both parts have learned that there is a demand for personalized podcasts in the Belgian market and that users were looking for short content, from 3 to 11 minutes.

The benefits of VRT Sandbox have been discussed elsewhere (Raats et al. 2018; MediaRoad 2017).[3] A project like this contributes to knowledge sharing and to advancing technological innovation in the sector. By providing a platform for start-ups to develop their products and assume a risk that private companies might be unable to take, the start-up can leverage expertise and access to audiences in a way which is not within the resources of most companies. Moreover, they can gain visibility with media investors as they retain the intellectual property (IP) for the product.

While the main benefit of this intervention for PSM includes a boost to its internal innovation and an opportunity to strengthen their relationships with stakeholders, this intervention also represents significant risk for the broadcaster including the ever-present danger of failure associated with innovation. As Van den Bulck (2007, p. 38) argues, PSM organizations must be careful "not to become a laboratory for expensive experiments without an actual aim or added value for (paying) individuals. It is not the task of PSB to support the expensive toys of the few." This must be a meaningful opportunity with which to extend the values of PSM to the digital landscape. We also see value in leveraging innovation which allows renewed vitality of PSM goals, rather than technology for its own sake.

In relation to both the supply base and innovation, PSM's role includes "growing symbiotic partnerships" (Mazzucato and O'Donovan 2016) and acting as "coordinators for all the media ecosystems conceptualized as 'innovation ecosystems'" (Ibrus et al. 2019, p. 4). The establishment of relationships with other media actors counters some of the crowding out thesis, and considers the public sector as "positive, co-productive agent" (Ibrus et al. 2019, p. 4). The relationship between public value and collaboration strategies has been highlighted by Raats et al. (2014, p. 267), and in the past few years there has been an increase in public-private collaborations in the media sector, mainly as a response to the increasing criticism of PSM's digital expansion (Wauters and Raats 2018, p. 176). The success of Roath Lock Studios or the Sandbox model, as examples, point to a new way to combine internal innovation and external collaboration. These kinds of collaborations contribute to strengthen PSM's role as "keystone species" (Wauters and Raats 2018, p. 188) who can mitigate some of the risks of the contemporary media market.

3 Conclusion

This chapter highlights the 'spill over' effects of PSM systems in media markets. We conclude that the framing of PSM in terms of risk allows for a useful vantage point for market impact, in order to add greater nuance to policy making and moves away from the problematic quantitative measure of things like the multiplier effect. It also offers a useful way in which to frame impact because of the considerable changes taking place within media markets and the expanded range of stakeholders who extract value from broadcasting (including property developers, city authorities, education providers, tourism bodies, etc.).

Our examples and analysis point to some of the ways that PSM mitigate some of the risks inherent within media markets. In two key areas we have considered the risks being negotiated in service of the wider market: supplier and labor capacity and innovation practices. In each area PSM can increase capacity over the long term which is then used by others, stimulating a further wave of economic growth. They are able to do this because of their scale and longevity relative to other creative bodies and business organizations. Rather than holding back private media, they are instead part of a risk reduction strategy which benefit the wider media market. However, cuts to their scale and resources diminish their agility and 'courage' to undertake systematic risk, but also their ability to leverage the rewards (the outcome of successfully negotiating risks). Therefore, we see considerable value in the role played by PSM in the effective functioning of media markets, and add our voices to those arguing for their protection in future funding settlements.

Acknowledgments This chapter is part of the activities of the research project (RTI2018-096065-B-100) of the Spanish State Program of R + D + I oriented to the Challenges of Society of the Ministry of Science, Innovation and Universities (MCIU), State Research Agency (SRA), and the European Regional Development Fund (ERDF) on "New values, governance, financing and public audiovisual services for the Internet society: European and Spanish contrasts."

Notes

1. We recognize that some political efforts are being made to rebalance the market for instance by imposing obligations to promote European content (European Commission 2020), or through fighting corporate tax avoidance by digital companies (European Parliament 2019).
2. The authors recognize the critical role that PSM can play in taking creative risks and innovating within genre, style, and forms as part of their program-making activities. However, for the purposes of this chapter, we focus on risk as a market-based concern.
3. The economic impact of VRT Sandbox was a 90% increase of the start-ups' staff and almost a 20 million euro boost of their capital (Raats et al. 2018). The success of the VRT Sandbox attracted international attention that eventually led to the establishment of the Sandbox Hub, a new platform launched in 2017 within the EU-funded project MediaRoad.

References

ABC. (2018). *Your ABC: Efficient, Trusted, Valued. Yours, Now & into the Future*. Retrieved June 10, 2020, from https://about.abc.net.au/wp-content/uploads/2018/02/FINAL_a11y_ABC_Efficiency_Paper_A4_Final-Ammended.pdf.

Aigner, R., Mattes, A., & Pavel, F. (2018). Es gibt weiterhin ökonomische Argumente für einen öffentlichen Rundfunk. *Wirtschaftsdienst, 97*(1), 45–52. https://doi.org/10.1007/s10273-017-2082-9.

Barwise, P., & Picard, R. G. (2014). *What If There Were No BBC Television? The Net Impact on UK Viewers*. Oxford: Reuters Institute for the Study of Journalism. Retrieved June 10, 2020, from https://reutersinstitute.politics.ox.ac.uk/sites/default/files/2017-06/What%20if%20there%20were%20no%20BBC%20TV_0.pdf.

BBC. (2004). *Building Public Value: Renewing the BBC for a Digital World: Renewing the BBC for a Digital World*. London: BBC.

BBC. (2013). *The Economic Value of the BBC: 2011/12 A Report by the BBC*. London: BBC. Retrieved June 10, 2020, from http://downloads.bbc.co.uk/aboutthebbc/insidethebbc/howwework/reports/pdf/bbc_economic_impact_2013.pdf.

Beck, U. (1992). *Risk Society: Towards a New Modernity*. London: Sage.

Benton, J. (2019, March 11). Trump Wants to Kill Federal Funding for PBS and NPR (Again); It Won't Happen, But It's Still Damaging. *NiemanLab*. Retrieved June 10, 2020, from https://www.niemanlab.org/2019/03/trump-wants-to-kill-federal-funding-for-pbs-and-npr-again-it-wont-happen-but-its-still-damaging/.

Bonet, M., Civil i Serra, M., & Llinés, M. (2008). Una década de políticas de gestión del espectro radioeléctrico en la Unión Europea (1997-2007). Análisis de las consultas públicas, el marco normativo y las prioridades estratégicas. *Observatorio (OBS), 2*(4), 40–61. http://obs.obercom.pt/index.php/obs/article/view/170/222.

Booth, P. (Ed.). (2016). *In Focus: The Case for Privatising the BBC*. London: Institute of Economic Affairs.

Brevini, B. (2013). European Commission Media Policy and Its Pro-market Inclination: The Revised 2009 Communication on State Aid to PSBs and Its Restraining Effect on PSB Online. *European Journal of Communication, 28*(2), 183–197. https://doi.org/10.1177/0267323112470227.

Burri, M. (2017). *Public Service Broadcasting 3.0: Legal Design for the Digital Present*. Abingdon: Routledge.

CECUV. (2015). *Bases para la renovación del espacio comunicativo valenciano y la restitución del servicio público de radiotelevisión*. Retrieved June 10, 2020, from http://hdl.handle.net/10234/179537.

Chalaby, J. K., & Segell, G. (1999). The Broadcasting Media in the Age of Risk: The Advent of Digital Television. *New Media and Society*, *1*(3), 351–368. https://doi.org/10.1177/14614449922225627.

D'Arma, A. (2018a). The Hollowing Out of Public Service Media: A Constructivist Institutionalist Analysis of the Commercialisation of BBC's In-house Production. *Media, Culture & Society*, *40*(3), 432–448. https://doi.org/10.1177/0163443717713260.

D'Arma, A. (2018b). How Do Public Service Broadcasters Make a Case for Themselves? An Analysis of BBC's "Charter Manifestos". *Journal of Information Policy*, *8*, 199–226. https://doi.org/10.5325/jinfopoli.8.2018.0199.

Donders, K., & Moe, H. (Eds.). (2012). *Exporting the Public Value Test: The Regulation of Public Broadcasters' New Media Services across Europe*. Gothenburg: Nordicom.

Donders, K., Raats, T., & Tintel, S. (2020). (Re)defining Public Service Media from an Economic Perspective: Damned If They Do, Damned If They Don't. In M. Bjørn von Rimscha (Ed.) in collaboration with: S. Kienzler, *Management and Economics of Communication*, (pp. 203–222). Boston/Berlin: De Gruyter Mouton.

Doyle, G. (2013). *Understanding Media Economics* (2nd ed.). London: Sage.

Doyle, G. (2019). Public Policy, Independent Television Production and the Digital Challenge. *Journal of Digital Media and Policy*, *10*(2), 145–162. https://doi.org/10.1386/jdmp.10.2.145_1.

EBU. (2012). Empowering Society. A Declaration on the Core Values of Public Service Media. Retrieved June 10, 2020, from https://www.ebu.ch/files/live/sites/ebu/files/Publications/EBU-Empowering-Society_EN.pdf.

EBU. (2019). Public Service Media: Contribution to Society Toolkit. May 2019. Retrieved June 10, 2020, from https://www.ebu.ch/publications/research/members_only/report/psm-contribution-to-society-toolkit.

European Commission. (2020). Audiovisual Media Services Directive. Online. Retrieved June 10, 2020, from https://ec.europa.eu/digital-single-market/en/audiovisual-media-services-directive-avmsd.

European Parliament Research Service. (2019, October). Understanding BEPS: From Tax Avoidance to Digital Tax Challenges. Briefing. October 2019. Retrieved June 10, 2020, from https://www.europarl.europa.eu/thinktank/en/document.html?reference=EPRS_BRI(2019)642258.

Evans, S. K. (2018). Making Sense of Innovation: Process, Product and Storytelling Innovation in Public Service Broadcasting Organizations. *Journalism Studies*, *19*(1), 4–24. https://doi.org/10.1080/1461670X.2016.1154446.

Fernández-Quijada, D., Bonet, M., Suárez Candel, R., & Arboledas, L. (2015). From Rhetorics to Practice: Implementation of Technological Innovation within Spanish Public Service Media. *The Journal of Media Innovations*, *2*(2), 23–39. https://doi.org/10.5617/jmi.v2i2.845.

Hjort, M. (2012). Introduction: The Film Phenomenon and How Risk Pervades It. In M. Hjort (Ed.), *Film and Risk* (pp. 1–30). Detroit, MI: Wayne State University Press.

House of Lords. (2020). Public Service Broadcasting: Impact on the Economy and Creative Culture. Debate on 5 March 2020. Retrieved June 10, 2020, from http://researchbriefings.files.parliament.uk/documents/LLN-2020-0067/LLN-2020-0067.pdf.

Ibrus, I., Rohn, U., & Nanì, A. (2019). Searching for Public Value in Innovation Coordination: How the Eurovision Song Contest Was Used to Innovate the Public Service Media Model in Estonia. *International Journal of Cultural Studies*, 22(3), 367–382. https://doi.org/10.1177/1367877918757513.

Kemeny, T., Nathan, M., & O'Brien, D. (2020). Creative Differences? Measuring Creative Economy Employment in the United States and the UK. *Regional Studies*, 54(3), 377–387. https://doi.org/10.1080/00343404.2019.1625484.

Komorowski, M., Wiard, V., Derinöz, S., Picone, I., Domingo, D., & Patriarche, G. (2018). A Mediapark in Brussels? The Media Industry and Its Regional Dynamics. *Brussels Studies*, 129, 1. https://doi.org/10.4000/brussels.1938.

Mazzucato, M., & O'Donovan, C. (2016). The BBC as Market Shaper and Creator. In N. Seth-Smith, J. Mackay, & D. Hind (Eds.), *Rethinking the BBC. Public Media in the 21st Century*. Margate: Commonwealth Publishing.

McElroy, R. (2020). Public Service Broadcasters: Interventions and Innovations for the Creative Economy? Online. Centre for the Study of Media and Culture in Small Nations. https://culture.research.southwales.ac.uk/news-and-events/news/psb-creative-economy/.

McElroy, R., & Noonan, C. (2019). *Producing British Television Drama: Local Production in a Global Era*. Basingstoke: Palgrave Macmillan.

McElroy, R., Nielsen, J. I., & Noonan, C. (2018). Small Is Beautiful? The Salience of Scale and Power to Three European Cultures of TV Production. *Critical Studies in Television: The International Journal of Television Studies*, 13(2), 169–187. https://doi.org/10.1177/1749602018763566.

Meade, A. (2018, July 25). 'Unprecedented Hostility': Murdoch, the Government, and an ABC Under Attack. *The Guardian*. Retrieved June 10, 2020, from https://www.theguardian.com/media/2018/jul/25/unprecedented-hostility-murdoch-the-government-and-an-abc-under-attack.

Mediapark.brussels. (2020). Ambition. Retrieved June 10, 2020, from http://mediapark.adt-ato.brussels/fr/zones-strategiques/ambition.

MediaRoad. (2017). What Are the Benefits for All Parties. Retrieved June 10, 2020, from https://www.mediaroad.eu/wp-content/uploads/2019/02/benefits-for-all-parties1.pdf.

Monk, D., Browne, F., Moseley, R., & Berry, M. (2019). *Ragdres Hwithrans Darlesor Gonis Poblek Kernewek Agwedh Onan—Studhyans Arhwilas Derivas. Cornish Public Service Broadcaster Research Project. Phase 1—Scoping Study*

Report. Retrieved June 10, 2020, from https://www.cornwall.gov.uk/media/40498119/cornish-public-service-broadcaster-research-project-scoping-study-report-july-2019.pdf.

Peacock, A. (2004). Public Service Broadcasting without the BBC? In A. Peacock (Ed.), *Public Service Broadcasting without the BBC?* (pp. 33–53). London: Institute of Economic Affairs.

Potschka, C. (2012). *Towards a Market in Broadcasting: Communications Policy in the UK and Germany*. Basingstoke: Palgrave Macmillan.

Raats, T., Donders, K., & Pauwels, C. (2014). Finding the Value in Public Value Partnerships. Lessons from Partnerships Practices in the United Kingdom, Netherlands and Flanders. In G. F. Lowe & F. Martin (Eds.), *The Value of Public Service Media* (pp. 263–280). Gothenburg: Nordicom.

Raats, T., Tintel, S., & Ballon, P. (2018). Is VRT Supporting Economic Growth? Brussels: SMIT. Retrieved June 10, 2020, from https://smit.vub.ac.be/wp-content/uploads/2019/05/Policy-Brief-20.pdf.

Ramsey, P. (2018). 'It Could Redefine Public Service Broadcasting in the Digital Age': Assessing the BBC's Proposals for Moving BBC Three Online. *Convergence, 24*(2), 152–167. https://doi.org/10.1177/1354856516659001.

Ramsey, P., Baker, S., & Porter, R. (2019). Screen Production on the 'Biggest Set in the World': Northern Ireland Screen and the Case of Game of Thrones. *Media, Culture & Society, 41*(6), 845–862. https://doi.org/10.1177/0163443719831597.

S4C. (2017). S4C: Pushing the Boundaries. Multi-Platform Welsh Language Media Service. Retrieved June 10, 2020, from https://www.s4c.cymru/gwthiorffiniau/pdf/S4C-Review.pdf.

Schrøder, K. C., & Ørsten, M. (2019). Demark. Reuters Institute Digital News Report 2019. Retrieved June 10, 2020, from https://reutersinstitute.politics.ox.ac.uk/sites/default/files/inline-files/DNR_2019_FINAL.pdf.

Sehl, A., Fletcher, R., & Picard, R.G. (2020). Crowding Out: Is There Evidence That Public Service Media Harm Markets? A Cross-national Comparative Analysis of Commercial Television and Online News Providers. *European Journal of Communication* (online first). https://doi.org/10.1177/0267323120903688.

Sieg, G., & Stühmeier, T. (2015). "Fixing What Ain't Broke" Through Public Service Broadcasting. *FinanzArchiv, 71*(4), 440–459. https://doi.org/10.1628/001522115X14425626525083.

TG4. (2018). Annual Report 2018. Retrieved June 10, 2020, from https://d1og0s8nlbd0hm.cloudfront.net/tg4-redesign-2015/wp-content/uploads/2019/11/TG4-Tuarascail-18-B.pdf.

Van den Bulck, H. (2007). Old Ideas Meet New Technologies: Will Digitalisation Save Public Service Broadcasting (Ideals) from Commercial Death? *Sociology Compass, 1*(1), 28–40. https://doi.org/10.1111/j.1751-9020.2007.00020.x.

Van den Bulck, H., & Donders, K. (2014). Of Discourses, Stakeholders and Advocacy Coalitions in Media Policy: Tracing Negotiations Towards the New Management Contract of Flemish Public Broadcaster VRT. *European Journal of Communication, 29*(1), 83–99. https://doi.org/10.1177/0267323113509362.

VRT. (2020). VRT Sandbox. Retrieved June 10, 2020, from https://sandbox.vrt.be/.

Wauters, D., & Raats, T. (2018). Public Service Media and Ecosystem Sustainability. Towards Effective Partnerships in Small Media Markets. In G. F. Lowe, H. Van den Bulck, & K. Donders (Eds.), *Public Service Media in the Networked Society* (pp. 175–191). Göteborg: Nordicom.

Williams, Ch. (2014, October 5). Netflix Chief Reed Hastings Takes on Telcos, Cinemas and Global Expansion. *The Telegraph*. Retrieved June 10, 2020, from https://www.telegraph.co.uk/finance/newsbysector/mediatechnologyandtelecoms/media/11141864/Netflix-chief-Reed-Hastings-takes-on-telcos-cinemas-and-global-expansion.html.

Zaragoza Fuster, M. T., & García Avilés, J. A. (2020). The Role of Innovation Labs in Advancing the Relevance of Public Service Media: The Cases of BBC News Labs and RTVE LAB. *Communication and Society, 33*(1), 45–61. https://doi.org/10.15581/003.33.1.45-61.

CHAPTER 11

Media and the Internet Access Providers in an Era of Convergence

Pierre-Jean Benghozi and Françoise Benhamou

1 Introduction

The media, and especially TV channels, have been transformed by a multifold movement triggered and supported by digitization. First, the scattering of content and audiovisual programs started with the proliferation of channels at the very beginning of the 1980s and was emphasized with new forms of production, distribution, and online access. Distribution of content becomes more and more dependent on Internet providers, giving birth to logics of concentration around dominant technical players. Second, delinearization developed in the framework of a platform economy (centered on new entrants).

P.-J. Benghozi (✉)
Ecole Polytechnique-CNRS, Paris, France

University of Geneva, Geneva, Switzerland
e-mail: pierre-jean.benghozi@unige.ch

F. Benhamou
Université Sorbonne Paris Nord, Villetaneuse, France

© The Author(s), under exclusive license to Springer Nature Switzerland AG 2021
M. Túñez-López et al. (eds.), *The Values of Public Service Media in the Internet Society*, Palgrave Global Media Policy and Business, https://doi.org/10.1007/978-3-030-56466-7_11

Thus, the emergence of information and communication technologies has challenged the existing rules of the game. In particular, the historical boundaries are blurred between media and telecom industries, with different means: diversifications, mergers, acquisitions, cooperations. Telecom companies got closer to TV companies in order to enrich their offers and TVs are looking for ways to develop their distribution by getting closer to telecoms and Internet players. Consequently, both industries have an interest in convergence, but project different strategies and visions behind the same term.

In the course of about 20 years, technological developments have thus precipitated the media companies into a vast set of communication media where sounds, images, and information of all kinds are mixed. From a public policy point of view, the consequences arise at both ends of the value chain—on the side of the providers of the service and on the side of the public that receives it. In the past, media regulation had to face technological changes on many occasions but has been able to adapt itself, benefiting from a double trigger ruling, national and European, which makes it easier to address some of the limits brought about. However, faced with a system that has reached its limits, the public player has to face today brand-new pitfalls since the new wave of transformation brought about by digital technology calls into question the very objectives and tools of media regulation. Telecom and internet regulation focus on infrastructures, competition, and on the protection of personal data. It is less interested in other aspects (ethic, cultural diversity, genre, etc.), which have historically formed the basis of the regulation of the audiovisual and media: they are difficult to implement on services that mix a logic of traditional linear TV and a logic of content aggregation platform.

Therefore regulation, whether for telecoms or audiovisual sectors, must rethink its traditional modes of intervention and change its paradigm: how to consider the definition of relevant markets, how to take into account the neutrality of networks, applications, and terminals, and, in a nutshell, how to migrate toward a regulation of platforms. In order to better understand such a change in industrial strategies and regulation, this chapter raises two main questions: while convergence has existed for a long time, how do firms revise their strategies in a new environment characterized by the market power of giant platforms? To what extent does this circumstance call for a reinvention of regulation? After recalling the challenges of convergence in Sect. 2, we expose the economic models of both industries (Sect. 3), and then we clarify the rationality of convergence (Sect. 4).

Section 5 stresses the importance of platforms and the way they disrupt the conditions of typical convergence. Section 6 raises the question of regulation and Sect. 7 concludes.

2   Main Challenges of Convergence

Technological breakthroughs have been an enabler and a major factor in the convergence of telecom operators and media (Xing et al. 2011). It can be considered the result of the parallel evolution of the telecom networks, the increase in throughput and capacity of and the emergence of new generations of terminals. Actually, these changes have accompanied and supported the development of technological upheavals in content distribution (Waterman et al. 2013).

Berec (2016) emphasizes that the process of "technological convergence" is at the origin of an economic de-compartmentalization in telecom industries but also in energy and transportation. These infrastructure networks were previously organized in silos and now face changing market boundaries. New strategies are emerging through a number of firms of network industries. They seek to exploit the same intangible resources (knowledge, information, etc.) or physical practicalities (infrastructure, technology, etc.) at different levels of the value chain. It potentially modifies the boundaries between these three industries and creates new synergies.

For many years, the debates on the convergence between networks and content have been the subject of numerous observations and appraisals in the academic literature (cf. Benghozi and Jäckel 1999).

In the same way, on the industrial side, the assumption has been the support of many movements. The takeover of media groups by telecom operators has rekindled the questions already raised in the early 2000s about the prospects for success of a "content-pipe convergence" strategy. Telecom operators have been active in the purchase of sports rights and film and series rights for the creation of TV channels or OTT (Over the Top) services, and even in the purchase or creation of audiovisual and/or film production companies. Moreover, it was also the justification for many strategies of mergers and acquisitions between telecom, cable TV, and media companies[1] (see Table 11.1 for the French case in 2018).

Regulators themselves have taken up the challenge by developing the concept of net neutrality (Wu 2003), in order to prevent the negative consequences of such industrial reorganizations.

Table 11.1 Top deals in technologies, media, and telecoms in France, 2018

Target	Buyer	Sector	Value (€M)
Gemalto NV	Thales Group	Technology	5424
Havas SA	Vivendi SA	Media	3733
Eircom Group Limited (64.5% stake)	Iliad SA; NJJ Holding	Telecom	2994
Sagem Sécurité	Advent Int. Corp. BPI France SA	Technology	2425
Aricent Inc.	Altran Techn.	Technology	1700
Bambora Group AB	Ingenico	Technology	1500
Asco Power Technologies, L.P.	Schneider Electric	Technology	1068
FPS Towers	ATC Europe	Telecom	727
SFR Group (4.13% stake)	Altice	Telecom	633
Dominion Web Solutions, LLC	Eurazeo, Goldman Sachs	Technology	625
Bouygues Telecom SA (1800 telecom towers)	Cellnex Telecom	Telecom	500
Grupo Media Capital, SGPS, S.A.	Altice	Media	440
Les Cinemas Gaumont Pathe SAS	Pathe	Media	380
Ausy SA	Randstad France	Technology	367
SES-Imagotag	Boe Techn. Group	Technology	356
SQS Software Quality Systems AG	Assystems Techn.	Technology	337
Exa Corporation	Dassault Systemes	Technology	325
Nextraq, Inc	Michelin	Technology	285
Teads Inc.	Altice	Media	285
AB Groupe SA	Media One Spac	Media	237

Source: PwC (2018)

Convergence between telecoms and media hang on a twofold challenge. Firstly, both media and telecom industries strive for increasing the number of consumers and subscribers thanks to network effects.[2] Secondly, they need to build and reinforce customers' loyalty, as well as to cope with wider competition. Contents appear as a tool for telecom operators in order to capture and care for a large number of subscribers so as to enhance, in addition to their financial power, their marketing know-how and real customer-oriented values. Therefore, there is a mutual interest of both industries for strategies of vertical integration and diversification in order to attract and lock in customers by supplying a diversity of contents and creating high switching costs for customers to stay in a closed ecosystem.

However, on close examination, one may wonder about this simple interpretation of convergence based on crossed and complementary strategies of telecom operators and content producers. Convergence seems paradoxical. On the one part, the rise of online digital platforms is shaking up a value chain that has simply sent operators and content producers back to the drawing board until recently. On the other part, the hypothesis of symmetrical convergence strategies has to be discussed: telecoms and media providers do not share the same goals, and their expectations are not necessarily reciprocal. Moreover, their economic models are quite different—and even opposed. For example, in France, telecoms do not want to pay for audiovisual content, while media companies argue that contents attract subscribers and increase their willingness to pay for Internet access. Consequently, regulators consider convergence-supported concentration may threat the independency of content producers and the neutrality of the Internet, which remains at the core of digital policies in Europe.

3 Two Economic Models with Different Economic Grounds

The main economic feature of convergence is that it is supported by network industries. Their architecture benefited from recent progress in the decoupling of the transport and service layers of the network (Santos et al. 2008). This means that, whenever a provider wishes to activate a new service, he can do so by defining it directly on the service layer regardless of the transport layer, thus making the services independent of transport details. Consequently, the efficiency of vertical integration is one of the reasons frequently put forward in order to explain convergence.

Beyond this generic observation, however, it is important to detail the more specific characteristics of the industries involved in convergence. Media and telecommunications are, on the one hand, fixed cost economies. On the other hand, they produce goods and services that generate externalities and network effects.

In both industries, fixed costs are very high while variable costs are very low. But there are deep differences in their economic models. The importance of fixed costs is much higher for telecoms, which can be qualified infrastructure economics, while they are much lower in the case of media, which are mostly economics of prototypes. Convergence players present both profiles. On the one hand, players for whom content distribution is an ancillary activity intend to increase the audience or traffic of a site, to increase the consumption of commercial sites, or to sell equipment. On the other hand, the business model of players for whom content distribution is the core activity and whose concerns are similar to those of traditional media players is based on the ability to aggregate and editorialize content: their revenues are proportional to the success of content whose risks are balanced.

In the case of telecoms, rapid entry and exit are difficult, since firms face irrecoverable investments supported for their telecommunication infrastructure: their rate of investment in relation to sales in Europe varies between 15% (UK) and 23% (France)! Operators are also facing a very significant increase in these investments in order to address the growing requirements for the renewal of their fixed and mobile networks (cf. Table 11.2). Those investments require a pretty long period of time in order to be amortized, compared with other industries (see Fig. 11.1).

Table 11.2 Investments of telecom operators, France, 2014–2018 (€ billion)

Years	2014	2015	2016	2017	2018
Mobile infrastructure	2.4	2.3	2.7	3.0	2.8
Fixed infrastructure	4.7	5.5	6.2	6.6	7.0
Total	7.1	7.8	8.9	9.6	9.8

Source: Fédération Française des Télécoms (2019)

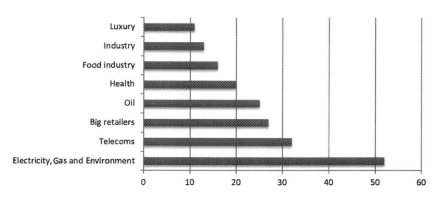

Fig. 11.1 Duration of return on capital invested (ROI) by sector, France, average 2013–2017, number of years (Source: Fédération Française des Télécoms, 2019)

On the one hand, they are made necessary by the rapid development of network technologies and protocols. On the other hand, they must respond to the growing needs of consumers (annually doubling, with, on average, the volume of data they consumed) and the necessity to differentiate from competitors by the quality and territorial coverage of their network.

Therefore, from the marketing viewpoint, firms seek a rise in the number of subscribers in order to lower the level of competition, by reducing prices, and wish to increase the average revenue per user (ARPU). Both actions are less contradictory than they appear. The strategy of firms in order to overcome this tension relies on locking consumers into their ecosystems through high switching costs.

In a fixed-cost economy, controlling and retaining a consumer base is an important advantage for stabilizing and securing revenues over the long term. It represents also an opportunity for a development based on an increase in ARPU. Therefore, operators seek for the monetization of new services.

Conversely, media rely on two-sided markets (Rochet and Tirole 2003) in which the value of ads depends on the ability of contents to attract a large number of consumers, and where, conversely, the monetization depends on the quality and attractiveness of the content—and especially the exclusive contents—provided to consumers. Content producers and distributors want to create portfolios of rights on a wide range of qualities in order to capture enlarged audiences. They need an access to powerful distribution networks to ensure the best possible distribution of their contents, to reach new audiences and to imagine new ways of making the most of them. In this way, television channels have expanded the audiovisual offer available on fixed broadband and very high-speed broadband networks by developing catch-up video solutions on their websites. The distribution of this non-linear content is based on the Internet access service, which offers any user the possibility to access the Internet at any time.

The growth of these investments goes beyond the audiovisual sector alone and more broadly concerns all rights holders, such as sport, for example (see Table 11.3).

Table 11.3 Premier League football TV rights value (€ billions)

Period	1992–1997	2001–2004	2007–2010	2013–2016	2016–2019
Value	0.3	1.6	2.3	4	6.9

Source: AFP

4 The Rationality of Convergence

Vertical integration is rooted in theoretical approaches that view the firm as an alternative to the market. It assumes that vertical integration allows internalization of costs and would result in economies of scale.

Such integration was natural and designed from the outset by the cable operators. Cable operators are in fact infrastructure players who have built their network for the sole purpose of delivering cable television. It is only recently that these cable operators have broadened their offer by also providing Internet access via their network.

Convergence is therefore a strategy inherited and revisited from early digital infrastructures. The logic of convergence is in the genes of cable operators who have always built a pipe / supply relationship for TV content. The situation has, however, changed considerably since the 1990s.

For TV channels (as it was for cable operators in the beginning), content distribution must be a profitable business, especially in the context of the overbidding in the ownership of premium rights. On the contrary, for telecom operators, the content strategy is not an end in itself, but essentially supports the development of their broadband subscriptions, both fixed and mobile. As a matter of fact, the TV business and investment in contents and rights acquisition are not necessarily directly profitable for them: the important point being that it enables them to win new subscribers or retain existing customers.

4.1 *A Basic Form of Complementarity Between Actors*

At first glance, convergence is justified on a basic form of complementarity between actors. Indeed, infrastructure operators need applications, services, and content to justify and provoke the use (and remuneration) of their networks. In such a framework, the recurring challenges of Telecommunications/Audiovisual convergence is part of a classical vertical integration perspective supported by a simplified vision of strategies of firms based on cost optimization and on the idea that controlling contents makes it possible to capture and develop consumer loyalty.

One hypothesis could be that convergence would allow actors to compensate for the weaknesses of their respective business models: attracting telecom subscribers by supplying a wide range of contents on the one side (at one bottom of the value chain) and ensuring the quality of content distribution (at the opposite bottom of the value chain) (see Fig. 11.2). Therefore the base of connected consumers, whose willingness to pay is high, is enlarging because such consumers benefit from a high quality of service and diversity in content supply.

One of the lever and consequence of the attractiveness of content is their wide availability and therefore a massive increase in data traffic over the networks. It means corresponding investment to upgrade networks (FttH, FttB, 4G and 5G) and equipments such as content delivery networks (CDN) contributing to enhance the viewer experience as well.

Convergence is the response to major changes in technology-driven behavior. Powerful and very affordable to buy and use, smartphones and touch tablets are driving this convergence. They are all the strongest because of the mobile nature of these tools. In a way, they confer the gift

		Value Chain from creators to their final audience				
		Part of the value chain in which telecom operators play a role				
	CREATION	PRODUCTION	EDITION	DISTRIBUTION	DIFFUSION	DEVICES
	Artists, moviemakers, composers, performers		Content editorialization, marketing	Sales, logistic	Transportation of the content to the audience	Screens
Traditional activities	id.	TV and music producers, studios, majors (ex. Lagardere Entertainment, Studio Canal, Universal Music Group, Ubisoft,...)	Ex. TF1, Canal+, Radio France, Amazon, Dunod, ...	Ex. CanalSat, Groupe M6, TF1 Video,...	Ex. FNAC, Pathé, UGC, Micromania, TDF, Eutelsat, ...	Ex. Samsung, Sony, LG
Digital activities	id.	Orange Studio	OCS, BBox, Amazon, iTunes, Pluzz, myTF1, Deezer	Bouygues, Orange, SFR, Amazon, iTunes, GooglePlay, ...	Bouygues, Orange, SFR, Amazon, ...	Bouygues, Orange, SFR, Amazon, Samsung, Sony, Apple

Fig. 11.2 Telecom operators in the content production value chain

of ubiquity through digital technology to their users. Such evolution rebounds the hyper-fragmentation of audiences due to the abundance of channels, sites, networks, and media brands, coupled with the delinearization of content consumption.

4.2 Convergence and Triple-Play Offers

With the spread of multiservice offerings, audiovisual content has become an element of the strategy of Internet service providers (ISPs). They support the new form of competition in the retail Internet access markets. Therefore, audiovisual distribution markets necessarily affect the fixed (and mobile) Internet access business models. Moreover, the prospect of accessing higher quality audiovisual content is an incentive for the migration to very high-speed Internet access.

In France, ISPs used the capacity of fixed broadband and very high-speed networks very early on to offer innovative audiovisual offerings. Curien and Moreau (2007) highlight that for network operators, content distribution appears to be an engine for growth. This was compulsory, given the decline in voice revenues driven by competition and the rise of VoIP (voice telephony over the internet).

Some 15 years ago, this led to the first mobile application platforms developed first in Japan and then in Europe, and this was the basis for major convergent takeover strategies (AOL Time Warner, Vivendi). At the same time, operators were also responding in the fixed-line networks. They launched the marketing of triple play multiservice offers that included Internet access, voice telephony over broadband, and access to an audiovisual package that generally included linear television offers of around 100 channels, including those broadcast on digital terrestrial television (DTT), followed by innovative non-linear services such as catch-up television.

The operator Free was the first to offer a unique subscription comprising the three services in France, in December 2003. The commercial success of triple-play offers, combined with the major technical developments experienced by fixed networks, has resulted in a significant proportion of households accessing television via their Internet connection. In 2016, 49% of households with at least one television set were equipped to receive television via ADSL or optic fiber cable and for 29% of households, wireline networks (including cable) are the only ways to receive television (source: CSA).[3] While the main operators have aggregated, within their multiple play offer, Internet access supply, and distribution of edited bundles or services, not all of them have moved up the value chain by adding content production to their business portfolio.

In a very competitive retail market for Internet access, revenues from additional services such as content represent only a minor share: 12% in 2015, according to Arcep, the national telecommunications regulatory authority. But they contribute to the attractiveness of offers, which gives players with rights to certain content a significant bargaining power and the ability to bring network externalities into play by favoring certain ISPs to the detriment of others.

4.3 The Variety of Strategies Relying on Convergence

The French, Italian, Israeli, and so on telecom markets have developed fierce price competition. But price wars have limits and companies began to develop distinct strategies of price discrimination in order to avoid the clipping of margins and the commoditization of supply. These strategies were substitutes or complements, depending on the case. In France, the biggest telecom company, Orange, focused on the quality of the network. Free, the more recent entrant company, put forward cuts in prices, without any direct investment in contents.[4] But simultaneously, Free aimed to be positioned on the layer just above via its box: the use and ergonomics of the consumption of contents.

The two other French operators SFR and Bouygues Telecom (BYT) have early chosen the integration of content and other services. Whatever the strategy, in all cases, content and services competition appeared progressively as a substitute for price competition. For example, Kiosque Premium launched by SFR offers an unlimited subscription to 450 newspapers and magazines at a price of €9.99 a month.

In a nutshell, one can say that the current convergence does not start from content publishers anxious to access a large market via new distribution channels and to find financial support (as in the Messier era—the chairman of Vivendi in 2000–2002), but from telecom companies trying to put an end to price wars and to prioritize product differentiation. Those competitive strategies are part of monopolistic competition where competition necessarily involves discrimination by the quality of goods and not, as in the case of a natural monopoly, by prices.

Such non-price strategy of product differentiation can be supported through three main levers: the size of catalogues, their variety, and their curation. Actually, distribution and production are not the only key to develop attractiveness of contents. In the context of hyper-offering provided through the Internet, aggregation of contents is a crucial issue since all contents are not alike (Benghozi and Benhamou 2010). Premium contents are a key element and operators can target some overpaid specific contents (namely sports or exclusive series) while aggregating as well long-tail, low-paid contents.

The importance of aggregation, cataloging, and therefore control of distribution has historically been the basis of the cable operators' bouquet and bundle strategies. In the current phase of maturity of the Internet, the appetite for convergence or integration movements has therefore increased for similar reasons. According to Bakos and Brynjolfsson (1999), the bundling strategy of selling a set of separate information assets for a single price often produces higher profits and greater efficiency than selling the same assets separately.

4.4 The Limits of Strategies Based on Convergence

One can wonder the degree of sustainability of convergence strategies. For network operators, sustainability is questioned by the ability to make major investments in infrastructures simultaneously with new investments to uphold the purchase and/or production of programs. Investing in content would distract resources from infrastructure development, at a cost for social and economic collective welfare. For content players, the situation is just as difficult. They are generally weakly capitalized structures, ensuring production investments in "project" mode, and must ensure very heavy investment plans in terms of both Capex (capital expenditure) and Opex (operational expenditure). Pogorel and Preta (2020) note that as more actors embrace ambitious one-stop shop strategy, with direct to consumer video services at the core, the jury is still out to value which "converged" services provider contributes in the best possible way to strengthening their audience and bottom line.

In France like in almost all European countries, telecom operators face a significant trade off or struggle between revenues and volume. On the one hand, they observe a regular decline in ARPU regarding the connectivity services they provide, in contrast to the increase in revenues from content aggregator platforms and customers' expenses on SVOD services. On the other hand, they have to address a growing volume of connections and data, mainly resulting from audiovisual non-linear services like Netflix.

Convergence strategies are considered as a solution to meet several objectives in tension: long-term value creation by securing the consumers with a relatively high willingness to pay for premium content, fueling margins by increasing ARPU, increasing the number of basic subscribers, being proactive by anticipating new business models based on data and advertising, and so on.

The risk for telecoms is that content costs are growing faster than revenue line. As a matter of fact, owning content is not necessarily a must-have to secure premium content provision to customers. Similarly, customers' loyalty, data aggregation, and revenue streams can also be secured by alternative services (banking, smart home services…).

5   Internet Platforms and Disruption

Online media consumption has risen sharply on all different devices (fixed PCs or smartphones on the move) to the detriment of linear consumption of broadcast or digital TV. Therefore, convergence becomes part of a three-way game that not only concerns content providers and telecoms, but the major Internet platforms as well. They have created new forms of intermediation different from technical infrastructures, but also from content publishers: OTTs provide services, hosting, and so on in the production and editorialization of content.

For telecoms, the evolution toward content seems difficult because they do not have a culture or an organization of their activity corresponding to that of the cultural world (short-term investments in risky projects, more creative training than engineers…). In this context, convergence does not only meet an objective of vertical integration or the economic targets described above. It also becomes a response of telecoms to the market power of OTT. By creating a privileged relation with media, they try to internalize the distribution of contents and to recapture the market power that platforms appropriate for themselves.

On the other hand, OTTs don't have the skills and the ways of thinking of media producers, but their considerable resources enable them to develop or/and purchase rapidly very rich programs with some worldwide successes (think of *House of Cards*) but also more uneven results. For example, in 2020, Amazon's SVOD offering has 150 million customers, formally almost as many as Netflix (167 million). However, the two are hardly comparable despite their growth in both cases and the attractiveness of the titles in their catalogs. The Amazon Prime Video catalog is on the one hand much smaller than that of Netflix. Secondly, the majority of

Prime customers subscribe primarily to take advantage of the benefits of free e-commerce delivery.

In any case, platforms disrupt the value chain by creating new playing field and preventing direct access to content for telecoms. Moreover, Google or Facebook don't hesitate to invest in infrastructure (fiber, network, etc.), creating an additional source of competition for telecom operators.

In addition, telecom networks sometimes show limit regarding the consequences of convergence. As a matter of fact, the growth of video distribution initiates network congestion on peak time or failures in case of large events. These economic and technological difficulties strengthen the integration movements undertaken by the OTTs toward infrastructure networks. Indeed, the main digital platforms are incented to control IP interconnection investing in networks (backbones, urban fiber networks…) and building their own CDN in telecom data centers.

The arrival of players from the Internet is thus introducing new competition for telecom operators; strategies combine mergers and acquisitions (see AT&T and Time Warner or Comcast and Sky), and deals and alliances (as in the cases of Deutsche Telekom and Netflix, Sky and Open Fiber, or Vodafone and Liberty Global).

Until now, their market has been essentially national in scope and coverage, but it is becoming increasingly international, driven by players, most often North American, who have the capacity to address a very large international audience and therefore to acquire rights on an almost global scale.

6 To What Extent Does Convergence Meet the Major Regulatory Challenges?

If firm strategies are somewhat convergent, it is not really the case for regulatory practices. The new configurations that are being put in place cover, in practice, different legal frameworks, actors, and fields of regulation. As a result, regulatory actions and decisions are themselves broken down into several segments.

Digital platforms obviously challenge the scope of regulation by imposing combined regulation dealing with personal data, market power, and net-neutrality. This raises, in particular, the following question: is *ex ante* regulation, prior to the implementation of the competition rules, appropriate? Should such intervention come from a sectorial regulator, who defines *a priori* the playground of the various economic actors? Or can it be carried out through the instruments available to the competition authority, which punishes abusive behavior *a posteriori*?

6.1 Why Should Convergence Be Regulated?

Converging environment changes the traditional regulatory dynamics. The Organisation for Economic Co-operation and Development (OECD 2016) emphasizes that in a constantly changing world of communications, policy makers and regulators are confronted with familiar challenges as well as new ones. The familiar challenges include the promotion of competition, investment, innovation, and consumer choice while meeting a number of social objectives such as universal service, emergency services, privacy, and security. However, new regulatory challenges emerge when technological developments turn of great magnitude and often disruptive and when services and applications are decoupled from networks. As Cortez (2014) points out, regulators are challenged by disruptive innovations and regulation can become stale and counterproductive. In a context of technological and economic disruption, regulators have to cope with different goals.

Regulators are focusing on two specific competitive risks in particular. The first risk corresponds to a possible vertical partitioning of the market. This can result from the vertical integration of players or the widespread of exclusivity legal provision. A second risk is the possibility of anticompetitive foreclosure strategies and market preemption in favor of dominant operators (Marty 2011).

To address these issues, the scope of regulation encompasses a series of levers. First, the definition of relevant markets, in order to assess the market power of companies, is quite important. What divisions of the telecoms and media markets are appropriate? Should we consider separately the mobile and fixed access to Internet? Should we consider media as a whole? Second, the consumer's benefits and losses should be identified, that is, restrictive access to contents, lock in, prices, and so on. Third, the indirect effect of mergers on the quality of Internet access infrastructures should be taken into account, and fourth, net neutrality, which is still in force in Europe, is questioned by convergence strategies.

One can wonder whether considerations linked to the peculiarities of content industries should be taken into consideration before framing and accepting the converging operations, partnerships, or mergers and acquisitions (M&A) in particular. In that respect, the questioning of traditional boundaries between industries entails risks for competition. For instance, Internet service providers pose a significant threat to traditional operators in the audiovisual market. Not only do triple play offers allow direct competition with TV channels, but also their technology offers telecommunication firms and consumers many advantages in term of non-linear uses of TV (replay, catch-up TV, and video on demand).

Moreover, in the field of telecoms, investments are national priorities in order for the whole population to be connected to Internet services. This point may be considered as a market failure leading to the need for regulation rules. For example, the promotion of cultural diversity can be considered as a goal of cultural policies, that can be better served by concentration than competition, or conversely.

6.2 The Tools of Regulation

Competition regulators, telecoms regulators, and TV regulators have to pay attention to the effects of convergence. Indeed, to what extent is it possible to accept converging bundles: are they compatible with new forms of competition? To address this question, public actors have a toolbox enabling them to tackle regulation from several angles. We can illustrate this from two complementary standpoints: the competitive approach and the preservation of net neutrality.

As for other M&A, in view of convergence competition, regulators first watch market power and evaluate the risk of abuse of dominant position, which is reflected, among other elements, in their market share and in the issue of prices.

When content providers and Internet service providers offer complementary goods or services, in the absence of integration, neither party internalizes the profit loss inflicted on the other party by raising its price: in consequence, vertical integration may reduce prices. Also, vertical integration may reduce the underinvestment that arises with independent parties, as the investment generates benefits for the firm producing the complementary product. In practice, the magnitude of these gains is unclear, but the empirical literature from other industries identifies many examples of efficiency gains from vertical integration (Lafontaine and Slade 2007).

In a two-sided market perspective, Belleflamme and Peitz (2020) review recent work that aims at better understanding the possible pro- or anti-competitive effects of convergence. They stress two specific non-price strategies: exclusivity as the contractual obligation to singlehome and price transparency as the disclosure of information about otherwise unobserved prices paid by users. Their results may sound paradoxical for regulators. They find that a monopoly platform is willing to remedy this problem by being transparent about all prices, whereas competing platforms would prefer more opaqueness in general.

Beside the competitive price dimensions, there is a broad consensus on the objectives of providing the widest possible access to online services and of encouraging access, innovation, and diversity of content and services. Anticompetitive concerns arise because an Internet service provider may offer its own services and charge termination fees for competing content providers, potentially leading to partial or full exclusion. Content providers are able to differentiate from competitors satisfying heterogeneous user tastes (Economides and Hermalin 2012). Then, vertical integration may lead telecom operators to favor their own contents and it is precisely to combat this risk that neutrality is aimed at. But a strict application by regulators may lead them to wrongfully exclude telecoms from activities linked to contents, in such a way that leading OTT platforms may finally take the economic power on cultural goods and services, as well as on networks infrastructure.

Nevertheless, regulators assume that an Internet service provider should be required to treat all data from all content providers in the same way, and they generally argue that net neutrality is essential because without it, Internet service providers could seek to control access to certain content according to their economic and strategic agreements. Net neutrality also prevents the possibility of providers charging end users an extra fee to access specific services. Yet, there is more discussion on implementation, that is, on the contours and limits of net neutrality and on its possible negative externalities. No consensus fully emerged in the literature regarding its characterization (e.g., Sidak 2006; Lee and Wu 2009).

As an illustration, Berec (2016) defines zero-rating as a situation "when an Internet Service Provider applies a price of zero to the data traffic associated with a particular application or class of applications."[5] But for Somogly (2016), zero-rating harms consumers if content is unattractive, whereas it improves social welfare in the case of attractive content.

Consequently, it is not automatically compatible with the principle of net neutrality and calls for regulatory scrutiny.

7 Concluding Remarks

Ultimately, the evolution of telecom networks, the generalization of nomadic screens, and changing consumer habits have created a framework that is favorable to advanced forms of integration or partnerships between content players and network players:

- Telecom industrials need contents to differentiate themselves and to increase ARPU,
- Telecom operators currently have investment capacities compatible with content financing and own the networks through which the bulk of content consumption is expected to take place in the coming years,
- Content industries need to find new growth drivers and outlets at a time when consumption is changing and traditional revenues are under pressure.

The issue of convergence is not radically new: it was a hot topic at the very beginning of the digital wave. Yet, the context of convergence differs deeply from 20 years ago. Firstly, the consumers have changed profoundly. They are connected and mobile, they want to get access to all content, anytime, anywhere, on any device. Secondly, digital technology is profoundly changing the economic landscape, with more competition, new players on the Internet, and the need to be able to provide the best possible service to consumers.

As a consequence, the content economy relies on over-abundance rather than scarcity. For both media and telecoms, the threat of "uberization" is strong. Each media must ensure that it is differentiated thanks to its catalog, creativity and production capacity. For its part, each network seeks, through non-price strategies, to avoid being reduced to a commodity, to a simple pipe.

Regulation should be revised correspondingly: the market power of platforms redefines convergence. The traditional regulation of convergence (through competition authorities) must move in order to integrate the regulation of platforms, which grab and capture contents. Regulation raises new stakes: access, cultural diversity, revenue sharing, and intellectual property rights.

The future of convergence oscillates between two scenarios. On the one hand, we can consider that the two models of media and telecoms are so different that, despite the multiplication and recurrence of convergence attempts, they will fail … as they did 20 years ago. But we can also assume, on the other hand, that there is an irretrievable movement, given the present multiplicity of mergers and alliances in a three players' game instead of two.

Further analysis should include a wider scope of convergence that does not concern only media and content players. The major operators are developing digital services for their industrial customers: smart cities, energy, on-board telematics, healthcare, and so on. In view of the recent movements observed among telecom operators, convergence also affects the world of finance, the world of smart homes, of online services, of cars, and industrial applications.

Notes

1. Pogorel and Preta (2020) consider AT&T/Time Warner, 21st Century Fox/Disney, and Comcast/Sky as the three most relevant examples of consolidation.
2. *Network effects* or externalities consist in an economic dynamic where the value and attractiveness of a good or services is increased by the numbers of users.
3. Cf. Avis n° 2016-1551of the Autorité de régulation des communications électroniques et des postes (ARCEP), 16 November, 2016, to a request of the Competition Authority about the takeover of TPS and Canalsatellite by Vivendi and Canal Plus Group.
4. Free does not invest in content directly, but Xavier Niel, its owner and founder, is present in newspapers and has launched a €500 million investment fund called "Media One."
5. https://berec.europa.eu/eng/netneutrality/zero_rating/.

References

Bakos, Y., & Brynjolfsson, E. (1999). Bundling Information Goods: Pricing, Profits and Efficiency. *Management Science, 45*(12), 1613–1630. https://doi.org/10.1287/mnsc.45.12.1613.

Belleflamme, P., & Peitz, M. (2020). The Competitive Impacts of Exclusivity and Price Transparency in Markets with Digital Platforms. *Concurrences, 1*, 2–7.

Benghozi, P. J., & Benhamou, F. (2010). The Long Tail: Myth or Reality? *International Journal of Arts Management, 12*(3), 43–53.

Benghozi, P. J., & Jäckel A. (1999). What Convergence for Which Media? First European Audiovisual Seminar Proceedings, University of Turin, December 5–8, 1998, University of West of England Press.

BEREC. (2016). BEREC Guidelines on the Implementation by National Regulators of European Net Neutrality Rules. Retrieved June 5, 2020, from http://berec.europa.eu/eng/document_register/subject_matter/berec/download/0/6160-berec-guidelines-on-the-implementation-b_0.pdf.

Cortez, N. (2014). Regulating Disruptive Innovation. *Berkeley Technology Law Journal, 29*, 175–228. https://doi.org/10.2139/ssrn.2436065.

Curien, N., & Moreau, F. (2007). The Convergence between Contents and Access: Internalizing the Market Complementarity. *Review of Network Economics, 6*(2), 1–14. https://doi.org/10.2202/1446-9022.1115.

Economides, N., & Hermalin, B. E. (2012). The Economics of Network Neutrality. *Rand Journal of Economics, 43*(4), 602–629.

Fédération Française des Télécoms. (2019). Les chiffres-clés 2019 du secteur des télécoms et des grands enjeux à venir. Retrieved June 5, 2020, from https://www.fftelecoms.org/etudes-et-publications/etude-economique-2019-telecoms-premiers-acteurs-numerique/.

Lafontaine, F., & Slade, M. (2007). Vertical Integration and Firm Boundaries: The Evidence. *Journal of Economic Literature, 45*(3), 629–685. https://doi.org/10.1257/jel.45.3.629.

Lee, R. S., & Wu, T. (2009). Subsidizing Creativity through Network Design: Zero-Pricing and Net Neutrality. *Journal of Economics Perspectives, 23*(3), 61–76. https://doi.org/10.1257/jep.23.3.61.

Marty, F. (2011). Convergence numérique et risques de forclusion des marchés: Quel partage des rôles entre politiques de concurrence et régulation sectorielle? *Concurrences, 3*, 28–34.

OECD. (2016). Digital Convergence and Beyond: Innovation, Investment, and Competition in Communication Policy and Regulation for the 21st Century. Retrieved June 5, 2020, from http://www.oecd.org/officialdocuments/publicdisplaydocumentpdf/?cote=DSTI/ICCP/CISP(2015)2/FINAL&docLanguage=En.

Pogorel, G., & Preta, A. (2020). Media and Telecom in an Age of Convergence Europe in a Transatlantic and International Perspective. Working Papers Telecom Paris Tech.

Rochet, J. C., & Tirole, J. (2003). Platform Competition in Two Sided Markets. *Journal of the European Economic Association, 1*(4), 990–1029. https://doi.org/10.1162/154247603322493212.

Santos, J., Gomes, D., Sargento, S., Aguiar, R. L., Baker, N., Zafar, M., & Ikram, A. (2008). Multicast/Broadcast Network Convergence in Next Generation Mobile Networks. *Computer Networks, 52*(1), 228–247. https://doi.org/10.1016/j.comnet.2007.09.002.

Sidak, G. J. (2006). A Consumer-Welfare Approach to Network Neutrality Regulation of the Internet. *Journal of Competition Law & Economics,* 2(3), 349–474.

Somogly, R. (2016). The Economics of Zero-Rating and Net Neutrality. CORE Discussion Papers 2016047, Université catholique de Louvain, Center for Operations Research and Econometrics (CORE). Retrieved from https://ideas.repec.org/p/cor/louvco/2016047.html.

Waterman, D., Sherman, R., & Wook, J. S. (2013). The Economics of Online Television: Industry Development, Aggregation, and "TV Everywhere". *Telecommunications Policy,* 37(9), 725–736. https://doi.org/10.1016/j.telpol.2013.07.005.

Wu, T. (2003). Network Neutrality, Broadband Discrimination. *Journal of Telecommunications and High Technology Law,* 2(1), 141–178. https://doi.org/10.2139/ssrn.388863.

Xing, W., Ye, X., & Kui, L. (2011). Measuring Convergence of Chinas ICT industry: An Input Output Analysis. *Telecommunications Policy,* 35(4), 301–313. https://doi.org/10.1016/j.telpol.2011.02.003.

PART IV

Democratic Reinforcement

CHAPTER 12

Media Capture and Its Contexts: Developing a Comparative Framework for Public Service Media

Marius Dragomir and Minna Aslama Horowitz

1 Introduction: Capture Is Everywhere

Far from retaining its independence from all vested interests, and delivering a critical and robust public interest journalism, the BBC is a compromised version of a potentially noble ideal: far too implicated in and attached to existing elite networks of power to be able to offer an effective challenge to them. (Freedman 2018, p. 4)

The British Broadcasting Corporation (BBC) is arguably the most revered—and heavily researched—Public Service Media (PSM) organization in the world. It has also served as a model of universality and quality

---

M. Dragomir
Central European University, Vienna, Austria
e-mail: DragomirM@spp.ceu.edu

M. Aslama Horowitz (✉)
University of Helsinki, Helsinki, Finland
e-mail: minna.aslama@helsinki.fi

for many emerging PSM efforts. As Des Freedman (2018, p. 11) argues, both the public service model and the reputation of the BBC have functioned as an antidote to the so called *media capture*, the concept that refers to media having failed to achieve or having gained and then lost autonomy and thus not exercising their core function of informing people (e.g., Mungiu-Pippidi 2013; Schiffrin 2018).

Even so, it could be argued that the BBC's governance and financial arrangements point to elements of capture, and various studies on news have indicated that the corporation has at times reinforced the views of political and economic elites (Freedman 2018). Recently, developments in the UK have increasingly shown symptoms of even more concrete influence of political interests in the public broadcaster's operations and editorial affairs.

The BBC, however, is by no means alone: signs of capture can be detected to various degrees in both emerging and mature PSM contexts (Dragomir 2019; Voltmer 2013; Wilson 2020), which points to the dual nature of the media capture phenomenon.

On one hand, the capture of PSM is context-specific and depends on a number of economic, political, and cultural realities (Milosavljević and Poler 2018). For example, media capture—and particularly the control of PSM—is especially pertinent in Central and Eastern Europe. The transformation of state media into PSM has generally failed, as governments in the region have maintained a tight grip on public service broadcasters thanks to their power to appoint key players in their governance structures and make decisions about their funding (Dragomir 2019; Milosavljević and Poler 2018; Ryabinska 2014). The experience in the Balkans highlights several tendencies that mark media capture by the region's governments, including the absence of independent journalism. The lack of public interest content in these countries also has to do with fierce competition from commercial players (Dragomir 2019; Milosavljević and Poler 2018).

On the other hand, while contexts may differ, the economic and political pressures on PSM are strikingly similar (Syvertsen and Enli 2018; Voltmer 2013). PSM are often politicized for broader ideological purposes; for instance, PSM organizations tend to be demonized by populist politics (Simon 2019), and recent developments in countries like Australia, Denmark, Switzerland, and the UK indicate significant political hostility toward PSM. Furthermore, the rapid commercialization and digitization of media markets are not endangering independent media solely in young democracies; the challenges faced by commercial legacy media in the digital economy have prompted questions about ostensibly unfair advantages enjoyed by PSM and their right to operate on commercial platforms (Van Dijck and Poell 2014), despite evidence showing that, contrary to what commercial competitors of PSM have argued, PSM seldom crowd out private media organizations (e.g., Sjøvaag et al. 2019).

One way to understand this interplay of similar but different manifestations of media capture is to deploy a four-component model to assess the degree of risk to editorial independence posed by media capture (Dragomir 2019). This model offers practical uses for companies and investors (to know when to enter and exit a captured market), journalists (to spot areas of serious risk to their autonomy), and regulators (to adjust the methodologies used to assess threats to media pluralism). The four components of the model are:

1. Regulatory capture (consisting of government control of the regulatory process that, due to the licensing powers of these authorities, affects the composition of the media market)
2. Control of PSM (consisting of mechanisms to control their governing structures and financial dependence on state bodies, which can turn these operations into government channels)
3. Use of state financing as a control tool (consisting of forms of public funding mechanisms, including public funding for state-administered media, state advertising, state subsidies, and market disruption measures, all of which are used to influence the operations and, indirectly, the editorial independence of media outlets)
4. Ownership takeover (consisting of forms of forceful takeover of commercial media through private enterprises close to the government)

For a country to exhibit the full extent of media capture, all these elements must be present. Using this model, media capture can be defined as a situation where a group of interests formed around a country's political and business power takes over and abuses the key regulatory and funding mechanisms, the public media, as well as a majority of the privately owned media to control the journalistic narrative with the long-term purpose of maintaining their grip on power and, with it, access to public resources. The capture can appear in countries with both poor and better press freedom records, the difference being that in the former the capture amplifies existing forms of control over the media.

The scope of capture, however, can vary, depending on the degree of control in each area. Capture clearly appears when the government and allied corporate interests achieve a level of control in the media that secures their success in the next electoral cycle. However, media capture is not coextensive with a complete lack of independent media but can manifest itself in various forms and at various levels within a given environment. This variety of contexts and pressures, despite certain similarities, calls for frameworks "within which it is possible to place the particular context facing each country at a particular moment" (Schiffrin 2018, p. 1039).

With this chapter, we answer Schiffrin's (2018) call and focus on PSM, which, in its ideal form, Schiffrin and others (Nelson 2017) see as the best antidote to capture. In reality, PSM is often the first media organization challenged by political forces. We purposely chose the concept of "Public Service Media": while the established term is still "public service broadcasting" (PSB; see, e.g., UNESCO n.d.), highlighting the multimedia nature of PSM emphasizes new forms of media capture that have emerged in the wake of digitization (Schiffrin 2018). We recognize the importance of studying PSM as connected to public service broadcasting institutions, many of which have a long tradition of mainstream broadcasting activities that they continue to undertake. At the same time, the question becomes whether PSB needs a broad remit when the online media landscape is so diverse, or whether public service broadcasters further distort the news business in the hypercompetitive environment (Syvertsen and Enli 2018). In other words, the very concept of PSM is an argument against those wanting to limit its independence.

We are writing this chapter during the COVID-19 pandemic, which has challenged all public communication, independent journalism, and national budgets, factors that could both encourage and curtail the future capture of PSM. This, we believe, is another powerful reason to propose a model to assess PSM capture. We aim to do so using a matrix that takes into account not only the concrete, structural forms of capture but also the kind of media systems and related contexts in which PSM operate, as well as discursive or cultural capture; that is, public discourses about PSM and their legitimacy. We focus on Europe due to its long and established history of public service broadcasting and the existence of a variety of PSM configurations in the different countries of the region.

2 Media Capture in Europe

European media, and public service broadcasting in particular, have served as a benchmark for independent and public interest journalism, as in academic and advocacy writings on media reform against market-driven media (e.g., McChesney and Nichols 2010). However, Europe has been by no means immune to media capture, although establishing with precision the date of media capture's appearance is difficult: elements of media capture appeared in various countries at many points in time over the past several decades.

Examples of high media ownership concentration and political interference abounded in the 1990s. Italy has always been cited as an extreme example of controlled media, because in the early 1990s, Prime Minister Silvio Berlusconi dominated both the private media market through his own conglomerate Mediaset and influenced to a high degree, through his political position, the editorial position of Radiotelevisione Italiana (RAI), the country's public service broadcaster. But that form of influence, or what scholars referred to at the time as the "Italian anomaly," (Mazzoleni and Vigevani 2005, p. 869) has since evolved into media capture, an extreme model of control that characterizes an increasing number of European media systems.

In media-captured environments, political interest groups and powerful businesses join forces to take control not only of a specific private media holding but of most of the country's privately owned media outlets. They not only try to influence the editorial perspective of the public broadcaster but also systematically purge public media of all critical journalists and manage these institutions as little more than state propaganda channels (see, e.g., Milosavljević and Poler 2018).

The first elements of media capture, particularly the growing role of the government in the market, whether directly through regulators, state media, and public resources or indirectly through groups of media owners associated with or indebted to the government, appeared in Central and Eastern Europe late in the first decade of this century. At that time, a global economic crisis combined with disruptive technologies that shook media structures worldwide to create an unprecedented opportunity for powerful governments and oligarchs to take over financially ailing media companies (Dragomir 2018). Those new realities alienated many of the foreign investors that had been operating across Central and Eastern Europe since the early 1990s. In the Czech Republic, for example, five large foreign publishers, most from Germany, left the market during the late 2000s, selling their assets to a clutch of wealthy businessmen with close ties to politics and investments in a wide array of industries. One of them, Andrej Babis, later became prime minister.

However, the media capture phenomenon is hardly limited to Central and Eastern Europe. The model has expanded globally in recent years, embraced by governments because it gives them powerful mechanisms to control the mainstream narrative and boost their electoral clout. Two of the most captured media environments in the world (if we exclude failed states and outright dictatorships) are Turkey and Hungary. In Turkey, following a failed coup in 2016, President Recep Tayyip Erdoğan and his allies took over almost all the country's media. In Hungary, Prime Minister Viktor Orban, with the support of a powerful oligarchy, has systematically taken over most of the media companies in the country. Europe's eastern periphery—countries like Moldova, Ukraine, and Georgia—is also experiencing capture, with a strong level of Russian involvement (Dragomir 2019).

Media capture is also becoming a predominant form of control in several Western European countries. In Spain's otherwise vibrant media market, an increasing number of media outlets, including the public service broadcaster RTVE, lack the autonomy to cover relevant issues under pressure from the government and corporations, especially banking groups (Minder 2015). The rise of right-wing parties in many European countries also created an opportunity for politicians to cement their control of the public media.

Another important trend is the cross-border expansion of oligarchic structures across Europe. For example, companies close to Hungary's Orban have recently invested in media outlets across Eastern Europe, including Slovenia, North Macedonia, and Romania. In the same five-year period, large financial groups from Slovakia and the Czech Republic made a series of major acquisitions across the region (Dragomir 2019).

3 Contextualizing PSM Capture for Comparative Assessments

The concept of media capture is well established. Country-specific studies ranging from nations in Central and Eastern Europe (Dragomir 2018b, 2019; Milosavljević and Poler 2018) to Hong Kong (Frisch et al. 2018) and Latin America (Márquez-Ramírez and Guerrero 2017) to Turkey

(Yeşil 2018) reveal two key observations discussed in the introduction. First, national media systems and contexts play an important role in the degree and forms of capture, and we can argue that each country is somehow a "special" case. Second, each situation still entails some consideration to both political and commercial challenges, including common themes that Schiffrin (2018, pp. 1035–1039) has described as new forms of capture: the challenges that digitization has brought about for the business models of journalism, the impact of the political transformations of the twenty-first century, and, in some cases, the role of philanthropy in funding journalism.

Following Dragomir's (2019) four-part model, PSM is but one component in possible manifestations of national and structural media capture. At the same time, PSM may be subjected to other forms of capture, such as public funding mechanisms. The key questions become, "How to dissect and understand the various roles played in the capture of and possible hardships faced by PSM, and how to compare features of one national context to another?" In our framework, we examine PSM by taking into account the specificities of each media form, but not in isolation from different forms of capture. Our focus is on the independence of PSM and on the actors that challenge it. It should be noted that media capture is not equivalent to what has been identified as political parallelism, that is the reflection of political parties in the structures of media systems and organizations (e.g., Hallin and Mancini 2004). In this model, media capture is understood as the *process* of intensification of political influence (over PSM in this case) in different ways.

Even so, it is crucial to address the role of PSM in a national media system when assessing media capture and PSM. This involves not only market share or funding model but also the broader sociocultural meaning of PSM in its national context. Another dimension is the variety of public discourses concerning, and especially opposing, the national PSM organization in question. Here, the notion of "cultural capture" (Woodall 2018, p. 1183; see also Kwak 2014) is helpful for our framework. Voices critical of PSM do not equal or necessarily precede media capture. Nonetheless, given that PSM organizations are often challenged on different fronts by commercial competitors and political adversaries alike, debates in the media can highlight how and by whom the legitimacy of PSM is challenged and whether regulators internalize the views of particular interest groups. Finally, at the core is structural capture, which is the different concrete forms of media capture and specifically the capture of PSM.

While we assume no direct causal relationship between these dimensions, together they allow us to better reflect on different cases, identify trends and patterns, and find possible responses to capture. Given the complex nature of the causes of and forms of capture, we have chosen to focus on a descriptive, qualitative approach founded on a framework based on three core questions.

1. *National media system: What is the role of the national PSM organization in the given media system?*

    Here, the focus is on describing essential characteristics of the national media landscape from the perspective of the PSM organization: What is its position historically? What kinds of content and services does it offer? Who are its competitors? What does it mean for audiences? We also highlight some comparative research and key statistics to position PSM in a national context.

2. *Current public discourses: How is the role of PSM discussed in the media? What aspects of PSM are especially highlighted?*

    Here, we depict key themes from media publicity from the past five years, including questions of content (genres), viewpoints, access, multiplatform services, and funding. To create these common categories for the analysis, we used Finland as a case study and examined some 140 critical media commentaries about the Finnish Broadcasting Company from March 2015 through January 2020 (Yle 2020a). We deliberately focus on public discussions instead of policy analysis, as policies to curb PSM can be considered a part of structural capture.

3. *Structural Capture: (How) Are PSM subjected to structural media capture?*

    Here, we use the model developed in "Media Capture in Europe" (Dragomir 2019). Do we witness a governance capture of PSM? Is it about financial pressures or regulatory measures that impact PSM? Finally, how do other possible forms of capture directed at other media affect the role of PSM?

4 Testing the Framework: A Five-Country Assessment

Our starting point in developing a comparative framework for assessing PSM capture lies in the premise that contextual factors matter. Even the selection of case countries for this chapter follows that approach. To choose the countries for comparison, we have employed two operationalizations and extensions of the renowned Hallin and Mancini (2004) model of three media systems. One operationalization has translated the model into comparable indicators depicting the inclusivity of the press market, journalistic professionalism, political parallelism, ownership regulation, press subsidies, and the status of public broadcasting. That study found distinct models of media systems that they call Central, Northern, Southern, and Western clusters (Brüggemann et al. 2014). A related study looked at specific media system clusters in Central and Eastern Europe (Castro Herrero et al. 2017).

We build on this modeling of media systems for two reasons. First, the original model and its reiterations are centered on the relationship between media and politics, which is undoubtedly a key factor to consider when assessing PSM capture. Second, the clusters may assist in understanding developments within relatively similar situations and perhaps point to transferable solutions. Accordingly, we have chosen countries to ensure that each cluster is represented: Belgium from the Western cluster, the Czech Republic from the Eastern-Central cluster (Castro Herrero et al. 2017), Finland from the Northern cluster, Spain from the Southern cluster, and the United Kingdom from the Central cluster.

Despite the comparative statistical elements that have informed the clusters in the research discussed above, we apply these clusters as guides for selecting countries rather than as the essence of our comparisons. In the cluster model, the role of public service broadcasting is quantified by its market share and revenue (Brüggemann et al. 2014). To provide a more nuanced picture, we apply a qualitative descriptive approach of each country to map specific systemic affordances, discursive challenges, and manifestations of capture in each context.

4.1 Belgium

Belgium belongs to the Western media system cluster of European countries (Brüggemann et al. 2014; see also Hallin 2016), which are characterized by a solid print media sector consisting of high-circulation newspapers that are both commercially driven and organized along party lines, a history of high political parallelism where media is seen as an institution with a mission close to parties and organized social groups, and relatively heterogeneous ownership regulation. The country sports a high Internet penetration rate of over 94% (Newman et al. 2020) and scores high in press freedom rankings; it was placed 12th on the Reporters Without Borders (RSF) 2020 World Press Freedom Index (RSF 2020).

The Belgian broadcasting market must be understood through the role that it plays in the broader Belgian society. Essentially, the Belgian broadcasting market reflects the structure of the Belgian state administration and society, which is divided into sociopolitical and linguistic pillars that exist and operate autonomously. In practice, the media follow these distinctions. As Belgium is divided into the country's two main communities, Flemish- or Dutch-speaking Flanders and French-speaking Wallonia, control over broadcasting is in the hands of the ministries of culture or media in the two communities. Belgium has three PSM companies: Vlaamse Radio- en Televisieomroeporganisatie (VRT, targeting the Flemish community); Radio-télévision belge de la Communauté française (RTBF, the public media company catering to the Wallonia community); and Belgischer Rundfunk (BRF, the public broadcaster serving Belgium's small German-speaking community).

Thanks primarily to the rules and regulations in place, Belgium's PSM have generally been insulated from outside pressures and political control. For example, the VRT developed its own newsroom statute in 1998; it ensures the independence of newsroom management. Moreover, the governance structure of both VRT and RTBF not only is determined by legislation and government-determined institutional arrangements but also results from the corporate culture within these organizations (Donders et al. 2019).

The independence of public service broadcasters in Belgium is, along with other factors, responsible for their strong audience figures. Both VRT and RTBF are leaders in audience figures in their language markets despite strong competition for RTBF from other French-language channels. At the same time, they are recognized as the top brands among news media outlets (Reuters 2019).

Despite this resilience to political attacks and pressure, the PSM in Belgium have been confronted with painful reforms in recent years, aimed primarily at trimming their finances. RTBF continues to be funded by license fees. Flanders, by contrast, ended its license fee in 2002 and replaced it with a government subsidy. In fall 2019, the government of the Flemish region announced plans to slash some €40m of the VRT's budget. Such measures, which will lead to job losses, are expected to profoundly and negatively affect the broadcaster's autonomy and editorial independence.

Although these setbacks are far from creating a discourse strong enough to destabilize the PSM in Belgium, the growing tendency of politicians to influence public media in that country has been worrisome (Raeymaeckers and Heinderyckx 2017). A report from the European Broadcasting Union (EBU) found a medium level of political pressure on PSM in Belgium, which is common in several European countries, but worse than in various Western and Nordic European countries with solid public media systems (EBU 2020b).

4.2 Czech Republic

The media system in the Czech Republic has followed an evolution common to other countries in Central and Eastern Europe, characterized by elements of the former communist state media, which stubbornly resisted change (Castro Herrero et al. 2017). The governing structures of PSM in these countries are highly politicized, and the systems of allocating state funds to the media lack transparency. In this type of media system, the political parties effectively "colonize" media outlets, using them as channels of communication in their own interest (Bajomi-Lázár 2014). These countries are characterized by a "business parallelism," a situation in which media owners are involved in both politics and other industries (Zielonka 2015). Due to economic problems in these countries (stemming from low advertising revenues and a lack of press subsidy mechanisms), media systems in this Eastern model also have a high level of media ownership concentration.

Within the Central-Eastern European typology, scholars identified three cluster of media systems: an Eastern one bringing together countries such as Romania, Bulgaria, and Hungary, a Northern one specific to the Baltic countries and Slovakia, and a Central one that includes countries such as Croatia, Poland, Slovenia, and the Czech Republic (Castro Herrero et al. 2017). The Central group to which the Czech Republic belongs is characterized by the relative strength of PSM and lower levels of foreign ownership.

As a result of the changes in media ownership after the economic crisis that began in 2007, the Czech media system is now highly captured. Since then, oligarchic groups have increased their dominance of the media through a wave of takeovers that pushed most of the foreign media owners out of the market. Unlike common media capture cases, where governments and oligarchs first impose control over state-administered institutions and regulators, the oligarchy and its allied political groups in the Czech Republic targeted the private media first. Since 2013, a group of powerful businesses operating in a wide range of industries has taken over most of the country's private media (Dragomir 2018b), In light of all these developments, it is not surprising that the Czech Republic ranks the lowest on the RSF Press Freedom Index among the five countries analyzed in this study, although it retains a respectable position (40th) in global terms (RSF 2020).

Unlike typical media capture cases, the Czech PSM have been the last to come under control. That was not necessarily a calculated decision of the Czech oligarchs, one of whom, Andrej Babis, became the country's prime minister in 2017; rather, it is a consequence of the resilience that the Czech PSM company had built over the years. Czech TV, the country's public broadcaster, is in fact one of the few public service broadcasters in Central and Eastern Europe that has managed to successfully stave off political attacks throughout the years. This reputation of relative independence and the track record of the Czech public media for quality productions (drama, political and current affairs shows, documentaries) have won them solid audience figures. With an audience share hovering around 30% for all its channels combined, public television fights for leadership on the television market with TV Nova, the largest privately owned broadcaster in the country. Moreover, the public service broadcaster is the news media brand with the highest recognition in the Czech Republic (Reuters 2019).

Nevertheless, as oligarchs have taken over most of the state structures during the past five years, attacks against the public media have intensified and, with them, an anti-public media narrative has emerged. The discourse against public media is captured (and led) by a string of private media that are visibly determined to tarnish the reputation of Czech TV, which is a major competitor in the local news production market. One of the most aggressive detractors of Czech TV is a group of interests around President Milos Zeman. Private media outlets supportive of the president, with TV Barrandov the most vocal, have been waging critical campaigns against the public media, primarily focused on alleged mismanagement of public money. Czech TV gets most of its funding from license fees, a tax of CZK 135 (€5) a month paid by each household that has devices technologically able to access television content. Czech Radio, the country's public service radio, is also funded to a large extent by revenues from (a separate) license fee of CZK 45 (€1.75) a month (Dragomir 2018b).

As in other countries, the narrative critical of the public media is also supported by political parties in the Czech Republic. The political rhetoric, however, tends to change significantly after an election, as the winning parties try to use their influence to gain access to the broadcaster while losing parties begin to attack the channel. In recent years, Prime Minister Babis has adopted a strategy of rapprochement with Czech TV in an apparent effort to win the support of the station's journalists. In recent years, the station's loudest critics have been left-wing and right-wing political forces (Dragomir 2018b).

4.3 Finland

Finland belongs to the group of countries that Trine Syvertsen et al. (2014) call "Nordic Media Welfare States." These countries are characterized, among other things, by universal media and communications services, strong and institutionalized editorial freedom, and cultural policies for the media.

While the Nordic countries are by no means uniform in their systems and communications policy approaches, these characteristics align with the dimensions of the media system model for the Northern cluster (Brüggemann et al. 2014): the wide reach of journalism, professional journalism, low levels of ownership regulation, and relatively low political parallelism. In addition, the Nordics all feature robust public service broadcasting, the national importance and popularity of which has not dramatically declined with the expansion of commercial television (Syvertsen et al. 2014). Finland fits well into the Northern cluster. In addition to the above dimensions, it is notable that Internet penetration in Finland is at 94% and that the country ranks at the top in terms of press freedom year after year; in 2020, Finland was second on the RSF Press Freedom Index (RSF 2020).

The role of the Finnish Broadcasting Company (Yleisradio Oy, or Yle) in the Finnish media system and Finnish society, is central and has remained so, even with the proliferation of commercial broadcasting and online media. Television broadcasting in Finland started as a distinctive mixed system based on the coexistence of public and private media. The commercial operator MTV would broadcast on Yle-owned channels and partly fund public broadcasting. Broadcasting licenses were not granted to other parties. This de facto Yle monopoly ended in the 1990s with the so-called managed liberalization of television broadcasting, which led to the creation of a genuinely dual system (Hellman 1999). As in many European systems, a significant part of Yle's funding was generated from license fees, but the fee was changed to a public broadcasting tax as of January 1, 2013. In 2020, this Yle tax is 2.5% of an individual's taxable income, up to a maximum of €163 a year.

Today, Yle remains well funded and has a notable reach. Its revenues in 2019 was €478m, an impressive figure in a country with 5.5 million inhabitants; moreover, Yle's funding level has not changed in recent years. In 2019, 96% of Finns accessed one of Yle's services at least once a week (Yle 2019). Yle boasts four television channels and six radio channels as well as Yle Areena, its popular streaming service. Yle's television channels accounted for 44% of the yearly audience share in 2019 (Finnpanel 2019). Both its broadcasting and online news are considered amongst the top news brands in the country (Newman et al. 2020, p. 69). Even so, Yle is struggling with and diligently seeking to solve the dilemma that many other PSM, including those in the countries examined in this chapter, are facing: how to reach younger audiences (e.g., Schulz et al. 2019).

While Yle has not been subjected to major attempts at capture, it has been at the center of public debates for decades. As Trine Syvertsen et al. (2014) note, Nordic public service broadcasting used to carry stigmas of both right- and left-wing biases, particularly in the 1960s, 1970s, and 1980s. This was due to several factors, including "careful political journalism" resulting from the broadcasters' overall loyalty to the "socialdemocratic order." Today, Yle serves audiences with diverse political views. The average level of trust in PSM news is high across the left, center, and right of the political spectrum (Schulz et al. 2019, p. 25).

Nevertheless, the Finnish Broadcasting Company is frequently criticized in the media, mainly by other media and political actors. Most recent discussions focus on the lack of diversity in content and biased political viewpoints. Many commentaries insinuate or openly allege that Yle may not be serving different audience groups equally, whether the issue is about age, language group, or region. There are also questions about Yle's remit, as the broadcaster produces popular content that competes unfairly—thanks to the Yle tax—with commercial media (Yle 2020a).

According to an EBU report (2020b) on PSM and trust, Yle fares well when it comes to perceived political pressure. In fact, among the five countries examined in this chapter, Finland is the only one with low perceived pressure on its PSM organization. An example of the relatively mundane challenges faced by the Finnish Broadcasting Company is an incident that might not have made waves in other contexts but elicited a major debate over Yle's role in 2017 and temporarily dropped the country's Press Freedom Index ranking down a few places. The affair known as "Sipilägate," named after the Prime Minister Juha Sipilä, involved his attempt to influence news coverage on the public broadcaster (Yle 2017):

> The PM admitted to sending around 20 emails to a Yle journalist reporting on a government decision to award €200 million in additional funding to the cash-strapped mine. Just two weeks later, the stricken mine awarded a half-million-euro contract to a company owned by Sipilä's relatives.... Sipilä reportedly applied pressure on the national broadcaster to kill further reporting on the matter, prompting two journalists to quit. They cited political pressure as the reason for their decisions, although senior management in the company denied caving to the Prime Minister's demands.

In general, however, debates for and against Yle are part and parcel of Finland's political debate culture. In early 2020, the fiercest foe was the right-wing True Finns party. In its program for media and cultural policy, True Finns claimed that Yle's coverage of the European Union and migration issues are especially biased and that Yle offers services of little use, such as Swedish-language programming for that linguistic minority group (Karkkola 2020). The party's highly unrealistic proposal was to do away with the Yle tax and introduce a pay service for television broadcasting. However, the shift from the license fee to tax-based funding for PSM could be a sign of laying the ground for pressure through funding decisions (Public Media Alliance 2019). While even commercial competitors like the largest Finnish daily Helsingin Sanomat praised Yle's COVID-19 coverage in spring 2020 (Kanerva 2020), the corona-induced challenges to the economy and the state budget may affect Yle's financing model, as the Finnish taxation system does allow for changes to the tax rate. Another sudden challenge emerged in June 2020, highlighting the challenges of Yle, even if it is the most trusted news source and a central actor in the media landscape. The Finnish Media Federation, an advocacy organization for private companies in the media and printing industries, had in 2017 filed a complaint with the EU Commission, claiming that Yle's textual online content is in conflict with EU state aid rules. Three years thereafter the government, after (unpublished) discussions with the Commission, considered amending the Act on Yleisradio accordingly, to limit its text-based web content mainly to support its audio and video content. In practice, this might mean less competition to commercial online news providers (Yle 2020b).

4.4 Spain

As in other Southern European countries, the mass media in Spain have traditionally been seen as means of "ideological expression and political mobilization," because of their involvement in the political conflicts that characterized the history of the country (Papathanassopoulos 2007). An important characteristic of the Southern cluster to which Spain belongs is a high degree of political parallelism (Brüggemann et al. 2014).

Spain's PSM—both the national broadcaster RTVE and the country's regional broadcast media—have been the targets of criticism for more than a decade, mainly because the politicization of these outlets has negative consequences on their reporting. In fact, government interference has characterized the Spanish PSM throughout most of its history (de Miguel et al. 2013).

The high level of capture of the PSM in Spain, as elsewhere, is achieved through two mechanisms: financing and by appointing the governing structures that manage and supervise the operations of these media. Spain's PSM legislation does not include provisions to prevent the politicization of RTVE. In 2012, Spain's parliament amended the law on public broadcasting to give itself the power to appoint the chair and members of the public broadcaster's governing board through a simple majority instead of a supermajority (two-thirds of all legislators), as had been the case until 2012. Notably, the board chair has the power to appoint all the key editorial positions. This procedure allows for the direct influence of politicians on the broadcaster's editorial policies and practices.

The governing structure model of the regional PSM largely mirrors the RTVE model. Regional parliaments, or in some cases regional governments, are in charge of appointing the governing boards of the regional public media and their general directors who, as with RTVE, have significant power in their outlets; they choose the people who will fill their stations' management structures (Fernández Alonso and Fernández Viso 2012). There are 13 public regional broadcasters, 12 of which are grouped in the *Federación de Organismos de Radio y Televisión Autonómicos* (FORTA), an alliance of regional public broadcasters. Some regional public broadcasters are actually for-profit corporations; others are public entities with an administrative structure similar to other public offices (Campos-Freire et al. 2020).

Beyond the power of appointment, the other mechanism used to control Spain's PSM in Spain is funding. The Spanish government spends vast amounts of money on the media. While that is not necessarily a bad thing, it has a negative impact on the outlets' editorial independence, particularly when those funds come with clear strings attached. In 2018, the government spent over €2bn on the media, including funding for RTVE and regional public media and financing for state advertising. That is nearly double the turnover of Atresmedia, the largest private media company in Spain (Campos-Freire et al. 2020).

RTVE is by far Spain's largest recipient of government media funding. In 2018, some 37% of RTVE's total budget of €916m came directly from the national budget, but the rest of its funding is also a disguised form of government aid, as it comes either from fees for broadcast spectrum rental or taxes imposed on private broadcasters and telecom firms. RTVE has been funded this way since 2009, when a law requiring the broadcaster to stop carrying advertisements took effect. The regional public service broadcasters had a combined budget upwards of €1.07bn in 2019, some 90% of which was contributed by regional governments (Campos-Freire et al. 2020).

Both the political influence in how PSM are managed and their privileged financial position have become key themes feeding a strong critical discourse around Spain's public media system. This criticism is both internal (fuelled by the broadcasters' own staff) and external (from various parts of civil society or industry players).

The criticism within the public media is triggered mainly by the political pressures that journalists working in these media must grapple with on a regular basis. Examples of reporters at RTVE mobilizing to stave off such attacks abound. In 2018, more than 50 RTVE employees launched an initiative to defend "an authentic free, independent and plural public radio and television" to "avoid abuse and reprisals" (Europa Press 2018). RTVE's News Council, an internal body working to guarantee independence and unbiased information, has repeatedly reported cases of manipulation by political authorities. For example, between July 2015 and January 2016, a total of 113 cases of bad practices were recorded (Nortes 2018). In 2019, plans to centralize RTVE's news programming at its headquarters, which journalists feared would have led to more control, came under fierce critical scrutiny, prompting MujeresRTVE, a group of the outlet's women reporters, to launch an online campaign denouncing political meddling in the broadcaster's affairs (Herrera 2019).

Similar protests regularly erupt among the regional public media. In an unprecedented protest, the staff of CRTVG, the public service broadcaster in Galicia, took to the streets in September 2018 and called on the government "to stop meddling in the station's affairs" (Media Power Monitor 2018).

The criticism and complaints of the journalists working in public media are exploited by the broadcaster's enemies, whose goal is to shape a narrative that will tarnish or even ruin the PSM's reputation in Spanish society. Two key players are central to managing this narrative: private media and political parties.

The attacks of private media against the public broadcasters were prompted until 2009 by RTVE's competition for advertising revenue, which is the main source of funding for privately owned media. Once RTVE stopped airing advertisements in 2009, it was expected that these attacks would cease. Nevertheless, because part of the public media budget comes from a tax imposed on private broadcasters and telecom firms, this critical narrative has continued unabated.

"RTVE, like all television channels, is at the service of its owner, in this case, the government in power and this, in turn, coerces the private sector to finance it," wrote Marc Fortuño, a journalist at El Blog Salmón, a digital portal. "The end result is a medium that serves as a transmission belt for the ideology of the government, especially in the news media" (Fortuño 2018). These problems often prompt experts and other observers to call for the closure of RTVE.

Political parties also exploit the critical narrative against public media for their own benefit. Ironically, though, their stance toward the public media is more tempered, as they know that the broadcaster will be a powerful tool if they take the reins of power. Criticism of RTVE's programming has come from almost every part of the political spectrum at one time or another. In recent years, complaints have come from key opposition parties, including the right-wing party Vox and the Popular Party. The central theme of their criticism was the alleged manipulation of the editorial line of RTVE by the ruling Spanish Socialist Workers' Party and Podemos, its junior coalition partner.

What is important to note, however, is that although the critical narrative surrounding the public media in Spain is clearly dominated and used to a large extent by opposition parties and receives ample coverage in the private media, the main arguments put forward by these critics hold true to a significant extent. That distinguishes Spain from highly captured media systems where such a critical discourse against PSM does not exist simply because an elite of politicians and oligarchs control both private and public media.

4.5 United Kingdom

In the media system cluster model (Brüggemann et al. 2014), the United Kingdom is an example of the Central cluster, defined by strong public broadcasting, strict ownership regulation, and low press subsidies. Indeed, public media has historically played a major role in British society, being accessed, accepted, and appreciated due to its independence and professionalism. The political independence of the BBC, which has made it extremely resilient to capture in many situations, was secured by a set of structural and normative sources of support. Structurally, the British broadcasting was created as a "formally autonomous system" rather than a politically affiliated one (Kelly 1983), which is an important distinction compared to PSM in other countries.

Much of the BBC's resistance to capture has been achieved through regulatory arrangements that are largely related to its governing structures and its funding model. The powers of the BBC, for example, are laid out in a Royal Charter (rather than ordinary parliamentary legislation) that has usually been reviewed once every ten years. The broadcaster has a supervisory trust in place that watches for any threats to the BBC's independence. All key executive appointments, except for its Director-General, are made by the BBC itself. The broadcaster's funding model is based on a license fee that all households in Britain equipped with audio-visual content-receiving devices must pay. All these rules enable internal editorial independence: only journalists have authority over journalists, and they all abide by editorial codes and guidelines (Blumler 2016).

Despite all these rules and mechanisms, BBC's independence has never been absolutely guaranteed (Hanretty 2011). British politicians have routinely attempted to influence how the media—especially the popular BBC—cover their work. That has forced the BBC to carefully manage its relations with the government, which are not free from open conflicts between journalists and politicians or even threats by the authorities against the BBC (Seaton 2015). Throughout its history, criticism of BBC coverage that culminated in the resignation of its Director-General has come from both the Labour and Conservative parties. However, in most cases, the BBC has responded with aplomb, rarely tempering or changing its coverage under pressure, unless it admitted wrongdoing or sloppy reporting.

However, the past decade or so has seen an intensifying series of concerted attacks against the BBC from a circle of powerful businesses associated with some of the largest private media in Britain, particularly those owned by Rupert Murdoch, and the Conservative Party. That has led to a consistent bias in some of the BBC's news coverage, particularly of the Labour Party (Dragomir 2016).

Although the BBC cannot be defined as a captured media, its editors and journalists still enjoying editorial freedom and independence, never in its history has the BBC come under such a targeted and fierce attack as under Boris Johnson's premiership. A product of Conservative-leaning newspapers, Johnson focused his onslaught on the BBC's funding model. In February 2020, he called for severe cutbacks at the BBC and confirmed plans to replace the license fee model (where households are legally obliged to pay the fee) with a subscription-based model, under which households will be offered the choice to pay the fee (PA Media 2020). Leading Conservative politicians suggested turning the BBC into a service that could imitate the success of Netflix, a video-streaming platform with more than 10 million UK users. However, the BBC and its supporters argued that it has a much wider focus than Netflix and reports on the news, which Netflix does not. The government's initial plans were to sack

450 members of the BBC News team and slash roughly £80m of its budget by 2022.

Some British observers noted that Johnson's ire was fuelled by the BBC's unflattering coverage of the Tories in the 2019 elections. However, a more in-depth analysis points to a deeper dissatisfaction with the BBC in the wider circle of Conservative politicians and media. The attacks on the BBC come at a time of growing public dissatisfaction with the license fee, under pressure from subscription-based content providers.

One key theme in the narrative against the BBC is the idea of overspending, which is used to negatively influence public opinion about how the corporation uses taxpayer money. These aspects have been excessively covered by some of the UK's Conservative-leaning media, especially those run by News Corp, Murdoch's media group. Headlines feeding into this narrative such as "Bloated BBC needs a boss who accepts it must change and represent more than the London media elite" (Wootton 2020) or "BBC paid out £1.6 million on flights in one year despite its push to go green" (Moriarty 2020) regularly appear in The Sun, one of News Corp's key titles in Britain. It is partly these developments affecting editorial independence that placed the UK 35th (respectable, but well behind the top performers) on the RSF Press Freedom Index (RSF 2020).

The government's plans to alter the BBC funding model will be extremely disruptive. In 2016, Damian Tambini (2016) wrote that "informal and pervasive timidity and self-censorship that may infect an organization that faces funding cuts, uncertainty about the future scope, and new funding burden, is worse than the prospect of direct editorial interference through regulation." That appears to be precisely the thinking behind the 2020 wave of attacks by the Conservatives against the BBC. Dismantling the BBC funding model will not only weaken the broadcaster's autonomy but will alter the very idea of public media in the UK. Moreover, it will have lasting repercussions on struggling PSM elsewhere that have closely followed and sought to imitate the BBC model, which is the case for many countries that have undertaken public broadcasting.

However, the crisis caused by the COVID-19 pandemic has led to significant changes in the narrative about the role of the public media. With Britons facing previously unimaginable challenges during the crisis, demand for accurate and objective news has surged since March 2020. Already recognized before the crisis as the leading news brand in the UK

(Reuters 2019), the BBC saw its audience, which was the largest in the country before the crisis at some 30%, grow by 44% between March and May 2020. Its iPlayer streaming service had a record 20.4 million requests to stream programs on March 23, 2020 (d'Ancona 2020).

Although this surge in popularity has changed the tone of the debate about the BBC, the corporation is still likely to face numerous challenges as consumption patterns and financing models continue to change. Even in the five months before March 2020, The Times reported that 82,000 households cancelled their license fees, either encouraged by plans (made public by the government before the crisis) to decriminalize failure to pay the license fee or forced by the financial challenges brought on by the crisis (Moore 2020). What the future of the BBC will look like is hard to predict, but its current financing model appears to be heading rapidly toward extinction.

5 New Context: Discussion

> [The BBC's] role helping the population grapple with a world muted by the pandemic has started to pacify the BBC's critics—a reversal in fortune when the public broadcaster started the year defending itself against attacks from both sides of the political divide and facing serious questions from Boris Johnson's government about the future of its funding. Tsang (2020)

We are writing this chapter in a new kind of context during the COVID-19 crisis, which has also been called an "infodemic" (e.g., Charlton 2020), given its vast challenges of inadequate and patently false dissemination of information.

In this situation, it seems that the value of PSM is being rediscovered. The pandemic is likely to temper or even scuttle the plans to disrupt the BBC's funding model, given the corporation's role in keeping its viewers abreast of the latest developments. The BBC is not alone in experiencing an uptick in appreciation and audience. An overview of news audience figures from 29 members of the EBU reveals that the average viewing share of PSM evening news was up 20% in March 2020 over the first quarter of 2019. In addition, younger audiences began to tune in, with an average increase of 44% over 2019. The daily PSM online and YouTube reach peaked in mid-March 2020 (EBU 2020a).

Despite this growing popularity, PSM are paradoxically facing numerous threats; some are triggered by continuously changing markets, technological advances, and antagonistic political voices, while others are sparked by the new realities that the pandemic crisis has created. In the UK, for example, although quality content is in high demand, harsh economic conditions are already forcing an increasing number of households to stop paying the license fee, which is likely to have a destabilizing effect on the BBC. The PSM financing model itself is being disrupted as the content industry rapidly evolves into a subscription-based environment. Moreover, whether genuinely prompted by the pandemic crisis or using it as a pretext, governments are showing signs of trying to control the public discourse even more by tightening their grip on national PSM.

The operation and remit of PSM are being shaped by both these emerging trends and the status and history of the PSM in specific contexts. Indeed, our framework for analyzing PSM capture in its contexts unsurprisingly reveals that the more deeply rooted the ethos and praxis of public service broadcasting is in a national media system, the more resilient PSM organizations are when facing pressure.

However, the framework calls attention to the fact that PSM are an essential front in the battle over meanings in political discourses and media policy decision-making throughout Europe. The more turbulent the economic and political conditions—precisely when independent, well-resourced media are most needed—the more likely public media organizations are to face hardship. Viewed through our model, the five countries examined, despite dramatic differences in context, exhibit the features discovered in other studies of media capture; namely, digitization and the political trends of the twenty-first century.

The proposed framework is by no means a predictive tool; nor does it signal that specific comparable quantifiable indicators could measure media capture. Rather, it showcases how easily PSM can be politicized and used in various ways as a symbol of bias, wasteful public spending, or the quality of content and reliability of information (Table 12.1).

Against this backdrop, the risk of destabilizing the BBC may not have completely disappeared with the pandemic. Even so, the framework depicted here may help to assess the state of media capture and prompt policy innovation in the post-crisis rebuilding era. Trust in the media is about not only the credibility of content but also the trustworthiness of the media—in this case, PSM—as an institution (e.g., Prochazka and Schweiger 2019). This framework helps to assess the latter which we believe is a prerequisite of the former.

Table 12.1 Summary findings based on the comparative framework for public service media

	Belgium	Czech Republic	Finland	Spain	United Kingdom
Role of PSM in the national media system?	Strong legal and cultural standing, despite linguistic divisions into different organizations and their varying models (including funding) (Western cluster)	Relatively strong standing in a highly captured media system (Eastern-Central cluster)	Strong, central, continued significant reach and trust (Northern cluster)	Significant national and regional player, but increasingly weakened by its highly politicized structure (Southern cluster)	Iconic cultural presence, with a set of structural and normative sources of support for independence (Central cluster)
Main discursive challenges to PSM?	No evidence that indicates a concerted attack on the role and operation of public media	Private media outlets supportive of the president waging critical campaigns against the public media	A recurring part of the political agenda: claims of distortion, especially regarding the challenging news market, bias, waste of public resources in an era of abundant digital content; challenged by populist politics	Critical voices by the opposition regarding both political influence in how PSM are managed and their privileged financial position; both reflect capture	Critical voices regarding elitism and biased content, mainly from political groups aligned with the interests of large commercial media conglomerates

(continued)

Table 12.1 (continued)

	Belgium	Czech Republic	Finland	Spain	United Kingdom
Structural capture?	Low possibility: growing political influence and cuts in financial resources	High possibility: one of the few public service broadcasters in Central or Eastern Europe that has managed to successfully stave off political attacks, but under intensified public attacks (see above)	Low possibility: from license fee to budgeted public funding; narrowing the content remit online	In place: government interference is typical through financing and the appointment of the governing structure	High possibility: attacks on the funding model are already financially destabilizing the public media, creating room for political pressures and interference

REFERENCES

Bajomi-Lázár, P. (2014). *Party Colonisation of the Media in Central and Eastern Europe*. Budapest: Central European University Press.

Blumler, J. G. (2016). To Be Independent or Not to Be Independent, That Is the Question. *Publizistik,* 61, 305–320. https://doi.org/10.1007/s11616-016-0284-6.

Brüggemann, M., Engesser, S., Büchel, F., Humprecht, E., & Castro, L. (2014). Hallin and Mancini Revisited: Four Empirical Types of Western Media Systems. *Journal of Communication,* 64(6), 1037–1065. https://doi.org/10.1111/jcom.12127.

Campos-Freire, F., Rodríguez-Castro, M., Rodríguez-Vázquez, A.I., Gesto-Louro, A., Juanatey-Boga, Ó., & Martínez-Fernández, V. A. (2020). Media Influence Matrix: Spain. Funding Journalism. Center for Media, Data and Society. Retrieved June 2, 2020, from https://cmds.ceu.edu/sites/cmcs.ceu.hu/files/attachment/basicpage/1632/mimspainfunding_0.pdf.

Castro Herrero, C. L., Humprecht, E., Engesser, S., Brüggemann, M. L., & Büchel, F. (2017). Rethinking Hallin and Mancini Beyond the West: An Analysis of Media Systems in Central and Eastern Europe. *International*

Journal of Communication, 11, 4797–4823. Retrieved from https://ijoc.org/index.php/ijoc/article/view/6035/2196.

Charlton, E. (2020). How Experts Are Fighting the Coronavirus 'Infodemic'. *World Economic Forum*. Retrieved June 2, 2020, from https://www.weforum.org/agenda/2020/03/how-experts-are-fighting-the-coronavirus-infodemic.

D'Ancona, M. (2020). The BBC Is Back. *Tortoise Media*. Retrieved June 2, 2020, from https://members.tortoisemedia.com/2020/05/04/the-bbc-is-back/content.html.

De Miguel, J. C., Casado, M. A., & Zallo, R. (2013). Crise et politisation de la radiotélévision de service public en Espagne. *Les Enjeux de l'information et de la communication*, 14(2), 51–65. https://doi.org/10.3917/enic.015.0051.

Donders, K., Van den Bock, H., & Raats, T. (2019). Public Service Media in a Divided Country: Governance and Functioning of Public Broadcasters in Belgium. In E. Polonska & C. Beckett (Eds.), *Public Service Broadcasting and Media Systems in Troubled European Democracies* (pp. 89–107). London: Palgrave Macmillan.

Dragomir, M. (2016). The BBC in the Dock Over Bias. *MediaPowerMonitor*. Retrieved June 2, 2020, from http://mpmonitor.org/2016/07/the-bbc-in-the-dock-over-bias/.

Dragomir, M. (2018). Media Influence Matrix: Czech Republic. Funding Journalism. Center for Media, Data & Society (CMDS). Retrieved June 2, 2020, from https://cmds.ceu.edu/sites/cmcs.ceu.hu/files/attachment/basicpage/1396/mimfundingczech_2.pdf.

Dragomir, M. (2019). Media Capture in Europe. Media Development Investment Fund. Retrieved June 2, 2020, from https://www.mdif.org/wp-content/uploads/2019/07/MDIF-Report-Media-Capture-in-Europe.pdf.

EBU. (2020a). COVID-19 Crisis: PSM Audience Performance. Updated Version (April 2020). Geneva: European Broadcasting Union. Retrieved June 2, 2020, from https://www.ebu.ch/files/live/sites/ebu/files/Publications/MIS/login_only/psm/EBU-MIS_COVID-19_Crisis_PSM_Audience_Performance-Public_UPDATE.pdf.

EBU. (2020b). *Market Insights: Trust in Media 2020*. Geneva: European Broadcasting Union.

Europa Press. (2018, September 2). Profesionales de RTVE crean una plataforma contra 'las represalias' y el 'intolerable número de ceses'. *El diario*. Retrieved June 2, 2020, from https://vertele.eldiario.es/noticias/Profesionales-RTVE-plataforma-atropello-represalias_0_2045495436.html.

Fernández Alonso, I., & Fernández Viso, A. (2012). ¿Cómo se gobiernan las radiotelevisiones públicas autonómicas?: órganos de gestión, injerencia política y fragilidad de los mecanismos de control. In J. C. Miguel-de-Bustos & M. A. Casado del Río (Eds.), *Televisiones autonómicas* (pp. 119–142). Barcelona: Gedisa.

Finnpanel. (2019). Finnpanel—TV Audience Measurement. Retrieved June 2, 2020, from https://www.finnpanel.fi/en/tulokset/tv/vuosi/pvatav/2019/pvatav.html.

Fortuño, M. (2018). Cerrar RTVE es la mejor solución para todos. El Blog Salmón. Retrieved June 2, 2020, from https://www.elblogsalmon.com/empresas/cerrar-rtve-mejor-solucion-para-todos.

Freedman, D. (2018). 'Public Service' and the Journalism Crisis: Is the BBC the Answer? *Television & New Media, 20*(3), 203–218. https://doi.org/10.1177/1527476418760985.

Frisch, N., Belair-Gagnon, V., & Agur, C. (2018). Media Capture with Chinese Characteristics: Changing Patterns in Hong Kong's News Media System. *Journalism, 19*(8), 1165–1181. https://doi.org/10.1177/1464884917724632.

Hallin, D. C. (2016). Typology of Media Systems. *Oxford Research Encyclopedia of Politics.*. https://doi.org/10.1093/acrefore/9780190228637.013.205.

Hallin, D. C., & Mancini, P. (2004). *Comparing Media Systems: Three Models of Media and Politics.* Cambridge: Cambridge University Press.

Hanretty, C. (2011). *Public Broadcasting and Political Interference.* Abingdon, UK: Routledge.

Hellman, H. (1999). *From Companions to Competitors. The Changing Broadcasting Markets and Television Programming in Finland.* PhD dissertation, University of Tampere, Tampere, Finland. Retrieved June 2, 2020, from https://trepo.tuni.fi/bitstream/handle/10024/67185/978-951-44-9914-2.pdf?sequence=1&isAllowed=y.

Herrera, A. (2019). *Uncertainty Continues for RTVE.* Public Media Alliance. Retrieved June 2, 2020, from https://www.publicmediaalliance.org/uncertainty-continues-for-rtve/.

Kanerva, A. (2020). Suomalaiset ovat päässeet kurkistamaan Jenni Vartiaisen kotistudioon ja nähneet Nordean analyytikon huonekasvit—näin koronavirus mullisti Ylen tv-uutisten ulkoasun. *Helsingin Sanomat.* Retrieved June 2, 2020, from https://www.hs.fi/kulttuuri/art-2000006472854.html.

Karkkola, M. (2020). Perussuomalaiset: Yle-vero pois, jos 'journalistinen taso ei nouse'—Tilalle vapaaehtoinen Yle-maksukortti. *Uusi Suomi.* Retrieved June 2, 2020, from https://www.uusisuomi.fi/uutiset/perussuomalaiset-yle-vero-pois-jos-journalistinen-taso-ei-nouse-tilalle-vapaaehtoinen-yle-maksukortti/dd7f1f4c-4b3b-4e46-8f82-7aa0a7f9c704.

Kelly, M. (1983). Influences on Broadcasting Policies for Election Coverage. In J. G. Blumler (Ed.), *Communicating to Voters: Television in the First European Parliamentary Elections* (pp. 65–82). London: Sage.

Kwak, J. (2014). Cultural Capture and the Financial Crisis. In D. Carpenter & D. Moss (Eds.), *Preventing Regulatory Capture: Special Interest Influence and How to Limit It* (pp. 71–98). Cambridge: Cambridge University Press.

Márquez-Ramírez, M., & Guerrero, M. A. (2017). Clientelism and Media Capture in Latin America. Center for International Media Assistance. Retrieved June 2, 2020, from https://www.cima.ned.org/resource/media-capture-clientelism-media-capture-latin-america/.

Mazzoleni, G., & Vigevani, G. E. (2005). Italy. In *Television across Europe: Regulation, Policy, and Independence, Volume 2* (pp. 865–954). Open Society Institute. Retrieved June 2, 2020, from https://www.opensocietyfoundations.org/uploads/c2f2d8d6-3c2c-459a-b2b7-e397987d9236/voltwo_20051011_0.pdf.

McChesney, R., & Nichols, J. (2010). *The Death and Life of American journalism. The Media Revolution That Will Begin the World Again*. Philadelphia: Nation Books.

MediaPowerMonitor. (2018, September 16). Galicia: Journalists Raise Against Manipulation. *MediaPowerMonitor*. Retrieved June 2, 2020, from http://mpmonitor.org/2018/09/galicia-journalists-raise-against-manipulation/.

Milosavljević, M., & Poler, M. (2018). Balkanization and Pauperization: Analysis of Media Capture of Public Service Broadcasters in the Western Balkans. *Journalism*, *19*(8), 1149–1164. https://doi.org/10.1177/1464884917724629.

Minder, R. (2015, November 5). Spain's News Media Are Squeezed by Government and Debt. *New York Times*. Retrieved June 2, 2020, from https://www.nytimes.com/2015/11/06/world/europe/as-spains-media-industry-changes-rapidly-some-worry-about-objectivity.html.

Moore, M. (2020, May 11). 82,000 Ditch TV Licence as Streaming Grows. *The Times*. Retrieved June 2, 2020, from https://www.thetimes.co.uk/article/82-000-ditch-tv-licence-as-streaming-grows-m0v2hw5hg.

Moriarty, R. (2020, February 15). BBC Paid Out £1.6 Million on Flights in One Year Despite Its Push to Go Green. *The Sun*. Retrieved June 2, 2020, from https://www.thesun.co.uk/news/10972806/bbc-million-flights-one-year-despite-push-go-green/.

Mungiu-Pippidi, A. (2013). Freedom without Impartiality: The Vicious Circle of Media Capture. In P. Goss, K. & Jakubowicz (Eds.), *Media Transformations in the Post-Communist World* (pp. 33–48). Plymouth: Lexington Books.

Newman, N., Fletcher, R., Schulz, A., Andi, S., & Nielsen, R. K. (2020). *Reuters Institute Digital News Report*. Oxford, UK: Reuters Institute of the Study of Journalism.

Nielsen, R. K. (2017). *Media Capture in the Digital Age*. Center for International Media Assistance. Retrieved June 2, 2020, from https://www.cima.ned.org/resource/media-capture-media-capture-digital-age/.

Nortes, S. (2018). Spain: 'Purge' at State-Owned RTVE Following Political Pressure. Index on Censorship. Retrieved June 2, 2020, from https://www.

indexoncensorship.org/2018/12/spain-purge-underway-rtve-political-pressure/.
PA Media. (2020, February 16). No 10 Could Scrap BBC License Fee in Favour of a Subscription Model. *The Guardian*. Retrieved June 2, 2020, from https://www.theguardian.com/media/2020/feb/16/no-10-launches-attack-on-bbc-as-licence-fee-comes-under-threat?CMP=fb_gu&utm_medium=Social&utm_source=Facebook&fbclid=IwAR1yOBROjKNCE9zULrd6nJnMQUvnRzhJcro8ILdAyf8hl-3KpreuMIC8rfc#Echobox=1581840315.
Papathanassopoulos, S. (2007). The Mediterranean/Polarized Pluralist Model Countries. In G. Terzis (Ed.), *European Media Governance: National and Regional Dimensions* (pp. 191–200). Bristol, UK: Intellect Books.
Prochazka, F., & Schweiger, W. (2019). How to Measure Generalized Trust in News Media? An Adaptation and Test of Scales. *Communication Methods and Measures, 13*(1), 26–42. https://doi.org/10.1080/19312458.2018.1506021.
Public Media Alliance. (2019). Changing Times for Public Media Funding. Retrieved June 2, 2020, from https://www.publicmediaalliance.org/changing-times-for-public-media-funding/.
Raeymaeckers, K., & Heinderyckx, F. (2017). Belgium: Instruments of Media Accountability Divided Along Language Lines. In R. Eberwein, S. Fengler, & M. Karmasin (Eds.), *European Handbook of Media Accountability* (pp. 14–23). Abingdon, UK: Routledge.
RSF. (2020). 2020 World Press Freedom Index—Reporters Without Borders. https://rsf.org/en/ranking.
Ryabinska, N. (2014). Media Capture in Post-Communist Ukraine. *Problems of Post-Communism, 6*(2), 46–60.
Schiffrin, A. (2018). Introduction to Special Issue on Media Capture. *Journalism, 19*(8), 1033–1042. https://doi.org/10.1177/1464884917725167.
Schulz, A., Levy, D. A. L., & Nielsen, R. K. (2019). *Old, Educated, and Politically Diverse: The Audience of Public Service News*. Reuters Institute for the Study of Journalism at the University of Oxford. Retrieved June 2, 2020, from https://reutersinstitute.politics.ox.ac.uk/our-research/old-educated-and-politically-diverse-audience-public-service-news.
Seaton, J. (2015). *Pinkoes and Traitors: The BBC and the Nation 1974–1987*. London: Profile Books.
Simon, F. (2019, July 10). Why Europe's Right-Wing Populists Hate Public Broadcasters. *European Journalism Observatory*. Retrieved June 2, 2020, from https://en.ejo.ch/media-politics/press-freedom/why-europes-right-wing-populists-hate-public-broadcasters.
Sjøvaag, H., Pedersen, T. A., & Owren, T. (2019). Is Public Service Broadcasting a Threat to Commercial Media? *Media, Culture & Society, 41*(6), 808–27.

Syvertsen, T., Enli, G., Mjos, O. J., & Moe, H. (2014). *The Media Welfare State: Nordic Media in the Digital Era*. Ann Arbor, MI: The University of Michigan Press.

Syvertsen, T., & Enli, G. (2018). Public Service in Europe: Five Key Points. In D. Freedman & V. Goblot (Eds.), *A Future for Public Service Television* (pp. 83–90). London: Goldsmiths.

Tsang, A. (2020, April 10). How the Beleaguered BBC Became 'Comfort Food' in a Pandemic. *The New York Times*. Retrieved June 2, 2020, from https://www.nytimes.com/2020/04/10/arts/television/bbc-coronavirus.html.

Tambini, D. (2016, January 27). Can the New Charter Protect BBC Independence? Retrieved June 2, 2020, from https://blogs.lse.ac.uk/medialse/2016/01/27/can-the-new-charter-protect-bbc-independence/.

UNESCO. (n.d.). *Public Service Broadcasting*. Retrieved June 2, 2020, from http://www.unesco.org/new/en/communication-and-information/media-development/public-service-broadcasting/.

Van Dijck, J., & Poell, T. (2014). Making Public Television Social? Public Service Broadcasting and the Challenges of Social Media. *Television & New Media, 16*(2), 148–164. https://doi.org/10.1177/1527476414527136.

Voltmer, K. (2013). *The Media in Transitional Democracies*. Cambridge: Polity.

Wilson, S. (2020). Public service media, an overview: Reflecting on news and trends. *Interactions: Studies in Communication & Culture, 11*(2), 253–259.

Woodall, A. (2018). Media Capture in the Era of Megaleaks. *Journalism, 19*(8), 1182–1195. https://doi.org/10.1177/1464884917725166.

Wootton, D. (2020, January 23). Bloated BBC Needs a Boss Who Accepts It Must Change and Represent More Than the London Media Elite. *The Sun*. Retrieved June 2, 2020, from https://www.thesun.co.uk/news/10807550/bbc-boss-accepts-change-london-elite/.

Yeşil, B. (2018). Authoritarian Turn or Continuity? Governance of Media Through Capture and Discipline in the AKP Era. *South European Society and Politics, 23*(2), 239–257. https://doi.org/10.1080/13608746.2018.1487137.

Yle. (2017). 'Sipilägate' Topples Finland from Top of Press Freedom Table. Retrieved June 2, 2020, from https://yle.fi/uutiset/osasto/news/sipilagate_topples_finland_from_top_of_press_freedom_table/9570235.

Yle. (2019). Economic Figures in 2019. Yle's Year 2019. Retrieved June 2, 2020, from https://yle.fi/aihe/yles-year-2019/economic-figures-in-2019.

Yle. (2020a). Ylen vastaukset (Answers by Yle)—Yleisradio. Retrieved June 2, 2020, from https://yle.fi/aihe/yleisradio/vastaukset.

Yle. (2020b). Gov't Aims to Limit Yle Web Publications—Yleisradio. Retrieved June 16, 2020, from https://yle.fi/uutiset/osasto/news/govt_aims_to_limit_yle_web_publications/11405119.

Zielonka, J. (Ed.). (2015). *Media and Politics in New Democracies: Europe in a Comparative Perspective*. New York: Oxford University Press. https://doi.org/10.1093/acprof:oso/9780198747536.001.0001.

CHAPTER 13

The Challenge of Media and Information Literacy for Public Service Media

José Manuel Pérez Tornero, Alton Grizzle, Cristina M. Pulido, and Sally S. Tayie

Media literacy, or Media and Information Literacy (MIL) as referred to by UNESCO, is the term used to describe the skills and abilities needed for conscious and independent development in the communication environment—digital, global, and multimedia—of the information society.

From an educational point of view, media literacy is now considered: (a) a basic skill included in most educational curricula in the world; and (b) a part of the essential right to education. Also, from the point of view of democratic citizenship, media literacy is considered essential for the

---

J. M. Pérez Tornero (✉) • C. M. Pulido
Universität Autònoma de Barcelona, Barcelona, Spain
e-mail: josepmanuel.perez@uab.cat; cristina.pulido@uab.cat

A. Grizzle
UNESCO, Paris, France
e-mail: a.grizzle@unesco.org

S. S. Tayie
Arab Academy for Science, Technology and Maritime Transport, Cairo, Egypt

© The Author(s), under exclusive license to Springer Nature Switzerland AG 2021
M. Túñez-López et al. (eds.), *The Values of Public Service Media in the Internet Society*, Palgrave Global Media Policy and Business, https://doi.org/10.1007/978-3-030-56466-7_13

247

exercise of (a) genuine active citizenship; and (b) an essential part of the various communication rights: freedom of expression, freedom of the press, right to information, copyright, and so on. In this context, several governments and international organizations have recently developed an intense legislative and political activity trying to consolidate the right to media literacy and trying to consolidate strategies and policies that try to promote it socially.

In this chapter we will briefly describe the long road that has led to this situation, and concentrate in particular on how the legal framework is pushing Public Service Media to integrate Media and Information Literacy policies in their strategic lines in the European context.

1 The Right of MIL Policies for Ensuring Democratic Societies

Nowadays, MIL policies are more necessary than ever due to the current challenges we are facing. The COVID-19 pandemic has demonstrated that Media and Information Literacy policies are necessary to confront fake news and misinformation that spread quickly through social networks and have negative effects on the individual and public health. Beyond the negative impact on health, fake news also impacts the quality of democratic societies that put trust in institutions at risk. Hence, supporting quality journalism able to maintain a relationship of trust with the citizens as a reliable information source is a must.

A recent Council of Europe study, 'Supporting Quality Journalism through Media and Information Literacy', was conducted with the purpose of "providing context and evidence (…) on media literacy activities in Europe supporting quality journalism" (Chapman and Oermann 2020). The study analyzed 68 MIL activities. One of the key findings is that:

> "Some of the MIL knowledge and skills required for people to recognise and value quality journalism in the digital age relate to knowing how the media is regulated and how the media is funded, understanding rights and responsibilities in relation to data and privacy, and having knowledge of how social media and search platforms operate" (Chapman and Oermann 2020).

According to the study, such a set of knowledge and skills, in which the role of the media appears, was found to be among the least included by the analyzed MIL initiatives. Accordingly, the authors recommend that in addition to reinforcing MIL's role in "promoting and protecting quality journalism in the digital age," it is essential to "create media literacy programmes that help citizens of all age groups to develop the MIL skills and knowledge that will support quality journalism" (Chapman and Oermann 2020).

Despite Media and Information Literacy being a relatively young field, there is a solid background on Media and Information Literacy policies (Carlsson and Culver 2013). Over the last decades, UNESCO and the European Commission have been the two main actors promoting and assessing MIL policies. A brief overview for the first 20 years is shown in Table 13.1 (Pérez Tornero et al. 2013) with other contributions added for this chapter:

Pérez-Tornero and Varis (2010) further contributed to defining media literacy under the humanism approach. One of their contributions is systematically organizing actors and spheres in relation to media literacy. Table 13.2 sums up this contribution as shown:

The advancement in the field of MIL in the first 20 years resulted in different recommendations that highlight Media and Information Literacy as the core of the competences required in the twenty-first century. Furthermore, Media and Information Literacy can help in advancing various sustainable development goals (SDGs), such as SDGs 11, 16, and 17 and Targets 4.7, 4.c, and 5.b, by raising citizens' critical awareness of information shared and received, how they communicate, their fundamental freedoms, and critical thinking that makes societies democratic, peaceful, inclusive, safe, and resilient. Media and Information Literacy is an enabler of social cohesion and fair societies in individual and collective contexts. But the question is what is the current status of development of MIL policies? We will focus on the two relevant actors who play a crucial role in defining, promoting, and assessing MIL policies in Europe and around the world—the European Commission and UNESCO.

1.1 Media Literacy by the European Commission

One of the recent developments in the European Commission (EC) has been the review of Audiovisual Media Services Directive (AVMSD) that strongly contributes to media literacy policies in Europe. Prior to the AVMSD, one of the crucial reports developed by the European Audiovisual Observatory in 2016 presented an overview of media literacy practices and

Table 13.1 A brief overview of media literacy/media and information literacy development

Timeline of media literacy development in Europe

Year	Date	Author	Title
1982	Jan, 1982	UNESCO	Grünwald Declaration on Media Education
1989	Oct, 1989	European Union	Television Without Frontiers Directive (TVWF)
	Oct, Nov 1989	UNESCO	General Actes
1990	Jul, 1990	UNESCO	New Directions in Media Education, Toulouse Colloquy
1991	Jul, 1991	European Commission	MEDIA Programme
1999	Jan, 1999	European Commission	Safer Internet Programme
	April, 1999	UNESCO	Congress in Vienna "Educating for the Media and the Digital Age"
2000	March, 2000	European Commission	Lisbon European Council
	May, 2000	European Commission	eLearning Programme. Designing tomorrow's education
	June, 2000	European Council	Recommendation 1466 (2000) of Media Education from the Parliamentary Assembly, Council of Europe
2002	Feb, 2002	UNESCO	"Youth Media Education Seminar in Seville"
	Nov, 2002	European Commission	Proposal for a decision of the European Parliament and of the Council adopting a multi-annual programme (2004-2006) for the effective integration of Information and Communication Technologies (ICT) in education and training systems in Europe (eLearning Programme)
	Dec, 2002	European Parliament	Recommendation 1586 (2002) The digital divide and education
2003	Sept, 2003	UNESCO	Prague Declaration "Towards an Information Literate Society"
2004	N/M, 2004	UK Film Council and BFI	*Promoting Digital Literacy* European Charter for Media Literacy

(*continued*)

Table 13.1 (continued)

Timeline of media literacy development in Europe

2005	Oct, 2005	UNESCO	L'éducation aux médias enjeu des societés du savoir
	Nov, 2005	UNESCO	The Alexandria Proclamation on Information Literacy and Lifelong Learning—Beacons of the Information Society
	Nov, 2005	European Parliament and Council	Recommendation of the European Parliament and of the Council on film heritage and the competitiveness of related industrial activities
2006	March, 2006	European Commission	The Media Literacy Expert Group
	Sep, 2006	Council of Europe	Recommendation Rec (2006)12of the Committee of Ministers to member stateson empowering children in the new information and communications environment
	Dec, 2006	European Parliament and Council	Recommendation of the European Parliament and of the Council on key competences for lifelong learning
	Dec, 2006	European Commission	Public consultation on Media Literacy. Making sense of today's media content
	Dec, 2006	European Parliament and Council	Recommendation of the European Parliament and of the Council on the protection of minors and human dignity and on the right of reply in relation to the competitiveness of the European audio-visual and on-line information services industry
	Dec, 2006	European Parliament and Council	Recommendation of the European Parliament and of the Council of 18 December 2006 on key competences for lifelong learning
	Dec, 2006	European Parliament	European Parliament resolution of 16 December 2008 on media literacy in a digital world
2007	Jun, 2007	UNESCO	Paris Agenda or 12 recommendations for media education
	Jun, 2007	UNESCO	L'éducation aux médias : avancées, obstacles, orientations, nouvelles depuis Grünwald: ver un changement d'échelle?
	Nov, 2007	European Commission	European i2010 initiative on e-Inclusion to be a part of the information society
	Dec, 2007	European Commission	Current trends and approaches to media literacy in europe (2007) European Audiovisual Media Service Directive (AMSD)

(*continued*)

Table 13.1 (continued)

Timeline of media literacy development in Europe

2008	Feb, 2008	European Parliament	Recommendation 1799 (2007) of Parliament Assembly of the Council of Europe of the image of women in advertising
	May, 2008	European Council	Council conclusions of 22 May 2008 on a European approach to media literacy in the digital environment
	Oct, 2008	European Union	Opinion of the Committee of the Regions on 'Media literacy' and 'Creative content online'
	Nov-Dec, 2008	European Commission	Working paper and recommendations from Digital Literacy High Level Expert Group e-Inclusion
2009	Jul, 2009	Council of Europe	Recommendation of the Committee of Ministers to member states on measures to protect children against harmful content and behaviour and to promote their active participation in the new information and communications environment
	July, Aug, 2009	European Commission	Study on assessment criteria for media literacy levels (2009)—A comprehensive view of the concept of media literacy and an understanding of how media literacy levels in Europe should be assessed Commission Recommendation on media literacy in the digital environment for a more competitive audio-visual and content industry and an inclusive knowledge society
	Nov, 2009	Council of Europe	Council conclusions on media literacy in the digital environment
2010	March, 2010	Council of Europe	Council Resolution on the enforcement of intellectual property rights in the internal market
	May, 2010	European Union	Opinion of the Committee of the Regions on regional perspectives in developing media literacy and media education in EU educational policy
2011	June, 2011	UNESCO	Fez Declaration on Media and Information Literacy
2012	May, 2012	European Commission	Communication from the Commission to the European Parliament, the Council, the European Economic and Social Committee and the Committee of the Regions A Digital Agenda for Europe EMEDUS European Media Literacy Education Study.
	June, 2012	UNESCO	Moscow Declaration on Media and Information Literacy

(continued)

Table 13.1 (continued)

Timeline of media literacy development in Europe

2013	June 2013	UNESCO-GAPMIL	Framework and Plan of Action for the Global Alliance for Partnerships on Media and Information Literacy
2014	May 2014	UNESCO	Paris Declaration on Media and Information Literacy in the Digital Era
2016	June, 2016	UNECO	Khanty-Mansiysk Declaration "Media and Information Literacy for Building a Culture of Open Government"
	July, 2016	UNESCO	Riga Recommendations on Media and Information Literacy in a Shifting Media and Information Landscape
	Nov, 2016	UNESCO	Youth Declaration on Media and Information Literacy
2018	Oct, 2018	UNESCO	Global Framework for MIL Cities

actions in Europe under the report "Mapping of media literacy practices and actions in EU-28" (Nickoltchev et al. 2016).

This report was based on responses from the national experts of each country, collected between May and September 2016, and revised by the members of the EU Media Literacy Expert Group. The questionnaire was elaborated in close cooperation with the European Commission, and the national experts are mainly: universities active in media literacy research, regulatory bodies with responsibility in this area, specialists in media literacy centers, and independent experts. The key questions addressed were identifying important media literacy projects in each country and providing a deep analysis for the most significant five for a case study.

The team responsible for the development of the report point out that there were methodological limitations which indicate the need to reinforce a common policy for implementing media literacy in Member States. These limitations were (Nickoltchev et al. 2016) (a) the absence of a common evaluation framework in order to make an effective comparison between a diverse range of media literacy projects, (b) the absence of a universally accepted definition of media literacy which influences the results, and (c) the absence of a common notion of what is "significant"; a multitude of cultural, social, and political factors are relevant in shaping how the level of significance is understood.

Table 13.2 Context, actors, competences, and processes

Contexts	Actors	Competences	Processes
Personal	Adults, children, and young people	Individual and personal competences in the consumption and appropriation of the media and ICTs	Conditions of access and use Individual development of skill acquisition
Family	Parents and guardians	Competences to authorize the use of the media and ICTs and for media education	Household conditions of access and use Family media education actions
	Children and young people	Competences for collective learning through the media and ICTs	Activity in family media education
Formal education	Legislators and authorities	Competences to regulate and impose sanctions in the realm of communication and media literacy	Conditions of access and use of ICTs Curricula and programs
	Teachers and educators	Institutional and collective competences of teachers in the realm of guardianship and media education	Media education activities Media production activities
	Parents and guardians	Personal competences of parents and professional competences of teachers and guardians	
	Students	Competences of collective learning and education	
Media	Legislators and authorities	Competences in media education policy and in media policy	Conditions of media regulation and participation
	Companies	Competences in promoting media education	Dissemination and promotion activities
	Professionals	Competences in media education policies	Public competences and participation
	Public (audience)	Collective competences in media literacy	
Citizens	Associations	Competences in the development and evaluation of media education projects and capacity for synergy	Conditions of citizens' regulation and participation
	Individual citizens	Civic competences	Design and promotion of media education activities Individual competences and participation

Source: Pérez-Tornero and Varis (2010, p. 47)

Once the responses were collected, 939 main media literacy stakeholders were identified. It is worth noting that over a third were categorized as "civil society" (305), followed by "public authorities" (175), and "academia" (161). A total of 189 networks were identified and the vast majority of them (135) are operating at a national level, while the others do not have a statutory responsibility in this area. This result shows that civil society has promoted more media literacy initiatives than other stakeholders that are responsible for that. This shows that more involvement by responsible institutions is required.

The report is extensive and full of details that serve for analyzing and identifying the difficulties and possibilities in current media literacy activities. The following is a selection of provided key findings that should be considered (Nickoltchev et al. 2016):

a) Civil society plays a very active role in media literacy projects, followed by public authorities and academia.
b) The majority of key media literacy stakeholders do not have a statutory responsibility around media literacy.
c) A total of 189 main media literacy networks were identified across the EU-28 countries, the vast majority of them (135) were categorized as operating at a national level.
d) The level of media literacy activity varies significantly across countries.
e) Providing front-line support to citizens is a priority for media literacy projects (outside the school system).
f) Skills linked to 'critical thinking' are the dominant skills across the projects in this study: 'Critical Thinking' was addressed by 403 out of 547 projects. The media literacy skill that is least addressed in the 145 'case-study' projects is 'intercultural dialogue', which was featured in 46 out of the 145 'case-study' projects.
g) Teens and older students are the most common audience group for the projects in the study.

Considering these findings, there are significant Media and Information Literacy activities but they need to be reinforced through a stronger common policy involving the public audiovisual authorities. As shown, the civil society is playing the most active role in promoting media literacy activities; this should be accompanied by better support and promotion from public institutions. The need to reinforce intercultural dialogue is another crucial point that should be highlighted especially now with the challenges of hate speech online. The revised Audiovisual Media Services Directive (AVMSD) lightened with measures proposed to Member States in this direction.

1.1.1 The Audiovisual Media Services Directive (AVMSD)

Media literacy (European Commission 2019) is one of the strategies promoted by the Digital Single Market led by the European Commission's Directorate-General for Communications Networks, Content and Technology, responsible to develop a digital single market to generate smart, sustainable, and inclusive growth in Europe. Before being included in this Directorate-General, the development of media literacy policies was linked to education. Media literacy is defined by the EC as follows:

> Media literacy, our capacity to access, have a critical understanding of, and interact with the media has never been as important as in today's society. It enables citizens of all ages to navigate the modern news environment and take informed decisions.
>
> Media literacy concerns different media (broadcasting, radio, press), different distribution channels (traditional, internet, social media) and addresses the needs of all ages. Media literacy is also a tool empowering citizen as well as raising their awareness and helping counter the effects of disinformation campaigns and fake news spreading through digital media (European Commission 2019).

In light of this definition, media literacy is understood as a tool that empowers citizens to take decisions in the current communication ecosystem. This definition incorporates the need to overcome the effects of disinformation campaigns and fake news. For this reason, media literacy now plays a central role in the current challenges that emerge in democratic societies. The European Commission's Expert Group of Media Literacy meets annually to identify good practices in media literacy, facilitate networking, explore synergies between different EU policies, and support media literacy initiatives.

The recently revised Audiovisual Media Services Directive (AVMSD) (European Commission 2020) reinforces the role of media literacy. It requires Member States to promote and consider measures for the development of media literacy skills (Article 33a). Every three years thereafter,

Member States shall report to the Commission how the implementation of media literacy measures is developing in their countries, and the EC should provide guidelines regarding the scope of such reports.

It is worth highlighting one of the points in the initial statement of the Audiovisual Media Services Directive. Point 59 states:

> 'Media literacy' refers to skills, knowledge and understanding that allow citizens to use media effectively and safely. In order to enable citizens to access information and to use, critically assess and create media content responsibly and safely, citizens need to possess advanced media literacy skills. Media literacy should not be limited to learning about tools and technologies, but should aim to equip citizens with the critical thinking skills required to exercise judgment, analyse complex realities and recognise the difference between opinion and facts. It is therefore necessary that both media service providers and video-sharing platforms providers, in cooperation with all relevant stakeholders, promote the development of media literacy in all sections of society, for citizens of all ages, and for all media and that progress in that regard is followed closely. (European Commission 2020b)

The approach to media literacy in the AVMSD goes beyond technological literacy. One of the crucial aspects emphasized is the promotion of critical thinking; the capacity to exercise judgment and analyze complex realities is needed now more than ever. The quality of democracies depends on whether or not institutions and citizens are implementing critical thinking linked to the values of humanism. This approach should be integrated in all policies developed and projects promoted.

Another key contribution of the AVMSD is Article 28b. One of the requirements stipulated in this article is that all Member States should ensure that video-sharing platforms provide effective media literacy measures and tools, in addition to raising users' awareness about them.

Last but not least, Article 30b focuses on the European Regulators Group for Audiovisual Media Services (ERGA). The European Commission (2018a) defines the composition of ERGA as "representatives of national regulatory authorities or bodies in the field of audiovisual media services with primary responsibility for overseeing audiovisual media services" and emphasizes that the EC participates in ERGA meetings. One of the tasks delegated to ERGA is "to exchange experience and best practices on the application of the regulatory framework for audiovisual media services, including on accessibility and media literacy". Thus, ERGA plays a crucial role in the promotion of media literacy.

1.1.2 Media Literacy to Overcome Disinformation

Overcoming disinformation is a priority in current media literacy policies. The communication "Tackling online disinformation: a European approach" (European Commission 2018b), presented in April 2018, initiated the path to promote several tools to tackle the spread and impact of online disinformation in Europe. One of the concerns addressed is ensuring the protection of European values and democratic systems that could be affected by the spread of false news and disinformation. The four principles that inspire the referenced communication are: (1) Improved transparency regarding the way information is produced or sponsored, (2) Diversity of information, (3) Credibility of information, and (4) Inclusive solutions with broad stakeholder involvement.

The communication referred to above assumes that the "open democratic societies depend on public debates that allow well-informed citizens to express their will through free and fair political processes" (European Commission 2018b). The role of the media is to guarantee quality journalism, providing information that enables citizens to form their own views on societal issues and participate in a democratic society, avoiding disinformation campaigns that erode trust in the institutions and in digital and traditional media, eventually harming our democracies. According to the communication (European Commission 2018b), today we are facing an unprecedented disinformation campaign addressed to personalized information spheres, which are becoming powerful echo chambers.

But how does the EC define disinformation? According to this 2018 communication, disinformation is described as:

> verifiably false or misleading information that is created, presented and disseminated for economic gain or to intentionally deceive the public, and may cause public harm. Public harm comprises threats to democratic political and policy-making processes as well as public goods such as the protection of EU citizens' health, the environment or security (European Commission 2018a, p. 4).

In this sense, the EC declares that there is not a single solution that could address all challenges related to disinformation. There are different principles and objectives recommended to be implemented in the different Member States, and one of them is Point 3.3: Fostering education and media literacy. The EC encourages Member States to mobilize resources and include in their educational policies digital citizenship, media literacy, the development of critical-thinking skills for the online environment, and awareness-raising activities on disinformation, among others.

The Code of Practice on Disinformation (European Commission 2018c) is the other initiative promoted by the EC. This code is the first self-regulatory set of standards worldwide to fight disinformation voluntarily, signed by platforms, leading social networks, advertisers, and industry. The code includes five main areas: (1) disrupting advertising revenues of certain accounts and websites that spread disinformation; (2) making political advertising and issue-based advertising more transparent; (3) addressing the issue of fake accounts and online bots; (4) empowering consumers to report disinformation and access different news sources, while improving the visibility and findability of authoritative content; and (5) empowering the research community to monitor online disinformation through privacy-compliant access to the platforms' data. Some of the platforms that have signed this code are Facebook, Google, Twitter, Mozilla, and Microsoft, among others. The last reports on the monitoring of the implementation of the Code of Practice are from Twitter (2019), Google (2019), and Facebook (2019).

The action plan against disinformation (High Representative of the Union for Foreign Affairs and Security Policy 2018), published on December 5, 2018 and developed by the European Commission, aims at reinforcing capabilities and strengthening cooperation between Member States and the EU in four areas: improving detection, coordinating responses, working with online platforms and industry, and empowering citizens to face online disinformation.

Finally, the European Digital Media Observatory (EDMO) was launched in June 2020. As defined by themselves (European Commission 2020a), "EDMO aims at creating and supporting the work of an independent multidisciplinary community capable of contributing to a deeper understanding of the disinformation phenomenon and to increase societal resilience to it." The five activities promoted by EDMO are: (a) mapping of the fact-checking organizations in Europe and training modules; (b) mapping and coordinating research activities on disinformation at the European level, including a global repository of peer-reviewed scientific articles on disinformation; (c) building a public portal providing media practitioners, teachers, and citizens with information and materials aimed to build resilience to online disinformation and supporting media literacy campaigns; (d) design of a framework to ensure secure and privacy-protected access to platforms data for academics researchers; and (e) support to public authorities in the monitoring of the policies implemented by online platforms to limit the spread and the impact of disinformation.

1.2 Media and Information Literacy by UNESCO

UNESCO is a key international institution leading the policies on Media and Information Literacy across the world. The approach is similar but there are some differences, the first one being the inclusion of information literacy. This came as a result of debates that have shown that media and information literacy should be unified as one discipline due to the relevance of both literacies. UNESCO further decided to promote a composite concept of Media and Information Literacy, presenting an integrated set of information, media, and digital competences.

UNESCO has a specific unit for coordinating the Media and Information Literacy policies, activities, and initiatives (UNESCO 2020). UNESCO's approach focuses on how our brains depend on information to work optimally, thus accessing quality information is a human need. The quality of the information that people access influences their perception, beliefs, and attitudes. In fact, MIL is linked with promoting intercultural and interreligious dialogue, peace, freedom of expression, and democratic societies.

The promotion of MIL depends on capacity-building resources according to its website through curricula development, policy guidelines and articulation, assessment framework, with a special focus on training. UNESCO promotes free and open online courses for MIL learning, besides promoting networking around the world. UNESCO facilitates networking and research through:

a) The Global Alliance for Partnerships on MIL (GAPMIL) is an initiative that was launched during the Forum for Partnerships on Media and Information Literacy which took place in Abuja, Nigeria. UNESCO brings support to this network offering more than 40 years of experience in Media and Information Literacy and supporting the creation of a solid network involving over 500 organizations since its beginning, all of them aiming to reinforce the global impact of Media and Information Literacy initiatives. GAPMIL[1] strengthened cooperation among other key MIL stakeholders such as the United Nation Alliance of Civilizations (UNAOC), UNICEF,

the Open Society Foundation, IREX, the European Commission, and other UN agencies and international development partners.
b) UNITWIN MILID (Media and Information Literacy and Intercultural Dialogue) Network[2] is the result of the collaboration between the UNESCO and UNAOC (United National Alliance of Civilizations) that together launched this network in 2011 in Fez (Morocco). This network is composed by universities of more than 20 countries around the world. They have engaged in research, publications, and guidelines for the promotion of Media and Information Literacy from an academic perspective and have obtained a solid theoretical framework that can be used in current and future research in order to advance this field of knowledge.
c) MIL CLICKS initiative (Media and Information Literacy: Critical-thinking, Creativity, Literacy, Intercultural, Citizenship, Knowledge and Sustainability)[3] is led by UNESCO with the collaboration of GAPMIL and other actors in Media and Information Literacy. The idea behind this initiative is to facilitate the acquisition of Media and Information Literacy competencies to people in their online daily environment, mainly through their interactions on social media sharing tips, resources, and also training with open courses. Individuals and institutions can be part of this initiative by agreeing to the pact to become a MILClicker and sharing in their own social media channels the content distributed by this initiative. Under the slogan "Think critically and Click wisely"[4] the individuals can commit to this initiative.

In order to understand how Media and Information Literacy is understood by UNESCO, Figure 13.1 explains this construct in detail.

UNESCO has a large trajectory in promoting assessment of MIL policies, training, and initiatives. Now that audiovisual platforms need to promote media literacy through their own media, it is time to join efforts. We selected some of them for consideration as part of the reflection in this chapter.

In that sense, UNESCO developed policy and strategies to promote MIL (Grizzle et al. 2013) and promoted a converging approach that interrelated different perspectives. UNESCO further identified the need for more collaboration and partnerships across government ministries to harmonize national and multilateral policies as one of the problems of policy strategy. For instance, MIL should be present beyond the education

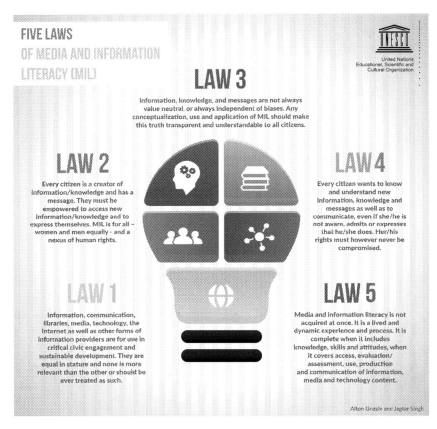

Fig. 13.1 Five laws of Media and Information Literacy. Source: http://www.unesco.org/new/en/communication-and-information/media-development/media-literacy/mil-as-composite-concept/

policy, forming part of communication and technology strategy besides cultural and other areas of public administration. The approach that involves the policies and strategies to promote MIL includes a combination of human rights, empowerment, knowledge societies, cultural and linguistic diversity, gender, and development approaches. MIL cannot be limited to technological learning; all these approaches are needed to promote an MIL in line with an effective humanistic approach.

The Curriculum of Media and Information Literacy for Teachers (Wilson et al. 2011) is a good resource to consider when promoting media and information literacy activities by different stakeholders. This curriculum was built by international experts from different countries with the definition of the different modules well developed, considering all the crucial aspects to promote MIL learning.

Another key document elaborated by UNESCO (2013) is the Global MIL Assessment Framework, which aimed at collecting data on the enabled environment, monitoring the extent to which citizens have acquired MIL competencies, specifically teachers in UNESCO's Member States. The idea behind this monitoring was to evaluate the effectiveness of the implementation of MIL policies and initiatives in the different UNESCO Member States. It would be useful to integrate data on the current website of UNESCO Data for the Sustainable Development Goals[5] focusing on MIL competencies acquired by citizens as a core competence for overcoming disinformation

Recently, two other key documents have been published and should be considered in this review. The first one is the Draft Global Standards on MIL Guidelines (UNESCO 2019a). This document contains the recommendations of Media and Information Literacy experts from 22 countries hosted by UNESCO in order to update UNESCO's model Media and Information Literacy Curriculum for Teachers and to make recommendations on Draft Global Standards for Media and Information Literacy Curricula Guidelines. And the second one is the proclaiming Global MIL Week signed by 193 countries that is a UNESCO resolution in November 2019 (UNESCO 2019b); now this is a global event that will be celebrated every year.

Due to challenges presented with the COVID-19 pandemic, UNESCO has elaborated a common strategy called UNESCO COVID-19 response[6]. The presentation of this strategy highlights that "more than ever the world needs professional journalism and reliable information to adapt its response to the spread of COVID-19, organize itself, learn from other countries' experiences and counter the increase of rumors and disinformation." They have included open education resources (OERs), networks of fact-checkers, Media and Information Literacy (MIL) resources to face the spread of disinformation, as well as the use of AI (artificial intelligence) and documentary heritage. Some of the initiatives shared in this common space are:

a) Actions to support media, enhance access to information, and leverage digital technologies in the fight against the pandemic;
b) UNESCO and radio stations mobilized to fight against COVID-19;
c) visuals, graphic, and social media messages to counter disinformation, fight discrimination, and promote best practices;
d) UNESCO and TV stations mobilized to fight against COVID-19. Short video messages in English, French, and Arabic for giving useful information and preventive measures for sharing in TV stations around the world;
e) code the Curve Hackathon;
f) mobilizing documentary heritage community amid the COVID-19 pandemic;
g) open solutions to facilitate research and information on COVID-19;
h) fighting COVID-19 through digital innovation and transformation;
i) the MIL Alliance response to COVID-19;
j) combating the *disinfodemic*: Working for truth in the time of COVID-19; and
k) communication and information webinars on COVID-19.

2 The role of Public Service Media Promoting Media and Information Literacy

In its handbook *MIL in Journalism: A Handbook for Journalists and Journalism Educators,* UNESCO emphasizes on the key role of professional media as "champions" in the process of promoting Media and Information Literacy:

> "There is an inclination to emphasise that MIL is a means of protection from the media. MIL is a process of transferring citizens/audiences to media partners and media to becoming champions of media and information literate societies." (Muratova et al. 2019).

The AVMSD indicates the need for both media service providers and video-sharing platforms providers to cooperate with all relevant stakeholders to promote the development of media literacy in all sections of the society and for citizens of all ages. The regulatory bodies of audiovisual media services play a crucial role, too. In order to explore some examples of how audiovisual platforms are promoting media literacy considering the principles of the AVMSD, we have selected two examples of audiovisual platforms (LUMNI and BBC-*Bitesize*) and one Observatory (Oi2 RTVE UAB).

2.1 LUMNI

https://educateurs.lumni.fr/images-et-medias

This platform was promoted by the French public service broadcaster *France-tv* in its origins, but is now supported by the collaboration of more French media organizations (ARTE, *France Television*, INA, *Radio France*, *Réseau Canopé*, RFI, and *TV5 Monde*). LUMNI offers audiovisual content for primary, secondary, and high school students. It is a repository of 3000 videos and audios. Its educational games for learning are particularly noteworthy and can be found in its entertainment section. It also offers free, quality content for teachers with whom they seek to encourage academic debate.

The catalogue of the *Lumni* platform includes specific content addressing media literacy and face news. In fact, the platform has as a special section dedicated to work with students and teachers, as illustrated in Figs. 13.2 and 13.3.

2.2 BBC-Bitesize

https://www.bbc.co.uk/bitesize/

Even though the UK is not a part of the European Union anymore, the BBC is still a good example to learn from. *Bitesize* is the BBC's online platform that compiles educational resources. Through this website, the British PSM organization makes available to the general public an

Fig. 13.2 *Fake news et complotisme, comment s'y retrouver?* Source: Lumni

Fig. 13.3 Education aux médias et à l'information. Source: Lumni

extensive catalog of resources supporting the education of students at primary, secondary, and post-16 levels. Facing the closure of schools throughout the UK due to the spread of Covid-19, *Bitesize* has daily updated its content in order to endure the lockdown and help families and students by guaranteeing more audiovisual content for learning purposes.

Regarding media literacy activities, *Bitesize* includes content on media studies for different ages, as well as a specific section called *Fact or Fake* aimed at acquiring competencies for the identification of fake news and disinformation.

One of the "star projects" of the BBC is the *BBC Young Reporter* (formerly BBC School Report), the BBC's journalism and media project encouraging young people aged 11-18 to share their stories and get their voices heard. This project is open to schools, colleges, home schools, youth organizations, and community groups in the UK and promotes the acquisition of media literacy competences, including lesson plans on how to be a journalist. By adopting a methodology based on "learning by doing," *BBC Young Reporter* (see Fig. 13.4) ensures the acquisition of media literacy competences. There are lessons planned step by step to get to know all the process of news production, including: (1) What is news?, (2) Finding news, (3) Gathering news, (4) Writing news, (5) Producing news for different platforms, and (6) Organizing and producing news for broadcast.

13 THE CHALLENGE OF MEDIA AND INFORMATION LITERACY FOR PUBLIC... 267

Fig. 13.4 *BBC Young Reporter*—lesson plans. Source: BBC

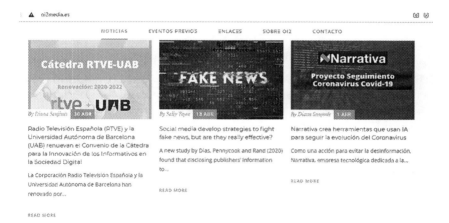

Fig. 13.5 Oi2

2.3 Oi2 RTVE-UAB Observatory

http://oi2media.es

OI2, the Observatory for Information Innovation in the Digital Society, is promoted by the Spanish PSM organization RTVE and the Autonomous University of Barcelona (UAB) as a partnership for monitoring the innovation in audiovisual information of Public Service Media, as well as the promotion of research. OI2 has promoted the reflection on debates on innovation, also integrating the contribution to media and information literacy in the past five years (Fig. 13.5).

Oi2 is now researching the application of artificial intelligence to the news making process, two of the crucial points being the development of specific report on detection of fake news through artificial intelligence (AI) and how can AI be used to promote the engagement of end-users in the audiovisual content, as another strategic line highlighted on Media and Information Literacy.

The above-mentioned initiatives demonstrate the essential role Public Service Media can play in disseminating MIL. As mentioned in UNESCO's MIL in Journalism handbook: "By promoting MIL, media are to simultaneously build a relationship with their audience while improving their quality and thus building and fostering the trust in media in general." (Muratova et al. 2019)

3 THE ROLE OF THE EUROPEAN PLATFORM OF REGULATORY AUTHORITIES

The European Platform of Regulatory Authorities (EPRA)[7] is another key stakeholder in the promotion of Media and Information Literacy guidelines. EPRA was set up in 1995 due the need for increasing cooperation between European regulatory authorities. It is now the oldest and largest network of broadcasting regulators in Europe, the European reference for interchanging information, cases, and best practices between different regulatory authorities. This network is composed by 53 regulatory authorities from 47 countries, while the European Commission, the Council of Europe, the European Audiovisual Observatory, and the Office of the OSCE Representative on Freedom of the Media are standing observers of the platform.

EPRA includes in its own portal a repository of laws, policies, and recommendations, developed by different countries. One of the most widely covered topics is Media and Information Literacy: there are now 58 last news, 6 events, and 67 documents from different countries. Thus, this repository contains the last developments in media literacy in relation to regulatory authorities and broadcasting agents (Fig. 13.6).

One of the relevant documents elaborated by EPRA was the *Media Literacy Networks Guidelines* (Chapman 2018). This document was elaborated with the objective to harmonize the way that the National Regulatory Authorities (NRA) could support MIL networks, to know what was been made in each country. The document summarizes some of the key points

Fig. 13.6 Keywords in EPRA search.
Source: EPRA

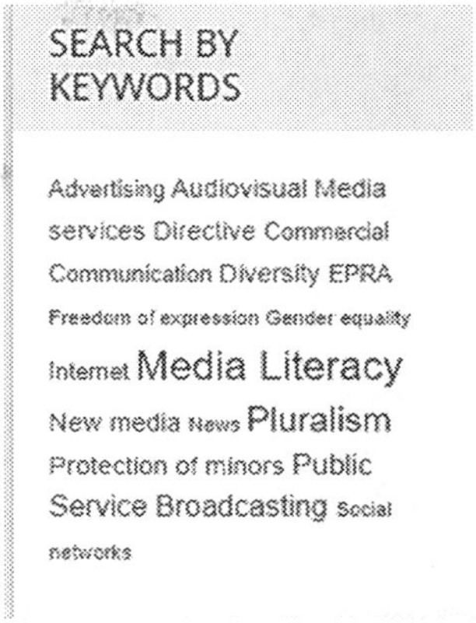

> **SEARCH BY KEYWORDS**
>
> Advertising Audiovisual Media services Directive Commercial Communication Diversity EPRA Freedom of expression Gender equality Internet Media Literacy New media News Pluralism Protection of minors Public Service Broadcasting Social networks

to learn from the experience of NRA supporting MIL networks. This document was prepared for the 46th EPRA meeting in Vienna in October 2017, where an agreement was reached on the promotion of MIL, complemented by a statutory regime that included the following points:

a) Raising awareness of existing rights and regulations,
b) addressing new regulatory challenges,
c) protecting constitutional values,
d) empowering citizens to manage their media use as a parallel to the regulatory mechanisms in place to help manage media use.

According to EPRA's guidelines, stakeholders who can be integrated as an MIL network include entities from the following fields: (a) Media (broadcasting, digital, print, games, community media); (b) Education (formal and informal, primary, secondary, third-level); (c) Commercial (e.g., companies and organizations who depend on digital transactions); (d) Digital intermediaries (social networks, search engines); (e) Civic society (foundations, community groups and networks, special interest groups, unions); (e) Government / Public sector (ministries, libraries, local authorities).

EPRA guidelines provide useful tips for creating MIL networks and ensuring the effectiveness of the activities promoted. The guidelines highlight the need to establish an evaluation framework that enables reviewing the results and the impact of the network. The need for continuous evaluation is equally crucial for all policies and MIL activities promoted.

4 Conclusions

This chapter presents a review of the latest developments in media literacy policies in Europe. One of the contributions worth highlighting is that audiovisual platforms have a crucial role to promote media literacy activities based on the AVMSD. The legal framework and policies reviewed encourage public service audiovisual media to become more active in the promotion of Media and Information Literacy policies.

Despite having a solid legal framework, public service audiovisual media need to reinforce their role becoming more engaged in MIL policies; the context is favorable, but more efforts are required from the side of public service audiovisual media.

The European Commission and UNESCO are currently focusing on MIL for overcoming disinformation. This comes as a result of a common concern regarding the negative effects of the infodemic caused by COVID-19 disinformation on democratic societies and public health.

Media literacy is a solid field, however monitoring systems are required to consistently and continuously evaluate the results of the policies implemented and promoted by audiovisual platforms and other media services. Coordination among different public audiovisual platforms and other agents is vital; this allows for sharing experiences of promoting media and information literacy. EPRA could contribute to reinforcing this goal.

There is a need to join efforts between traditional agents that have provided media literacy activities over the last 25 years, and the new agents that are currently developing media literacy activities, in order to guarantee the quality of training offered.

More success stories of people who have acquired MIL competencies should be shared through audiovisual platforms to demonstrate how MIL empowers to overcome disinformation. Public service audiovisual media could play an active role to serve this aim.

Notes

1. GAPMIL: https://en.unesco.org/themes/media-and-information-literacy/gapmil/about

2. Unitwin MILID University Network: https://en.unesco.org/themes/media-and-information-literacy/milidnetwork/Members
3. MIL CLICKS: https://en.unesco.org/milclicks
4. MILCLICK's PACT: https://en.unesco.org/sites/default/files/mil_clicks_pact_english.pdf
5. UNESCO Data for the Sustainable Development Goals http://uis.unesco.org
6. UNESCO COVID-19 Response: https://en.unesco.org/covid19/communicationinformationresponse
7. EPRA: https://www.epra.org/articles/general-information-on-epra

References

Carlsson, U. & Culver, S. (Eds.) (2013). *MILID Yearbook 2013: Media and Information Literacy and Intercultural Dialogue*. Sweden: Nordicom

Chapman, M. (2018). *Media Literacy Networks - Guidelines*. European Platform for Regulatory Authorities (EPRA).

Chapman, M., & Oermann, M. (2020). *Supporting Quality Journalism through Media and Information Literacy*. Council of Europe. Retrieved June 2, 2020, from https://rm.coe.int/prems-015120-gbr-2018-supporting-quality-journalism-a4-couv-texte-bat-/16809ca1ec.

European Commission. (2018a, November 21). European Regulators Group for Audiovisual Media Services (ERGA). Retrieved from https://ec.europa.eu/digital-single-market/en/audiovisual-regulators.

European Commission. (2018b). Tackling online disinformation: a European Approach—COM(2018) 236. Retrieved June 2, 2020, from https://eur-lex.europa.eu/legal-content/EN/TXT/PDF/?uri=CELEX:52018DC0236&from=EN.

European Commission. (2018c). EU Code of Practice on Disinformation. Retrieved June 2, 2020, from https://www.hadopi.fr/sites/default/files/sites/default/files/ckeditor_files/1CodeofPracticeonDisinformation.pdf.

European Commission. (2019, April 05). Media literacy. Retrieved June 2, 2020, from https://ec.europa.eu/digital-single-market/en/media-literacy.

European Commission. (2020a). EDMO. Retrieved June 2, 2020, from https://ec.europa.eu/digital-single-market/en/european-digital-media-observatory.

European Commission. (2020b, June 22). Audiovisual Media Services Directive (AVMSD). Retrieved June 2, 2020, from https://ec.europa.eu/digital-single-market/en/audiovisual-media-services-directive-avmsd.

Facebook. (2019). *Facebook Baseline Report on Implementation of the Code of Practice on Disinformation*. Retrieved June 2, 2020, from https://ec.europa.eu/information_society/newsroom/image/document/2019-5/facebook_

baseline_report_on_implementation_of_the_code_of_practice_on_disinformation_CF161D11-9A54-3E27-65D58168CAC40050_56991.pdf.

Google. (2019). *EC Action Plan on Disinformation—Google May 2019 Report*. Retrieved June 2, 2020, from https://ec.europa.eu/newsroom/dae/document.cfm?doc_id=60042.

Grizzle, A., Moore, P., Dezuanni, M., Asthana, S., Wilson, C.,Banda, F., & Onumah, C. (2013). *Media and Information Literacy: Policy and Strategy Guidelines*. UNESCO. Retrieved June 2, 2020, from https://unesdoc.unesco.org/ark:/48223/pf0000225606.

High Representative of the Union for Foreign Affairs and Security Policy. (2018). Action Plan against Disinformation. Retrieved June 2, 2020, from https://eur-lex.europa.eu/legal-content/EN/ALL/?uri=CELEX:52018JC0036.

Muratova, N., Grizzle, A., & Mirzakhmedova, D. (2019). *Media and Information Literacy in Journalism: A Handbook for Journalists and Journalism Educators*. UNESCO. Retrieved June 2, 2020, from https://en.unesco.org/sites/default/files/mil_eng.pdf.

Nikoltchev, S., Capello, M., Cabrera-Blázquez, J., & Valais, S. (2016). *Mapping of Media Literacy Practices and Actions in EU-28*. Strasbourg: European Audiovisual Observatory. Retrieved June 2, 2020, from https://rm.coe.int/1680783500.

Pérez-Tornero, J. M., & Varis, T. (2010). *Media Literacy and New Humanism*. UNESCO Moscow: Institute for Information Technologies in Education. Retrieved June 2, 2020, from https://iite.unesco.org/pics/publications/en/files/3214678.pdf.

Pérez-Tornero, J. M., Pulido, C. & Tejedor, S. (2013). Advancing MILID. In U. Carlsson & S. H. Culver (Eds.), *Media and Information Literacy and Intercultural Dialogue* (pp. 99–113). Göteborg: Nordicom. Retrieved June 2, 2020, from https://milunesco.unaoc.org/wp-content/uploads/2013/04/Media_and_Information_Literacy_and_Intercultural_Dialogue.pdf.

Twitter. (2019). Twitter May Update: Code of Practice on Disinformation. Retrieved June 2, 2020, from https://ec.europa.eu/newsroom/dae/document.cfm?doc_id=60043.

UNESCO (2013). *Global Media and Information Literacy Assessment Framework: Country Readiness and Competences*. UNESCO. Retrieved June 2, 2020, from https://unesdoc.unesco.org/ark:/48223/pf0000224655.

UNESCO (2019a). *Belgrade Recommendations on Draft Global Standards for Media and Information Literacy Curricula Guidelines*. Belgrade: UNESCO. Retrieved June 2, 2020, from https://en.unesco.org/sites/default/files/belgrade_recommendations_on_draft_global_standards_for_mil_curricula_guidelines_12_november.pdf.

UNESCO. (2019b). 193 Countries Proclaimed Global Media and Information Literacy Week. Retrieved June 2, 2020, from https://en.unesco.org/news/193-countries-proclaimed-global-media-and-information-literacy-week-it-now-official.

UNESCO. (2020). Media and Information Literacy. Retrieved June 2, 2020, from https://en.unesco.org/themes/media-and-information-literacy.

Wilson, C., Grizzle, A., Tuazon, R., Akyempong, K., & Cheung, C. K. (2011). Media and Information Literacy Curriculum for Teachers. Paris: UNESCO. Retrieved June 2, 2020, from https://unesdoc.unesco.org/ark:/48223/pf0000192971.

CHAPTER 14

Electoral Debates in Television and Democratic Quality: Value Indicators

Iván Puentes-Rivera, Paulo-Carlos López-López, and José Rúas-Araújo

1 Trust, Politics, and Democracy

Trust is the magic word that can explain almost everything, in many orders of life and, of course, also in politics and communication. Maslow's (1943) theory places trust almost at the top of his well-known pyramid, very close to the height of self-fulfillment and at the same level as success, recognition, and the respect of others. However, if we broaden the meaning that

---

I. Puentes-Rivera (✉)
Universidad de A Coruña, A Coruña, Spain
e-mail: i.puentes@udc.es

P.-C. López-López
Universidade de Santiago de Compostela, Santiago de Compostela, Spain
e-mail: paulocarlos.lopez@usc.es

J. Rúas-Araújo
Universidad de Vigo, Pontevedra, Spain
e-mail: joseruas@uvigo.es

© The Author(s), under exclusive license to Springer Nature Switzerland AG 2021
M. Túñez-López et al. (eds.), *The Values of Public Service Media in the Internet Society*, Palgrave Global Media Policy and Business, https://doi.org/10.1007/978-3-030-56466-7_14

Maslow gives to this concept, going beyond the trust in oneself and focusing in the sense of security that we primitively and vitally need in our social relations, it can be said that there are few issues that are more defining, instinctive, and basic to humanity than trust.

Trust, its presence or absence, can explain the historical development of our species, from the configuration of the first communities to the creation of ancient civilizations, the development of trade, art and feudalism, the bourgeois revolutions, the rise and fall of great dictatorships, or the current representative democracies. We can talk about physical security, cooperation, outrage, and so on, but in the end what underlines is always trust or mistrust in the system, in the political, social, and personal environment of any given time. Such trust and mistrust are, therefore, the true driving force of human action. This statement can be easily noted at this time, marked by a pivoting economic recession since over a decade, a crisis which has been defined by many as a crisis of trust in the markets (Martínez Campuzano 2007), but also by the crisis of the traditional system of political parties, the rise of worldwide populism, the questioning of classic democratic structures, the instability of international polity, and even the more recent fight against phenomena that were deemed unexpected today, such as pandemics, which increase the growing mistrust derived from all the above mentioned phenomena, a crisis, in essence, of trust (Callejo and Ramos 2017).

If we add to the described situation the increasing concern for information quality, mainly because of fake news and their influence in democratic quality (particularly during election periods), we can draw the full picture of this trust crisis that has been defining the current public opinion. There is a growing trend toward social and government concern about institutional trust and the quality of democracy, a concern that has jumped to the front page of the agenda setting after the confirmation of the interference of foreign powers, with Russia playing a leading role (Meseguer 2017), in democratic processes as delicate as the referendum on the continuity of the United Kingdom in the European Union (Rose 2017; Fresneda 2017), the 2016 presidential elections in the United States (Guess et al. 2018; Kaiser 2020; Velarde 2019), or the suspicions, in Spain, that the Kremlin might have been behind certain social media actions in favor of the Catalan referendum and independence (Guimón 2017; Cervera 2017). This is an underground work, mainly in social networks (De Miguel 2018; EFE 2018), that is always based in the spread of false information with multiple origins and intentions, from the specialized communication agency that develops a campaign with a one-off objective, to great geopolitical strategies prompted by old and emerging powers attempting to configurate a new global order, gaining influence at the expense of internally weakening their competitors.

As pointed out before, both governments and society as a whole are becoming aware of the importance of an issue that in 2018 was deemed as a threat to democracy by 83% of European citizens, highly concerned (74% of Internet users) by online disinformation during electoral periods (EUvsDisinfo 2018). Moreover, within the European Union, State Members decided to act jointly and launch a far-reaching action plan against disinformation (EU 2018), which in most cases, such as in Spain, is directly coordinated as part of the national defense and security strategies, which illustrates the magnitude of the problem. Previously, the European External Action Service had already established in 2015 *EU vs Disinfo* (euvsdisinfo.eu), a project focusing mainly in the detection of and response to the disinformation campaigns coming from Russia and targeting the destabilization or interference in EU matters, in any of the Member States or in any other European country.

Media organizations are facing the growing social need to professionally contrast information, as well as the historical opportunity to recover their role as strategic mediators that the digital revolution had in part taken away from them (Vázquez-Herrero et al. 2019; López-Borrull et al. 2018). In this context, media organizations are prompting initiatives and alliances focusing on verification or fact-checking tools that fight against the spread of hoaxes and fake news. In Spain, some examples of these strategies have materialized in projects such as *Newtral* (www.neutral.es) or *Maldita.es* (www.maldita.es), whose impact and social benefit are easily evidenced by the fact that they have become the target of fierce criticism and of professional discredit campaigns powered by relevant social and political agents whose involvement in the spread of fake news has been repeatedly proven (Pastor 2020; El Cazabulos 2020).

However, despite the magnitude of these data, it is remarkable that only 3% of the Spanish population places the spread of fake news as one of the three main problems of the country (CIS 2020), something invisible or, at least, not that worrisome for 97% of the Spaniards.

Considering this, the solution that is most frequently pointed out for the abovementioned crisis is always the same: the development of what some have already branded as the "trust economy" (PRNoticias 2019). This is a value that should be transversally nurtured in all fields of society, also in the area of communication and as a basic objective for public relations (Cuenca-Fontbona and Puentes-Rivera 2019). Its growing relevance can be observed in different studies on the subject, such as the European Communication Monitor (ECM) (Zerfass et al. 2015, 2017), that in 2019 (Zerfass et al. 2019) rose trust to the maximum degree of importance, dedicating to it the core section of the research under the title "Exploring trust in the profession, transparency, artificial intelligence and new content strategies."

It is in this context of political crisis and growing importance of trust that the bet on the quality of political debates in television makes sense. Television debates are powerful tools for the mobilization of citizen participation in the elections (Campo Vidal 2017, p. 75), as they are perfect scenarios, almost unique within an electoral campaign, for the contrast of the information and arguments raised by the candidates (Campo Vidal 2017, p. 18), as true personnel selection tests, as defined by Allan Schroeder (Campo Vidal 2017), to which the candidates for the presidency of a country's government apply, which places them outside of their comfort zone (rallies and perfectly planned and controlled electoral campaigns) and, ultimately, as one of the very few occasions when citizens have the chance to see their candidates as they are, beyond the advertising product of these campaigns (Bassat 2012).

Electoral debates are thus great opportunities for politicians to gain the trust of the voters (Puentes-Rivera et al. 2020), but above all they are a tool at the service of the citizens. As they subject their candidates to the filter of the debate, the confrontation and contrast of arguments from each side and the observation of how they resolve such confrontation, they have the chance to enrich their opinion with new perspectives or, at least, to qualify previous concepts and stances, which will take them to a greater level of trust in their representatives and in their decisions, to strengthen their links with the political dynamics of their country (that they will perceive as less distant), and, in the end, to an increase in trust in public institutions. More debates are always a symptom of more democracy.

2 Key Aspects in the Organization of Television Debates

Electoral debates have a double soul: they are power tools at the service of democracy, and, at the same time, they are television shows that must respond to the logics of this medium. The better they work as an entertaining television show, without losing information accuracy, the greater their audience figures will be and, thus, greater influence they will have in the improvement of the aforementioned democratic quality. It involves balancing audience and credibility: the first one widens the effects of the debate, and the second one provides them with depth (Campo Vidal 2017, p. 20).

They are a formula that is strictly related to classic television genres and formats, as they contain "conflict, stars, high risk, a competitive structure and great consequences" (Schroeder 2017, p. 10). Whatever the country, debates thus get massive television audience figures, only comparable to those of big events and major sport broadcasts, reaching over 10 million viewers in Spain, around 40 million in Mexico, and many more in the United States (US). Television thus works in this case as "one of the few windows of information opened for everybody" (Campo Vidal, 2017, p. 18).

Therefore, the programming and directing of debates as a television product is one of the key aspects that have to be acknowledged when organizing events of this kind and developing value indicators for them, along with the specific format of the show and the transparency and the fact-checking that must preside every political or public action.

2.1 Programming and Direction of the Debates

The first essential condition is the live broadcast, as all the emotion, tension, unpredictability, and thus, generation of trust within the voters depend to a large extent on the citizens knowing that they are watching what is really happening, without prior scripts or edition, at the same time that it is taking place. Moreover, this is the formula that intimidates and tenses the candidates the most, due to the vertigo that the unknown always generates within an electoral campaign and because a live debate can never be controlled (Schroeder 2017).

It is equally key the programming time, especially in terms of their placement in prime time slots, in order to gain extent and viewers without succumbing to the temptation that many programmers could have to extend it beyond this time schedule, dragging the pull of audience figures to the late night, but generating discomfort among the citizens, as it already happened in Spain in 2016, something that received criticism from several viewers organizations due to the disrespect to conciliation (Campo Vidal 2017, p. 164). Along with this, the length of the show is also important. It must combine enough duration to be informatively useful and, at the same time, the required brevity to be followed in its entirety. Balancing both premises with the logics of television, their total length should be between 90 and 120 minutes (Schroeder 2012), the typical running time of Spanish prime time television shows. However, they must differentiate themselves from the programming logics of these time slots in terms of advertising breaks, desired by the operators, but this is risky because they break the tension and the dynamics of the debate. Since 1993, electoral debates in Spain only include one advertising break that allows the candidates to take a break while allowing the operators to generate advertising incomes.

Unlike in other countries, in Spain there is a certain tradition by which the *Academia de Televisión (Television Academy)* organizes electoral debates, as it is deemed as a neutral and representative body separated from the different television operators. Aside from party suspicions, what underlines this decision is the need to gain extension, distributing the signal to all television channels that want to broadcast the debate, thus adding the audience figures of all of them and understanding the show as a real public service. As a result of this, the broadcast must take place in free-access television channels and be accessible for all audiences, avoiding pay-TV platforms.

Another distinctive aspect of the Spanish format is the fact that the show begins before and continues after its celebration (Rodríguez 2009), with the broadcast of the arrival and the departure of the candidates that even without sound can offer a great detail of information on the participants, their moods, attitudes, personalities, and so on, outside of the theatricality of the set. Several examples of this feature can be provided: the bags under the eyes of Felipe González (PSOE) and his tiredness when he arrived to the first debate in 1993, the anger of José María Aznar (PP) as he left the second one, or the loneliness and unease of Albert Rivera (*Ciudadanos*), unable to socialize with the rest of the candidates at the end of one of the debates of 2019. Due to the crucial importance of the debates, it is also imperative to pay attention to the "debate of the debate"

(Campo Vidal 2017), that is to say, all the previous and following programs aimed at discussing the expectations and the results of the debate, as they also have an influence on the audience and on shaping their opinion about it. A similar influence that the self-promotion spots broadcasted by the TV channel and the debate of the debate in their entertainment shows have, cultivating the infotainment genre and multiplying the effects of the debate (Puentes-Rivera et al. 2019).

Electoral debates must expand not only in duration, but also to second screens. Media and information consumption today are clearly multiplatform, and several sectors of population are informing themselves almost exclusively through social media, growingly key for the development and the result of electoral campaigns (Campo Vidal 2017, p. 15), so this cannot be an alien environment for television debates. Besides the political parties' efforts to stimulate their respective digital eco chambers (Gómez Ponce 2012), the organization of the debate must plan its diffusion on the Internet, from the streaming broadcast through different channels to the production of specific content.

Finally, the direction of the debate must not be confused for a minor factor, as the selection of a shot, the lighting, the sound, or the decoration of the set must faithfully communicate what is taking place in the debate, without interferences nor beneficial or unfavorable orientations toward any of the participants, taking great care to avoid any type of technical failure that could distract the audience (Navarrete 2009). For that purpose, listening shots are essential (Campo Vidal 2017, p. 66), as they enable the audience to observe the candidates' reactions when, for instance, they are invoked, although the same number and size of such shots must be maintained (Campo Vidal 2017, p. 70) in order to balance the limelight, a task for which a split screen can be a useful solution (Campo Vidal 2017, p. 192). The design of the set—an object of frequent discussion—must tend toward neutrality, simplicity, credibility, and transparency, while at the same it must be consistent with an audiovisual aesthetic (Rodríguez 2009, p. 165).

2.2 *The Format of the Debate*

Despite the multiple discussions between political parties, there is a certain consensus among scholars that the face to face format is the most demanding type of debate for the candidates (Campo Vidal 2017, p. 26), the easiest one to understand for the viewer (Bassat 2012, p. 27) and the one that stimulates greater participation in the elections (Campo Vidal 2017, p. 75). The direct confrontation between two candidates does not have to come at the expense of plurality, as different face to face debates can be organized with different candidates. Moreover, the face to face debate between the two candidates who are most likely to become president can be framed in the context of other collective debates.

Both this topic and all the other aspects that conform to the format of the program, such as the logic of the political parties, eager not to leave anything to chance and to have everything under control, usually clashes with the logics of television, that involve spectacle and entertainment and, therefore, loose norms that leave some space for surprises (Campo Vidal 2017, pp. 154–5), a matter that is also appreciated from the point of view of the public interest. For this reason, the media must act as a countervailing power and impose their conditions as well. Only this way can there be a dialogue, a real face to face, and a verbal confrontation between the candidates, a specific value of the Spanish debates (Schroeder 2012, p. 20). This is also why flexibility in the definition of the thematic blocks, the limitation on the number of graphics and items that the participants are allowed to display, the amount of documentation allowed to access the set, and so on, are extremely valuable features. However, in the face of this value of improvisation, Campo Vidal (2017) and other authors also highlight the importance of the so-called final golden minute, obviously scripted and with no room for improvisation, but very useful in terms of creating empathy with the audience and drawing the profile of each candidate, contrasting this image with the one displayed during the show.

From the point of view of the format, it is also key the role played by the moderator, who must stick to a required neutrality (Schroeder 2017, p. 8), at the same time that they have to be able to qualify, reconduct, and ensure the public interest, without becoming the star of the show (Schroeder 2012, p. 21). In line with the same willingness to ensure plurality, and following the French model, it is also valued that, in case there are multiple moderators, they belong to different media organizations (Campo Vidal 2017, p. 37) and that gender parity—a growing value across all areas of society—is guaranteed. This is because the topics, concerns, and even the interaction among candidates and moderators is different depending on this variable (p. 114).

Moreover, the definition of the number of actors who are present in the debate is crucial. On the one hand, the number of political parties, and which ones, that are going to be represented at the debate is important.

Should it be just those which had obtained representation in the previous elections, as defined by the Spanish electoral commission, or should all those parties that, even if they are new, are already playing a major role in current policies, which seems more reasonable when we are speaking about the future and not the past? (Campo Vidal 2017, p. 152). On the other hand, a decision has to be made regarding whether the candidates and moderators are going to be alone in the set, or if other journalists or even an audience will have the chance to participate as well. These are the three debate formulas established by Alan Schroeder (2012, p. 21): debates with moderator, a panel of journalists, and town hall debates. None of these models is better than the others and all of them present advantages and disadvantages, so a properly balanced combination of the three formats can be the most attractive option, mixing the vibrant rhythm of an open discussion among politicians, with the unease and unpredictability of the journalists' questions and the doses of reality and the expression of the concerns of the people provided by the questions of the citizens. In any case, there must be at least a block in which the candidates debate directly, because of the advantages already mentioned regarding direct confrontation.

Finally, another aspect that can be considered is the presence of an audience in the place where the debate takes places, as it is done in some US formats, which requires a greater level of concentration from the candidates, as the bubble effect that in some cases derives from the isolation in the set is broken.

2.3 Transparency and Fact-Checking

Considering radio and television as a public service and debates as a powerful electoral weapon at the service of democratic quality, it is obvious that transparency must be a transversal guiding principle for all aspects of their organization. Therefore, considering legal and social imperatives, if we discuss the quality of the debates, we must consider the degree to which citizens know in detail aspects ranging from the total cost of the show to the procedures followed for the allocation of speaking time or the placement of the candidates in the set, something that some organizers already decide through the public drawing of lots (Puentes-Rivera et al. 2019, p. 184), not forgetting the decisions on the thematic blocks or the ability to supervise intervention times. Likewise, it is necessary to make public the negotiations that always take place between the political parties and that condition the development of the debate to a great extent, like for example the notarially authenticated agreement between PSOE and PP for the celebration of the 1993 face to face debate (Campo Vidal 2017, p. 223).

Transparency also requires an exercise of accountability by the organization, meeting the demands of the interested media and distributing all types of relevant information related to the event, developing an "open doors" or "total transparency" strategy that enhances the interest and the audience of the debates (Gallego Reguera 2009, p. 139). Similarly, the diffusion of tracking surveys of the show is also important, as well as the development of ways to interact and effectively communicate with the audiences. This has to be done under pluralistic premises and considering the specific and, in many cases, accessibility needs of the citizens. For instance, blind or deaf people have to be able to follow the debate as well, so sign language interpretation should always be an option, one that is preferred instead of automatic subtitles, as it is much easier to follow.

Finally, regarding the so-called era of post-truth and the widely proven influence of hoaxes and fake news in several electoral processes (Campo Vidal 2017, pp. 15–21), the development of fact-checking tools and their integration within televised electoral debates, that will allow for real time verification of the statements made by the candidates, is imperative (Mazaira-Castro et al. 2019). This allows for a newer understanding of the US journalist Walter Lippmann's claim regarding 1960's debate between Kennedy and Nixon, after which he referred to television as "a machine to find out the truth" (Schroeder 2017, p. 12).

3   Indicators of Value for Television Electoral Debates

According to what has been developed above, and assembling the key aspects that influence the organizations of televised electoral debates, in this section we provide a proposal of indicators of value for the assessment of such debates, so that they can be used both as a planning guide and as a tool to compare them under equal and standardized grounds.

As it can be seen now, the proposal consists of 50 indicators organized in three categories: programming and direction (20 indicators), format (18 indicators), and transparency and fact-checking (12 indicators).

A. *Programming and direction*
   1. Is the show broadcasted live? It is not an edited program, nor a delayed broadcast (a show recorded without cuts).
   2. Is it scheduled during prime time, the slot with the biggest audience figures?
   3. Is its running time between 90 and 120 minutes?
   4. Is it a shared broadcast? Either because it is organized by an entity or operator that freely distributes the signal to other TV channels or because it is organized by several operators belonging to different media groups.
   5. Is it broadcast free-to-air? Non in pay-TV channels with a coded signal.
   6. Are there no advertising breaks, or is there just one?
   7. Is the arrival of the candidates broadcasted?
   8. Is the departure of the candidates broadcasted?
   9. Regardless the arrival of the candidates, is there any program before the debate and about the debate?
   10. Regardless the departure of the candidates, is there any program after the debate and about the debate? The debate about the debate.
   11. Does the media organization or the organizing institution plan its diffusion in second screens, mainly through social media? Beyond the diffusion made by the participating political parties themselves.
   12. This diffusion in second screens, does it go beyond the proposal of a hashtag and/or sporadic posts, that is to say, is there a full diffusion of the content or a full broadcast via streaming of the show in their social media and website?
   13. The media organization that broadcasts the debate, does it broadcast self-promotion spots of such debate?
   14. Does the holding of the debate become also a content, after or before it takes place, within other entertainment or infotainment shows of the channel?
   15. Does the debate include listening shots of the participants?
   16. Are the listening shots of all the participants similar in terms of size and duration?
   17. During direct confrontations between two candidates, is a split screen used regularly?

18. Are the set or stage properly soundproof? No sounds external to the show are broadcasted.
19. Are there no technical failures of any kind? Lighting, sound, broadcast, and so on.
20. Is the set neutral? No associations in shapes or colors with none of the participating political parties at the expense of others.

B. *Format*

21. Is it a face to face format? Only two candidates are confronted.
22. Within the same electoral campaign, are there other televised debates with a different (collective) format or a face to face where different candidates are confronted?
23. Beyond the required acceptance of the political parties, are the conditions and the format of the debate generally established by its organizers and not from a unilateral agreement between the candidates?
24. Are the rules relatively loose and provide space for improvising?
25. Is there an actual dialogue between the participants, with crossed interpellations, replies, and counter-replies? Not a sequence of monologues.
26. Are the thematic blocks generic enough so that there is room for improvisation and for the candidates to be able to speak about different topics within them? A debate without encapsulated topics.
27. Do the participants have a limited number of graphs, documents, and other resources that they are allowed to show to the camera during their interventions?
28. Do the participants have any limitations, explicit or implicit (the absence of a stand or a table, for instance), on the amount of documentation that they can check during the debate?
29. Is there a golden minute? Final and direct interpellation to the viewers, without interruptions, by each of the candidates.
30. Is the moderator playing their role neutrally? They don't express opinions nor interpret the interventions of the participants.
31. Respecting the previous matter, does the moderator have capacity to cross-examine, ask for clarifications, or qualify some issues?

32. In the case of the participation of several moderators, do they belong to different media organizations and media groups?
33. Do the represented political parties play a leading role nowadays and, if the debate is a collective one, are there no political parties of such consideration excluded?
34. Is there a plural panel of journalists posing questions to the participants?
35. Either live or through the internet, are citizens allowed to pose questions to the candidates?
36. Besides the previous matters, is there at least a section of the show with no external interventions, when the candidates are only debating with each other?
37. Among the moderators, the panel of journalists, and the participating citizens, if that is the case, is there gender parity between men and women?
38. Is there an audience live at the debate? Beyond advisors, professionals, and other accredited staff.

C. *Transparency and fact-checking*

39. Is it broadcasted, or, at least, is there any prior information about how the assignation of the speaking times was decided?
40. Is it broadcasted, or, at least, is there any prior information about the selection of the different thematic blocks or sections of the program that was decided?
41. Is it broadcasted, or, at least, is there any prior information about how the placement of the participants in the set was decided?
42. Before the broadcast, are the aspects regarding the negotiation between political parties and/or the organization, conditioning the debate, published?
43. Does the organization establish through its communication department a strategy of previous information on all the aspects related to the debate? Attending the media, interviews, press releases, and so on.
44. Is the cost of the program made public?
45. Are the audience surveys made known in the broadcasting media organization? This allows for a better interpretation of the real impact of the program.

46. Are there participation channels for the viewers to express their suggestions, complaints, or comments on the show?
47. Is the audience able to see the time control of the candidates' interventions, either in the set or on the screen?
48. Is the broadcast accessible to all people with functional diversity, mainly deaf and blind people?
49. In the case of deaf people, is sign language interpretation available in any of the platforms?
50. Is the audience provided with fact-checking tools that enable the verification of the participants' most outstanding statements during the broadcast?

4   The Value of Debates and Public Service Media

The development of value indicators for televised electoral debates is relevant as they provide a tool that allows for objective and measurable comparisons among this type of programs, broadcasted in different geographical areas, but also by different types of broadcasters, regional and national, and, of course, public and private.

The type of ownership of the broadcasting company has proven to be one of the most defining features when deciding on the kind of electoral debate to be developed, that is, when choosing between a classic, aseptic, and clearly informative type, which is likely to be hosted by a Public Service Media organization; and another type closer to infotainment and to emotional communication, even including features from reality and talent shows, resulting in a hybrid debate show, more likely to be developed by private broadcasters. This is not a haphazard difference: it is linked to the greater editorial freedom, the lower legal requirements and the lower control by public powers that private broadcasters operate under.

The other side of the coin is, however, the greater social compromise that public service broadcasters have, even legally, when shaping the public opinion and exercising their safeguarding function over the effective compliance of the citizens' rights included in the constitutions of any democratic country: the right to freely communicate and to receive truthful information, the right of access to the media for all significant social and political groups, or the respect for pluralism.

In the end, linking this vital role played by Public Service Media to the important role that electoral debates play from the point of view of the democratic quality of a country and the level of citizens' trust in their institutions, it is appropriate to conclude that the value indicators listed in this chapter are particularly relevant when assessing electoral debates organized by public service broadcasters. It is within their duties to guarantee the plural access of the citizens to the different political options, respecting the principles of neutrality and through quality information, without this leading to a give up entertainment nor certain features of motional communication that are part of the new debate formats.

Acknowledgments The research developed for this chapter is part of the activities of the research project of R + D + I (Challenges) "DEBATv, Televised Electoral Debates in Spain: Models, Process, Diagnosis and Proposal" (CSO2017-83159-R), funded by the Ministry of Science, Innovation and Universities (MCIU) of the Government of Spain, the State Research Agency (SRA), and the European Regional Development Fund (ERDF).

References

Bassat, L. (2012). El debate a dos, el mejor formato para el ciudadano. En M. Gallego Reguera (Coord.), *Debate del Debate 2011. España* (pp. 25–29). Madrid: Dykinson.

Callejo, J., & Ramos, R. (2017). La cultura de la confianza en tiempos de crisis. Análisis de los discursos. *RES: Revista Española de Sociología, 26*(2), 185–200. https://doi.org/10.22325/fes/res.2017.12.

Campo Vidal, M. (2017). *La Cara Oculta de los Debates Electorales*. Barcelona: Arpa Editores.

Cervera, J. (2017, November 11). Internet y «fake news», así ha sido la injerencia rusa en la crisis catalana. *La Razón*. Retrieved June 10, 2020, from https://www.larazon.es/espana/internet-y-fake-news%2D%2Dinjerencia-insidiosa-rusa-JH16889624/.

CIS: Centro de Investigaciones Sociológicas. (2020). *Barómetro Especial de Abril 2020. Avance De Resultados. Estudio n° 3279*. Retrieved June 10, 2020, from http://datos.cis.es/pdf/Es3279mar_A.pdf.

Cuenca-Fontbona, J., & Puentes-Rivera, I. (2019). Relaciones Públicas Avanzadas: Confianza. *Trípodos, 45*, 7–12. Retrieved June 10, 2020, from http://www.tripodos.com/index.php/Facultat_Comunicacio_Blanquerna/article/view/683/733.

De Miguel, B. (2018, December 5). ¿Cuántas 'fake news' retiran cada mes las redes sociales?. *El País*. Retrieved June 10, 2020, from https://elpais.com/internacional/2018/12/05/actualidad/1544020888_112000.html.

EFE. (2018, October 25). Reino Unido multa a Facebook con 565.000 euros por el escándalo de Cambridge Analytica. *El País*. Retrieved June 10, 2020, from https://elpais.com/internacional/2018/10/25/actualidad/1540460489_978436.html.

El Cazabulos. (2020, April 15). Vox se inventa un nuevo bulo para atacar a los verificadores independientes: es falso que emitan dictámenes para Twitter. *El Diario.es*. Retrieved June 10, 2020, from https://www.eldiario.es/tecnologia/Vox-verificadores-independientes-dictamenes-Twitter_0_1016999460.html.

EU. (2018). *Action Plan against Disinformation*. Retrieved June 10, 2020, from https://eeas.europa.eu/sites/eeas/files/action_plan_against_disinformation.pdf.

EUvsDisinfo. (2018). *Understanding the Threat and Stepping up European Response*. Retrieved June 10, 2020, from https://www.dsn.gob.es/es/actualidad/sala-prensa/uni%C3%B3n-europea-plan-lucha-contra-desinformaci%C3%B3n.

Fresneda, C. (2017, November 17). La trama rusa del Brexit. *El Mundo*. Retrieved June 10, 2020, from https://www.elmundo.es/internacional/2017/11/17/5a0dbd3446163f23128b4623.html.

Gallego Reguera, M. (2009). Un debate transparente. In M. Gallego Reguera (Coord.), *El Debate de los Debates 2008* (pp. 139–145). Barcelona: Àmbit.

Gómez Ponce, M. (2012). El debate preelectoral Rajoy-Rubalcaba en Twitter: Políticos y ciudadanos en el debate 2.0. In M. Gallego Reguera (Coord.), *Debate del Debate 2011. España* (pp. 67–75). Madrid: Dykinson.

Guess, A., Nyhan, B., & Reifler, J. (2018). *Selective Exposure to Misinformation: Evidence from the Consumption of Fake News During the 2016 U.S. Presidential Campaign*. European Research Council. Retrieved June 10, 2020, from http://www.ask-force.org/web/Fundamentalists/Guess-Selective-Exposure-to-Misinformation-Evidence-Presidential-Campaign-2018.pdf.

Guimón, P. (2017, December 21). El Parlamento británico investiga la injerencia rusa en Cataluña. *El País*. Retrieved June 10, 2020, from https://elpais.com/politica/2017/12/19/actualidad/1513667125_373603.html.

Kaiser, B. (2020, January 27). I Blew the Whistle on Cambridge Analytica—Four Years Later, Facebook Still Hasn't Learnt Its Lesson. *The Independent*. Retrieved June 10, 2020, from https://www.independent.co.uk/voices/us-election-trump-cambridge-analytica-facebook-fake-news-brexit-vote-leave-a9304421.html.

López-Borrull, A., Vives-Gràcia, J., & Badell, J. I. (2018). Fake News, ¿Amenaza u Oportunidad para los Profesionales de la Información y la Documentación? *El Profesional de la Información, 27*(6), 1346–1356. https://doi.org/10.3145/epi.2018.nov.17.

Martínez Campuzano, J. L. (2007, August 18). Una crisis de confianza. *Cinco Días*. Retrieved June 10, 2020, from https://cincodias.elpais.com/cincodias/2007/08/18/economia/1187549744_850215.html.

Maslow, A. H. (1943). *A Theory of Human Motivation*. Eastford, Conética: Martino Fine Books.

Mazaira-Castro, A., Rúas-Araújo, J., & Puentes-Rivera, I. (2019). Fact-Checking en los debates electorales televisados de las elecciones generales de 2015 y 2016. *Revista Latina de Comunicación Social, 74*, 748–766. https://doi.org/10.4185/RLCS-2019-1355.

Meseguer, M. (2017, December 12). La injerencia rusa: ¿Hasta qué punto puede manipularnos un bot?. *La Vanguardia*. Retrieved June 10, 2020, from https://www.lavanguardia.com/internacional/20171211/433569713164/injerencia-rusa-manipularnos-bot.html.

Navarrete, F. (2009). Claves para realizar un debate electoral. In M. Gallego Reguera (Coord.), *El Debate de los Debates 2008* (pp. 117–120). Barcelona: Àmbit.

Pastor, A. (2020, April 10). El bulo en WhatsApp sobre Newtral.es. *Newtral.es*. Retrieved June 10, 2020, from https://www.newtral.es/el-bulo-de-whatsapp-sobre-newtral/20200410/.

PRNoticias. (2019, June 27). Kreab organiza la jornada 'En transición hacia la economía de la confianza'. *PRNoticias*. Retrieved June 10, 2020, from https://prnoticias.com/comunicacion/clubagencias/kreab/20174450-kreab-jornada-transicion-economia-confianza?utm_source=general+grupo+pr&utm_campaign=35888bc3a6-EMAIL_CAMPAIGN_2019_06_28&utm_medium=email&utm_term=0_2f89044ab7-35888bc3a6-9631653&ct=t(EMAIL_CAMPAIGN_2019_06_28).

Puentes-Rivera, I. Fernández-Souto, A. B., & Vázquez-Gestal, M. (2020). Prólogo. En I. Puentes-Rivera, A. B. Fernández-Souto y M. Vázquez-Gestal (Coords.), *Debate sobre los debates electorales y nuevas formas de comunicación política* (pp. 9–12). La Laguna (Tenerife): Sociedad Latina de Comunicación Social. Retrieved June 10, 2020, from http://www.cuadernosartesanos.org/2020/cac171.pdf.

Puentes-Rivera, I., López-López, P. C., & Vázquez-Gestal, M. (2019). Seducir a la audiencia televisiva: la autopromoción permanente. In E. Conde-Vázquez, J. Fontenla-Pedreira & J. Rúas Araújo (Eds.), *Debates Electorales televisados: del antes al después* (pp. 171–192). La Laguna (Tenerife): Sociedad Latina de Comunicación Social. Retrieved June 10, 2020, from http://www.cuadernosartesanos.org/2019/cac154.pdf.

Rodríguez, D. (2009). En España los debates empiezan antes. In M. Gallego Reguera (Coord.), *El Debate de los Debates 2008* (pp. 163–167). Barcelona: Àmbit.

Rose, J. (2017). Brexit, Trump, and Post-Truth Politics. *Public Integrity, 19*(6), 555–558. https://doi.org/10.1080/10999922.2017.1285540.

Schroeder, A. (2012). Los Formatos de los Debates Televisivos. In M. Gallego Reguera (Coord.), *Debate del Debate 2011. España* (pp. 19–24). Madrid: Dykinson.

Schroeder, A. (2017). Prólogo. In M. Campo Vidal (Ed.), *La Cara Oculta de los Debates Electorales* (pp. 7–12). Barcelona: Arpa Editores.

Vázquez-Herrero, J., Vizoso, A., & López-García, X. (2019). Innovación tecnológica y comunicativa para combatir la desinformación: 135 experiencias para un cambio de rumbo. *El Profesional de la Información, 28*(3) https://doi.org/10.3145/epi.2019.may.01.

Velarde, G. (2019, April 10). Qué tienen en común el procés independentista, el Brexit y la victoria de Trump. *ElEconomista.es*. Retrieved June 10, 2020, from https://www.eleconomista.es/economia/noticias/9814795/04/19/Que-tienen-en-comun-el-proces-independentista-el-Brexit-y-la-victoria-de-Trump.html.

Zerfass, A., Moreno, Á., Tench, R., Verčič, D., & Verhoeven, P. (2017). *European Communication Monitor 2017. How Strategic Communication Deals with the Challenges of Visualisation, Social Bots and Hypermodernity: Results of a Survey in 50 Countries*. Brussels: EACD/EUPRERA, Quadriga Media Berlin. Retrieved June 10, 2020, from http://www.communicationmonitor.eu/2017/06/04/ecm-european-communication-monitor-2017-social-bots-visualisation-hypermodernity-benchmarking-strategic-communication/.

Zerfass, A., Verčič, D., Verhoeven, P., Moreno, A., & Tench, R. (2015). *European Communication Monitor 2015. Creating Communication Value Through Listening, Messaging and Measurement. Results of a Survey in 41 Countries*. Brussels: EACD/EUPRERA, Helios Media. Retrieved June 10, 2020, from http://www.zerfass.de/ECM-WEBSITE/media/ECM2015-Results-ChartVersion.pdf.

Zerfass, A., Verčič, D., Verhoeven, P., Moreno, A., & Tench, R. (2019). *European Communication Monitor 2019. Exploring Trust in the Profession, Transparency, Artificial Intelligence and New Content Strategies. Results of a Survey in 46 Countries*. Bruselas: EUPRERA/EACD, Quadriga Media Berlin. Retrieved June 10, 2020, from http://www.communicationmonitor.eu/2019/05/23/ecm-european-communication-monitor-2019/.

CHAPTER 15

Trends on the Relationship Between Public Service Media Organizations and Their Audiences

Carmen Costa-Sánchez, Barbara Mazza, and Ana Gabriela Frazão-Nogueira

1 INTRODUCTION

In the era of converging television (Jenkins 2004), there is a radical transformation of the relationship between the television system and the audiences which also affects public broadcasters.

C. Costa-Sánchez (✉)
University of A Coruña, A Coruña, Spain
e-mail: carmen.costa@udc.es

B. Mazza
Sapienza University of Rome, Rome, Italy
e-mail: barbara.mazza@uniroma1.it

A. G. Frazão-Nogueira
Fernando Pessoa University, Porto, Portugal
e-mail: ana@ufp.edu.pt

© The Author(s), under exclusive license to Springer Nature
Switzerland AG 2021
M. Túñez-López et al. (eds.), *The Values of Public Service Media in the Internet Society*, Palgrave Global Media Policy and Business,
https://doi.org/10.1007/978-3-030-56466-7_15

If at the basis of this change lie digital technologies that create multimedia and interactive environments in which the user can assume an increasingly interactive and participatory behavior, the real challenge lies not so much in the combination of platforms for non-linear consumption, but rather in defining new content in a logic that is both top-down and bottom-up. Content and new relational uses are the key elements to establish a future where Public Service Media (PSM) meets the needs of citizens.

This new environment is characterized by (Bonini 2017) in the following way:

- emphasis on PSM as a "liberator" to a two-way approach that promotes dialogue and interaction;
- transition from "one-to-many" to a more personalized approach that satisfies a wider range of needs for a varied quality in a diversified society;
- transformation from a closed or fortress-like institution to an open institution linked to networks of people, communities, culture organizations, and civil society.

So, changes associated with convergence, globalization, and privatization have produced a new set of challenges to public broadcasters and policy makers (Syvertsen 2003). Public broadcasters have traditionally enjoyed privileges like political support, relatively secure funding, and longevity (Iosifidis 2007), but economic constraints and a new television environment push for an adaptation to actual ecosystem and relation with young audiences becomes a necessary issue. Previous studies (Costa-Sánchez and Túñez-López 2017) have identified the coincidence of working in online environments with simulative interactive participation with audiences, but this is not real 2.0 participation, it still can be considered directional communication (1.0).

The urgency of changes is even more evident if we consider the data on television consumption, especially in Europe. As reported by EBU (2019), although most people continue to be reached by television every week, there is a gradual decline in the long run. The average TV viewing time was 3h 35m in 2018 and the weekly flow rate was 85.3% in 2018, down 2.7 percentage points compared to five years ago. Among young people it reaches just 1h 40m. Weekly coverage of young people in 2018 stood at 65.7%, down 10.8 percentage points from 5 years ago.

The drop in weekly coverage of PSM was also in line with all the decline in television and stood at 60% in 2018, down 4.1 percentage points from

5 years ago. Among young people, the daily market share of the PSM stood at 16.9% in 2018, up 0.8 percentage points in 2017 and 1.7 percentage points compared to five years ago. Performance suggests that PSM is better at retaining its audience than its competitors.

This trend is also visible in the data collected on the sample of Internet users segmented by the age of 16–24 in Europe. The data show that, among individuals between 16 and 24 years old, eight out of ten watch TV online and more than half of the group uses on-demand services, especially in Spain. On the Portuguese and Bulgarian markets, the penetration of broadcasters on demand is more than double compared to individuals aged between 16 and 74. In Portugal, for example, 100% of young people between 16 and 24 use the Internet, 90% of whom use it to watch TV content or video services and 50% routinely use on-demand services. In Italy, the penetration of on-demand services among young people corresponds to 30% of 90% of Internet users. There is, therefore, both a decline in the vision of traditional television and a strong fragmentation of the public on multiple platforms, particularly among young people.

Abreu et al. (2017) studied the motivation that guides people to look at the contents on the different platforms (video on demand, social networks, mobile, etc.) instead of just on their televisions. The main reason seems to be due to the lack of content availability on broadcast TV (42.5%). According to the authors, 69% of videos have the same success online and offline, 16% of videos are unsuccessful on any platform, and only 15% benefit from their online availability. It also appears that users can gain greater control or empowerment over their multimedia experiences, the different ways of watching TV.

TV broadcasters are aware of this trend and have started offering dedicated applications for viewing non-linear TV content on the Internet. In Europe, from the 30 countries analyzed, 20 already offer recovery TV services, while 37 major Pay-TV operators offer Catch-up TV, with a prominence in England and Portugal.

This chapter focuses on the PSM of the three southern European countries (Spain, Italy, and Portugal) to find out how they are facing the challenge of attracting and retaining young audiences with new usage habits in a multiplatform and successful context of online video.

RTVE, RAI, and RTP are consolidated examples of the tradition of public service and historical leadership in their respective countries, but what initiatives are being proposed to build relationships and community with young audiences?

2 THE RTVE CASE IN THREE KEY-POINTS: REALITIES, PLAYZ, AND LAB

Times have changed for television corporations in an especially accelerated way these recent years. The habits of television consumption have diversified. The characteristics of the public largely determine the coexistence between traditional uses (based on the consumption of streaming television) and the new uses (on the Internet and in the networks, in a prosumer or, at least, interactive way). While older audiences maintain traditional television consumption, younger audiences consume television on multiple screens, fragmented, everywhere and any time, multitasking and interactively.

The emergence of new operators, new catalogs, and marketing strategies in the Spanish television panorama has led to a strong competitiveness of providers and content (Costa-Sánchez and Guarinos 2018). In 2015, the offer of new video-on-demand subscription platforms such as Netflix burst in Spain, and in 2016, HBO Spain and Amazon Prime Video launched their services in Spain as well, to cite some of the most outstanding globally.

RTVE must face the change of scenery paying attention to the present and future audiences. In particular, young audiences are the most desired and the most difficult to conquer by European Public Service Media (Azurmendi 2018). As Guerrero (2018) concludes, the younger sectors of the population—millennials and younger generations to come—show an audiovisual behavior that prioritizes always-connected and customizable services, as opposed to rigid and closed offers, they are attracted by those products that give them an active role, also as programmers and producers, placing them at the core of the stories that interest them.

Throughout this brief case study, we will review RTVE's strategic line for relations with a young audience, in order to identify strengths, weaknesses, opportunities, and threats in the post-broadcasting era (Tse 2016).

2.1 Three Lines of Relationship with Younger Audiences: Reality TV, Playz, and RTVE's Lab

RTVE's relationships with its younger audiences is specified in terms of television audience through the reality shows *Operación Triunfo* [Operation Triumph] and *Maestros de la costura* [Sewing masters]. Both are successful reality shows (Gordillo 2009), the first one focused on the musical field (the contestants enter a musical academy to make them into successful stars) and the second one on sewing/fashion.

Even if the traditional audience figures are becoming weaker for *Operación Triunfo*, a format that has been around for many years in Spain, it should be noted that, recently, the space has gained a significant community of followers on social networks. Specifically, more than 600,000 followers on Instagram, 350,000 on Twitter, and an average of 30,000 people following the 24-hour YouTube broadcast every day. From engaging traditional audiences to successfully engage social media audience.

In the case of *Maestros de la costura*, the most recent format, now in its third edition in Spain, the audience figures for the current edition are allowing TVE to maintain a large portion of the television cake, in direct competition with the offer of the private broadcaster Telecinco, which has bet on that particular day, for fiction.

Apart from reality TV formats, which may present certain doubts and criticisms regarding the convenience of their use by public service television, the most innovative initiatives in the public sector aimed at young audiences take shape in two specific activities: Playz, the RTVE youth platform, and RTVE Lab, specialized in the development of new interactive stories. Both platforms operate exclusively in the online environment.

Playz (https://www.rtve.es/playz/) is a platform with its own entity that develops content for young people based on novelty and interactivity. These contents are framed both in the hypergenre of fiction (online series) and in the informational one (through reporting and interactive documentary, fundamentally). It should be noted that interactivity has become a denominator of all its content and in turn a hallmark, generating, for example, interactive narratives in which users can decide the next step in the story or interact with the presenters of the program. Playz has its own app and its own social media profiles, differentiated from those of RTVE, specifically, Facebook, Twitter, Instagram, YouTube, and mobile application. According to López-Golán et al. (2019), Playz has become a leading brand in the digital environment from the point of view of immersive and interactive narratives.

The RTVE Lab (http://www.rtve.es/lab/), meanwhile, has produced various multimedia pieces since 2016 (webdocs, virtual reality, multimedia reports, transmedia products, 360 videos, etc.), linked to topics of public interest and deepening in key aspects for society. Despite the fact that the content developed by the RTVE Lab may be suitable for young audiences, due to its dynamics and participation possibilities, there is low use of social networks used under a proactive strategy of attracting audiences (Zaragoza and García-Avilés 2018).

2.2 From Networks to Screens

The Spanish public channel faces, like the other traditional television channels, the management of a brand and relational projection space, which until now did not need or had available (Costa-Sánchez and Túñez-López 2017). Social media platforms have transformed the way organizations communicate, a new wave to which public television must rise to establish and maintain relationships with the youngest.

Audiovisual promotion strategies today are based on bringing audiences from the networks to the screens, in a context of an overabundance of supply and, therefore, of high competitiveness among the contents. This type of proactive strategies would be of great interest for the products that RTVE produces both in Playz and through the Lab.

Having quality products and/or suitable for a young audience profile is not enough. They must be made known, singled out, and promoted. Creating interest, advancing content, and using the potential of each platform could be three fundamental keys to accompany audiences from the space in the networks to that of content.

3 RAI: Digitalization and Identity Project

Broadcasters typically use digital platforms to create a universe to support the brand and to direct users from television programs to mobile and online services, and back to television (Enli and Syvertsen 2016). And this happened, obviously also in Italy. Rai, like all consolidated broadcasters in Europe and in the rest of the world, both public and private, has, in fact, developed great awareness of the role of social media as new platforms for content distribution. Multiplying devices also means multiplying and differentiating the possibilities and methods of using communication content, migrating between a screen. The personalization of television viewing is given by a mix of equipment: broadband diffusion, multiplication of the media on which it is possible to see live television content, possibility of viewing television programs for individual segments, and multiplication of on-demand and paid television channels.

The objective of Italian public television has been twofold: on the one hand, to keep one's identity intact, modernizing and updating it to current needs and technologies, on the other hand, to try to recover the attention and appreciation of young people.

To do this, in 2016, for the first time, the company rebrands all the channels transmitted, from generalists to specialized ones. It focuses on Rai 4, modifying its schedule according to the tastes of young people: international TV series on the crime/thriller, sci-fi/fantasy genre, action, and formats created specifically.

Also in 2016, RaiPlay was launched, replacing and expanding the previous Rai.tv, available on various Android, iOS, Windows phone, browser, and Smart TV platforms. In response to the new trend of use of digital and on-demand video content, the service is presented both as an online catalog and as an app, so that the contents can be viewed online and offline. The service allows you to see all the 14 Rai channels live, consult a catalog with documentaries, films, cartoons, and review the contents broadcast up to seven days from the broadcast. By registering for free to the service, the user can customize the experience on the platform, thanks to categories such as "last viewed," "look after," and more, which also allows to resume viewing the content from the moment it's stopped.

RaiPlay achieved moderate success, positioning itself as the first on-demand player in Italy (EBU 2018). In fact, in the first two months of activity (October–November 2016) the results reported by the Rai Press Office are quite positive: 75.5 million media views from 15 million devices with a 74% increase in online traffic on Rai services and 50% in the user base.

Despite this, in 2017, Auditel still confirms the typical trend of having high percentages of spectators in the mature segment of the population, with little appeal precisely in the young adults target very difficult to attract, registering a 9%, which is a much lower figure than the one from its competitors. In that year, Rai recorded a drop in the age groups between 4 and 14 years (-2%), 15 and 24 years (-1%), 3 and 44 years (-2%), and 45 and 54 years (-2%). It remains stable in the 25–35 years (5%) and 55–64 years (18%) groups, registering an increase for those over 65 (+7%).

Only after two years there is a slight improvement. In 2019, 9.7% of the population over the age of four years, watch live or on-demand television programs on screens other than television, connecting to fixed or mobile devices. Smartphones, in this year, exceeded television sets for the first time, and smart TVs and external devices that allow a traditional television screen to be connected to the web grew by 20.6% compared to 2017 (Auditel-Censis 2019).

In general, again in 2019, about the content offered, among the three generalist networks, Rai 1 obtained the highest rating (with a score of 7.8), slightly higher than the overall Rai offer. Follows Rai 2 (7.7) and Rai 3 (7.6). The semi-generalist contents of Rai 4 (7.9) is highly appreciated. All the genres offered reach good levels of popularity; in particular the Rai production fiction (8.3) and culture (8.0), followed by the fiction and serial purchase and sports events (both at 7.9). The popularity index of the digital Rai offers for the first half of 2019 (Rai 2019), measured on a scale of 1–10, is equal to 6.9. The score is stable, compared to the previous year, with all the individual sites/apps showing generally positive scores. The best rating is obtained by RaiPlay (7.4), followed by RaiPlay Radio (7.2), Rai.it (6.6), Rai News (6.5), and Rai Sport (6.5).

The Rai.it site is used as a "bridge" for access to the other group sites that offer multimedia content and that contains the area dedicated to corporate. Users believe that accessibility to on-demand products and the speed of navigation within the site should still improve, while appreciating the quality/completeness/access/updating of content, the quality of images/audio, and ease of use. RaiPlay is the digital platform appreciated for the quality/completeness/updating of the proposed contents, the quality of the images/audio, the comprehensibility of the graphic layout adopted, the ease of use, the accessibility to the program guide, and the programs transmitted in the last seven days.

To bring young people closer, Rai has activated specific channels (Rai Scuola, Rai Gulp, Rai Yoyo), but above all it has developed some projects dedicated to young people with the aim of enhancing the offer on digital channels, from a cultural point of view, but also of greater awareness and participation.

3.1 *Rai Brand Project*

Rai Porte Aperte is the offline project dedicated to young people, from kindergarten to university, conceived and launched in 2017. The goal of the project is to bring young people closer to the Rai brand, making them know the company closely and the professional skills of their media workers and it is the result of the observation of some activities already carried out independently by the 4 production centers and the 17 regional offices of the company. The mission is to tell about Rai and the Rai product, trying to increase engagement and improve its brand image.

Four targets were identified, divided by age (5–10, 11–13, 14–19, and university students) to whom specific activities are addressed. For the younger ones, up to the age of 13, the following are provided: recreational and educational visits, educational visits to all the production centers (in Rome, Milan, Turin, Naples) and to all the editorial offices, educational visits to the Museum of Radio and Turin TV, educational workshops with the Rai Symphony Orchestra and with "The Rai archives." For older ones (14–19 years), professional orientation educational visits, educational modules of school-work alternation, educational visits to the Research and Technological Innovation Centre of Turin, to the Technical-IT Infrastructure Management also in Turin, and to the Museum of Radio and TV, or educational workshops ("Che fuori tempo che fa", "The Rai Archives"). Finally, for university students, internships are planned in all the corporate structures, educational visits to the Research and Technological Innovation Centre of Turin, and to the Technical and IT Infrastructure Department also in Turin, and finally to the Museum of Radio and TV.

To date, the Rai Porte Aperte project has involved 21,807 students with its initiatives, 5207 of which in 2017 (year of birth) and 16,660 in September 2018. There were 111,000 visits on the website, of which 45,000 were in 2017 and 66,000 in 2018, showing positive and constantly growing data.

Rai is not present on Facebook, Instagram, and Twitter with its own channel that represents the entire broadcaster but is only present on Youtube with 1.4 billion views. During the search, pages were found on the social networks, but dedicated to the individual channels of the PSM organization. The Rai Porte Aperte project also has the limitation of not having an active page on social media. Only on Instagram, by typing the name, is there a link to a hashtag, but it is not possible to interact or inform your audience about the latest news or create interaction. The total absence from social channels is, for a project born a year ago and aimed at young people, certainly a limit that must be overcome.

Also, in terms of co-creation, self-productions were tested on the Rai 4 thematic channel, which however were not successful. Perhaps it would be desirable to use the Rai Play streaming service to create a section with exclusive content for young people, if not the opening of a dedicated online channel (as BBC and ZDF did). Dialogue with young people (and not only) on a digital platform representative of the brand (with a greater number of visitors), could be more attractive and very effective.

In summary, in just four years, Rai has made a big step forward in digitalization aimed at improving relations with its audiences, but it still has to do a lot, above all, to satisfy its main objective of returning to being a fundamental reference point for young people.

4 RTP: A Trail of Public Service Toward a Youth Approach

In 2015, the Television Law, which regulates access to television activity and exercise in Portugal, has been enhanced. The new regulation guarantees the "production and transmission of educational and entertainment programs aimed at young people and children, contributing to their formation" (Law No. 78/2015, of 29/07, 5th version), as well as participation in "educational activities for the Media, ensuring, in particular, the transmission of programs oriented towards this objective" (*idem*).

Since 1957 Portugal has had another entertainment and information media: the Rádio e Televisão Portuguesa. However, the Internet has brought a new audiovisual space and, at a time when the content offer is wide and diversified, the discussion of the television public service's place acquires an extra importance, especially at two fronts: the youth and the media survival.

Founding member of the European Broadcasting Union (EBU) and of the Ibero-American Telecommunications Organization, RTP has as its main objective to get closer to the Portuguese citizens, and "Always Connected" is its signature. In fact, RTP is today seen by millions of people across the planet, through its eight national and international channels. In 2006, RTP designs its online identity, enhancing all its contents either by streaming or IPTV, through *RTPplay*, and with feeds, Instagram, Facebook, and news Apps it completed (and expanded) its digital process, a scenario that, as written before, truly pleases young people.

4.1 The Educative and Informative Proposes in Youth Programming

Within the different RTP's digital educational and youth entrepreneurship spaces and support, online museum, and archives, for this chapter, *RTP Teaches* [https://ensina.rtp.pt/] stands out: a partnership with the

Ministry of Education in which an educational portal organized by RTP was created, where useful programs are found for topics such as citizenship, philosophy, economics, media education, junior education, among others. However, the idea isn't new. Giving a pedagogical use to the newcomer media, between 1965 and 1987, *Telescola* (school on TV) had live regular broadcasts that complemented the national education network, which allowed thousands of students apply to exams and complete basic education, raising the country's school success rate.

Today, in terms of youth programming, RTP insists on keeping an eye on young people with active, dynamic, informative, and educational formats. *Radar XS* (2020) [https://www.rtp.pt/programa/tv/p37709], brings forward the model of *Diary XS* (2010–2015), a daily television news format that, aimed at ages from 8 to 12 years old, wants to encourage critical thinking and conscious citizenship by combining complicated themes in a simple and objective discourse. Through *Reporter XS, Radar* goes out on the street and, through social networks, the program aims to promote global participation through dialogue and debate.

In fact, the bet on children's journalism comes since the *Quiosque* (Kiosk) (2006–2008), and the PICA (2010), a cultural magazine with daily news and reportages of interest to young people, presented as a fictional program, "guarantees the transmission of information in a differentiated, that is, with an audiovisual vocabulary and language suitable for the public" (Dias and Borges 2012). In reality, "public television aims to offer programming based on content that differs from commercial programming. It must obey quality parameters and serve society" (*idem*) as, for example, *Destemidas* (2020), an animation series that tells stories of fearless and exceptional women.

In fiction, the successful Sofia's Diary (2005–2006) returned in 2017 and, as the title indicates, it refers to the daily life of a teenager, first in high school and then, in the year before university. In entertainment, RTP always presented several contests, challenging children and youth either in general knowledge, kitchen, sports, and/or language. The most recent, and in the field of social responsibility, is "Movement of Gentleness" where, with the support of UNESCO, the Portuguese Olympic Committee and the Portuguese Government, youth dynamics is "One gesture and one person is enough to change the world. Start now!" [https://media.rtp.pt/zigzag/programa/movimento-gentil]. But one can also highlight the eight episodes of *Jogos Reais* [Royal Games] (2017): challenges between teams, based on worldwide classic children's books and short stories or, in international cooperation, *Yes, I can do it* (2017), a set of documentaries in which young people (8 to 12 years old) from several countries, make themselves known and meet a challenge. However, within the same age group, all those are very discreet compared to the promotion of programs adaptations such as *Chefs Academy Kids*, 2014; *The Voice Kids*, which returns in its 2nd edition, and *Joker Kids*, also launched this year.

4.2   Connected to the Future

Digital and social diversity and pluralism are concepts and practices that must be more and more protected in nowadays current media ecosystem. On the other hand, televisions are incorporated in info-communication models and formats, expanding its capacity to articulate with technological, transmedia, and social system.

Aware that the pleasure of watching television in young people is to break with the routine of simultaneity, locating consumption "at the moment they decide" (Vilela 2016), RTP, also through this autonomy of consumption given by the wide access to its contents, reflects a bet on the development of critical conscience of the youngest, with educational programming and promotion of citizenship.

Therefore, in addition to the social purpose of television, the responsibility for the production and distribution of content that should also "deviates from the standard of programming aimed exclusively to conquer audiences" (Paulino et al. 2016) as well as, in view of a technology constantly updated, the concern with media literacy - namely through didactic and quality programming - "for all audiences" (*idem*), since this consumption autonomy redefines the concept of family mediation and Media competition, in short, of the Individualization Paradigm that is perfected in the hands of new generations.

5   Conclusions. Public Service Media in Spain, Italy, and Portugal: Points of Convergence and Common Challenges

The focus of this chapter is the relationship of public broadcasters in Italy, Portugal, and Spain with youth through different initiatives, contents, and dynamics in new platforms.

The converging aspects mainly concern objectives, commitment, and awareness that public televisions have assumed, especially in the last 15 years, but with a clear acceleration in the last 5 years. RTVE, RAI, and RTP have started a process of digitalizing the platforms and innovating content but, above all, they have chosen to act in a manner consistent with their mission. This is very important because, as noted from data reported in this essay, young people recognize the characteristics of the offer that they can expect from a public TV.

In fact, the three European broadcasters show that they have accepted the challenge of innovation not only for market reasons, but precisely to respond to their institutional public service task. The common thread is the ability to enhance culture, the transmission of values, and the enhancement of their social and national service, with the awareness of operating in an increasingly global and interconnected world. For this reason, RTVE underlines the need to pursue the quality of content and the creation of value for the country, RAI considers that the modernization process must enhance the identity of the company and around it encourage inclusion and a sense of belonging, and RTP wants to be the connection point between the population and the rest of the world.

In conclusion, this means that for all three broadcasters, technological innovation means further enhancing their offer as a public service. It is not enough to become an "open institution," but to ensure that it becomes a fertile territory for the growth of the younger generations. The projects carried out by RAI to involve different school and university age groups, such as those developed by RTP with the Ministry of Education, are clear examples of this effort. In the same way, all three—and above all RTVE—focus on the generation of quality content, very careful to cross styles, languages, and formats dedicated to young people.

The other aspect of convergence is linked to the desire to intercept and meet the needs of young people. Personalization, participation, access to content that is not found in traditional and generalist programming and greater control of one's multimedia experience: these are the reasons that push the audiences, especially the younger ones, to the use of the digital offer. The public system of the three countries wants to meet these needs of its young audience, through interactive and multitasking platforms and applications. Young people appreciate having no time constraints, being able to make a hybrid consumption on different devices and platforms. In this way, public TV must become a "non-place" (Augé 1995) and, above all, a common sphere of action and interaction, of construction and sharing of collective meanings (Lotz 2014; Gray and Lotz 2019).

However, despite current efforts, the important challenge of building a joint space with younger audiences on virtual platforms remains ahead. For this, Public Service Media must enter, if not in the fight for the audiences, yes in the tough *competition for attention*. In the three countries analyzed, content is developed (that is, created and launched) with the youngest in mind, but this is useless if such proposals fail to overcome the barrier of saturation of advertising and informational messages to which they are exposed. Today, the work of television (and public television in particular) does not end in the offer: it continues in the promotion of said offer that, otherwise, will fall into the anonymity of the mountain of content that is available to them, every day.

Young people, on their own initiative, do not go to public television, either for information or entertainment. Therefore, it must be public television that approaches them, tells them what it has been doing, and why it may be of their interest. And for that, the logical thing is that the dialogue begins in the networks, in which the so-called generation Z moves habitually and comfortably, from there, leading it to concrete proposals that make public television visible as a benchmark for quality information and entertainment.

Today's young audiences will be the ones to judge tomorrow the desirability and need of a public television system that programs content and culture outside of commercial interests. If public channels do not focus their attention on them, fail to present themselves as a benchmark for innovation, quality, and novelty, it will be difficult for them to know and recognize the reasons for continuing to finance a public service that they will not use tomorrow.

In the age of digitization, the role of Public Service Media continues to confirm its importance, to affirm national identity and to be a cultural reference point, and to respond to the information and entertainment needs of its population. And this is possible if Public Service Media companies continue to increase quality and diversity in general, as well as acting as a "digital locomotive," driving the transition to information societies as innovation and risk-taking (Storsul and Syvertsen 2007).

References

Abreu, J., Nogueira, J., Becker, V., & Cardoso, B. (2017). Survey of Catch-up TV and other Time-Shift Services: A Comprehensive Analysis and Taxonomy of Linear and Nonlinear Television. *Telecommunication Systems, 64*(1), 57–74. https://doi.org/10.1007/s11235-016-0157-3.

Auditel-Censis. (2019, October). Secondo Rapporto. Tra anziani digitali e stranieri iperconnessi, l'Italia in marcia verso la Smart TV. Retrieved June 4, 2020, from http://www.censis.it/sites/default/files/downloads/Secondo%20Rapporto%20Auditel%20Censis.pdf.

Augé, M. (1995). *Non-places: Introduction to an Anthropology of Supermodernity*. London: Verso.

Azurmendi, A. (2018). Reconectar con la audiencia joven: Narrativa transmedia para la transformación de la televisión de servicio público en España, Francia, Alemania y Reino Unido. *Revista Latina de Comunicación Social, 73*, 927–944. https://doi.org/10.4185/rlcs-2018-1289.

Bonini, T. (2017). The Participatory Turn in Public Service Media. In M. Glowacki & A. Jaskiernia (Eds.), *Public Service Media Renewal. Adaptation to Digital Network Challenges* (pp. 101–116). New York: Peter Lang.

Costa-Sánchez, C., & Guarinos, V. (2018). Gestión de marca corporativa online de los canales públicos de televisión en Europa. Propuesta de indicadores para su medición. *Revista Latina de Comunicación Social, 73*, 895–910. https://doi.org/10.4185/rlcs-2018-1287.

Costa-Sánchez, C., & Túñez-López, M. (2017). Análisis de la información corporativa en línea de las televisiones publicas europeas: transparencia, finanzas, RS, ética y relaciones con la audiencia. *Comunicación y Medios, 36*, 125–139. Retrieved from https://comunicacionymedios.uchile.cl/index.php/RCM/article/view/45100.

Dias, A. S., & Borges, G. (2012). Jornalismo para crianças: um serviço público da televisão portuguesa. *Estudos em Jornalismo e Mídia, 9*(2), 1984–6924. https://doi.org/10.5007/1984-6924.2012v9n2p397.

EBU. (2018). Media Consumption Report 2017. Retrieved June 4, 2020, from https://www.ebu.ch/publications/media-consumption-trends-2018.

EBU. (2019). *Audience Trends Television 2019*. Public Version Media Intelligence Service. Retrieved June 4, 2020, from https://www.ebu.ch/publications/audience-trends-television-2019.

Enli, G., & Syvertsen, T. (2016). The End of Television—Again! How TV Is Still Influenced by Cultural Factors in the Age of Digital Intermediaries. *Media and Communication, 4*(3), 142–153. https://doi.org/10.17645/mac.v4i3.547.

Gordillo, I. (2009). *La hipertelevisión: géneros y formatos*. Quito: CIESPAL.

Gray, J., & Lotz, A. D. (2019). *Television Studies*. John Wiley & Sons.

Guerrero, E. (2018). La fuga de los millennials de la televisión lineal. *Revista Latina de Comunicación Social, 73*, 1231–1246. https://doi.org/10.4185/rlcs-2018-1304.

Iosifidis, P. (2007). Public Televisión in Small European Countries: Challenges and Strategies. *International Journal of Media & Cultural politics, 3*(1), 65–87. https://doi.org/10.1386/macp.3.1.65/1.

Jenkins, H. (2004). The Cultural Logic of Media Convergence. *International Journal of Cultural Studies, 7*(1), 33–43. https://doi.org/10.1177/1367877904040603.

López-Golán, M., Rodríguez-Castro, M., & Campos Freire, F. (2019). La innovación de las radiotelevisiones públicas europeas en la comunicación digital y las comunidades de usuarios. *Cuadernos.info, 45*, 241–255. https://doi.org/10.7764/cdi.45.1350.

Lotz, A. D. (2014). *The Television will be Revolutionized.* New York University Press.

Paulino, F. O., Guazina, L., & Oliveira, M. (2016). Serviço público de média e comunicação pública: conceito, contextos e experiências. *Comunicação e Sociedade, 30*, 55–70.

Lei nº 78/2015, of 29/07, 5ª versão. "Lei da Televisão e dos Serviços Audiovisuais a Pedido". Procuradoria Geral Distrital de Lisboa, Ministério Público. In: http://www.pgdlisboa.pt/leis/lei_mostra_articulado.php?nid=923&tabela=lei_velhas&nversao=5&so_miolo=.

Rai. (2019). Sintesi Qualitel. Retrieved June 4, 2020, from https://www.rai.it/trasparenza/Gradimento-della-Programmazione-6f45656e-f8cd-4f87-9893-3858f88366be.html.

Storsul, T., & Syvertsen, T. (2007). The Impact of Convergence on European Television Policy: Pressure for Change—Forces of Stability. *Convergence, 13*(3), 275–291. https://doi.org/10.1177/1354856507079177.

Syvertsen, T. (2003). Challenges to Public Television in the Era of Convergence and Commercialization. *Television and New Media, 4*(2), 155–175. https://doi.org/10.1177/1527476402250683.

Tse, Y. (2016). Television's Changing Role in Social Togetherness in the Personalized Online Consumption of Foreign TV. *New Media & Society, 18*(8), 1547–1562. https://doi.org/10.1177/1461444814564818.

Vilela, R. S. (2016). Jovens e cultura audiovisual: novos modos de ver televisão. *Revista Famencos: mídia, cultura e tecnologia, 23*(2), 1–10. https://doi.org/10.15448/1980-3729.2016.2.23173.

Zaragoza, M. T., & García-Avilés, J. A. (2018). Desarrollo de la innovación periodística en la televisión pública: El caso del RTVE Lab. *Hipertext.net: Revista Académica sobre Documentación Digital y Comunicación Interactiva, 17*, 11–21. https://doi.org/10.31009/hipertext.net.2018.i17.02.

CHAPTER 16

State Media and Digital Citizenship in Latin America: Is There a Place for the Weak?

Natalí Schejtman, Ezequiel Rivero, and Martín Becerra

1 Introduction

In undertaking an analysis of the experiences of state-run audiovisual media in Latin America, one encounters the challenge of specifying what exactly is meant by the term "public media." Part of the academic production, as well as documents from international organizations, have upheld for decades that a series of attributes must be present for such media to be considered public services. These attributes are rarely fully met in the experiences found in the Latin America media landscape.

The absence of a Latin American model of state-run media based on some basic consensus—for instance, on the quality and stability of programming, and on the autonomy with respect to political and economic

---

Natalí Schejtman was an executive producer for Primal and worked at Canal Encuentro between 2012 and 2017.

N. Schejtman
FONCyT, Universidad Nacional de Quilmes, UBA, Buenos Aires, Argentina

E. Rivero • M. Becerra (✉)
CONICET Universidad Nacional de Quilmes, UBA, Buenos Aires, Argentina

© The Author(s), under exclusive license to Springer Nature Switzerland AG 2021
M. Túñez-López et al. (eds.), *The Values of Public Service Media in the Internet Society*, Palgrave Global Media Policy and Business, https://doi.org/10.1007/978-3-030-56466-7_16

powers to define their financing and forms of governance and control—leads to an especially fragmented and heterogeneous map. This map reveals the most diverse experiences, some of them virtuous, albeit lacking the regularity to become established in the long term, mainly due to their pendulous and naturally short-term relationship vis-à-vis the incumbent administrations. Common and stable features over time are a governmental imprint of varying intensity and, with a few exceptions, a low incidence in terms of audience.

This scenario of the state media in the region has long faced the challenge of recreating itself virtually after the technological shock experienced by the media sector (Castells 2009), and of translating core questions and answers about the mission of state media into their online, digital versions.

At the same time, the discussion on digital citizenship that emerges at the intersection of state media and digital networks involves rights and responsibilities that are under construction, mingling such issues as access to technology and culture, digital divide, freedom of expression, pluralism, and participation. It is, from the conceptual and regulatory point of view, a discussion in progress, posing multiple difficulties, some of which have to do with the global nature of the issues as well as with the inevitable dependence on large commercial technological platforms, which today act as mediators in the exercise of the abovementioned rights.

In this framework, this chapter examines to what extent state media in the region can face the challenges of technological transformation and the online circulation of cultural and news content in order to contribute to shape a digital citizenship that is able to fully exercise its rights, and to what extent this intervention adds another layer of complexity in relation to technological platforms, and the rights to diversity and access to information and participation. That is to say, considering the differential traits of state-run media compared to private media, what ideal of digital citizenship does the state media model propose, and what rights do state TV stations call into question and could call into question through their convergence strategies?

2 State-Run Media in Latin America

In Latin America, most countries have state-run media (see Arroyo et al. 2012). By action or omission, the governments of most countries in the region have maintained some type of policy for the media they manage. These are experiences with dissimilar characteristics, time frames, and outcomes, which makes it hard to establish a comparison. However, case studies available enable us to recreate some particular scenarios. On the one hand, expansionary processes are observed, in general terms, which are associated with the injection of greater resources for content production, equipment acquisition, creation of new channels, or the launch of online services. On the other, we find moments of retraction in which the state media systems have been diminished in their benefits, reducing their budget, productive capacity, and headcount.

The strong government dependence on state channels, in almost all the countries of the region, implies often drastic twists and turns, whenever there is a change of administration. Expansion initiated during one period of government may be wholly or partially halted by another (or even during the same administration); however, some continuity efforts may survive over longer periods of time. In other words, governments with state media retraction policies may keep the state media system alive for years thanks to the legacy received from previously expansive periods. Two other possible scenarios are, on the one hand, an absolute retraction and the reconfiguration of the system after expansive periods, and on the other, a relative retraction, whereby after making adjustments to a preexisting management design, a state-run station continues to operate under a new structure, with downsized services maintaining a minimum level of production and quality.

At this point, it is key to note that the expansive periods of the state media system do not necessarily maintain a linear relationship with or a greater impact on the audience or an expanded social role. This is partly due to the historical structuring of media systems in Latin America under an almost exclusively commercial logic and with extremely high levels of concentration (Becerra and Mastrini 2017). Conversely, it could be the case that an attempt to privatize or close down a state-run station may arouse some kind of reaction from a section of society, which may end up giving the station greater prominence on the public agenda.

In Argentina, the state media system lived an expansive period at least between 2006 and 2015, under the Néstor Kirchner and Cristina Fernández de Kirchner administrations. When Mauricio Macri was elected to office (2015–2019), a period of retraction started, but leveraging the legacy that had been received. In this same country, the Encuentro educational channel, created in 2007, could be considered what we have defined as a form of relative retraction, since in 2016 its management limited its operations, reduced its staff and budget, and passively accepted a downgrade in its positioning within the grid of the main cable operator, to a much more marginal place; however, the channel managed to keep a minimum of original productions, with good acceptance in international broadcast circuits. In Brazil, the expansive period of the state media system had its corollary in 2007 with the creation of the Brazil Communication Company (EBC). The controversial political transition started in 2016 with Michel Temer after the impeachment of Dilma Rousseff, and the deepening of the turn of events in 2018 when Jair Bolsonaro became president started a period of retraction that in 2020 was heading toward a complete overhaul of the system as it had been conceived.

In Colombia, the Álvaro Uribe administration created in 2004 RTVC, a state company that runs, among other media, Señal Colombia, which managed to position itself as a benchmark in the production of quality television products at documentary and cultural level. The period ended in 2018 amid layoffs of producers and journalistic reports of censorship, after the arrival of Iván Duque to the presidency. For its part, TV Peru is an example of a succession of expansive periods followed by a relative retraction with certain continuities. While the Ollanta Humala (2011–2016), Pedro Pablo Kuczynski (2016–2018), and Martín Vizcarra (2018–) administrations made a clear governmental use of the station, which resulted in successive changes in its authorities and editorial line, in those periods relevant projects were launched and sustained, such as a children and youth channel, an international station and a policy of news programs spoken in native languages. Finally, Televisión Nacional de Chile, which is entirely financed by advertising and until 2014 had been the leader in terms of audience, had an expansive period until that year, when the concurrence of a crisis in its corporate governance model, the interference by political power in internal management, and changes in the local media system plunged it into a long period that is consistent with a situation of crisis and deep retraction.

The moment of expansion that state media experienced in certain countries of the region can be understood in some cases from the perspective of the "de-demonization of the state" (Rabotnikof 2008), involving a "repositioning [of the state] as a symbolic reference" (2008, p. 44). At the same time, this move led to greater state dependency and a shift in the discussion on plurality as an issue of less importance compared to investment, the upgrade of equipment, the improvement of the technical construction of content, and the increase in the number of production hours. Faced with the discussions about new regulations for the concentration of media in various South American countries, the internal plurality of state media was either removed from the center of the discussion or purposefully rejected: in such countries as Argentina between 2009 and 2015, or

Venezuela, from 2003 to the present day, having governments in confrontation with certain media groups, the arch of official voices advocated for the use of public media to give the government's side of the story, allegedly hidden from view by the efforts of some of the major commercial media outlets. In these cases, which combined a momentary impulse and a strong use of state media by governments in discussions about the situation, although internal pluralism ceased to be a value to be pursued, that same impulse cascaded down toward other values of public media such as aesthetic quality and formats, emergence of new genres and innovation.

3 State Media and the Public Sphere

The lack of adherence to prescriptions and ideal models that postulate good practices for this type of institutions, and their low penetration in terms of audience, combined with the fact that in Latin America these state-run media take the place of "public media," suggests the need for a revision of the conceptualizations around the meaning of "public" and its relationship with the media. As Nora Rabotnikof systematized, we could indicate, at least, three criteria to define what is public and its difference with what is private: what is of common interest or utility to all; what is and develops in daylight at plain sight, or is manifest and ostensible, and what is of common use or readily accessible to use (Rabotnikof 2008, p. 38).

In Latin America, the supremacy of commercial media outlets over state-run ones is overwhelming. According to Orozco Gómez and Franco Migues (2019), in the 23 countries of Ibero-America there are 103 privately owned free-to-air TV channels versus 49 state-owned channels (run by the federal government), and most of the latter are concentrated in just four countries: Cuba (5), Mexico (4), Panama (6), and Venezuela (8). In the rest of the countries there are only one or two state-run TV stations. In all cases, TV channels of "national" scope were analyzed, whether through subsidiaries, repeaters, or the sale of content to regional stations. In any case, in addition to the numerical supremacy of the private media offering, state media do not represent, with a few exceptions, any type of competitive pressure for private licensees (Orozco Gómez and Franco Migues 2019). Findings from audience measurement company Kantar Ibope processed by Obitel (Vasallo de Lopes and Orozco Gómez 2019) show that in countries such as Argentina, Brazil, Colombia, and Peru, public broadcasters obtain marginal figures on the total share of free-to-air TV, and they come in the last place. The exception is Televisión Nacional de Chile (TVN), which despite having lost its leadership, continues to boast a significant share of the audience, with programming that is mostly commercial in nature.

The public sense of such media outlets, meaning what is common to all, could be challenged by such findings. In economic terms, "the public sphere" should comprise not only the level of supply but also of demand. This leads to the need for constantly redefining the notion of what is public, particularly in contexts where the commodification of the media scene (Schuliaquer 2014) has such a consolidated tradition, which in turn leads to rethinking the role of state media. On the other hand, taking into account the meaning of public sphere as opposed to "that which is secret, preserved, hidden" (Rabotnikof 2008, p. 38), the state-run channels in the region evidence a wide range of variability in terms of their approach to institutional transparency: while Channel 22 of Mexico has on its portal a link to the national transparency platform where anyone can search for information on budgets and salaries, and RTVC of Colombia makes part of its information available to the public, Channel 7 of Argentina hardly publishes on its portal any information on public tenders and purchases. In Chile, TVN allows access to all its financial statements since 2008 from its institutional website, including the evolution of its payroll and the salary of its managers, among other data.

On the other hand, Latin American state media outlets have generally maintained their imperative of gratuitousness and have sought to develop quality and diverse content that distinguishes their proposition from the commercial one (Arroyo et al. 2012; Rincón 2005; Fuenzalida 2005).

In accordance with Mateo and Bergés Saura (2009), it is in the characteristics of programming that the key to defining television as a public service (2009, p. 20) is to be found, considering such indicators as the type of programs, their arrangement in the programming grid, and the volume of hours allocated to each genre. Although these ideas are partially challenged by the deprogramming that characterizes the supply and consumption of audiovisual goods by online fixed and mobile platforms, their validity lies in the fact that the reproduction of linear TV content is still the main policy followed by the state channels of Latin America on the internet. For Valerio Fuenzalida (2005), "the public sphere" does not occur with the mere broadcasting of a program or piece, but rather requires an effective public audience, that is, not elitist or marginal, and that it be as broad as possible. Thus, "what is public" in a mass media outlet is defined by effective public consumption and not only by its form of broadcasting (2005, p. 165).

Finally, one might think that another meaning of what is considered public has to do with a distinctive mission in terms of democracy, and its relationship with its appeal to audiences not in the role of consumers, but rather in the role of citizens. Rincón (2010) summarizes it this way, "the only defense and possibility of public media is to think having the citizens at the starting point" (Rincón 2010, p. 26).

4 State Media in the Public Sphere on the Internet

Much has been written about the democratic implications and potential of the internet. And it is not by chance that the field of communication has become fascinated during the new century (Lunt and Livingstone 2013) with the notion of the public sphere that Jürgen Habermas described from the 1960s onwards. Considering the new developments brought about by the emergence of a growing capitalist bourgeoisie in the eighteenth century and its articulation with the written press, Habermas described the public sphere as the aspect of our social life in which something similar to public opinion could be formed, with guaranteed access to all citizens (Habermas 1984, p. 49 in Lunt and Livingstone 2013, p. 2). His skepticism regarding the capacity of mass media for contributing to a public sphere found a match in his subsequent view regarding the progress of the Internet in democratic societies. Rasmussen (2014) historicizes the different reactions and forecasts that the existence of an online public sphere has caused among those who studied what is meant by public. Both Habermas and Benjamin Barber were skeptical faced with the new social media in relation to "the public sphere." Barber observed that, due to its speed, simplicity, tendency to polarize, its base on solitary users, its bias toward the image to the detriment of the text, and its resistance to hierarchical mediations, among other things, the new media did not contribute to improving the public sphere (Rasmussen 2014, p. 1321). Cass Sunstein joined the list of skeptics of the 'Daily Me' and the personalized Internet described by Negroponte in 1995, pointing out that its impact undermined the "general interest" (Sunstein 2001) and, later, creates an impossibility of forming public opinion due to its segmentation and polarization (Sunstein 2009 in Rasmussen 2014, p.1321).

There were, of course, more optimistic as well as more pragmatic views. Michael Shudson argued that the integration of digital media into democracy would require expanding the concept of citizenship beyond the original idea of the basic condition of the informed citizen, while Youchai Benkler did conceive of new media as a prodemocratic development, in the sense of their multidirectionality and engagement in the public sphere (Rasmussen 2014, p. 1322), but at the same time he perceived the effects of the commodification of the public space in digital networks.

In line with Benkler, De Balkin (2012) noted the "range of opportunities to express, create and publish" offered by ICTs, as well as the decentralization of "control over culture, the production of information and access to mass audiences" (2012, p. 56).

As some authors have noted (Jakubowicz 2006; Moe 2008a, b; Miguel-de-Bustos et al. 2011), privately owned media usually transfer to the new digital environment the same characteristics they have in their traditional broadcasting versions, strongly marked by standardization, commodification, and homogenization. In this connection, state-run media could function as a means to ensure diversity, while commercial actors, who need to monetize new businesses, adopt a more conservative behavior in the contents they supply, as they are less prone to experimenting and distributing content with low profit potential. If in the world of networks and digitization the process of commodification of information and culture is greater than in times of traditional media, an opportunity may be there for national states to seize, and that is putting together, in the landscape of the digital metamorphosis of communications, an agenda that is not purely driven by business interests, and for such purpose, state-run media can serve as a strategic tool.

The intersection of the traditional audiovisual industry with the Internet, which in commercial media put traditional business models in crisis, has allowed in certain experiences—and not by mere chance—a nimbler, more innovative response from state-run channels, used to not necessarily asking about a model of sustainable business. Certainly, state-owned channels in general were more innovative and less reluctant to make their contents available on the Internet: the BBC launched its first portal in 1994 and by 2004 it was offering its service on demand; TVE launched its portal in 2000 and in 2005 added online video capabilities. In Latin America, for example, Brazil's TV Cultura landed on the web early in 1996. For its part, Argentina's Channel 7 implemented since 2009 and almost in isolation compared to the rest of the country's open channels, a policy of mass publication of content on the network for an undetermined period of time, which was upheld almost unchanged in its logic until 2016, after the change of administration. This does not mean that commercial broadcasters did not have an online presence through institutional sites also since the mid or late 1990s. However, state-owned media moved with more agility and less calculation when initially making their linear content also available on the Internet (Rivero 2014).

In a recent paper, Karen Donders (2019) studied in depth the public media in the United Kingdom, Ireland, Flanders (the Dutch region of Belgium), and the Netherlands and described five phases in the public media response to the advancement of digital communications: first, a phase of experimentation, in which public media understood that they could cocreate content with audiences and develop apps; second, a phase of panic, in which these aging institutions noted how other competitors, or even individuals on their own, were more successful than they were in attracting audiences, leading to multiple unfocused strategies; third, a phase of expansion, in which public media attempted to "maximize their presence online, placing more value on this than on their public service mission" (2019, p. 1013); fourth, a phase of consolidation with an emphasis on the on-demand distribution of content, which led to a reorganization of internal teams and budgets, and fifth, the current phase of maturity, in which it was possible to combine an online proposal that includes public service missions and the relationship with the audience, with the need to negotiate with platforms such as YouTube or Netflix, although this can coexist with features from other phases (p. 1013).

In Latin America, the level of development of Internet services is uneven. However, in recent years there has been an incipient rapprochement between state media and private actors with great power in content production and distribution. In Argentina, state-owned Channel 7 was the first screening window and the coproducer of the series that became popular on Netflix, El Marginal (2016–). It also partnered with Cablevisión Flow, the video-on-demand platform of the country's main pay TV operator (whose largest shareholder is media group Grupo Clarín), to coproduce the miniseries El Mundo de Mateo (2019), as did the Argentine university channel Un3 for the distribution of the Gorda series (2018). For its part, Canal Once in Mexico sold to Netflix the distribution rights for the period series Juana Inés (2016).

In general terms, state media contribute their conception of digital citizenship in a field driven by the concentrated commodification of the global distribution of digital products. The digital revolution builds information-driven societies that seek to motivate expression and also promote access to educational, cultural, and informative resources. However, for this to take place, rights need to be recognized, for example, in the access to information products and services.

If citizenship is related to the exercise of rights, in the "information societies" the regulatory frameworks, infrastructure, and practices that define those rights are precisely under construction and discussion. In Latin America, structural inequality is a conditioning factor for the exercise of rights associated with such "information societies."

5 From Broadcasting to Digital Service

The mass use of digital platforms represents both an opportunity and a challenge to corroborate or recreate a public sense that is not always clear and evident in the state media.

From the point of view of the commercial sector, Miguel-de-Bustos (2011) states, "in a field such as the Internet, without the limitations that the radio space had, private content providers are capable of offering content that is diverse and pluralistic enough," and therefore the service of public media online has been called into question in terms of their raison d'être, particularly in European countries and in the United States, since these operations that rely on state money are seen as a form of unfair competition by private companies.

In the European context, the questioning of the online operations of public broadcasting companies is found in cases such as the BBC (United Kingdom), and ARD and ZDF (Germany), which have relevant services on the Internet. Private actors are asking them to keep their Internet offer in the "program-related" realm, and to refrain from overstepping the sphere eventually covered by private activity. At this point, the scarce prominence of most state media in media systems in Latin America is at the same time a drag that they transfer to their online versions, with a negative impact on them, as seen in the difficulty of building their brand among younger segments of the population, but this also presents an opportunity, given that in general, they are not seen as mighty competitors by their private counterparts, at least in regard to digital services.

However, the existence of a large number of content in circulation is not a guarantee of diversity in itself. In this regard, Zallo (2016) argues that diversity does not only have to do with content, but also with platforms that act as gatekeepers, which are, ultimately, the ones that determine the terms of circulation of those contents. Indeed, the author argues, "in this field there is little diversity. The platforms are controlled by a handful of companies, most of them in the United States" (Zallo 2016, p. 239). On a similar note, Emili Prado adds:

> Each new wave of innovation in communication technologies applicable to the audiovisual sector has stimulated euphoric stories about the advent of a diversity of contents that would become accessible to citizens, following the train of thought of an equation expressed as follows: multiplicity (of channels) = diversity (of content). (Prado 2016, p. 365)

Managing the abundance of online content becomes an additional challenge due to the difficulties it represents and the skills required for meaningful access and use of content that do not result in the opening or widening of new digital gaps (Van Dijk 2006). At this point, platforms play a decisive role in granting or denying visibility to contents bearing diversity, and the opportunities to be found by audiences depend on editorial policies, sometimes mediated by algorithms that "in their attempt to customize results tend to make invisible products that could potentially be of interest to the user but which will be difficult for them to get to know if only products that match their already known tastes are recommended" (Prado 2016, p. 329). As this author warns, except for those minorities that have differential search skills, many contents of cultural, educational, and social interest will become buried in the network, and in the absence of public policies that promote diversity, this leads to the imposition of the standardizing and homogenizing forces of the market. In sum, neither the so-called Internet "platforms" nor the algorithms they hinge on are unbiased or neutral mechanisms; on the contrary, they are the result of human creation, express political and editorial decisions, and operate by creating "regimes of visibility" (Morozov 2016, p. 176) and, thus, they reactivate the old problem of diversity in what is shown (Napoli 1999).

The notion of "platform capitalism" (Srnicek 2018) allows us to define, among other phenomena, the current moment in which the production and distribution of audiovisual content on a global level is increasingly led and directed by a few companies. These global corporations rely on the extraction of personal data, the deployment of monopoly trends driven by the network effect, the use of cross-subsidies to capture different groups of users, and the possession of a central architecture (hardware and software) with which they control the possibilities of interaction.

Although for the purposes of this analysis platform capitalism affects public and private actors around the world, not all of them are equally positioned to insert themselves more or less competitively in the new environment. The difficulties faced by the European public television stations themselves on the Internet, many of them with a long tradition of public service and competitiveness in terms of audience lead to questioning the low role played by public TV and radio in Latin America and their real possibilities of an expansive and relevant development on the Internet from a peripheral position, taking into account the media context that is increasingly leaning toward globalization.

If free access to content is part of one of the digital rights sought by state media, it is precisely there that a complex overlap exists between the mission of public media and ubiquitous private platforms including Facebook and YouTube. This tension is also seen in the content distribution phase: today public media depend on commercial companies to massively distribute their content, so interests overlap in terms of both access and institutional missions. This has an impact on the digital citizenship models that public broadcasters appeal to. Thus, authors such as Castells (2009) warn that, paradoxically, the success of the commercialization of content distribution by public media implies distorting its essence and, by generating genuine resources with this activity, the production process of such public media becomes impregnated with a commodifying conditioning. As Maria Michalis observes, in the case of audiovisual content, the logic of the TV market was disruptive for the open foundations of the Internet and not the other way around (Michalis 2018, p. 198).

In Latin America, "the imbalance of human, financial, and technological resources, against which corporations from developing countries or emerging markets need to contend, set the conditions for unequal competition due to the high cost of the required infrastructure in internet distributed television" (Piñon and Rivero 2020), and therefore for the most part content distribution networks, which allow optimizing network traffic and other essential digital intermediaries, are a few companies (Akamai, Amazon CloudFront, CloudFlare, Imperva Incapsula, Stack Pack), mostly owned by US capitals.

This has posed quite a few dilemmas for converging strategies, which depend on the position of the state media in their own digital ecosystems: should the state media prioritize technological sovereignty—hosting their content on their own servers or at least on servers of national origin—or the reach afforded by hosting contents on the global digital platforms? Should they partner to produce content or compete against these 'new' actors?

The state-run media have a specific challenge in building citizens who hold digital rights. If we think of them more in terms of functions than of organizations, as Hjarvard (2018, p. 60) suggests, one could think of their role in social networks not as an isolated strategy but as part of a "wider, converging media infrastructure in which PSM and other media jointly influence information flows and debates that unfold in and between various media" (2018, p. 70). In other words, the role of public media in platform capitalism to materialize a differential in terms of configuring digital legal persons exceeds the space of the media proper, going beyond the production and communication of its quality content, and must spill over to become relevant throughout the digital ecosystem. For this reason, the researcher proposes three public service tasks for public media in the online era: curation, moderation, and monitoring (op cit., p. 70). The question that arises would then be: what is the level of legitimacy of the state media in Latin America to become the organizers of public discussion? Undoubtedly, state media start from different realities, but the task implies an interesting challenge for this era.

6   From Users to Digital Citizens

In Latin America, neither state regulation nor the state strengthened in its role as operator of its own media, in those countries where these processes occur, have managed to institute a public media system as such. In addition to economic and political independence or the mandate of pluralism and diversity that can be expressed in a normative plexus, citizen access is a key aspect (Monje 2015), a mission that in Latin America has been more linked to the non-profit media sector rather than to the state media. In this sense, it is probable that the relationship between state media and citizens lacks a tradition, insofar as, due to its strongly governmental nature, the link has been spasmodic with citizens in their role as adherents to political party factions, and not as part of a broad and inclusive call for citizenship.

In a similar approach to Lowe's for the European case, in Latin America the public media should assume the role of helping citizens, offering services that allow individuals to explore a variety of topics to better understand the world around them and to be able to fully develop in it, while having the ability to express their concerns and participate actively in the social and political sphere. (Lowe 2008 in Arroyo et al. 2012, p. 166)

While, on the one hand, traditional media had a decisive involvement in the cultural and civic literacy of a large portion of the population (Martín Barbero 1987), digital networks today are the indispensable continuators in this task.

The information revolution, and the processes of content digitization in the cultural industries, can be executed based on premises that are discriminatory or inclusive (Becerra 2015). The type of citizenship that is built in the information society will depend on that, and it is precisely here that the state-run media could play an especially virtuous role.

But, as previously stated, the very definition of digital citizenship is under debate. According to Bernardo Sorj (2005), the idea of citizenship has on the one hand a normative application, which focuses on the conformation of civil society, and, on the other hand, an ambiguous application that is conditioned by rights and practices, which becomes more relevant when it comes to Latin America. Citizenship is for Sorj

a collective construction that organizes the relationships between social subjects, formed in the very process of defining who is, and who is not, a full member of a politically organized society. This affiliation character of citizenship is generally ignored since it is defined in terms of individual rights. (Sorj 2005, p. 21)

Assuming the opposition between the individual and the collective as productive in analytical terms, the construction of digital citizenship underpins the construction of collective identities. There are examples that speak of this concern in Latin American state-run media which correspond to the phase that Donders referred to as "experimental," in which co-creation emerges as a way of getting the public involved, in the context of expansive periods according to the description made at the beginning of the chapter.

The case of Cuentos de viejos, by Señal Colombia, is especially interesting: it is a transmedia and transgenerational project that had its first season in 2013 and consisted of collecting stories about childhoods in the voice of older adults for a website, and making animated pieces based on those stories for the channel's screen, in addition to complementing them with an educational project to recreate the experience and promote intergenerational dialogue. Cuentos de viejos has won relevant awards for the public media sector such as the Japan Prize (2014) and Iberoamerican Prix Jeuneusse (2013).

In Argentina, Canal Encuentro developed a coproduction together with the National Film Board of Canada that consisted of a platform called Primal, "a collaborative experience on the expression of our most vivid feelings through the construction of an eternal and collective cry." The project (IDFA 2014 selection) featured an acoustic and nomadic booth that traveled through Argentine schools to collect entries, and a guide on primal expression in art. In this case, a coproduction between state agencies of two countries emerges and meets global citizenship, while it addresses at least two different countries with a production in Spanish, English, and French that shows Argentine and Canadian youths.

Citizenship is a complex category that gathers practices, identifications, rights, and the imaginary of social groups (Becerra 2015) and also, as Silvio Waisbord (2013) suggests, involves participation, expression, and the affirmation of rights. These are aspects to be taken into account by the public media, if they want to complement their lack of massive reach with a relevant and fundamental role in terms of citizenship in the digital age.

There are different ways in which state-run media can contribute to strengthening the rights to a more comprehensive digital citizenship. Perhaps what remains to be done is to finalize a digital proposition that articulates them as transparent, open media, with broad coverage both geographically and of the different social groups, and accessible to build a sincere and relevant dialogue with citizens.

References

Arroyo, L., Becerra, M., García Castillejo, Á., & Santamaría, Ó. (2012). *Cajas Mágicas: El renacimiento de la televisión pública de América Latina*. Madrid: Editorial Tecnos (Grupo Anaya, S. A.).

Balkin, J. M. (2012). El futuro de la libre expresión en una era digital. *Derecho y humanidades, 20*(2012), 41–62.

Becerra, M. (2015). *De la Concentración a la Convergencia: políticas de medios en Argentina y América Latina* (1ra ed.). Paidós.

Becerra, M., & Mastrini, G. (2017). *La concentración infocomunicacional en América Latina (2000–2015): nuevos medios y tecnologías, menos actores.* Universidad Nacional de Quilmes y OBSERVACOM editores.

Castells, M. (2009). *Comunicación y poder.* Madrid: Alianza Editorial.

De Mateo Pérez, R., & Bergés Saura, L. (2009). *Los retos de las televisiones públicas. Financiación, servicio público y libre mercado* (1ra ed.). Comunicación Social Ediciones y publicaciones.

Donders, K. (2019). Public Service Media Beyond the Digital Hype: Distribution Strategies in a Platform Era. *Media, Culture and Society, 41*(7), 1011–1028. https://doi.org/10.1177/0163443719857616.

Fuenzalida, V. (2005). Programación: por una televisión pública para América Latina. En O. Rincón (Ed.), *Televisión Pública: del consumidor al ciudadano* (1ra ed., pp. 133–172). La Crujía.

Hjarvard, S. (2018). Public Service in the Age of Social Network Media. *Public Service Media in the Networked Society, 2018,* 59–74. Retrieved from https://bit.ly/2yRI4CV.

Jakubowicz, K. (2006). *PSB: The Beginning of the End or a New Beginning in the 21st Century.* RIPE p.14 y ss. Retrieved from http://ripeat.org/wp-content/uploads/2010/03/Jakubowicz_KeynotePaper.pdf.

Lunt, P., & Livingstone, S. (2013). Media Studies' Fascination with the Concept of the Public Sphere: Critical Reflections and Emerging Debates. *Media, Culture and Society, 35*(1), 87–96.

Martín Barbero, J. (1987). *De los medios a las mediaciones. Comunicación, cultura y hegemonía.* Barcelona: Ediciones G. Gili.

Michalis, M. (2018). Distribution Dilemmas for Public Service Media Evidence from the BBC. *Public Service Media in the Networked Society, 2018,* 195–210.

Miguel-de-Bustos, J. C., Galindo Arranz, F., & Casado del Río, M. Á. (2011). De la radiotelevisión pública a Internet, la adaptación de las autonómicas y sus contenidos al entorno digital. In *X Congreso AECPA "La política en la red", Área IV. GT 4.7: Televisiones públicas e internet. Redefinición política y servicio público.* 7–9 de septiembre, Universidad de Murcia, Murcia. Retrieved from https://bit.ly/2JY08xv.

Moe, H. (2008a). Dissemination and Dialogue in the Public Sphere: A Case for Public Service Media Online. *Media, Culture and Society, 30*(3), 319–336.

Moe, H. (2008b). *Public Broadcasters, the Internet, and Democracy: Comparing Policy and Exploring Public Service Media Online.* PhD thesis, University of Bergen, Norway.

Monje, D. (2015). El país que no cabe. Políticas de acceso ciudadano a sistemas públicos audiovisuales en Sudamérica. *Chasqui: Revista Latinoamericana de Comunicación, 2015*(129), 41–59.

Morozov, E. (2016). *La Locura del Solucionismo Tecnológico.* Katz Editores.

Napoli, P. (1999). Deconstructing the Diversity Principle. *Journal of Communication*, 49(4), 7–34.

Orozco Gómez, G., & Franco Migues, D. (2019). Reconocimiento del campo iberoamericano de la Televisión Pública. In G. Orozco Gómez & G. Torres Espinosa (Eds.), *Agenda digital para la TV pública en Iberoamérica* (1ra ed., pp. 25–46). Gedisa.

Piñon, J., & Rivero, E. (2020). Distribution, Infrastructure, and Markets: SVoD Services in Latin America. In T. Havens, C. Brannon Donoghue, & P. McDonald (Eds.), *Media Distribution in the Digital Age* (1st ed.). New York University Press.

Prado, E. (2016). Desafíos para la diversidad audiovisual en internet. En L. Albornoz & M. T. García Leiva (Eds.), *El audiovisual en la era digital. Políticas y estrategias para la diversidad*. Madrid: [mimeo] Cátedra.

Rabotnikof, N. (2008). Lo público hoy: lugares, lógicas y expectativas [The Public Sphere Today: Places, Logics and Expectations]. *ÍCONOS*, 32, 37–48.

Rasmussen, T. (2014). Internet and the Political Public Sphere. *Sociology Compass*, 8. https://doi.org/10.1111/soc4.12228.

Rincón, O. (Ed.) (2005). Televisión pública: del consumidor al ciudadano. Buenos Aires: La Crujía.

Rincón, Ó. (2010). "La obsesión por que nos amen: crisis del periodismo/éxitos de los telepresidentes", en Amado Suárez, Adriana (ed.): La palabra empeñada: investigaciones sobre medios y comunicación pública en Argentina, Buenos Aires, Friedrich Ebert Stiftung, pp. 13–16.

Rivero, E. (2014). *Televisión Pública, Internet y Democratización: El caso de Canal 7 online (Tesis de maestría)*. Buenos Aires: Universidad Nacional de Quilmes.

Schuliaquer, I. (2014). *El poder de los medios. Seis intelectuales en busca de definiciones*. Buenos Aires: Capital Intelectual.

Sorj, B. (2005). La democracia inesperada, Prometeo, Buenos Aires.

Srnicek, N. (2018). *Capitalismo de Plataformas* (1ra ed.). Buenos Aires: Caja Negra.

Sunstein, C. (2001). *Republic.com*. Princeton, NJ: Princeton University Press.

Van Dijk, J. (2006). Digital Divide Research, Achievements and Shortcomings. En *Poetics 34* (pp. 221–235). Holanda: University of Twente, Enschede.

Vasallo de Lopes, M. I., & Orozco Gómez, G. (Eds.). (2019). *Modelos de distribuição da televisão por internet: atores, tecnologias, estratégias* (1ra ed.). Sulina.

Waisbord, S. (2013). *Vox populista. Medios, periodismo, democracia*. Buenos Aires: Gedisa.

Zallo, R. (2016). Políticas culturales y comunicativas para la diversidad de las expresiones culturales: una aproximación. En L. Albornoz & M. T. García Leiva (Eds.), *El audiovisual en la era digital. Políticas y estrategias para la diversidad*. Madrid: [mimeo] Cátedra.

Index[1]

A

Accessibility, 14, 61, 113, 115–116, 257, 284, 300
Accountability, 9, 47, 112, 119, 120, 141–144, 284
Adblocking, 65
Advertising, 6, 7, 23–27, 32, 46, 51, 53, 65, 69, 95, 99, 101, 102, 133, 140, 160, 174, 205, 219, 227, 233, 234, 259, 278, 280, 306, 312
Algorithms, 23, 49–51, 54–56, 60–64, 67–71, 88, 319
Amazon, 49, 54, 96, 100, 165, 174, 205
Amsterdam Treaty, 31
Applications, 52, 53, 65, 84, 87, 94–96, 98, 101, 103, 104, 114, 117, 118, 122, 123, 142, 162, 166, 168n3, 184, 194, 200, 202, 207, 209, 211, 257, 268, 295, 297, 299, 300, 302, 305, 317, 322
Artificial intelligence (AI), 13, 65, 67, 70, 71, 263, 268, 278
Audience
   data, 61
   engagement, 24, 65
   participation, 12, 13, 24, 47, 104
Audiovisual Media Services Directive (AVMSD), 141, 249, 256–257, 264, 265, 270
Authority, 16, 86, 93, 119, 145, 185, 207, 210, 219, 234, 236, 255, 257, 260, 268, 269, 312
Automation, 62–66, 69, 71

B

Big data, 13, 65, 67
Blockchain, 12, 13, 93–106
Board of directors, 138, 142–146

---

[1] Note: Page numbers followed by 'n' refer to notes.

328 INDEX

Brand, 12, 16, 32, 67, 100, 117, 202, 226, 228, 230, 237, 297, 298, 300–302, 318
British Broadcasting Corporation (BBC), 5, 7–11, 27, 32, 33, 35, 53, 54, 63, 132, 133, 137, 139, 140, 145, 178–180, 182–184, 217, 218, 235–239, 265, 266, 301, 316, 318
Broadcasting, 3, 4, 6, 8, 10, 13, 14, 24, 26, 28, 30–32, 46, 47, 51–53, 86, 103, 112–115, 117, 119, 122, 123, 131–145, 147, 156–161, 166, 167, 169n11, 174–177, 179, 182, 183, 185, 220, 225, 226, 230–232, 235, 237, 256, 268, 269, 287, 288, 314–316, 318–321
Business model, 4, 5, 12, 15, 24–27, 51, 54, 63, 79, 95, 99, 100, 166, 198, 201, 202, 205, 223, 316

C
Canadian Broadcasting Corporation (CBC)/Société Radio-Canada (SRC), 157, 159, 161, 163, 167
Capture, 15, 64, 180, 196, 199, 201, 210, 217–239, 319
Catch-up, 4, 53, 199, 202, 208, 295
Censorship, 99, 105, 134, 312
Children, 14, 83, 84, 117–118, 302, 303, 312
Citizens, 3, 8, 9, 11, 12, 16, 21, 22, 24, 26–29, 31–33, 35, 47, 53, 55, 63, 67, 78–82, 86–89, 104, 105, 113, 115, 117–120, 122, 123, 140–142, 248, 249, 255–259, 263, 264, 269, 277–280, 283, 284, 287–289, 294, 302, 315, 316, 319, 321–323

participation (*see* Participation)
Citizenship, 23, 26, 33, 147, 247, 248, 303, 304, 316, 318, 321–323
Civil society, 119, 233, 255, 294, 322
Co-creation, 25, 47, 141, 147, 301, 322
Collaboration, 25, 47, 65, 85, 86, 118, 179, 184, 185, 261, 265
Commercial
  activities, 6, 27, 31
  broadcasters, 10, 23, 25–27, 31, 34, 35, 140, 183, 317
Commissioning, 181
Communication rights, 16, 248
Community, 9, 22, 49, 53, 69, 80, 84, 87, 113, 115–117, 120, 123, 129, 136, 137, 139, 140, 145, 158, 179, 183, 226, 259, 264, 266, 269, 276, 294, 295, 297
Competition, 3, 5, 7, 12, 22–27, 29, 30, 66, 131, 136, 159, 160, 162, 165, 174, 180, 194, 196, 199, 202, 203, 206–208, 210, 218, 226, 232, 234, 297, 304, 306, 318, 320
Concentration, 193, 197, 208, 221, 227, 283, 311, 312
Content
  aggregators, 51, 67, 204
  production, 4, 59–61, 63, 64, 69, 165, 201, 203, 311, 317
  programming, 61
  strategies, 54, 200, 278
Convergence, 12, 15, 25, 52, 87, 112, 113, 131, 159, 294, 304–306, 310
Co-production, 163, 164, 323
Corruption, 82, 84, 119
COVID-19, 10, 11, 88, 180, 220, 232, 237, 238, 248, 263, 264, 266, 270

Creative
  cluster(ing), 182
  economy(ies), 176, 182, 183
Credibility, 16, 123, 147, 239, 258, 279, 281
Critical thinking, 120, 121, 249, 255, 257, 259, 261, 303
Crowd(ing) out, 63, 177, 178, 185
Crowdsourcing, 100
Cultural
  exception, 158, 162
  identity, 82, 123
  industries, 50–52, 82, 95–101, 105, 106, 106n1, 162, 322
  intermediaries, 50, 66, 69–71
  minorities, 116–117
Culture, 4, 11, 13, 14, 17, 21, 31, 35, 36, 45–56, 62, 63, 67, 72n2, 79, 81, 85, 86, 88, 117–119, 123, 129–131, 142, 147, 148, 156, 157, 159, 161, 162, 164, 167, 168n3, 180, 184, 205, 226, 231, 294, 300, 305, 306, 310, 316
Czech TV, 228, 229

D

Decentralization, 97, 102, 130, 131, 139, 316
Democracy, 15, 25, 55, 56, 79, 82, 112, 138, 176, 218, 257, 258, 275–279, 315, 316
Deregulation, 29, 131, 132
Dialect, 116–117
  See also Language
Digital
  challenge, 35
  citizenship, 16, 258, 309–323
  competencies, 115, 260
  divide, 310
  economy, 5, 15, 52, 182, 219
  influencers, 64, 65
  intermediation, 59–71
  media, 4, 61–63, 66, 69, 72n1, 121, 174, 176, 256, 316
  platforms, 5, 6, 13, 16, 22, 23, 34, 50, 63, 64, 95, 114, 156, 162, 197, 206, 298, 300, 302, 318, 321
  transition, 8, 22–23
Digitalization, 22–25, 31, 61, 66, 78, 113, 131, 141, 298–302
Digital Terrestrial Television (DTT), 22, 30, 34, 99, 202
Disinformation, 256, 258–260, 263, 264, 266, 270, 277
Disruption, 161, 205–207, 219
Distinctiveness, 13, 32, 55, 71, 174
Diversity
  cultural, 55, 81, 112, 194, 208, 210
  linguistic, 133, 165, 262
Dual model/system, 78, 230

E

Ecology, 10, 51, 180
Economic interests, 24, 52, 174
Education, 9, 31, 35, 78, 86, 88, 112, 120, 121, 137, 185, 247, 256, 258, 261, 266, 269, 302, 303
Elections, 116, 135, 143, 144, 147, 166, 229, 237, 276, 278, 282, 283
Electoral debates, 16, 275–289
Employment, 82, 136, 164, 181
Entertainment, 6, 11, 23, 26, 31, 32, 60, 80, 84, 86, 88, 101, 105, 118, 134, 137, 163, 265, 281, 282, 285n14, 289, 302, 303, 306
European Broadcasting Union (EBU), 6, 9–11, 47, 65–67, 79, 112, 141, 147, 174, 179, 227, 231, 238, 294, 299, 302

European Commission (EC), 4, 5, 16, 131, 141, 174, 186n1, 249–261, 268, 270
European Digital Media Observatory (EDMO), 259
Europeanization, 132
European Regulators Group for Audiovisual Media Services (ERGA), 257
European Union (EU), 6, 7, 12, 14, 27, 30–31, 78, 111–124, 129, 130, 140, 231, 232, 253, 255, 256, 258, 259, 265, 276, 277
Ex ante
 regulation, 5, 206
 test, 30 (*see also* Public value, tests)

F
Facebook, 6, 46, 49–51, 53, 63, 88, 206, 259, 297, 301, 302, 320
Fact-checking, 259, 277, 279, 283–284, 287
Fake news, 11, 13, 65, 86, 88, 95, 98, 101, 102, 121–123, 147, 248, 256, 265, 266, 268, 276, 277, 284
Federation of Autonomic Radio and Television Entities (FORTA), 122, 136, 139, 233
France, 11, 16, 27, 54, 135, 140, 158, 196–198, 202–204
Funding, 4–7, 12, 13, 22–27, 30, 31, 33, 34, 82, 96, 106, 112, 132, 134, 136, 139–141, 147, 148, 159, 165, 175–178, 186, 218, 219, 223, 224, 229–231, 233–238, 294

G
Gamification, 121
Gatekeeping/gatekeepers, 5, 13, 51, 61, 62, 70, 71, 102, 319
Gender parity, 282, 287

Globalization, 131, 162, 163, 294, 320
Google, Apple, Facebook, Amazon, Microsoft (GAFAM), 50, 51, 94–96, 102, 166
Governance, 12, 14, 15, 79, 106, 129–148, 218, 224, 226, 309
 models, 14, 136, 312
Government, 3, 7, 22, 28, 29, 31, 33, 46, 53, 54, 78, 82, 88, 113, 130, 133–139, 141–148, 155–158, 161–167, 168n2, 177, 218–222, 227, 228, 231–234, 236–239, 248, 261, 269, 276–278, 310, 311, 313
 influence, 28, 29, 134, 142

H
Hallin, D.C., 53, 112, 130, 147, 223, 225
Homogenization, 30–31, 316

I
Impartiality, 27, 29, 120
Independence, 7, 9, 14, 15, 28–30, 47, 105, 111, 112, 115, 132, 133, 138–143, 147, 165, 217, 219, 220, 223, 226–228, 233–237, 276, 321
Independent production, 174, 180, 183
Indicators, 16, 112, 113, 119, 120, 160, 179, 225, 239, 275–289, 314
Information societies, 131, 247, 306, 318, 322
Infrastructure, 49, 50, 52, 56, 69, 97, 157, 174, 182, 183, 194, 195, 197, 198, 200, 204–207, 209, 318, 320, 321

INDEX

Innovation, 8, 9, 12–15, 22, 32, 47, 61, 63, 64, 66, 79, 81, 88, 95, 105, 112–114, 124, 142, 147, 148, 175, 180, 183–186, 207, 209, 239, 264, 267, 305, 306, 313
Instagram, 46, 50, 51, 64, 81, 88, 297, 301, 302
Instrumentalization, 112, 131
Integration, 97, 118, 119, 132–134, 139, 147, 196, 197, 200, 203–210, 284, 316
Intellectual property (IP), 95–98, 184, 206, 210
Interactivity, 24, 174, 183, 297
Intermediaries, 49, 50, 52, 55, 60, 65, 66, 69–71, 95, 96, 99, 101, 102, 113, 269, 320
Interventionism, 156, 157

J

Journalism
  local, 51, 113
  quality, 248, 249, 258
  robot, 65, 71
Journalists, 25, 60, 61, 65, 68, 70, 112, 119, 165, 181, 219, 221, 229, 231, 234, 236, 266, 283, 284, 287
  data, 60, 83

L

Labor, 15, 61, 180–183, 186
Language, 14, 81–84, 86, 103, 112, 115–117, 133, 140, 157, 158, 181, 226, 231, 284, 288, 303, 305, 312
Legitimacy, 5–8, 13, 29, 46, 49, 63, 66, 67, 112, 122, 132, 141, 147, 157, 167, 220, 223, 321

Liberalization, 48, 53, 159, 168n4, 177, 230
Licence fee, 27, 178
Literacy, 14–16, 113, 116, 120–124, 146, 247–270, 304, 322
Literature review, 12
Lobbying, 165

M

Management, 8, 13, 23, 33, 35, 55, 61, 66, 83, 88, 98, 99, 112, 132, 137–147, 226, 231, 233, 298, 311, 312
Mancini, P., 53, 112, 130, 147, 223, 225
Market
  failure, 28, 30, 31, 176, 180, 208
  impact, 5, 15, 30, 31, 173–180, 185
  logic, 13, 23, 105
  power, 4, 5, 194, 205–208, 210
  risk (*see* Risk)
  shaping, 180
Media
  capture (*see* Capture)
  ecosystem, 11, 47, 53, 59, 122, 182, 185, 304
  literacy (*see* Literacy)
  local, 113, 123, 312
  non-profit, 321
  regional, 112, 117
  regulation, 26, 30, 66, 194
  systems, 15, 16, 26, 53, 131, 220, 221, 223–225, 227–230, 233, 235, 239, 311, 312, 318, 321
Misinformation, 11, 64, 122, 183, 248
  See also Disinformation
Mixed model, 12, 26, 27, 32, 34, 35
  See also Funding

Mobile, 24, 78, 81, 83, 84, 87, 112, 114, 117, 123, 183, 198, 200–202, 207, 210, 295, 297–299, 314
Multimedia, 16, 23, 34, 46, 79, 84, 87, 113, 115, 220, 247, 293, 295, 297, 300, 305
Multiplatform, 24, 25, 32, 33, 35, 82, 85, 224, 281, 295
Multiplier, 178, 179, 185
Multi-stakeholder, 28
  See also Stakeholders

N
National
  identity, 36, 158, 306
Neoliberalism, 12, 29, 156
Netflix, 14, 49, 51, 53, 54, 99, 100, 102, 155, 156, 161–167, 168n2, 168n6, 168n8, 168n11, 169n13, 174, 182, 184, 204–206, 236, 296, 317
Net neutrality, 15, 195, 206–210
Network society, 59–71
New
  media, 14, 24, 25, 30, 66, 67, 79, 80, 87, 112, 123, 159, 160, 177, 315, 316
  technologies, 12, 13, 22–25, 32, 33, 67, 81
News, 5, 6, 11, 13, 23–25, 29, 46, 59, 63, 65, 70, 71, 81, 84, 86–88, 95, 98, 101, 102, 104, 106n1, 115, 118, 121–123, 137, 138, 147, 177, 218, 220, 226, 228, 230–232, 234, 236–238, 248, 256, 258, 259, 265, 266, 268, 276, 277, 284, 301–303, 310, 312
  local, 161

O
Ombudsman, 119, 120, 123, 146
Over the Top (OTT), 99, 195, 205, 206, 209

P
Paradigm, 13, 48, 49, 55, 82, 141, 194, 304
Participation, 12, 14, 16, 24, 30, 31, 47, 79–82, 85, 88, 103–106, 106n3, 113, 116, 117, 119–121, 123, 136, 141, 142, 147, 148, 159, 164, 278, 282, 287, 288, 294, 298, 300, 302, 303, 305, 310, 323
Participatory turn, 47
Personalization, 4, 70, 71, 116, 183, 298, 305
Pillarization, 145
Platform
  capitalism, 53, 319–321
  ecosystem, 50
  society, 50, 56
Platformization, 12, 13, 45–56
Pluralism, 7, 22, 26, 31–33, 82, 89, 131, 141, 147, 183, 219, 288, 304, 310, 313, 321
Podcasts, 51, 81, 118, 184
Policy, 12, 14, 15, 17, 28–31, 51, 55, 69, 70, 88, 116, 118, 131, 132, 155–167, 168n3, 174–177, 180, 182, 185, 194, 197, 208, 224, 229, 231, 233, 239, 248–264, 268, 270, 283, 294, 310–312, 314, 317, 319
Political
  economy, 13, 51, 52, 156
  parties, 7, 134, 135, 143, 156, 166, 223, 227, 229, 234, 235, 276, 281–283, 285–287, 321

pressure, 7, 27, 177, 218, 227, 231, 234
Politicization, 136, 142, 148, 232
Populism, 79, 132, 276
Power
 relationships, 50
Pressures, 7, 10, 15, 22, 27, 30, 50, 51, 131, 132, 177, 210, 218, 220, 222, 224, 226, 227, 231, 234, 236, 237, 239, 313
Privacy, 101, 207, 248
Privatization, 25, 26, 134, 137, 294
Production, 4, 10, 13, 14, 22, 24, 26–29, 31, 49–51, 59–69, 71, 77, 78, 80, 81, 83, 87, 94, 97, 103, 105, 117, 118, 137, 139–141, 156, 158, 159, 161–167, 168n11, 169n13, 169n15, 174, 175, 179–183, 193, 195, 201, 203–205, 210, 228, 266, 281, 300–302, 304, 309, 311, 312, 316, 317, 319–321, 323
 original, 6, 181, 311
Programming, 11, 16, 26–28, 31, 61, 65, 68–70, 103–105, 114, 118, 158–160, 169n12, 181, 231, 234, 235, 279–281, 284, 285, 302–305, 309, 314
Promotion, 14, 15, 82, 102, 103, 112, 117, 122, 165, 207, 208, 255, 257, 260, 261, 267–270, 298, 304, 306
Propaganda, 50, 133, 135, 221
Proximity, 13, 14, 80, 82, 88, 89, 112–124, 157, 159, 165
 media, 13, 80, 82, 112–114
Public discourse, 15, 220, 223, 224, 239
Public good, 9, 71, 157, 180, 183, 258

Public interest, 9, 26, 28, 217, 218, 221, 282, 297
Public opinion, 16, 34, 132, 237, 276, 288, 315
Public remit, 30
Public Service Platforms, 13, 48–56, 82
Public sphere, 9, 14, 17, 79, 104, 130, 313–318
Public value, 5, 8, 9, 12, 23, 26, 28, 30–33, 52, 54, 144, 174, 178–180, 183, 185
 tests, 178 (*see also* Ex ante, test)
À Punt Mèdia, 13, 81–86, 89

Q
Quality, 9, 11, 12, 16, 26–29, 31–35, 66, 67, 79, 81, 82, 86, 88, 111–124, 132, 142, 143, 180, 199, 201–203, 207, 217, 228, 239, 248, 249, 257, 258, 260, 265, 268, 270, 275–289, 294, 298, 300, 303–306, 309, 311–314, 321

R
Rádio e Televisão de Portugal/Radiotelevisão Portuguesa (RTP), 16, 54, 136, 139, 145, 295, 302–305
Radio-télévision belge de la Communauté française (RTBF), 120, 122, 136, 139, 145, 182, 226
Radiotelevisione Italiana (RAI), 11, 16, 53, 54, 135, 139, 146, 221, 295, 298–302, 305
Reality TV, 296–298
Recommender systems, 52, 59, 63, 65, 67–69

334   INDEX

Regulation, 5, 12, 14, 15, 23, 26, 28–31, 66, 119, 129–136, 141–143, 157, 158, 160, 162, 165, 169n11, 179, 194, 195, 206–208, 210, 211n3, 225, 226, 229, 235, 237, 269, 302, 312, 321
Remit, 4, 8, 11, 16, 27, 60, 173, 175, 220, 231, 239
   See also Public remit
Research & Development (R&D), 183
Risk, 6, 7, 15, 56, 173–186, 186n2, 198, 205, 207–209, 219, 239, 248, 279
RTVE, 7, 11, 16, 47, 54, 135, 136, 139, 146, 222, 232–235, 267, 295–298, 305

S
S4C, 133, 178
Social
   audience, 297
   media, 4, 12, 13, 23–24, 33–35, 46, 48, 49, 63, 64, 67, 70, 71, 104, 105, 248, 256, 261, 264, 276, 281, 285, 297, 298, 301, 315
   responsibility, 123, 124, 143, 303
Spectrum, 3, 23, 62, 111, 157, 176, 177, 230, 233, 235
Stakeholders, 8, 11, 17, 23, 35, 63, 113, 143, 175, 181, 184, 185, 255, 257, 258, 260, 263, 264, 268, 269
   See also Multi-stakeholder
State
   aid, 4, 27–29, 131, 232
   financing, 219
   media, 16, 136, 138, 218, 221, 227, 309–323
Supply base, 15, 175, 180–183, 185

Support, 7, 11, 14, 30, 51, 62, 67, 87, 105, 116, 131, 133, 146, 157, 161, 165, 174, 178, 181, 185, 195, 200, 202, 203, 222, 229, 232, 235, 249, 255, 256, 260, 264, 268, 294, 298, 302, 303
Sustainable Development Goals (SDGs), 249, 263
Switchover, 22–23

T
Telecommunication, telecoms, 14, 15, 52, 64, 139, 156–159, 183, 194–198, 200, 201, 203–211
Training, 86, 121, 181, 182, 205, 259–261, 270
Transmedia, 4, 12, 13, 77–89, 117, 297, 304, 322
Transparency, 30, 31, 55, 82, 97, 101–103, 105, 112, 142, 147, 148, 209, 227, 258, 278, 279, 281, 283–284, 314
Trust, 7, 11, 94, 144, 147, 175, 230, 231, 235, 239, 248, 258, 268, 275–279, 289
Twitter, 46, 50, 53, 63, 259, 297, 301

U
UNESCO, 16, 112, 158, 220, 247, 249, 260–264, 268, 270, 303
United Kingdom (UK), 6, 7, 11, 15, 16, 28, 32, 53, 54, 133, 140, 178, 179, 182, 198, 218, 225, 235–239, 265, 266, 276, 317, 318
Universal access, 16, 23, 31, 32, 67, 81, 103, 158
Universality, 9, 13, 24, 47, 111, 112, 116, 142, 147, 217

V

Value, 3–17, 21–23, 26–33, 35, 36, 45–49, 52–55, 65, 67–70, 79, 81, 85, 94, 100, 102, 103, 105, 106, 112, 120–123, 130, 133, 139, 141, 143, 144, 146–148, 158, 162, 169n13, 174, 175, 178–181, 183, 185, 186, 196, 199, 200, 204, 205, 238, 248, 257, 258, 269, 275–289, 305, 313, 317
Value chain, 13, 66, 96, 97, 162, 195, 197, 201, 203, 206
Value for money, 67
Veracity, 95, 113
Video on Demand (VOD), 6, 24, 54, 161, 208, 295, 296, 317
Visibility, 60, 64, 65, 85, 86, 184, 259, 319
VRT, 117, 118, 120, 122, 136, 139, 145, 178, 182, 184, 226, 227

W

Websites, 11, 12, 14, 49, 53, 65, 68, 83–85, 95, 111–124, 199, 259, 260, 263, 265, 285, 301, 314, 323

Y

Yle, 139, 224, 230–232
Young audiences, 6, 13–16, 123, 294–298, 305, 306
Youth, 7, 84, 85, 117–118, 266, 297, 302–304, 312, 323
YouTube, 6, 23, 46, 49, 51, 53, 64, 78, 85, 88, 160, 238, 297, 301, 317, 320

Printed in the United States
by Baker & Taylor Publisher Services